The Study of Real Skills
Volume 4

Social Skills

The Study of Real Skills

Series Editor: W. T. Singleton, *Applied Psychology Department, University of Aston in Birmingham*

Volume 1
The Analysis of Practical Skills

This book attempts to bridge the gap between laboratory studies of human skill by experimental psychologists and behavioural studies of man at work.

Volume 2
Compliance and Excellence

Reviews the methods used in skills analysis from work study to process control study with detailed analyses of two extreme kinds of jobs and effort: Compliance, where the individual learns to cope with a hostile situation; and excellence, where the individual dominates the situation with superb performance.

Volume 3
Management Skills

Reviews the conceptual background to management skills with the emphasis on a systems approach.

Volume 4
Social Skills

Reviews the conceptual background to social skills with emphasis on the variety of criteria for effective communal effort from productivity to quality of life.

The Study of Real Skills
Volume 4

Social Skills

Edited by

W. T. Singleton MA DSc

Professor of Applied Psychology
University of Aston in Birmingham

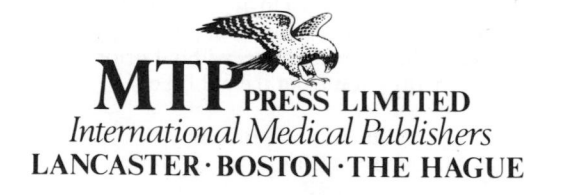

MTP PRESS LIMITED
International Medical Publishers
LANCASTER · BOSTON · THE HAGUE

Published in the UK and Europe by
MTP Press Limited
Falcon House
Lancaster, England

British Library Cataloguing in Publication Data

Social skills. —(The study of real skills; v. 4)
  1. Interpersonal relations
  I. Singleton, W. T.   II. Series
  302   HM132

ISBN 0–85200–092–8

Filmset and printed by
Mather Bros (Printers) Ltd Preston

Contents

A taxonomy of learning conversations
Challenging the robot
The need for three related dialogues
The management of learning
Learning managers

Contributors

D. E. Ager

University of Aston
Department of Modern Languages
Birmingham B4 7ET

Educated at Ilford and London he obtained degrees in French and Russian Studies and a PhD on 'Teaching Linguistic Register in French'. After completing National Service and some years of language teaching in a Grammar School he joined the staff of the new University of Salford as Lecturer in French. In 1971 he was appointed to the newly-created Chair of Modern Languages in the University of Aston. His research interests relate to the use of language, particularly the French language, in defined communication situations. He also works as a consultant in language learning problems.

Chris Barker

University of Aston
Department of Applied Psychology
Birmingham B4 7ET

Read Mathematics at Cambridge and then took a Master's degree in Operational Research from London School of Economics. After working as an operational research analyst, he went to the University of California, Los Angeles, to take his doctorate in Clinical Psychology. He presently lectures at Aston University, does research in clinical and community psychology, and is a part-time counsellor at Aston University Student Health Service.

Doreen Caney

Central Birmingham Health District
The School of Physiotherapy
Queen Elizabeth Medical Centre
Edgbaston
Birmingham B15 2TH

Doreen Caney is the Principal of the Queen Elizabeth School of Physiotherapy, Birmingham. She gained clinical physiotherapy experience at Reading and Stoke Mandeville before qualifying as a teacher. She was made a Fellow of her profession in 1980 and obtained an honours degree in social science from the Open University in 1981. She is a keen advocate of the need to analyse and evaluate professional skills in the interest of greater competence in patient care.

Guy Cumberbatch

University of Aston
Department of Applied Psychology
Birmingham B4 7ET

Guy Cumberbatch graduated in psychology from University College, Cardiff and obtained his PhD from Leicester University where he studied human memory. He carried out postdoctoral research at the Centre for Mass Communication Research in Leicester and since 1972 has been a lecturer in Applied Psychology at Aston University. He has engaged in police research for the last five years and is currently completing an evaluation research programme on community policing for the Home Office. Publications include *Mass media violence and society* which he co-authored with Dennis Howitt (London: Elek).

M. M. Goodfellow

Ribston Hall High School
Stroud Road
Gloucester GL1 5LE

Conventional path through the profession—grammar school, university, heavily subject-oriented teaching in grammar schools but with easy relationships and activities shared with pupils. Experience in a large comprehensive school with broader social attitudes among staff and pupils. Progress up normal hierarchical ladder, though missing a few rungs and avoiding anything labelled 'pastoral' in the belief that this is an integral part of any teaching and should not be compartmentalized. Education has become too serious; school teaching is about children and, however infuriating, they can be fun and learning can still be a delight.

K. M. Hay

5 Temple Road
Dorridge
Solihull
West Midlands B93 8LE

Studied medicine at St Bartholomew's Hospital and Cambridge University, qualified in 1939. After working as a resident doctor in hospitals in London and Midlands joined the RAFVR, work included the training of aircrew in the use of night vision, demobilized as a Squadron Leader in 1946. Held some postgraduate appointments in hospitals in the Midlands, followed by a research post at the Birmingham and Midland Eye hospital working on the nature of migraine headaches. Entered general practice in Acocks Green—an industrial suburb of Birmingham—as a principal in 1950. One-time chairman of the Midland faculty of the College of General Practitioners, followed by a term of office as Provost. Now retired.

R. J. Loveridge

The University of Aston
Management Centre
Nelson Building
Gosta Green
Birmingham B4 7DU

Mature student at Ruskin College, Oxford, and Churchill College, Cambridge, after previously working as an engineering apprentice and draughtsman. At that time he was a shop steward and later was National Research Officer of a federation of Civil Service Unions. One-time lecturer at London Business School and London School of Economics. Currently Professor of Manpower Management, University of Aston Management Centre and Joint Principal Investigator, SSRC Work Organization Research Centre. Also acts as a consultant to a wide range of industries.

P. Moorhouse

3 Chichester Lane
Hampton Magna
Warwick CV35 8SR

After graduating from Queen Mary College (University of London) in Mathematics with Social Sciences, he attended Stirling University to read a Master's degree in Psychology. He then joined Dunlop Limited, Central Personnel Division, as a management trainee and through a collaborative postgraduate scheme with Aston University undertook doctoral research into management skills to assist in Company management development activities. Subsequently took a position within the commercial management team of Dunlop Aviation Division. Currently he works for British Aerospace.

J. Brian Morgan

Devon and Cornwall Constabulary
Force Headquarters
Middlemoor
Exeter
Devon

Commenced his police service in the Metropolitan Police where he served in the CID and uniform in West and East Ends of London. He transferred to the West Midlands Police as a Detective Inspector and served throughout the force area finishing as Chief Superintendent in charge of Wolverhampton. He was seconded to the Home Office from 1974 to 1976 in charge of the Police Research Services Unit. Appointed Assistant Chief Constable to Devon and Cornwall in 1976 and Deputy Chief Constable in 1982.

He received a BA degree from the Open University in 1973 and an MSc from Cranfield in 1980. Research interests include police operation systems, community policing and police relations with other agencies. Current research is on the process of criminal investigation.

Michael Potter

64 Howards Lane
London SW15 6QD

Michael Potter's career spans sales, personnel and training management with an international food group. He held appointments up to national level in divisions serving a diverse range of consumer markets—from grocery retailing to farming. His final post with this company, then employing 35 000 people, was Group Training Manager.

He left them in 1978 to help set up a training consultancy which operates in two important though diverse fields; firstly, management development, marketing/sales management, and selling techniques; and secondly, security training, covering both the training of specialist security staff and the security awareness training of line managers. He himself specializes in sales and sales management training, from basic selling techniques upwards.

Stephen J. Singleton

The University of Leeds
Department of Medicine
The General Infirmary
Leeds LS1 3EX

After graduating from Leeds he worked in medicine and surgery in various hospitals. In 1980 he was appointed Lecturer in Pathology at the University of Leeds. He has subsequently worked in Clinical Haematology and is currently a Teaching Fellow in Medicine in the Professorial Medical Unit of the Leeds General Infirmary. He also works in Accident and Emergency Medicine.

W. T. Singleton

University of Aston
Applied Psychology Department
Birmingham B4 7ET

After graduating in Natural Sciences and in Moral Sciences (Psychology) he stayed in Cambridge as a member of a research unit in the Department of Psychology. Later he worked for six years in the industrial Midlands on Human Performance and spent a similar period at the College of Aeronautics, Cranfield, in engineering production. For fifteen years he was Head of the Department of Applied Psychology, University of Aston in Birmingham. He now works mainly as a consultant to high-technology industries and to United Nations organizations.

D. A. D. Slattery

Rolls-Royce Limited
PO Box 31
Derby DE2 8BJ

After qualifying in Medicine at St Thomas' Hospital he served with the RAMC, first in England and later in Malaya, in the field of tuberculosis. After leaving the army he joined the gas industry in Sheffield as Medical Officer where he worked for ten years. He then moved to the British Steel Corporation as Medical Officer and later Manager, Safety Health and Welfare at the Rotherham group of works. In 1973 he took up his present position as Chief Medical Officer, Rolls-Royce Limited. He has been intimately concerned with the development of Occupational Health services in industry and the application of the Health and Safety at Work Act.

Laurie F. Thomas

Centre for the Study of Human Learning
Brunel University
Uxbridge

Laurie Thomas has first degrees in Engineering and Psychology and was awarded a PhD in 1962 for a study of the Psychology of Judgement and Decision-making applied to Industrial Inspection. He served an apprenticeship in precision engineering, did his national service as a Captain in REME and spent some years as Progress and Planning Officer and Production Manager. He then went on to make a career as teacher and research worker in Industrial and Educational Psychology. Since 1969, he has been Director of the Centre for the Study of Human Learning at Brunel University.

John J. Thornhill

80 Cockshead Road
Liverpool L25 2RB

After graduating from the University of Hull he gained a Diploma in Education and Psychology at Edinburgh University and attended the University of Dundee to read a Master's degree in Education and Psychology. He currently holds a post as Senior Lecturer at a constituent college of Liverpool University and is engaged in doctoral research into the causes of stress for match officials. He has refereed association and rugby football at professional level officiating at both Hampden Park and Wembley and is a licensed referee instructor with the Football Association. He is also an international athletics official.

The Hon. Mr Justice W. A. N. Wells

Judges' Chambers
Supreme Court
Adelaide
South Australia 5000

Educated at Adelaide and Oxford Universities. Graduated with LLB (Adelaide Stow Scholar, Rhodes Scholar) and with MA, BCL (Oxon. Eldon Scholar). Called to the Bar in England (Inner Temple) and to practice in South Australia. Queen's Counsel, 1963. Appointed Solicitor-General for the State of South Australia 1969. Justice of the Supreme Court of South Australia since March 1970. Particular interests as a judge include the proper management of trials by judge and jury, and the relationship between the community and the courts.

Introduction

W. T. SINGLETON

THE CONCEPT

This is the fourth in a series of books devoted to the study of real skills. A skilled person is one who achieves his objectives effectively, that is by an optimal expenditure of effort, attention and other resources working within his native capacities of strength, vision, intelligence, sensitivity and so forth. It is difficult if not impossible to measure in a quantitative sense. There is, however, no question about its presence or absence. The differences between a highly skilled performer and a mediocre one are so readily manifest that there is no ambiguity. The student of skill is a person interested in what these differences are and how they originate.

The importance and the difficulty of skill study is that the concept is a universal one for human activity. The movement of one limb can be skilled or unskilled within the context of a task, so also can the way a leader addresses a large meeting of his followers. For these and other equally disparate activities there are certain descriptive terms which always seem to be applicable: continuity, sequencing, timing, together with a subtle combination of sensitivity, adaptability and imperturbability. What happens at any instant is set precisely with the flow from what has already happened to what is going to happen. The order of events has a determinate logic which may not be obvious to the observer except with the benefit of hindsight. Timing also is just right and is controlled intuitively with extraordinary precision. Each action is modified as a consequence of knowledge of the results of earlier actions so as to adjust to the situation without losing the essential direction of progression—unless it is becoming clear that the immediate objective cannot be achieved, in which case there will be a smooth, unnoticeable switch to another more readily attainable objective still within some higher goal.

1

Such wide generalization may become clearer with the aid of an illustration. Consider what happens as one person goes into the office of another person so as to obtain agreement on some issue. There is an obvious need for continuity and sequencing in the way one person opens a door, walks through it, shuts the door again and walks towards the desk, unless he is very nervous nothing will go awry in this series nor with the reaction of the host who has a highly complex series of movements in getting out of his chair to greet his visitor. In ordinary people such activities are so highly skilled that they proceed immaculately and without conscious attention but slight variations will not go unnoticed. There are considerable subtleties in the timing, how quickly the visitor shuts the door and moves forward, how the host delays or hastens his looking up and rising, all have implications for the interaction which is to follow. The extremes are socially crude and unskilled, the door slam and the rush to the desk, the refusal by the other party to look up for five seconds or so indicate unusually hostile behaviour, it is the fine timing within fractions of a second which has meaning within a more normal encounter. No one practises these things with a stopwatch; it would not help because it is interactive phasing not instants in real time that are significant and these are arrived at on the occasion without conscious intervention. The verbal exchange which follows will be highly adaptive depending on the responses from each side and the sensitivity of the recipients to these responses. As the dialogue progresses there will usually be an adjustment of objectives on both sides—a compromise. If one or both is highly skilled he will be aware of just how much and why he is adjusting his position, or alternatively why he is refusing to do so. Each person has a curious position almost as an intermediary between himself and the other person, it makes sense to say that adjustments are made after self-consultation which may be either conscious or unconscious. Paradoxically, although skill usually implies awareness of and anticipation of what is going to happen a skilled practitioner will not plan the progress of a meeting of this kind in detail. The meeting is taking place because he wants to know more about the position of the other party and as he acquires this knowledge during the meeting he adjusts his position accordingly. Awareness that the other party is changing his position is satisfying not just for political reasons but because it signifies that real communication is taking place. Conversely there is nothing more frustrating than attempting to communicate in this way and detecting no movement on the other side, this indicates that the communication has failed. It is analogous to controlling a machine and finding that pressing buttons and pulling levers appears to have no consequential response. The reaction in this situation is either to attack the machine with greater vigour or to walk away from it. Similarly in the office meeting if there is no response then one party will either lose his temper or withdraw. This vignette illustrates not only the essentially progressive and phased nature of skilled performance already mentioned, but also that there are similarities between man–machine interaction and man–man interaction. The issue gets more complicated if the total environment to which a person is adapting is not just the physical world but also contains one or more other people, but the principles of adaptation and communications do not change. The communication/action processes of an individual are sustained by underlying mechanisms which are very complex and are not currently identifiable physiologically but nevertheless we have some knowledge of how they must function. These are the concepts of skill.

In this series of studies of skill it seemed reasonable to begin by examining practical skills of interaction with the physical world and proceed through interaction involving people in the structured settings of management to the people interactions within society more widely. At each stage some attempt has been made to establish the principles which emerge about skilled performance and these principles extend as more and more complex performances are considered. The topic of this book, social skills, is regarded as the most complex area of skilled performance.

Some care is needed in considering precisely what is meant by complexity. Manifestations of social skill are clearly evident in the behaviour of many higher animals which live in groups or interact with people as do domestic dogs and no one would suggest that this behaviour is 'higher' than that of say a research scientist conceptually exploring the physical universe. Nonetheless it does seem that the behaviour of the scientist is the more readily susceptible to description in skill terms. The research scientist appears in the second book and this, the fourth book, will consider social skills.

THE PRECEDING BOOKS

The first book in this series contains descriptions of skilled performance in a sample of jobs across the primary, manufacturing, service and information industries. This range of jobs can also be described in terms of the degree of technical support provided, from aids to muscle power as in farming, to aids to decision making as in information systems. All these jobs had in common the need to cope with the vagaries of the physical world.

In the second book the range of jobs was selected in terms of two dimensions of difficulty. First the difficulty of external constraints from hazardous environments such as that under the sea and secondly the difficulty of internal constraints such as hearing impairment. There was considerable exploration of how excellence is achieved in the expert performer such as the golfer or the professional musician. The search was for insights into skilled performance as it emerges in the overcoming of difficulties and in the achievement of performance far above the average.

The third book dealt entirely with managers. This was not an appreciable limitation because of the variety of management-type jobs in the community. Again these ranged from the farm through manufacturing to the service and information industries. Because management is fundamentally a people-organizing task, there was much in common in the description of the component tasks in the various management jobs and also in the identification of strategies used by successful managers.

The objective of the series is to underline the generality of skill concepts and the commonality of skill themes which emerge from the study of such different jobs. The series is also arranged in order of increasing task complexity and as the books progress, skill concepts become more elusive but not more elaborate. There is an inherent unity and simplicity in the mechanism underlying skilled performance.

SKILL SO FAR

Skill is the consequence of learning and appears as one of the two fundamental kinds of directed behaviour, the other is instinctive behaviour. Although skilled performance is essentially continuous and homogeneous, there have been attempts to classify skills based on the sequence of information processing within the organism. These include the separation into perceptual skills and motor skills and also the separation into input, output and cognitive skills. It is acknowledged that there must be social skills which do not fit within these two schemes. Motor skills are regarded as the mechanisms behind output routines which utilise the complex skeletal and muscular systems in such dexterous ways. Perceptual skills are essentially mental models regularly supplemented by incoming sensory data, in skilled performance the reaction is to the model rather than directly to sense data. In this way the organism can cope coherently with large sets of data and need not react immediately in real time. Introspection and inference affirm the presence of mental activity which has no direct output or input and this is described as cognition. If cognition is just thinking, then the phrase cognitive skill is something of a misnomer because skill implies action. There must be at least a verbal output before there is any manifestation of skill. Input skills as related to cognitive skills are to do with selection and identification of the cues from a highly 'noisy' sensory environment. Output skills are the same as motor skills.

These approaches are limited in the same way that the underlying information concepts are limited in not being able to escape from time sequencing. Thus the essential gestalt quality of skill does not emerge. Skills are simultaneously integral and hierarchical. There are skills within skills but a total skilled performance is homogeneous in space and time. The skilled operator is simultaneously developing a model and using it as a map to navigate in the real world. These models or schema are most readily thought of as mental pictures although symbolic abstractions such as language are involved and so also are more primitive models based on the use of the body image. The individual or self seems to be at once the model and also the observer of the models as expressed in action. This elaborate self-monitoring goes on at all levels from the use of kinaesthetic feedback to overall self-appraisal. The skilled operator's control is maintained by taking note of the unpredicted. Behaviour at all levels has an associated internal record which is also a prediction of what it is anticipated will happen. If things go according to plan no further modification of the record is needed but when they do not then the consequent information must be processed and the internal model is modified accordingly.

The extensive hierarchical nature of this activity would suggest that there must be an overall plan, an executive programme which orchestrates the skills concerned with subsidiary aspects. It is sometimes convenient to use this concept, for example in identifying excellence with the ability to 'put it all together' and in locating fatigue as an overall dislocation. This apparent master plan may turn out to be an illusion fostered by the entirely integrated nature of skilled activity. Thus, executive skills merge into perceptual skills. Correspondingly, perceptual skills merge into motor skills. Perceptual skills are organized on the basis of strategies or categories of action and motor skills are organized on the basis of identifying a relevant stream of input of information. There is thus a severe limit to the usefulness of identifying perceptual skills with early stages of information processing and motor skills with later stages. It seems to be more fitting to think in terms of enactive modelling which is 'inside looking out' as distinct from pictorial modelling which is 'outside looking in'. Again, however, this distinction may not be as definitive as it appears at first sight because of the facility which the skilled person has for switching rapidly between the two, and for shifting information between them. In most real skilled activity the operator seems to behave with several different schema supporting him so closely that it begins to look like one hybrid model.

The set of schema used by one person is uniquely determined by his own capacities and his own total previous experience, they are thus the source of individual differences and the manifestation of one individual.

SOCIAL INTERACTION

A social skill, in common with every other kind of skill, is a hypothetical construct, inferred from observation of performance. Analysis of social skills is bound to be more complex than analysis of physical skills because there is adaptive reaction on both sides and hence the variety of what can happen increases by another order. The physical world changes passively according to the actions of a person; a skilled person will have predicted these changes before they happen and he will check, using sensory information, whether the actual changes correspond or not to the predicted changes. Practical skilled performance of this kind involves an interaction but an adaptation on one side only and hence it is relatively straightforward. The increased complexities following two-sided adaptation are daunting.

Consider, by way of analogy, the skilled operator of a manually-guided missile. Suppose he simply wishes to guide his missile towards a concrete bunker, all he has to do is align the missile between himself and the bunker and keep it on that line. This is typical of practical skills. Suppose alternatively that he wishes to guide his missile to hit a tank which has freedom to manoeuvre and may even be equipped with anti-missile devices. There is now two-sided adaptability and the strategies adopted by the missile operator are much more complex. He will not aim directly at the tank, the tank in these circumstances would take avoiding action. He will probably aim away from the tank and choose precisely the right moment, when it is too late for the tank to move, to redirect the missile towards the tank. On the other hand, the tank commander may be aware of this strategy and may indulge in an even more complex manoeuvre of avoidance. This is analogous to the deployment of social skills in a hostile situation. Fortunately most social interactions are not hostile and a closer analogy would be one in which the missile contains not explosives but perhaps mail and the tank is actually trying to catch the missile. In these collaborative circumstances mutual adaptation can increase the chance of success because one side can compensate for errors on the other side. There remains, even with good will on both sides, the possibility of getting at cross-purposes which can confuse the whole situation.

Misunderstandings can occur at many levels particularly with an individual who for personal or cultural reasons habitually expresses himself obliquely. At the level of the verbal exchange it is surprisingly easy to convey or receive a totally wrong impression. Hence the common hiatus within a dialogue when there is agreement about the words used but differences about the meaning. The extreme of this is expressed in the no doubt apocryphal story of the University Senator credited with the statement, 'I know you believe you understand what you think I said, but I am not sure that you realise that what you heard is not what I meant'.

Presumably the reason why the highly indirect and ambiguous approach to negotiating encounters is encouraged in so many cultures is that it enables the two sides to develop during the process a compromise without ever having revealed that when the discussion began the respective positions were far apart. To clear a starting position might discourage even the attempt to reach a mutually satisfactory outcome and there might be too much loss of face if the extent of the retreat is obvious.

At a higher level communications can be confused if one side starts with the wrong impression of the objectives of the other side so that the reasons for particular moves within the interaction are totally misconstrued. This is the basis of 'situation comedy' where the audience have been made aware of the objectives of each side and can perceive why the actors drift further and further into a state of mutual incomprehension. This phenomenon can be a very serious matter in national or international negotiations between politicians or administrators. This is why experienced negotiators are always sensitive to the need to identify the real objectives of the other side and are prepared to put much effort in the search for hidden cues within what is said.

CONTEXT AND PURPOSES

In all skill studies what is happening makes sense with reference to the context. The context of practical skills is relatively straightforward, the skilled operator is functioning within a physical environment which can be observed. There may be some wider social influences affecting the action but they cannot be allowed to dominate it, otherwise there will be interference with the physical activity. This does happen particularly in games between two people such as tennis or squash, but allowing it to happen is not the way to win. Management skills are exercised within the formal context of the organization. In most organizations there is a consistent culture or climate or style which is continuously reinforced by rewarding conformity and punishing deviance. These organizational mores are reinforced not only within the day-to-day interactions but also by the criteria adopted for selection, training and appraisal. The skills analyst has to understand this culture within any organization in which he works but this is not too difficult because it is consistent.

One of the difficulties of studying social skill is that the cultural context is diffuse and highly variable. Culture in the wider society where social skills are practised is much more difficult to understand, describe and take account of. Within one profession, as in one organization, there are established mores, standards and values which facilitate communication between professionals but inhibit communication with outsiders. Within purely social encounters there is an attempt to establish as quickly as possible the occupation, education, economic status and so on of a stranger so that the likely irritants and lubricants to the conversation can be estimated. (In English society accent used to be a valuable cue to this preliminary clarification but this is now frowned upon.)

The concept of purpose also becomes much more elusive when dealing with the total range of social skills. People interact with each other differently when they are working and when they are at leisure. In the leisure situation there may be no purpose beyond a general interest in another human being but usually one person either wishes to learn something from another (even if it is no more than guidance in geographical direction) or seeks some other kind of aid. This asymmetrical encounter (one suppliant and one donor) is perhaps the most common kind of social interaction, the donor's incentive may vary from general goodwill to the opportunity to acquire some social credit either of status or of an investment to be drawn on at a later date when there may be a role reversal.

Fundamentally people are social animals, their need to interact with each other is much more basic than mere personal gain. This basic need for social interaction is overlaid with other features arising from the structure of society particularly mutual dependence because of specialization of function. Each individual cultivates some specialized skills which he practises as his personal contribution to the collective activity of ordinary life—usually he calls the exercise of these functions his work. This is the background to the concept of a *role* which describes and summarizes what an individual is doing, how he is doing it and why he is doing it without resorting to any attempt to uncover the layers of complexity of individual drives and incentives. In the analysis of social skills it is not essential to search for motives.

SKILLS ANALYSIS

For the analysis of practical skills it was suggested in the first volume of this series that the main techniques were observation and detailed discussion with skilled practitioners. This communication can be reinforced by using various focusing techniques such as use of critical incidents and identification of sub-goals. What happens during formal training can provide insights and so also can experimental checks of specific hypotheses which arise from the observation. In the second volume there was increased emphasis on the good/poor contrast method in its widest sense of the study of excellence, but there remained some support from experimental evidence and psychological theory. The sources of evidence shifted in emphasis from the performance itself to introspections about it and there was an increased input of personal experience from the analyst himself. In the third book about management skills all the analysts were or had been practitioners themselves so that the above trend continued. There was almost no utilization of currently fashionable concepts from professional psychology and no reliance on experimental methods. The analysis became more of a systems approach but, of course, emphasizing people-based and behaviourally-based systems. Social skills appeared as one of the central features of behaviour in the structured field of management. The stage was set for a closer look at social behaviour in a wider community context.

Analysing social skills is not something which can be done by following a standard procedure. As described above purposes are often obscure and the contextual variables can dominate. A slight change in context might result in the total switch in the mode of operation of the skilled performer. Conversely a less skilled performer might repeat an interaction and obtain a totally opposite result because of a change of context to which he was sufficiently sensitive.

Nevertheless some of the established constancies in skills analysis should remain; the effect of experience, the value of contrasting excellent with indifferent performance and the importance of the dialogue between the analyst and the practitioner—itself, of course, a situation requiring the practice of social skills.

Each of the chapters which follows deals with a particular occupation with the exception of the three final chapters which treat more general issues and the first chapter which explores what psychologists know about individual differences.

1
Individual Differences

W. T. SINGLETON

INTRODUCTION

The skills of any one person are the product of his unique history as an individual. He was born with particular potential into a particular culture, brought up in a particular family and community, and educated and trained in particular institutions at particular times. As an adult he has behind him his personal set of experiences in work and leisure. All these influences have steered the development of his repertoire of skills.

The study of individual differences has always been a central theme in psychology. The work of Sir Francis Galton in England in the mid-nineteenth century is commonly regarded as the foundation of this line of inquiry. In common with most early scientists, Galton had wide interests—from meteorology to mental imagery—but he is best known as the founder of eugenics. This last interest led him to follow Shakespeare in distinguishing between nature and nurture. Galton was a relative of the Darwin family which no doubt stimulated his interest in hereditary genius. He pioneered the use of statistical techniques, classification methods and questionnaires but his direct measurements were restricted mainly to physical characteristics; he used educational and scientific achievement as measures of mental attributes. It was his younger contemporary Ebbinghaus in Germany who laid the foundations for mental measurement; he worked mainly on memory but also devised intelligence tests.

INTELLIGENCE TESTS

Ebbinghaus's intelligence tests are interesting in that they allowed for multiple correct answers and thus had some of the characteristics of the more recent tests of divergent intelligence. The French pioneer, Binet, introduced the graded-difficulty approach. The subjects—in his case children—were asked questions in increasing order of difficulty and the measurement was based on the level of difficulty with which the child could cope. The questions were also devised so as to rely on general experience, which ought to be common to all the children, rather than on specialist scholastic study. At about the same time—the first decade of the twentieth century—Cattell in America was attempting to relate test scores to academic success for university students, and Spearman following in Galton's footsteps at London University was correlating test scores and academic success for schoolchildren.

Based on the pattern of correlations obtained, Spearman put forward the theory that intelligence consisted of a general factor 'g' with specific factors related to kinds of question. In particular: reasoning ability, vocabulary ability and arithmetic ability. This contrasts with the multi-dimensional concept of intelligence regarded as a set of overlapping factors again distinguished by kind of question or kind of problem.

Intelligence tests were first used on a large scale by the American Army during World War I. The objective was primarily to eliminate men of such low intelligence that they were not of military value (one of the two main tests was designed for the illiterate) and secondarily to identify men of superior intelligence for rapid promotion. This use of tests placed a premium on ease of scoring; open-ended questions were eliminated in favour of covergent questions requiring unambiguous answers.

The controversy between the general factor and the specific factors theories of intelligence continued through the period between the two world wars and reinforced the emphasis on tests capable of generating simple numerical measures which could readily be manipulated statistically. The statistical methods of factor analysis became more sophisticated and considerable attention was paid to methodological distinctions. For example, the two facets of reliability: test/retest reliability over time and internal consistency; and the many facets of validity: face validity—does it seem satisfactory?, concurrent validity—is it consistent with other intelligence tests?, predictive validity—does it match some other criterion such as occupational success? and construct validity—is it satisfactory theoretically and operationally? There was also extensive effort devoted to principles of text construction including the importance of norms, efficiency as measures by time and cost of administration and so on. The emphasis on these and other aspects of test technique increased as testing became more important in selection and allocation within the armed forces in World War II (Vernon and Parry, 1949) in selection for educational streaming (Vernon, 1956) for occupational choice (Anastasi, 1961) and as a diagnostic tool in clinical psychology (Wechsler, 1958).

Unfortunately the rapid development of the technique tended to obscure the intractable underlying scientific issues. The emphasis on the use of norms and the need for large-scale testing resulted in intelligence measurement becoming nothing more than a way of allocating individuals to categories distinguished only as broad bands of intelligence levels. Questions such as the definition of intelligence, its place within the spectrum of individual differences, its importance in relation to the individual as a member of society and so on were all debated at length but inconclusively. The effort to acquire empirical evidence was related to test measurements, not to the questions as to why it was thought to be important to have such measures.

During the 1950s there was increasing dissatisfaction with the direct question/multiple-choice answer test. Guilford (1950) reminded psychologists of the importance of creativity and he reintroduced the distinction between convergent and divergent thinking as a research topic. Getzels and Jackson (1962) demonstrated that there is more to a gifted child than is measured by a high score in traditional intelligence tests; they identified 'creative children' by tests which were scored by variety and complexity, appropriateness and originality of ideas rather than deductive reasoning. Hudson (1966) using similar tests produced some evidence that undergraduates in science subjects are better at convergent thinking while undergraduates in arts topics are better at divergent thinking.

The vast amount of work on intelligence testing has not made a contribution to knowledge of skill. Intelligence studies moved rather in the opposite direction in attempting to eliminate learned aspects of behaviour and thus isolate intelligence as a feature of genetic endowment. More recently, Cattell (1965) has distinguished between fluid and crystallized ability. Fluid ability is essentially innate capacity and crystallized ability is the expression of this as expanded and consolidated by personal experience.

At the practical level it is obvious that there are other individual attributes which affect educational attainment, career choice, career success, mental illness and so on. Tests of these other factors are generally called personality tests as distinct from intelligence tests although, if personality is intended to mean those factors which identify a person, then obviously the spectrum of 'personality' must include intelligence.

PERSONALITY TESTS

Any test is a formalized standard situation to which a person, the testee, is invited to react. The tester has two general problems; how to construct the best situation and how to measure the response of the testee. The tester, whether he is concerned with intelligence or personality, has a wide choice in what he does and in the guidelines he uses to direct his choice.

Ideally the guidelines should be provided by an agreed comprehensive theory of personality. Such a theory would provide the context in which a particular study could be set both in terms of what is being measured and how it is being measured. Unfortunately there is no such theory. The classical definition of personality is due to Allport (1937): 'Personality is the dynamic organization within the individual of those psycho-physical systems that determine his unique adjustments to his environment'. There are many more recent definitions but the concept remains consistent, namely that personality studies are about how to describe individuals as opposed to much other psychology which is about how the standard person thinks and behaves (perception, learning, memory and so on). It also has to be assumed that in spite of the uniqueness of each individual there are always enduring features of a personality which make the concept and the pursuit of measurement worthwhile. Most, if not all, theories assume that personality is integral and holistic. As Sanford (1963) points out this does not mean that personality cannot be analysed but rather that the analysis must include not only the identification of parts but also an exposition of how the parts relate to the whole.

Unfortunately this requirement is not met by current personality tests. Because measurement is so difficult, studies often concentrate on the measurement itself, and precisely how the particular dimension measured relates to personality as a whole is not explored. Dimensions can be identified by commonsense observations of people either in ordinary life or in the clinic or by factor-analytic techniques applied to correlations between tests applied in batteries. The difference between these two approaches is not as clear-cut as it might appear at first sight. The factor analyst inevitably uses his personal knowledge of people particularly when he indulges in labelling his factors using words already in use in ordinary language or in psychology. The complexities of personality have tempted even the most distinguished psychologists into making a rather arbitrary stab at a dichotomy; two words which define extremes of a dimension along which people differ: hence extraversion/introversion, cyclothymic/schizothymic, viscerotonic/cerebrotonic, manic/melancholic and so on. Eysenck (1947) provides a list of 14 dichotomies of personality types and 15 personality traits. The traditional distinction between a type and a trait is that types imply separate groups (an underlying bimodal distribution) while traits imply continuous gradation with most people near the average (an underlying normal distribution). Eysenck and Cattell have, however, used types to mean constellations of traits. Both these terms refer essentially to the conative field as distinct from the cognitive field where the equivalent term is abilities. Again, traditionally personality refers to the comprehensive complex of individual differences (conative, cognitive and physical) while temperament is restricted to emotional differences, but this distinction also has become blurred. Personality now usually indicates conative differences because intelligence has been separated out and the attempts to relate physical characteristics to behaviour have not been successful, e.g. Sheldon's (1942) ectomorph, endomorph and mesomorph. Many personality tests have followed the orthodox psychometric approach developed for intelligence testing. For example the Minnesota Multiphasic Personality Inventory (MMPI), Cattell's Sixteen Personality Factor questionnaire (16PF) and Eysenck's personality inventory (EPI). For descriptions of these and other tests see Peck and Whitlaw (1975) and Kline (1976). These tests are used extensively in psychotherapy, guidance and, less frequently, in selection and man-power allocation. They are also used within psychological research when attempting to distinguish the behaviour of certain kinds of people in particular circumstances. For example are introverts more competent than extraverts in the performance of inspection tasks? Nevertheless, perhaps because the measurement problems always seem to take priority over the conceptual problems there seems to be little contribution to psychological theory in general or personality theory in particular.

The opposite trend is exemplified by the psychoanalytic approach which is relatively strong on concepts but weak on measurement. The clinical situation has stimulated a variety of personality theories which rely for demonstration of validity on the contribution to diagnosis and therapy or more generally to understanding and describing the patient's problems. Freud (1940) identified three basic personality factors: the id, the ego and the superego. The id is the basic feature of personality, its interaction with the outside world is modulated by the ego and monitored by the superego. This theory does not simplify the concept of 'self'. Self is distributed across the id which is the underlying self, the ego which characterizes the adaptation to the environment and the superego which represents the enduring influence of moral teachers, particularly parents. However, it seems not unreasonable to accept that the self is complex, made up of genetic endowment on to which is superimposed the influences of experience and of standards accepted from other people.

Psychoanalytic theory might be regarded as the progenitor of projection tests, the second main kind of personality test. The testee is presented with a highly ambiguous situation and asked to say what it means to him. It is assumed that the specific interpretation must reflect some attributes of the interpreter. The test material used varies from ink-blots (the Rorschach Test) to drawings of scenes containing people (the Thematic Apperception Test [TAT]). The insurmountable difficulty is how to score these tests in any way which might make it possible to reliably position the response of one individual in relation to the responses of other individuals. This, of course, does not preclude the effective use of these tests in a clinical situation, but it does mean that, once again, it is not possible to use such results to build a structure of knowledge about personality.

There is a third kind of test which explores personality indirectly by measuring related attributes such as interests and values. The best known ones are the Strong Vocational Interest Blank (SVIB) and the Kuder Interest Tests. These tests are self-report inventories where the testee is asked to state his likes–dislikes and interests in specific contexts. There are two objections to these tests, which apply particularly for intelligent testees: the scoring consequences of a particular answer can be guessed so that a testee can, if he feels so inclined, design an artificial set of interests on the spot and there is often a forced choice where it is not possible to say 'a plague on both your houses'. These objections may be academically strong but in a practical situation such as that of an ordinary rather muddled person genuinely seeking vocational guidance they do not interfere with the successful use of such tests. On the other hand, yet again, the tests do not contribute any penetrating insights into the basic structure of personality.

So far, the intellectual yield from personality testing or from psychometrics generally seems to be mediocre. Test results have some value in the clinical or counselling situation where an individual is looking for help and at the opposite extreme where vast numbers of people have to be drafted into new jobs when a nation goes to war. Academically, the test situation, in comparison with the experimental situation, seems to have even less of the desired simultaneously disciplinary and yet catalytic effect of enforcing precise thinking about what is happening and why. Heim (1970) states that, 'Insofar as personality tests do assess aspects of temperament and character, the aspects chosen are arbitrary and variable'. Bromley (1979) states that 'it can be argued that the personality testing movement and the study of individual differences are off-course, if not completely misdirected . . . personality study should shift its emphasis towards the study of individual tasks and develop systematic case-law'.

ATTITUDES

There is a cluster of related terms which includes needs, attitudes, beliefs and opinions. *Opinions* are stated positions on a point about which there is not, often cannot, be conclusive evidence. The opinion is therefore a consequence of some evidence and some attributes of the person commenting on the evidence. A *belief* is a proposition which a given person would accept or not. Compared with an opinion it reflects the person more than the evidence and it need not be overtly expressed. An *attitude* is a disposition which influences the way in which evidence is evaluated and action is taken, it is similar to a belief but broader and more enduring. *Need* is an ambiguous term which sometimes indicates a personal state or a parameter of an individual which relates to his choice of action (in this sense it overlaps with attitude); it might also mean the requirements for a given course of action. 'I need a holiday, I need a camping holiday and I need a tent to go camping'. The above set of terms incorporates a concept which is of fundamental importance in relation to human behaviour both operationally and theoretically.

Operationally, the assessment of collective beliefs and opinions is the basis of democracy. The method varies from the traditional ballot box to the public-opinion poll but the common adjective is to find out what the people want in terms of their own government. At a more mundane level, a competitive society dominated by the market must spend considerable effort in finding out what the customers want and also in attempting to influence their beliefs in what they want. These are consumer preference studies and advertising respectively. As relatively new areas for the application of psychology there is still considerable scope for expansion.

Theoretically, knowledge in the general area of attitudes and beliefs is fundamental to the understanding of the person and of interpersonal communication. Anglin (1973) in describing Bruner's work writes that 'his investigations of attitudes convinced him that they served important functions for their holders—to align them with reference groups, to externalize their internal systems of beliefs, and to test their hypotheses'. Russell (1948) points out that sentences usually contain an indicative idea—a fact or an hypothesis about the external world and also an expression of an attitude towards that idea on the part of the speaker. For example the sentences: 'I believe it is going to rain', 'Oh dear, it's going to rain!' and 'I wonder if it is going to rain' all contain the same indicative idea but different attitudes, respectively an assertion with some doubt, an expression of dislike and an interrogation. Thus, in communicating verbally one is simultaneously indicating a topic and attaching an attitude to it. Sherif and Sherif (1967) consider that attitudes are characteristic, consistent and selective; they are acquired or learned. The individual uses a set of categories for comparing and evaluating items within the stimulus domain with varying degrees of positive or negative affect. A change of attitude is inferred from the individual's acceptance–rejection pattern which in principle at least is susceptible to measurement.

The acquisition of evidence about attitudes has been attempted using the test method and the experimental method. Predictably the premature switch to empiricism has tended to trivialize the subject. The test psychologists have got into difficulties because they are not clear about whether the objective is to identify consistent biases in behaviour or the attitudes which underpin these biases. The result is ludicrous debates about the relationships between attitudes, self-opinions about attitudes and behaviour resulting from attitudes. A summary of this approach in the 1960s is provided by Thomas (1971). The experimentalists have concentrated on a few simple phenomena related to attitudes which happen to be susceptible to relatively easy control in the classroom or the laboratory. The best known one is Festinger's (1957) Theory of Cognitive Dissonance according to which the holder of two beliefs or impressions (cognitions) which are incompatible will tend to feel uncomfortable, and will attempt to reduce the dissonance. For example, he might selectively perceive new evidence which will support a choice between beliefs to which he is already committed by some action.

The difficulty of making progress with concepts such as attitude has resulted in a switch of terminology so that psychologists are now more likely to discuss cognitive styles rather than attitudes. See for example Warr (1970). This might be a step forward in that it emphasizes the gestalt nature of the phenomena and it has some flavour of dynamic development but the corresponding disadvantage is that the acquisition of new evidence becomes even more difficult.

MOTIVATION

There are a number of so-called theories of motivation but they are theories only in the sense of belonging in the realm of speculative thought. Even their most enthusiastic proponents would not defend the position that they are hypotheses which have been confirmed by arrays of evidence. One of the difficulties is that the concept of motivation is sometimes scalar and sometimes vectorial. Organisms are seen as having different levels of arousal, energy or excitement and consequently they respond with more or less enthusiasm to particular stimuli. We talk about a person being 'highly motivated'. More directionally, organisms are regarded as different because the patterns of their interests and enthusiasms are not the same. Thus motivation straddles the two areas of psychology; the behaviour of the standard person and the differential behaviour of individuals. Not surprisingly there are many different approaches. Evans (1975) lists some of the differences as *mechanism versus cognition*—this is the traditional philosophical distinction between a mechanical and a teleological explanation, *push versus pull*—explanation can be devised in terms of either drives or incentives, *innate versus learned*—we can catalogue instincts or consider how motives are acquired through experience and *conscious versus unconscious* which emphasizes the unique approach of the psychoanalysts. Hilgard (1963) divides approaches to motivation into those with a learning orientation, a biological orientation and a personality–social orientation, he considers that such general terms survive within psychology not because they are precise but because they are convenient. Warr (1976) separates seven different kinds of motivation theory and relates them to nine different general reasons for action.

Within applied psychology the approach is eclectic with clinical psychologists using the psychoanalytic and behavioural theories, the educational psychologists using learning theories (which are mostly based on animal studies) and the occupational psychologists who relate motivation to organizational theories.

In the occupational context, motivation is considered as the background to the interest in work design (Davis and Taylor, 1972), quality of working life (Davis and Cherns, 1975), job satisfaction (Sell and Shipley, 1979) and worker participation (Wall and Lischeron, 1977). Collectively these represent the 'job enrichment' movement which flourished in the sixties and early seventies when the western world was still in a period of full employment and there had been several decades of continuously increasing prosperity.

The basic theory was that due to Maslow (1943), who proposed that human needs could be usefully classified into five groups: physiological (food, water, sleep, etc.), safety (minimal threat and maximal stability), love (membership of groups), esteem (by others and also self-) and self-actualization (self-fulfilment). The originality of this theory lies in the postulates that these needs are in a hierarchy and that there is prepotency—that is when the needs at one level are satisfied the needs at the next level up become dominant. In organizations in Western societies it is assumed that workers' dominant needs are in the top two levels—hence the emphasis on work restructuring which will make the fulfilment of these needs feasible.

Another theory with originality is that due to Herzberg *et al.* (1959). They proposed that the factors associated with satisfaction are not the same as those associated with dissatisfaction. The former, called *motivators*, include achievement, recognition and responsibility, the latter, called *hygiene factors*, include financial remuneration, working conditions and social relationships.

Both of these propositions have an intuitive appeal. Maslow is suggesting, for example, that if a person is hungry or under threat he doesn't worry about self-actualization. Herzberg is suggesting that an unsatisfactory salary will result in dissatisfaction but real satisfaction will not be achieved simply by increasing the salary, this will depend on factors which encourage self-fulfilment. There is a considerable literature reporting studies attempting to support and refute these theories but since it mostly depends on question-naire-type studies and these studies necessarily use all the rather hazily understood terms mentioned earlier, it is scarcely surprising that the results are conflicting.

Progress in this field is slow because of the sheer complexity of the issues. Complexity arises from the number of behavioural factors and from their inherently dynamic nature. The situation changes continuously for each individual as he learns and ages and as his circumstances change and also for the standard man as economic and social conditions of society change. For a review of the current position taken by psychologists see Duncan *et al.* (1980).

TAXONOMIES

Recognition that each individual is unique does not remove the psychological problems of classifying people into categories. Even if we restrict ourselves to the work situation, each of the three advanced world economies; the EEC, USA and USSR has about one hundred million workers. The big developing economies such as India and China have even more. We cannot comprehend the human factors relating to work by trying to consider all these individuals separately but equally it is an overgeneralization to make statements about 'the worker'. Defining kinds of people or kinds of worker is a problem of taxonomy.

A *taxonomy* is a classification system based on a theoretical background and relating to some practical issues. As Miller (1975) puts it 'The application of a taxonomy to a set of facts or observations results in adding more information to these facts or observations in the sense of revealing patterns, enabling predictions and the giving of guidance to various kinds of action. A taxonomy is therefore a way of simplifying a complicated universe of individual events and objects according to some useful way of identifying and labelling the way in which groups of individuals (or observations) have things in common and differ from other groups of individuals.' (Miller, 1967). Unfortunately taxonomies of people are usually neither rigorous nor comprehensive, that is, respectively, the categories are not mutually exclusive (memberships overlap) and there are people who don't fit into any of the categories except the final one labelled 'miscellaneous'. The simplest way of dividing people into groups is by sex; with a negligible number of exceptions, individuals can be categorized rigorously and comprehensively as either male or female but for many purposes, particularly those related to work, this categorization is not useful. The only other reasonably tidy taxonomy is that based on age-groups and this can be a valuable descriptor of a group of people and a predictor of performance.

Classification using other less general taxonomies usually depends on defining the purpose of the exercise; it is necessary to begin by stating the reasons for dividing people into the particular groups. People taxonomies are needed for all kinds of human resource development and utilization including education, selection, guidance, training, placement and work design. Operationally the criteria of a good taxonomy are to do with fitness for purpose rather than conceptual rigour, although in the long term the two sets of criteria coincide. Taxonomies can refer directly to tasks or abilities rather than to people; task taxonomies are described in the second book in this series. Gagne (1975) suggests that there are five major categories of learned human capabilities: motor skill, verbal information, intellectual skill, cognitive strategy and attitude. By attitudes he means learned dispositions which influence choices of personal action, by verbal information he means knowledge. Thus he is proposing that education leads to individual differences in knowledge, attitudes and three kinds of skills: motor skills, intellectual skills and cognitive strategies.

Cognitive strategies are to do with ways of doing things (how to think) whereas intellectual skills are to do with achieving specific objectives (thinking as problem solving). Wallis *et al.* (1966), looking at individual differences from the point of view of military training rather than education, use a similar set of skill categories (Table 1.1) but add also group skills including leadership, deployment of resources and team activity. Table 1.1 compares these two taxonomies with the taxonomies of skill used in this series of books. This figure is intended to be used for ease of presentation and comparison rather than as a precise indicator of different skill levels. It has been emphasized previously that skills do not form a neat orderly hierarchy. Most skilled performance involves a hybrid mix of mechanisms.

Table 1.1 Taxonomies of ability/skill

Gagné (education)	Wallis et al. (military training)		Singleton (real skills)	
motor skills	physical fitness procedural skills routine skills control skills	inside/out	body-image	enactive iconic
			pictorial	
verbal information	acquisition of information			
			symbolic	abstract
intellectual skill cognitive strategies	intellectual skills	outside/in		
attitudes	character building group identification			
			social skills	
	managerial skills system activities			

A less ambitious approach to taxonomic discussion is to separate out from the total population a particular category which is likely to have special properties and to be worthy of specific study. Hence 'the disabled', 'immigrants', 'gifted children', 'qualified scientists and engineers' and so on. As with all such people classifications it proves very difficult to define precisely the borderlines between those just inside and just outside the category.

PRINCIPLES OF COMPLEX MEASUREMENT

The underlying concept is that we are trying to define one position in an abstract multi-dimensional space. To do this unambiguously we have to construct axes within this space and we have to produce scales of measurement along each axis. Ideally as in Euclidean space there is a universal zero, a number of axes orthogonal to each other and a linear scale along each axis.

The people measurement problem can be approached in many ways. We can start by using some arbitrary scales which we have invented by devising particular tests and we can place the individual at a point on each scale. We can then speculate about how each of these scales relates to an abstract concept such as intelligence either by a process of reasoning relating the abstract concept to real behaviour, or rather more formally by trying to construct some less arbitrary axes to which the scores relate as in factor analysis. This is the psychometric approach. Alternatively we can start from manipulable situations and measure behaviour in these situations until certain consistencies begin to emerge as we manipulate the external variables. In this way we define categories of phenomena which eventually might fit together so that we have a structure of the behavioural universe. This is the experimental approach which has been supremely successful in dealing with the physical world. When one considers the way it has been possible to reduce all the variety of physical substances and phenomena to one unambiguous structure there remains some hope that the world of the psyche might also yield to the same treatment. Unfortunately it looks increasingly unlikely because psychologists are always faced with processes rather than structures and the behavioural experiment must include people who bring in an unknown but relevant past and a conscious awareness of the situation itself and its context.

One alternative is to start with a population of people and attempt by observation to locate certain consistencies which make it possible to divide people or tasks or abilities into categories either in the form of a comprehensive series of sets or selected subsets of the whole. This is the taxonomic approach. It has been widely used in the biological sciences. It is useful in applied psychology in dealing with issues of education and training.

Another alternative is to start with the recognition that individuals learn; behaviour and the individual are continuously and irreversibly modified by experience. Psychology then becomes a matter of identifying how these processes function and the underlying metric space is constructed on the basis of the different mechanisms which promote the processes. This is the developmental approach of which skills can be regarded as a special case. Inevitably these and other approaches are not mutually exclusive. Currently they remain competitive as measured by success in making sense of behaviour and there need be no objection to an eclectic strategy, each alternative has its own degree of success in particular fields.

Taxonomic approaches relate to the skills approach because so many taxonomies are based on form, structure or process. It is also implicit in skills theory that human function involves categorizing, which would indicate that the construction of taxonomies is quite fundamental within skilled behaviour. It seems that we need categories which are the analogue of axes in the metric space before we can think about measurement, but conversely we may need the inspiration of measurement to clarify our concepts of categories (Singleton and Spurgeon, 1975).

In general the study of individual differences is impeded by the twin difficulties that the concepts are not easily progressed without obtaining new empirical evidence and yet the accumulation of reliable evidence awaits the classification of the concepts. Incidentally this might well be the epitaph of much of twentieth-century psychology. However, there is another approach to individual differences which holds promise—this is to find out how each individual structures his universe and hence distinguish that individual by his personal constructs.

PERSONAL CONSTRUCT THEORY

Kelly (1955) reorientated the study of personality along more idiosyncratic lines. He proposed that each individual should be regarded as constructing his personal version of events and interactions in which he is involved. This enables him to make sense of the world and in particular to predict what is likely to happen. This fundamental and universal anticipatory procedure is based on an internal model of the world made up of what Kelly called 'constructs'. *Constructs* are bipolar ways of categorizing similarities and differences which are detected in the environment, they may or may not have explicit verbal labels such as black/white or friendly/hostile (Bannister, 1966). An individual's constructs fit together into a hierarchical network. There are constructs within constructs and each construct has a range of *convenience*. That is, there is only a limited set of events or interactions to which a particular construct can be applied. Each individual develops continuously his own set of constructs and their inter-relationships. In measuring and describing this set or network of constructs we are studying and describing the personality of that individual. Thus Kelly is suggesting that we should not look for a universally valid set of dimensions along which to measure the personality, rather we should try to find out which dimensions the individual is using to construct his world and these dimensions together with the way he uses them will define his personality.

Kelly's contribution consists not only of a plausible theory but also a consequential method of measurement. He suggested a technique called *The Repertory Grid* which is half-way between the two standard clinical procedures of the test and the structured interview. A list of people, roles or phenomena related to the subject and his behaviour are developed with or without his involvement and he is presented with these in sets of three. For example, one set might be employer/wife/brother. He is then asked, for each set of three, what two of them have in common which is not shared by the third. For the above example he might say that his employer and his wife are unco-operative and bossy, but his brother is co-operative and sympathetic. This gives us one of his constructs: co-operative/unco-operative which might apply to others within the list of roles. By this kind of procedure, with many variations depending on the objectives of the study, it is possible to indirectly elicit a set of constructs from the subject which he would not have been able to provide by direct introspection and discussion. Although various statistical techniques, including factor analysis, can be applied to the results of such a study the approach is essentially a clinical one aimed at finding out about a particular individual rather than placing him in a category or ranking him in relation to others.

The Repertory Grid is one formal approach to self-characterization (Bannister and Fransella, 1971). An allied theory of personality which also places great emphasis on the self is that due to Rogers (1959). This is a

client-centred humanistic formulation of the principle that a person continuously appraises himself and his behaviour; if this appraisal indicates consistency and not too far a departure from some personal norm—the 'ideal self'—
then all is well. If not then the individual is in personal difficulties which might
result in him appearing in the clinic of a counsellor such as Kelly or Rogers.
There seem to be two main types of theory currently in vogue in counselling
practice: humanistic theories such as those just described and behavioural
theories in the Pavlov/Skinner/Eysenck tradition (Nelson-Jones, 1982).

The former are much more closely allied to theories of human skill. The
common ancestry is in gestalt psychology by contrast with behavioural
psychology. There are common principles of the individual monitoring his
own behaviour, continuously categorizing, predicting the future, comparing
actual performance with expected performance and modifying not only his
performance but his own internal structures on the basis of experience. In
terms of skills the repertory grid would seem to provide access only to higher
level skills which involve language. Enactive and iconic skills are not so readily
analysed introspectively. The concept of self is confirmed in importance but
remains resistant to explanatory analysis, so also does motivation.

ORGANIZATIONALLY IMPORTANT DESCRIPTIONS
OF INDIVIDUALS

Most of what is known about individual differences has arisen from studies in
the clinical and educational fields. The issues which arise in the occupational
field are different because competitive organizations cannot be student-
centred as in educational psychology, or client-centred as in clinical psychology. The worker is rewarded as a servant of the system and it is necessary
to have individual assessment techniques which lead to differential rewards in
the form of pay, promotion and changes in training exposure and job specification. Here we are on very weak ground conceptually. Because the vast
majority of psychologists, either academic or applied, have concentrated on
educational and clinical work, there has been a tendency to transfer their concepts too uncritically into the world of work and other activities of ordinary
adults. The only recognized parameter of the mind which has universal cur-
rency is intelligence and the importance of this in ordinary life is considerably
overrated by those who have spent their lives in education. The qualities of
subordinates and peers which employers or managers always seem to seek are
reliability, perseverance, commitment and integrity. Individuals do differ considerably along these dimensions but at present we have no means of measuring these attributes and no theory which will fit them into an integral context.

However, social skills are important to all fields of psychology and the
studies of particular occupations in the chapters which follow come from
education, research, the law and sport as well as from industry and commerce.

References

Allport, G. W. (1937). *Personality: a Psychological Interpretation.* (London: Constable)

Anastasi, A. (1961). *Psychological Testing.* (New York: Macmillan)

Anglin, J. M. (1973) (ed.). *Beyond the Information Given.* (London: George Allen and Unwin)

Bannister, D. (1966). A new theory of personality. In B. M. Foss (ed.) *New Horizons in Psychology.* (Harmondsworth: Penguin)

Bannister, D. and Fransella, F. (1971). *Inquiring Man: the Theory of Personal Constructs.* (Harmondsworth: Penguin)

Bromley, P. B. (1979). Personality appraisal. In K. Connolly (ed.) *Psychological Survey No. 2.* (London: George Allen and Unwin)

Cattell, R. B. (1965). *The Scientific Analysis of Personality.* (Harmondsworth: Penguin)

Davis, L. E. and Cherns, A. B. (2 vols.) (1975) (eds.). *The Quality of Working Life.* (London: Collier–Macmillan)

Davis, L. E. and Taylor, J. C. (1972). *Design of Jobs.* (Harmondsworth: Penguin)

Duncan, K. D., Gruneberg, M. M. and Duncan, K. D. (1980) (eds.). *Changes in Working Life.* (Chichester: Wiley)

Evans, P. (1975). *Motivation.* (London: Methuen)

Eysenck, H. J. (1947). *Dimensions of Personality.* (London: Routledge and Kegan Paul)

Festinger, L. (1957). *A Theory of Cognitive Dissonance.* (New York: Harper and Row)

Freud, S. (1940). *An Outline of Psychoanalysis.* (London: Hogarth Press)

Gagne, R. M. (1975). Taxonomic problems of educational system. In W. T. Singleton and P. Spurgeon (eds.) *Measurements of Human Resources.* (London: Taylor and Francis)

Getzels, J. W. and Jackson, P. W. (1962). *Creativity and Intelligence.* (New York: Wiley)

Guilford, J. P. (1950). Creativity. *Am. Psychol.*, **5**, 444–54

Heim, A. (1970). *Intelligence and Personality.* (Harmondsworth: Penguin)

Herzberg, F. B., Mausner, M. and Snyderman, B. B. (1959). *The Motivation to Work.* (New York: Wiley)

Hilgard, E. R. (1963). Motivation in learning theory. In S. Koch (ed.) *Psychology: a Study of Science, Vol. 5.* (New York: McGraw-Hill)

Hudson, C. (1966). *Contrary Imaginations.* (London: Methuen)

Kelly, G. A. (1955). *The Psychology of Personal Constructs.* (New York: Norton)

Kline, P. (1976). *Psychological Testing.* (London: Malaby Press)

Maslow, A. H. (1943). A theory of human motivation. *Psychological Review*, **50**, 370–95

Miller, R. B. (1967). Task taxonomy: science or technology? In W. T. Singleton, R. S. Easterby and D. Whitfield (eds.) *The Human Operator in Complex Systems.* (London: Taylor and Francis)

Miller, R. B. (1975). Taxonomies for training. In W. T. Singleton and P. Spurgeon (eds.) *Measurements of Human Resources.* (London: Taylor and Francis)

Nelson-Jones, R. (1982). *The Theory and Practice of Counselling Psychology.* (London: Holt, Rinehart and Winston)

Peck, D. and Whitlaw, D. (1975). *Approaches to Personality Theory.* (London: Methuen)

Rogers, C. R. (1959). A theory of therapy, personality and inter-personal relationships as developed in the client centred framework. In S. Koch (ed.) *Psychology: A Study of Science, Vol. 3.* (New York: McGraw-Hill)

Russell, B. (1948). *Human Knowledge.* (London: George Allen and Unwin)

Sanford, N. (1963). Personality: its place in psychology. In S. Koch (ed.) *Psychology: A Study of Science, Vol. 5.* (New York: McGraw-Hill)

Sell, R. G. and Shipley, P. (1979) (eds.). *Satisfaction in Work Design.* (London: Taylor and Francis)

Sheldon, W. H. and Stevens, S. S. (1942). *The Varieties of Temperament.* (New York: Harper Row)

Sherif, M. and Sherif, C. W. (1967). *Attitude, Ego Involvement and Change.* (New York: Wiley)

Singleton, W. T. and Spurgeon, P. (1975) (eds.). *Measurements of Human Resources.* (London: Taylor and Francis)

Thomas, K. (1971). *Attitudes and Behaviour—Selected Readings*. (Harmondsworth: Penguin)

Vernon, P. E. (1956). *The Measurement of Abilities*. (London: University Press)

Vernon, P. E. and Parry, J. B. (1949). *Personnel Selection in the British Armed Forces*. (London: University Press)

Wall, T. D. and Lischeron, J. A. (1977). *Work Participation*. (London: McGraw-Hill)

Wallis, D., Duncan, K. D. and Knight, M. A. G. (1966). *Programmed Instruction in the British Armed Forces*. (London: HMSO)

Warr, P. B. (1970). *Thought and Personality—Selected Readings*. (Harmondsworth: Penguin)

Warr, P. B. (1976). Theories of motivation. In P. Warr (ed.) *Personal Goals and Work Design*. (London: Wiley)

Wechsler, D. (1958). *The Measurement and Appraisal of Adult Intelligence*. (London: Bailliere, Tindall and Cox)

2
The School Teacher

M. M. GOODFELLOW

INTRODUCTION

We are all consumers of the education system but the product is intangible and society, represented by parents, employers and politicians, is very demanding of teachers.

Education is not an industry; schools are not factories for churning out socially and academically acceptable young persons for the minimum outlay. Pupils do not form a homogeneous group; they are individuals and, to maximize potential, they should be treated as such; their social needs are as varied as their academic capabilities. Staff are normally selected for their potential contribution to the social development of the children in the context of that particular school as well as for their practical and academic ability.

Education is an open-ended process subject to constant modification as a result of teacher–pupil interaction and other factors. Teachers are concerned to offer something that goes beyond mere training or instruction. Although being directly responsible for specific children for only a short period, their interest continues throughout life and often to the third generation. Pupils, however independent they claim to be, cannot avoid the influence of school and usually have a loyalty to their school.

THE TEACHER–PUPIL RELATIONSHIP

The teacher's first contact with a pupil is in an accepted role; the skilled teacher knows how to maintain and trade on this inherited ethos while gradually earning respect as a person. Once a teacher's reputation has been established, whether good or otherwise, it tends to be self-sustaining; attitudes made clear in one class will send ripples in wide circles so that action is rarely needed by the strong disciplinarian after the initial period thus encouraging a more relaxed attitude. This, in turn, opens the way for the development of more interesting and stimulating methods which elevate the teacher, and the subject, in the opinion of the pupils. The image of mastery can be further reinforced by colleagues, either unconsciously or as a result of agreed policy. A child must be under firm control if it is to learn, and allow others to learn; the success of the education system will be measured in terms of evidence of that learning. Given that the necessary academic knowledge and practical skills are adequate, the social skill of the teacher lies in persuading the pupils to provide the environment most suitable for the learning process with the minimum opposition and maximum co-operation.

A high academic level may be achieved when there is a degree of respect and discipline, even if the degree of empathy is small. This is more likely to be encountered when children are highly motivated and the teaching is subject-orientated, but this ideology is less common than the pupil- or client-orientated approach which is more demanding of the empathic ability of the teacher. Empathy in the most idealistic terms poses considerable problems. It is in a constant state of flux; the transitory nature might baffle the inexperienced teacher and lack of response could be a constant source of disappointment. The effects of compatibility, or lack of it, become more obvious as the child becomes older and more aware of others. Very few teachers are called upon to apply their skills across the whole age range, from infants to young adults, or through the whole ability range, but all are concerned with children of widely differing abilities, upbringing and aspirations. A rigidly structured programme of instruction of infants is necessary to establish group discipline and a repertoire of habits appropriate to the new situation of a larger community whereas similar treatment of older children will merely antagonize. Initially, in all circumstances, the objective should be to instil acceptance of requests and instructions leading to the establishment of confidence on both sides with subsequent facility for relaxation, discussion and corporate decision-making. A senior class will normally accept the need to defer this stage but will take unkindly to total repression with little possibility of participation at some time. If the teacher is totally dominant for too long, there will be a brake on the assumption of self-discipline and a desirable work ethic; the child will also be incapable of assuming responsibility for others. These deficiencies of social progress will be evident in the difference in behaviour when supervised and when left to continue private study or group activity.

Children have a tendency to deal with life in compartments and, generally, do not transfer inter-relationships when staff change. Thus each teacher must establish his own standards within each group which he teaches and the general tone of the whole school will be a reflection of the established patterns. Once the demands and responsibilities of the group as a unit have been accepted, it is possible to identify sub-groups for attention and, within these, to establish communication with individuals. The firmest ground for the first steps is that of the academic work which has defined boundaries. This can be assessed relatively easily on an objective basis; it enables the teacher to establish that he is knowledgeable, to set the standard required and to be seen to be accurate and 'fair' in marking. This period can be most profitably used to identify group loyalties, to note the leaders and the more isolated children. The most urgent targets are the strong personalities who could be potential trouble-makers. Attention to these, diverting them, applying the 'divide and rule' principle, mixing them with the rest of the class and giving responsibility and praise, even if the effort is minimal, could pay dividends later, especially if they have a strong following. It is important that the tasks given are such that one would expect them to be fulfilled with success. If pupils thus gain favourable recognition, desirable changes in attitude may be effected not only in the leaders but also in lower status pupils.

It takes longer to determine if the quiet ones are reluctant, inadequate or merely of a retiring nature, and there is always the danger of neglecting the apparently happy, conforming child who, nevertheless, might perform at a higher level, both socially and academically, if given attention on occasion. Frequently, children behave as they think they are expected to behave and find it increasingly difficult to act in a manner which does not conform to their reputation whether it is as an aggressive extrovert or, in contrast, an aloof, solitary being. Skilled indeed is the teacher who can effect a total change, harnessing the energy of the former and giving the confidence to ignore the pressures of the peer group or involving the latter in group activities.

Pupils' self-esteem is influenced by their treatment at the hand of others; those who experience repeated educational failure are likely to become bored and apathetic, or even antagonistic, with a decreasing estimate of their capabilities. Thus, evaluation of a child's ability and talents, with judicious use of approval in classroom teaching to emphasize success rather than failings, can have a marked influence on the morale of an individual and set the tone of the whole group. However, reward should be tempered by constructive criticism if a child is to develop, and excessive use of praise, or reward, is self-defeating, since it becomes undervalued. Ideally, the aim should be recognition and stated appreciation of success at any level by members of the peer group. The skill of listening, with only occasional interjections, is of considerable value in dealing with problems as well as in establishing contact. The child with a grievance can air it in private and be treated as a reasonably responsible individual rather than a potentially subversive element. The better the relationship, the more ready will be the child to accept criticism of work or attitude; if this can be delivered in a bantering manner it is usually accepted without rancour. Education should be enjoyable with an element of fun.

What are the pupils' demands of the teacher? Discipline, attention, patience, kindness, enthusiasm, expertise, humour, integrity . . . and so on. To satisfy these demands, the teacher must be able to adjust according to the mood of the moment, to be able to assess if anger will be more beneficial than tolerance, to judge the correct time to bring antagonists together to extract an apology, and to decide if a pupil is ready to accept more responsibility in the knowledge that, if the moment is allowed to pass, action might be too late.

THE TEACHER–PARENT RELATIONSHIP

Parents, although strictly speaking they are secondary, probably consider themselves as the primary consumers of the education system since their offspring are too young to make decisions at the beginning of their schooling. They often expect the type of education they experienced with emphasis on strict discipline and rote learning; the more informal approach, alien concepts and group teaching may create a climate of suspicion at the outset. This may change with time; if it does not, the teacher will need to take active steps to explain the methods used and the aims of the curriculum otherwise the child's development will be hindered.

The parents' first formal introduction to the school will probably be at a meeting for the new intake; the aim of this exercise is usually to make the child's transition from pre-school to infant, or junior to secondary, as untraumatic as possible for all concerned. Parental attitudes and co-operation are especially important at this stage before the pupil has made his own judgements. If the child is interviewed at the same time, the sense of unity will be encouraged and it is possible to assess the interaction between parents and child. The size of the school and local organization will determine, to a large extent, the method adopted. In a small school, which includes most primary schools and some secondary, the Head should be able to see everyone, which enhances the feeling of importance and involvement. In a large school, various staff must be involved in seeing parents and dealing with the essential paper work which will entail careful planning if the meeting is to be worthwhile on the social level. Some staff are very skilled at establishing rapport quickly, especially if they know the neighbourhood or are sufficiently interested to determine if there are any family connections with the school.

It is socially valuable to address a parent by name; this is taken as a compliment if the child is not present but to be unable to do so when the pupil is at hand is not readily forgiven. The primary school teacher is at an advantage in this respect as parents usually collect young children from school and bring them in if they happen to be late so that the parent is easily identified with the pupil. An increasing problem is the number of pupils who do not have the same name as the mother. Implied criticism of the family may provoke indignation as one cannot assume that the presence of two parents together means that they live as a family. A skill which is frequently needed at interviews or consultations is the ability to terminate discussion without the parents feeling that they are being dismissed.

Happy relationships depend on conveying the implication that the views of the parents will be considered, even if they are not accepted eventually. Phraseology is all important; 'I will see what can be done' is essentially the same as 'I cannot deal with the matter now' but the positive attitude is usually more acceptable. A request for an appointment can be caused by almost any aspect of school life; making time to respond quickly can save time if it is trivial; if it is more serious, the possibility of a problem growing out of all proportion is prevented. On the rare occasions when a telephone call is made to thank or compliment a teacher, it gives a considerable boost to morale. The fact that the relationship is two-way frequently becomes overlooked or obscured; few parents realize how effective in encouragement a personal word of appreciation can be.

Time and patience on the part of the Head can usually defuse conflict between parents of different pupils, parents of a particular pupil or parents and a teacher. The major skill called into use on such occasions is the ability to listen, refrain from personal comment and appear to be sympathetic to all sides if there is not clear-cut blame. Assessing the accuracy of information may pose some difficulty since children, naturally, give their version of an event rather than all the facts. Interviewing the child in the presence of the parents usually settles the matter in a few minutes and puts it in perspective.

The most difficult counselling relates to selfish behaviour on the part of parents which is obviously having a detrimental effect on the child, physically or mentally. Again, no firm guidelines can be followed; the skill lies in being able to assess the situation and respond accordingly. When more than one person is involved, it may be necessary to play the part of the firm chairman, even if the protagonists would like a referee. The majority of parents contribute much in terms of material benefits and time and should be made aware that their efforts are appreciated.

THE TEACHER–COLLEAGUE RELATIONSHIP

Direct social interactions between members of the staff of a school differ little from those of any profession in which there is a fairly well-defined hierarchical structure but, in this case, there is the third dimension of the pupils who may affect relationships either directly or indirectly. Children are notorious for their inclination to set one person off against another if it will make life easier for themselves; the experienced teacher never believes any tale before checking but, of course, the unguarded comment may be reported and sour relationships.

Go into any staff-room and one can find the spectrum of types and behaviour patterns which are readily recognizable. The probationer, at the bottom of the pecking order, is liable to feel isolated if there is no one else in a similar position unless care is taken to ensure integration.

Teachers are generally jealous of status and possessions, probably because they have been hard won. The sensitive teacher shows due deference to those in authority, encouraging the pupils to do likewise, and does not act selfishly. The self-centred one, who has little idea of communal living and is not prepared to sacrifice or contribute to the common good, can cause considerable friction in the common-room. If this extends to empire-building, and the pursuit of personal ambition as the mainspring of activity, repercussions will, almost certainly, be felt throughout the school. The current review of the whole curriculum will highlight these aspects, but it is unlikely to cause modification of the attitudes of the strongly subject-orientated teacher, especially in the secondary sector where subject requirements frequently govern allocation of resources.

The Head of Department should be able to relate well to the sub-group to facilitate effective organization and involvement and to maintain enthusiasm but he should also be able to regard general school requirements in an objective manner. The Deputy Head in overall charge of the staff-room plays a key role in keeping a balance, being aware of any social problems and filtering information in both directions. Ideally he should be a firm, kindly, efficient, impartial organizer known to be able to respect confidentiality and prepared to deal with any routine or emergency business with calm good humour. The relationship of the Head to the rest of the staff will depend to some extent on the relationship with the Deputy. A delicate balance needs to be maintained between a very authoritarian approach and contact sufficiently relaxed to be able to appreciate the personality of the teacher outside the classroom without encouraging familiarity. Accessibility, willingness to delegate and encouragement for all to feel that they can take responsibility for some administration and that their views on policy formulation will be heeded are all useful attributes. Consultation with the senior teachers, knowledge of family background and consideration in times of stress will help to foster a sense of group loyalty which can alleviate difficulties caused by industrial action, should it occur. The head of any school still exercises some control over appointments and allocations, if only through recommendation, and must be seen to be acting fairly. The slow movement within the profession at the present time makes good social relations among the staff even more important and much skill is required to maintain the spirit of working for the good of the pupils without undue consideration of reward in financial terms. Corporate decision-making can help toward this end but is of little value in the absence of corporate responsibility.

OTHER RELATIONSHIPS

The position of ancillary staff in schools is often misunderstood by those outside the profession. Absence of the secretary or the caretaker makes an immediate impact: they are involved in most aspects of the running of the school. Normal commonsense and consideration will allow them to make most effective use of the limited time available and facilitate smooth operation; forward planning, strict enforcement of time schedules and regulations and the occasional word of appreciation will help to alleviate frustration. A particular teacher will probably not meet most of the domestic staff but will meet some of them and can play a part in fostering a sense of belonging to the community by acknowledging their presence and encouraging the pupils to be aware of them as members of the school. Ignorance of the work of the ancillary staff and of the system can lead to action which may cause unhappiness or complete breakdown in relations to the detriment of all.

The role of the governors varies considerably in different establishments from near-total management in independent schools to one of general support in many maintained schools. The Head has most contact with the governing body as a whole and it is his responsibility to be able to relate to all members to create cohesion and trust, to keep them informed of the activities of the school and to introduce them to staff. The advent of statutory teacher representatives on the governing body of a school has brought the working of this group to the attention of the staff. Alienation and antipathy, which could arise from differences in political views or disagreement over the operation of the school, does sometimes occur. Care taken to explain facets of the work, aims and achievements, will usually minimize opposition and has been known to bring about reversal of opinion.

CAREER DEVELOPMENT

One hopes that the teacher develops throughout professional life as experience is gained and contact broadened. He will normally have some ambition or may take the opportunity to progress through the hierarchical structure, and must be able to adapt, especially if progression is within one establishment. He will find a change in emphasis of the skills required as his position changes.

He starts as a probationer who has to make a mark but is expected to remember his place as a member of a department and the common-room. He will be expected to be able to accept criticism with good grace and to accede to requests of more senior colleagues. At the end of the year he is considered to be an experienced assistant and expected to take responsibility within the school and have departmental work delegated to him. If he has not already been in this position, he will now have to acquire the skill of approaching colleagues in such a way as to get their full co-operation. In a secondary school he might by this time be second in department with the additional task of organizing others and, possibly, monitoring their work if there is corporate management.

The Head of a large department, or senior teacher in a small school, is in a superior position with demands being made from below and above. The ability to assess the strengths of junior staff in order to delegate, to absorb disciplinary and other problems within the department, to influence and encourage other staff and to act as liaison with Head or LEA representatives is expected. So, too, is a greater commitment to the general organization of the school. The Departmental Head must have his own needs as a priority but he should also be able to relate to others in the same position and recognize their claims to the available resources. Ideally, discussions of such matters as overall curriculum development should be amicable and objective since they may lead to policy decisions to be implemented throughout the school.

Above this level are the realms of management with a smaller teaching load so the social relationship with the children, as well as the staff, changes in a subtle manner. The role of Deputy Head and the Head will depend on the size and structure of the school; in smaller ones their duties are very broad-based, in larger schools there is usually division of labour between administrative and pastoral responsibilities. The Deputy in the latter position will normally need to exercise social skills at all levels with little respite. The officers of the LEA are so remote from the daily lives of those at the chalkface, other than the Head and secretary, that they are not usually regarded as persons but referred to collectively as the inanimate 'County Hall' or its equivalent. The general staff will rarely see an adviser or inspector, will meet education officers only if they appear at social functions, and will know the Director of Education and the Chairman of the Education Committee only by name. Nevertheless, contact is necessary, on occasion, and the Head of Department who collaborates with the subject adviser will be in a better position to make requests to gain benefits for the department. The Head is in a different position; having established a sound relationship, he must be able to judge when unheeded polite requests should be superseded by orchestrated action which is less acceptable to superiors but produces a response, thus encouraging staff and parents. The administrative skill of negotiating the maze of bureaucracy has some value in furthering confidence in dealing with social problems when pastoral or financial help is required.

THE COMPETENT TEACHER

The achievement of competence must be based on a genuine interest in education and sympathy with, or at least tolerance of, the prevailing interests of the young. The teacher must have the ability to gain respect and to act always with dignity and authority. Other relevant attributes include humour, a sense of proportion, objectivity, fairness and the ability to think on one's feet. The techniques of providing encouragement and expressing unopinionated opinions are valuable. Perhaps the most important skill emerges as awareness of people and their situation, particularly of course young people, and empathy with their activities and aspirations.

THE VIRTUOSO TEACHER

Many trainee teachers will have all these characteristics but the experienced teachers develop also the ability to foresee the possible lines of development of a situation and guide these in a desirable direction either by reinforcement or by blocking. It is a fairly simple exercise to create situations in order to achieve a desired position, or end, and to manipulate children in a covert manner to persuade them to attempt tasks which they consider to be beyond their capabilities or to take an unfamiliar stance.

Ideally, one aims to foster a public-spirited attitude and to transfer responsibility to the group or sub-group. Peer group pressure may be towards anti-social, non-conformist behaviour; this may be used effectively by making it the subject of open discussion in a controlled debate thus alleviating tension. The essential sensitivity and the ability to communicate with individuals without interrupting the flow of a lesson is established almost without notice. Action is often more effective than words. The bright look, sidelong glances, unnatural behaviour, attention concentrated on the teacher, all make the experienced practitioner somewhat suspicious. Familiarity with a class or child will enable rapid assessment of the degree of mischief—is it serious or can it be treated as a joke? Complete mastery of the lesson content enables one to proceed with that at a level of lower consciousness, while the conscious mind is freed to explore the social planes.

It is sometimes better to play the part of the ignoramus in order to elicit information, either factual or explanatory, rather than to appear to be knowledgeable and, perhaps, brusque or abrasive. Gradual application of pressure, always leaving room for manoeuvre but not withdrawing, usually avoids use of the ultimate sanction. Eventually, one should get beyond the concept of giver and receiver to sharing lessons and other activities so that both teacher and pupils enjoy the experience, reaching the end with a feeling of satisfaction. The potentially dreary lesson, a breeding ground for trouble or apathy, can be tackled together as a challenge to beat boredom, so that even a low level of content satisfaction can be balanced by a high degree of social rapport.

Openings need to be created for the less extrovert children. Periods of working quietly in class gives the opportunity to devote attention to the apparently non-participating pupils. The easiest point of contact is the work in hand which may be used to reveal other interests— or none! The teaching skill of providing variety should be sufficient to identify the totally withdrawn child. An unfamiliar class and younger children sometimes respond more readily to the impersonal use of roll number rather than being called upon by name. Requests for assistants to linger after the lesson will frequently produce a response which will not be elicited by a show of hands. Similarly, a time and place set aside for casual contact, quite distinct from detention or remedial provision, preferably with an objective in the nature of special books or displays, will give shy children scope to discuss their interests and find others of like mind.

The tiresome colleague presents a more difficult problem in many ways. Thoughtlessness on the part of a basically co-operative person will usually be corrected if he is approached in a straightforward manner and the effects of his action clearly demonstrated. Almost total self-centredness in an adult is very wearing. The most successful approach will be determined by the relationship with other members of staff. Good humoured comment, especially if reinforced by those not directly concerned, may be used if the general relationship is relaxed but some find this irritating. Even if reform is slow, this approach will probably not further sour attitudes. Constant reminders sometimes achieve a satisfactory change and taking matters to a higher authority should be considered only if all else fails.

Timing

There are some obvious occasions when timing is crucial. Nothing will be gained by tackling a sullen child who arrives late with every symptom of a recent confrontation, even if it appears that bad manners are tolerated. The necessary time and space must be created for a private interview thus giving the child more scope for explanation and avoiding aggravation. In all inter-relationships, listening to others and selecting the right time to intervene in a suitable manner is a skill which is worth cultivating. It can be used to stimulate, to direct, to prevent further comment, to inspire confidence or to give shy children a chance to contribute orally. Noting the more successful methods is of value, but the chance to improve upon them is rare because of the constantly changing conditions and mood of the group. A bad mistake should never be repeated, however, as it usually reflects some deficiency in basic technique.

CONCLUSION

The key to the success of a teacher is encompassed in one trait—awareness, a sense of the needs of others coupled with a sense of time and place, sharpened by experience.

The exercise of social skills is not a function of intellectual capacity. Indeed, academically gifted individuals are frequently disastrous as teachers. One can distinguish the social skills of teaching, the basic routine attitudes applied to the age range being taught, from the skills of the teacher which are much more diverse. It is possible to inculcate good habits by repetition and example but the scale of the exercise and the frequently changing pupils make constant effort a necessity. The teacher must deal with hundreds of individuals, sub-groups, groups and the whole. Those clamouring for attention are not necessarily those who need it most; the pitfall of mid-group attention with the fringe being ignored should be recognized. Through constant vigilance it may be possible to prevent a child establishing an undesirable pattern of behaviour and a reputation for non-conformity. This awareness must be accompanied by adaptability and flexibility with the facility to make an individual feel that he is the most important person at that time. The realities of a teacher's task are extremely complex and some of the skills defy analysis. Why is it that an apparently weak, helpless teacher, infuriating to colleagues, is protected by the pupils whilst another, similar, one is massacred? Why will verbal abuse be accepted from one teacher but not from another? The social skills practised in a school are inextricably bound with the practical skills and both can be assessed only through the performance of the pupils, sometimes years after they have been directly influenced by a particular teacher. To acquire per-ceptual or motor skills requires instruction and guidance; the result is known and feed-back is readily available. The area of social skills is less definable; one is not always sure of the result and rarely is there any feed-back, but how rewarding it is to find a youth returning to the primary school, to have letters telling of success 'you believed in me when I doubted, now I have reached my goal' or to meet erstwhile worried parents who can live more happily.

3
The University Teacher

W. T. SINGLETON

INTRODUCTION

University students are always the product of some form of selection scheme. The selection criteria vary from one country to another and from one era to another within a country, but broadly speaking it can be assumed that the ordinary student comes from a family with a belief in the value of education and that he or she is above average in intelligence, in ambition, and in interest in the particular subject of study. This would seem to be a very positive foundation on which to base the tertiary educational phase but there are also some negative factors. In the United Kingdom at the present time the ordinary student has a low standard of living in that the disposable income is much smaller than that of contemporaries who have started to earn a living; this has many repercussions such as difficulties in finding an adequate private study environment, the steady reduction of the habit of book buying, inadequate diet, a shortage of cultured or exciting leisure pursuits and perhaps most important of all, a low morale because of the feeling not only of lack of privilege but even lack of sympathy from the supporting community.

The university teacher is under similar pressures in that his standard of living has, comparatively, been on the decline for many years and so also have the resources he can devote to a student in terms of facilities and his own time. However, these pressures are not yet so severe as to reduce the demand for student places or to cause the teachers to move to other occupations on any appreciable scale. Thus the context is still one of dedication and shared intellectual beliefs. There is clarity and urgency in objectives in that examinations are never very far in the future. This can sometimes conflict with interest in the subject in its own right.

OBJECTIVES

The task of the university teacher is to transfer his expertise in a particular discipline to his students. This expertise is made up of an acquaintance with what is known, where to find it, how to use it, how to add to it, how to assess it, and how to communicate it.

Advance in knowledge is achieved by communication within a generation of academics (research) and by communication between successive generations (teaching). All this communication depends on the agreed conceptualizations of the particular topic. In skill terminology it depends on devising and sharing pictorial and symbolic models. The older academic (the university teacher) condenses his own intellectual activity into models which he passes on to the younger academic (the student). The latter is thus in an advantageous position because he has a mind which is fresh but equipped with the achievements of previous minds. He is hoisted, as it were, on to the intellectual shoulders of his predecessors. This is the basic function of a university.

Some students will have the drive and the intellectual capacity to take up the challenge of this privileged position but the majority will not. There is no selection procedure which will identify the academically gifted minority before a university course and so universities have a secondary function. They educate and train people to take up tasks other than advancing knowledge such as teaching younger pupils and taking up other jobs which depend on having some expertise in the subject. Practising the trade in this way is not necessarily inferior to studying it academically. There is a distinction here between arts and sciences. On the whole the professors of physics are the great physicists but the professors of literature are not the greatest novelists, playwrights or poets. This is because physics is a mechanistic abstract discipline where communicable pictorial and symbolic models are the core of skill but literature is a humanistic discipline where success in practice depends on enactive models. The technologies—medicine and engineering—are in an intermediate position. The advances and highest levels of achievement may come from either the pure or the applied workers.

If the graduate is to become a practitioner with a market value in the world external to the university he needs some certification. This is provided by his teacher who must therefore also be an assessor or examiner. This role is actually inextricable from the continuous activity of teaching because the teacher's feedback from the practice of his skill must itself be a form of assessment of how much the student has learned. The student cannot learn without continuous feedback related to his degree of success and similarly the teacher cannot teach skilfully without continuous feedback about his degree of success. The teacher's knowledge of results refers partly to individual students and partly to the collective reaction of the group of students.

Similarly, the student assesses his position not only in an absolute sense of his rate of learning but perhaps mainly in a relative sense of his performance compared with that of his fellow students. The teaching/learning situation is obviously a group process as well as an interaction between one teacher and one learner.

In summary there are two objectives for the university teacher:

(1) He provides his own successors at the frontier of knowledge.
(2) He provides practitioners in professions related to the discipline.

To achieve these objectives he must not only convey information and skill, he must assess continuously how much is being conveyed and terminally how much has been conveyed.

THE LEARNING PROCESS

It is possible that learning in the sense of acquiring factual information can be a one-way communication process. Skills, however, always require participative learning. A teacher cannot transmit a skill, he can only persuade a learner to make the effort to acquire it himself. Fortunately it seems that knowledge of results can reinforce the learning process in two separate ways. Providing that the goal matters to the participant, knowledge of results provides a profound incentive to go on learning and simultaneously knowledge of results will aid orientation by providing reinforcement of successful actions. Annett (1969) maintains that these two effects are, from some theoretical viewpoints, not as distinct as they might appear. Regardless of this academic argument the teacher is attempting to maintain both rate and direction of progress. Steering a student is like steering a boat, one needs a propeller and a rudder and neither is of very much use without the other. Correspondingly a boat has no meaning without an occupant who wishes to go somewhere. Teacher and learner co-operate in agreeing the goal and in finding ways of moving towards it. From this viewpoint the teacher is the leader of the class and he needs the skills of a leader which are just those mentioned above, namely to be able to articulate the objective and to formulate acceptable ways of achieving it.

The psychological literature is much concerned with separating types of learning; for example, conditioning, verbal learning, perceptual–motor skills learning, problem-solving (Melton, 1964). These distinctions are necessary to understand psychological research but they are not of great relevance to the business of practical teaching. Types of learning are used also as a basis for describing the conditions of learning (Gagne, 1970) but again the university teacher rarely formulates the instructional process in such detail. He is concerned with the patterns of learning over several years rather than within a few days.

The university student usually works through a teaching programme for a university year which, in terms of weeks, takes up about half a calendar year. The end of a teaching year is followed by examinations although there will be an intervening period of several weeks allocated to private study and revision.

The basic teaching vehicle is the lecture which lasts about one hour and is mainly a one-way communication from teacher to students. There will be some feedback. Questions may be possible and the experienced teacher will gain information from the individual postures of students, where they look, how much and how quickly they write and so on. He is continuously assessing the collective level of arousal and attention and how it changes during the lecture. In some factual topics such as engineering the lecture may be used to convey comprehensive information, everything the student needs to know is written on the blackboard or in the handout. More usually the lecturer is conducting a guided tour of the topic extensively referenced so that students can locate details later. The tour is a progressive one moving through the key features at a pace which the average student appears to comprehend. The underlying purpose is not to convey information but rather to demonstrate how the lecturer's mind works in appraising a particular topic.

More participative learning is encouraged by tutorial discussions with associated essay writing, laboratory experiments with associated reports, seminars, computer-directed learning exercises, class experiments, case studies, group projects and workshops.

In order to conduct this whole process effectively the university teacher must, often together with other teachers, be involved in the following tasks:

the design of the structure and content of the course—the curriculum;

the design of the pattern of teaching processes: lectures, laboratories, tutorials and so on;

the selection and induction of the students;

the teaching;

the assessment.

The students are not present at the first two stages but there are social skills in making progress with a group of fellow teachers. These are also required for the collective assessment. Thus the practice of skills can be subdivided into peer group interaction and staff–student interaction.

PEER GROUP INTERACTION

University teachers participate in many collective development activities and decisions. These processes can be divided roughly into three categories according to purpose: the continuous modification of the curriculum, the teaching activity and the assessment.

Curriculum discussions

These may take place at any level from formal course committees to a casual encounter between two individuals concerned about a specific issue. Cues which support the need for a change come partly from the written work of students but mainly from social interactions with either students or colleagues. In the course of conversation someone will say something which provokes an unintended or secondary reaction in the listener. Apart from the primary reaction to what has actually been said, the listener will get a sudden insight that the speaker has revealed something about his state of knowledge if he is a student, or his reaction to the course if he is a teacher which indicates that the curriculum is at fault. The curriculum is not doing its job as revealed by the style and attitude rather than content of what the speaker said. Sensitivity to this kind of cue is clearly a consequence of a social skill. The listener must have a mental model which incorporates expected characteristics of the course effects and the individual speaker which enables him to predict how the speaker should behave, but there is a clash and a discontinuity—the speaker is not conforming to predicted behaviour. There is a close analogy with skilful behaviour in the physical world. Any skilled individual has an internal model of the outside world which he is manipulating. The model develops in parallel with changes in the real world and new sensory data should confirm the match between the two. When the behaviour of the real world begins to depart from the model then new sense data will originate a signal of mismatch. Here is information which must be processed by modifying the model. This description applies equally to a man walking along a pavement or a man discussing a teaching issue with a colleague. Information is generated when things cease to go according to prediction. The increased complexity of the latter situation is due to the fact that the physical cues—the spoken word, the gesture, the posture and so on are themselves secondary indications of what the listener is actually modelling, namely the knowledge and attitudes of the speaker and how they must have arisen. Thus there are several stages of inference between the source of information—the model in the speaker's mind and the destination of the information—the model in the listener's mind. It is hardly surprising that conversations of this kind are muddled, repetitious and fraught with misunderstandings. Discrepancies may abound in terms of detailed disagreements stated verbally but the underlying differences in the two models are not readily identifiable again because these may be several orders removed from the spoken word. Much of the conversation will be at this meta-level where the speaker analyses his own statements in the form, 'I support this position because fundamentally I believe . . .', equally the listener will try to probe the different levels by questions such as 'When you say that, is it because you think . . .?' The pedantic person who insists that he said something just because that is what he meant is being unhelpful in refusing to explore the more basic levels of his own thinking. When identified, the real source of disagreement often turns out to be a value judgement about the relative importance of various aspects and although these are not easily susceptible to change by rational argument it is useful to expose them.

All these problems are easier to solve between two people or within a group where there has been co-operation over a long period. Their models are likely to be very similar, they merely need to be recalled and updated for smooth communication to take place. Colleagues who have stayed together are likely to have similar underlying values, partly because their values have converged and partly because they were similar anyway which has encouraged continuing co-operation. A newcomer to such a group takes some time to make an effective contribution because he either struggles to develop the group model or he challenges it or most probably, does something of both. In any case he is bound to temporarily slow down the performance of the group. There is great pleasure to be had in operating as a member of a group of this kind—there is a feeling of a collective mind in action. This is not necessarily diminished by newcomers who, if they are able, will modify the collective mind and will be welcome to do so. The manifestation of this collective mind is in the close similarities of the relevant models carried in the minds of the individuals.

The development of such a consensus is the essential base for a coherent course from which students will receive an unambiguous message albeit from a number of different teachers. Agreements about hours and syllabi are the relatively trivial details built on this base. The group of teachers on any course or programme must spend considerable time in joint discussions essentially to maintain this base in the form of an agreed model. Written communication, for example, of modifications in a syllabus are not an adequate substitute for group meetings.

Team teaching

The current meaning of this title conveys the concept of several teachers in the same classroom. This rarely happens in universities but nevertheless there is usually a team involved not only in curriculum development but also in the teaching process where several methods such as the lecture, the laboratory and the tutorial may proceed in parallel and may be intended to be complementary and yet each might be the responsibility of a different teacher. Communication between the teachers in this situation will take place mainly through the students. A tutorial discussion after a lecture will obviously reveal not so much what the lecturer said but what he succeeded in conveying to the students. As a fellow expert, the tutor will know reasonably well what the lecturer was trying to convey and he will probably agree that this is what should be conveyed but his task is to supplement in this context what the students appear to have learned. Equally in his interactions with the students he is noting also their interests and anxieties as well as their current level of knowledge. Regarding this as a skill, it is very difficult to envisage what the mechanism is which can simultaneously support all this mental activity. Sticking to our basic concept of the mental model as continuously developing schemata this particular one is massive in that it contains or has access to an academic topic, some attributes of a lecturer and the individual and team attributes of a group of students. The output, what the tutor actively says and does, is a function of the academic topic conditioned or modulated by all the other more individual and individual interaction parameters. The sense of competence of the tutor is clearly determined mainly by these modulatory effects rather than the basic knowledge of the topic. Curiously this highly complex task is usually given to junior academics such as doctoral or immediately post-doctoral students. In a simple form such a mechanism or schema will consist of several parts, a central one of academic knowledge of the topic within a learning process where the students are currently at a particular point of development and other different ones relating to individuals: the lecturer and his style, each student with his own capacities and interests and one which describes the position of the student group not merely intellectually but also emotionally. The puzzle is how such disparate streams actually cohere or interact to generate the skilled unitary action of the tutor within the tutorial. Part of the answer is that it is a difficult task and it is rare to find high competence in it. Good performance probably does not arise through great simultaneity of mental activity. What happens is that the tutor has a first shot at saying something relevant based on the learning processes, and he then modifies this according to the degree of comprehension or otherwise reactively demonstrated by the students. This implies that he is rapidly switching between the relevant sub-schemata listed above. In this context it would seem that the mechanisms underlying social skills are in no way different from those underlying skills in academic exposition—indeed they are interdependent within the tutorial performance.

Examination boards

The formal assessment of a student is always the responsibility of a Board rather than an individual academic. The Board will consider each individual separately but also by comparison with other students on the same course. There are two sources of evidence; the examination/course marks, and the individual recollections which some members of the Board will have of that particular student. The Chairman will initiate a discussion of a student by effectively asking the question—'here is the profile of marks—is it what we expected?' Those who know the particular student will assent or dissent and make various relevant comments. Those who do not know him will listen carefully and check the comments against the written evidence—asking further questions if there seem to be inconsistencies. Here there is an inter-action of very different schemata—some based simply on presented data—others very complex, long-term recollections of a student performance over several years. Members of the Board will have no difficulty in communicating with each other from these different bases but they may have difficulties in arriving at a decision which depends on some weighting of the different kinds of evidence. The discussion will often shift away from the student to the abstract principles of what the members of the Board are doing. This seems to be so easy most members will not even notice it has happened until the chairman refocuses on the issue because he at least is conscious of the limited real time available. Individual examiners seem to manipulate a hybrid multi-dimensional model incorporating such features as a global view that an individual should become a graduate in a particular class together with all kinds of different marks for different efforts within one student performance and between students' performances. Other features such as actual perform-ance versus expected performance will be incorporated without any explicit agreement about their relative weighting. In spite of all this complexity and fuzziness a decision will emerge which usually satisfies everyone. Again it is difficult to conceptualize the underlying mechanism either in the examiners' minds or in their collective procedure. There is a strong impression that any attempt to overformalize the activity will reduce its effectiveness. If it could be formalized then a computer would do it better than a Board but such a proposition is absurd.

STAFF–STUDENT INTERACTION

University teaching is necessarily the work of a team in that it takes quite a large group of teachers to ensure that there is available the total expertise needed to take a student through to an honours degree. The group activity of the teachers has been described above, when in contact with students they invariably operate as individuals. Thus the standard teaching situation con-sists of a relatively homogeneous group of students interacting with one very different person—the teacher. Before the teaching can take place, however, there is another social process—the selection of students regarded as the most suitable for the course.

Selection

Final selection for most courses is still carried out on the basis of a personal interview between a teacher and a potential student. As in all good inter-viewing this is a two-way assessment. The student is finding out about the teacher, the course, the department and the university just as the teacher is finding out about the student. There is a strong element of self-selection, the student will develop an impression, 'I would like to come here' or 'I would not like to come here'. Being 18 or 19 years old the student's reaction and decision is very much a straightforward intuitive and emotional one but nonetheless it can be valid if the teacher involved is representative of the staff of the department. Among other evidence on which to base his decision the teacher will be observing this reaction. He will weight the student response very highly. The main things he is looking for are indications of commitment by the student to the topic, the course and the department. Intellectual level and scholastic achievement so far are secondary. They are almost certainly adequate if the student has got as far as an interview and the primary issue to be settled by the interview is that of potential commitment. Students very rarely, if ever, fail or drop out from a degree course because they are intellectually inadequate—invariably the problem is one of involvement and motivation. How the teacher makes effective decisions in this situation and gets better at it by experience is very difficult to analyse. He may begin by noting the available information traditionally emphasized by trainers in interviewing techniques; physical appearance, self-confidence, self-expression and so on but he will also be aware of the more current psychological theories of the interview as a form of transactional analysis and an essentially dynamic process. He may have certain key questions which he inserts at the appropriate point, partly to maintain the momentum of the interview and partly so that he can check the response against what he expects from the ideal student and also what he predicts from knowledge of the particular student acquired so far. The total response includes not only what the student says but also the order and timing of his reply with its accompanying physical response of facial movements, hand activity and adjustment of total posture. The interaction if it is proceeding satisfactorily will be highly empathic. The teacher is modelling the student, putting himself in the position of the student not just mentally but also posturally and trying out his own enactive reaction to the question from the student's point of view as he puts it to the student. If the student is sympathetic he will receive not only the verbal questions, his total perception will include the teacher's use of posture as an anticipatory model of what the student is expected to say. The student is not, of course, consciously doing all this and even the teacher's activity may have a fairly superficial conscious content. Nevertheless the two are behaving in this transactional situation not only as observers of each other but also each observes the other as a mirror of himself. In this way the teacher develops his enactive model of what the student is really like and vice-versa. Each can then use this model, embellished by all the detailed factual information which has been exchanged, as a basis for a personal decision. Clearly such a wide-band exchange can only take place in the one-to-one interview situation for which there is no substitute.

The skills of the interviewer are based on some awareness of the total complexity of this situation, the facilitation of the communication and the steering of the interview so that this empathic interaction develops to the optimal extent. Because this is a relatively primitive skill, any development is partly dependent on being able to dispose of the inhibitions which arise in what is seen as an important formal occasion.

Teaching

The university teacher in a class situation usually considers himself as a lecturer. He expounds something of what he knows tailored to the stage of learning development which the average member of the class ought to have reached. He is simultaneously a source of information, a guide, a mentor, a leader and an actor on a stage. Ostensibly data is being transferred from the teacher's notebook to the student's notebook, but this is only the most superficial aspect of a complex process. The communication should be of beliefs and enthusiasms rather than mere facts. A skilled lecturer will convey the excitement of moving forward into new areas of knowledge and the sense of privilege in catching up and comprehending what earlier high-quality minds have already explored albeit not completely. Further explorations are still needed and the opportunity is available for the students to undertake these when they are fully equipped to do so. This equipment includes skills in the methods and techniques relevant to the particular study. Acquiring these skills involves extensive practice by the students in the laboratory, the workshop, and the real world. In these situations, again, the lecturer has the roles of guide and leader. The lecturer's success in achieving these objectives will, of course, depend on extensive preparation as a basis for the on-line performance. During this preparation and performance he is relying on an image of how the average student is going to approach and react to whatever he is presented with.

Advanced teaching is easier than more elementary teaching because in the former the teacher has a smaller shift to make from his own present intellectual position. Dialogue in any teaching situation takes the form of cajoling the student to extend his personal view of the issues and persuasion so that the individual or the group develop their own schemata in line with those held by the lecturer. The lecturer can only provide the opportunity and the incentive to learn. The learning itself is a personal activity by the individual student.

The behaviour of the class as a group depends on the will of the majority. If the majority have been captured by the exposition of the lecturer then they will reinforce each other and him, although there may still be a few stragglers who are not going along. There is nothing more disheartening for a lecturer than the realization that the majority are not with him. In these circumstances he can try to keep going by concentrating on the few but more usually the situation reinforces itself and his performance gets worse. It is impossible to lecture well to an unco-operative group, but a co-operative group will continuously reinforce a good performance. This, of course, is true of leaders and actors in all situations. Communication with others is a basic and natural characteristic of human behaviour; sensing its presence is bound to be profoundly stimulating and rewarding. The consequent performance is exhausting. It is not possible to lecture at this level for more than two or, at the most, three hours in one day and this assumes comprehensive technical knowledge of the topics under discussion. The optimal size of class is 10 to 30 students, very large classes become more of a stage performance and less of an intellectual interaction. Viewed as a manifestation of skill the lecturer's performance is an exposition based on previous knowledge and planning and steered continuously by the reaction of the audience. This reaction is perceived by an enormous variety of detailed cues coming from the behaviour of individual members of the audience. It rises into consciousness, if at all, only as the collective behaviour of the class. The collective percept is used immediately to reinforce and guide what is said and how it is said in terms of speed, repetition, changes of tone and loudness and so on. In musical terms it is more similar to jazz than to classical music, the basic script is available either on paper or in the head of the lecturer but the embellishment is highly impromptu. The audience is the conductor. A lecture which is literally read from a script is not a teaching performance, because in these circumstances the lecturer cannot fully receive and use the audience reaction.

Skills in the university teaching situation

To summarize it emerges that, as for all communicators, the lecturer's degree of success depends on how closely he can understand the intellectual and emotional position of his audience and can react accordingly. This is true also of the content, when the lecturer is organizing the material he can include and it is true of the on-line situation where he reacts to the continuous response of the audience. It is entirely typical of the general social situation where communication is required except that there is also a high intellectual context. Assuming that the lecturer knows his material then in skill terms he becomes similar to an actor, a team captain, a salesman and others whose profession is basically to communicate. The basis of good performance is in the ability to appreciate the minds of the recipients—what they want, what they need and how far they have gone along the road the communicator wishes them to take. This 'road' is a developing schema or a group of schemata.

This applies also to all the other background communication within the teaching team as organizers of a course and as selectors and assessors of students. The student must have the capacities, abilities and interests to undertake his further development. Interests are perhaps no more than a recognition of success in using capacities and developing abilities. The underlying motivation is the need to explore and develop and also, because man is a fundamentally social animal, to encourage others to explore and develop.

CONCLUSION

It is sometimes argued that the university lecturer does not need the skills of communication and leadership which are essential for success in school teaching. The university teacher should simply be an expert in his chosen field and the effort to extract this expertise should come entirely from the student. If the student does not have both the wish and the capacity to make this effort then he should not have gone to the university. This elitist and simplistic viewpoint may have been tenable when there were only two or three universities in any one country and when only a minority of those students were there for the intellectual rather than the social life, but it hardly seems to fit the current concept of a university. The university is now a further place of education for quite a large proportion of school leavers and it is also the initial training centre for most of the professions. As such it must be a centre of teaching expertise.

This expertise is essentially social, it involves communication within groups of students and teachers, between a student group and a teacher, and between individual teachers and students. The purpose of all this personal communication is not primarily to convey knowledge, knowledge is most unambiguously obtained from the written word. The direct communication is mostly about intellectual guidance; seeking it and providing it. The student learns how and what to learn and the lecturer learns how and what to teach. There seem to be at least three different kinds of skills:

skills used in the practice of the particular academic discipline;

learning skills to be acquired by the student and understood by the lecturer;

teaching skills to be acquired by the lecturer.

The second and third group are almost independent of the first group and are probably general across all university work. The third group are the social skills which are the focus of interest for this chapter. It is possible to be more specific about some of these skills while others remain elusive. The tasks in which these skills are deployed by a lecturer can be divided into three categories: individual interactions with a student, interactions with student groups, and interactions within the staff group. For each of these tasks the central skill is demonstrated by sensitivity to the intellectual position, emotional drives and required direction of progress demonstrated by another person. A lecturer seems to achieve this by creating within himself a model which incorporates the above facets of this other person. He acquires this model partly by listening to what the other says and partly by watching what he does. From previous experience of communicating with many other people in similar circumstances he has acquired certain key features which act as bench marks indicating the person's position. These may be in the form of standard attitudes, standard procedures, standard questions and probably most important, standard errors. The skill consists of this repertoire of identifiable cues and an associated set of categories into which the person concerned can be temporarily fitted. The categories define what to do. The slotting into a category does not mean eliminating all specific individual features of the person concerned. It is used rather to suggest a strategy of how to respond to this person, but the general strategy will, during the response, be tailored to the specific needs of the individual. This tailoring includes how to do it as well as what to do; the style is as important as the content. This seems to be how the basic skill works.

Dealing with a group is an extension of the sensitivity to individuals. The individuals within a group are scanned and minor cues are picked up from selected members of the audience and then put together, e.g. in noting the proportion who are manifestly not attending or who are looking baffled so that the lecturer has in his mind a model of the group which is at the pictorial or partially iconic level. At this stage the lecturer is outside the group, he is not a member of it, but he has some understanding of it and he can communicate with it. He does communicate by taking from his other schemata about the topic of study certain elements of information which he can now present to the group shaped into the most readily acceptable form. He can represent things, modify them, express them in different ways, approach them from different viewpoints and so on as he watches the degree of understanding growing in the audience. This is the normal good teaching situation.

Occasionally the rapport between the audience and the lecturer will grow to the point where he becomes one of them. He identifies entirely with them and they with him. He switches from a pictorial view of his audience to an enactive view. This is the true collective mind situation mentioned already. In these circumstances the lecturer can readily shift much academic material from his superior store to the minds of his students. He is aware that he is doing it but not how he is doing it. Similarly the audience are aware of this rapid growth of insight with little awareness of the actual mode of communication. This is a satisfying and often an inspiring experience for all those involved.

It is not achieved as frequently as it should be because it makes high demands on all those involved. The lecturer must have the teaching skills, the audience must have the learning skills. In addition both sides must have a high level of personal commitment, security and self-confidence so that they are prepared to allow the ideal situation to develop. Any antagonism or self-doubt detracts from this potential development within the serial performance of a lecture. A lecture must start with two isolated sides observing each other. The lecturer begins to speak, the audience begins to react. If communication develops successfully both sides will be using pictorial/iconic models with symbolic detail from the languages in use. These models will grow continuously during the interaction. If the circumstances are ideal then there will be, after 10 or 15 minutes, a switch to the much closer identification afforded by enactive modelling. This will exhaust everyone after half an hour or so and there will be a retreat to the pictorial position again followed by a disengagement as the lecture ends.

Although these are obviously social skills it is not clear how they differ from other skills, e.g. the practical skills of coping with the physical world. In all cases contact has to be established and engagement take place; complete identification may or may not emerge. The central activity is a pictorial schema, a picture in the mind established and detailed by symbolic descriptors and this may take over the person as a whole by becoming enactive. A social skill is unique only in that it has a unique set of key features which the observer is seeking within the total performance going on in front of him. Attached to the sets of key features are categories of action strategies. Level of skill is indicated by the range and subtlety of the available key features and action strategies and the ease with which they are located and used.

References

Annett, J. (1969). *Feedback and Human Behaviour*. (Harmondsworth: Penguin)
Gagne, R. M. (1970). *The Conditions of Learning*. (New York: Holt, Rinehart and Winston)
Melton, A. W. (1964). *Categories of Human Learning*. (New York: Academic Press)

4
The General Practitioner

K. M. HAY

INTRODUCTION

It is, perhaps, unfortunate that in the NHS the word 'health' has never been properly defined. Different people and groups expect different things. Crichton Millar's 'ideas of health' would be as good as any, they are:

the will to live;

ability to enjoy all normal biological functioning;

enough feeling of self-mastery to maintain an adequate independence of circumstances and environment;

a scale of values whereby experiences and memories that have purpose and significance are preferred to those that lack them;

a readiness to face conflict, internal and external, with a minimum recourse to evasion;

a social effectiveness characterized by:
a reasonable trust in one's fellow men,
a broad toleration of human idiosyncrasies,
that sense of social responsibility which only manifests itself in those who recognize in social contribution a prerogative rather than a duty.

If a failure in one or more of these categories is what brings patients to the doctor's surgery, it follows that the need for professional help is almost unlimited, and no political system can supply the resources necessary to maintain health. The fourth paragraph in the list deals with 'values' and these form highly contentious subjects for debate. The values of the patients, their doctors and society can vary over a wide range and they must be understood sympathetically and discussed in terms of what is possible with the means available to meet a particular need against a wide background of conflicting interest.

The word 'cure' can be an unfortunate one which gives rise to misconceptions in a patient's mind. Most cures depend on nature's own healing and regenerative powers. When surgeons operate, it is to remove or repair a damaged organ when these powers are inadequate or have failed. The general practitioner intervenes by providing the treatment for, or advising the patient on the necessary conditions for the healing, regeneration or control of a disability to be effective to the best possible extent. He needs to be honest, and not make facile promises, while maintaining the patient's hope and morale. A surprisingly large number of people can show personal courage and resource in meeting the penultimate category of the list, given the proper support which is available both from the personal doctor and the state.

Health is a very personal side of life, and it is necessary that all playing a part in its provision and maintenance should come to understand each other better through regular local meetings. There is no place for 'facelessness' or remote impersonal committees when urgent problems have to be resolved for the promotion of health.

COMMUNICATION IN THE SURGERY AND THE HOME

The meeting of doctor and patient is usually a brief one and is personal. On occasions, other members of the patient's family may be present or such professional people as nurses and non-medical surgery staff: there can be a need for chaperones or witnesses sometimes. The scenario is the doctor's surgery or the patient's home on domiciliary visits. The latter are particularly valuable to the doctor as he learns a lot about a patient's family, his interests, his aesthetic tastes, and his literary and television preoccupations. These are valuable non-verbal clues in communication and understanding.

One can assume that the purpose of the meeting is to resolve or contain a problem centred on a feeling of ill health. The patient is the suppliant, the seeker of aid and explanation. What follows next are series of transactions which can only be described in terms of various models of behaviour. Such research as has been done is based largely on taped and video-recorded consultations in which the patients and the doctors are aware that they are performing in front of a potentially large if anonymous audience.

A good model for describing how doctors and patients communicate is that based on the theories and experience of Berne's (1969, 1975) transactional analysis. From the doctors' point of view his behaviour is conditioned by factors described under four headings by Byrne and Long (1976):

Behaviour which stems from the doctor's need to know, i.e. to get a clear understanding of the symptoms. This would include diagnostic measures to establish a diagnosis.

Behaviour which stems from the doctor's need to 'control', i.e. to limit the patient to a defined area.

Behaviour which stems from the recognition of the patient's undeclared needs, i.e. dealing with apparent anxieties.

Behaviour which stems from a belief in the ability of the patient to make decisions and to be involved in his own treatment.

In the first the doctor has the role of detective. In the second he has the role of stage manager. In the third he is the interpreter of myths, analogies, metaphors, and fairy-tales in which patients can wrap or rationalize their inner feelings. Lastly, in the fourth category he is 'the doctor', that is to say the teacher from the root of the Latin word 'doceo', to teach.

Berne's (op. cit.) transactional analysis model states that everybody carries within them three ego states; the parent, the adult, and the child, and that the prevailing ego state at any time can be one of these. To complicate matters the overt transactions and communications can overlie more covert aims which the participants do not declare openly, or of which they may be only partially aware. The doctor is usually in the parent or adult ego state. As the 'parent' he is acting as he has been taught to act by his cultural background and his professional training. When the cultural background is a foreign one this can be difficult. For instance, the Hindu family traditions are closer than those now prevalent in the western societies, and each may have very different assumptions and prejudices, which need to be known and appreciated. Essentially, the 'parent' exercises controlling and nurturing functions both physical and emotional.

The adult ego state is the one where reason, logic, scientific observation, detachment and problem solving can operate. If both doctor and patient can communicate at this level both are acting together without much misunderstanding. This is a desirable form of medical transaction, and is to be achieved if possible.

The child has been described by Zygmond (1981, a, b) as the natural spontaneous self-centred, curious, creative, impulsive, demanding and unashamed creature who will laugh or cry without embarrassment: and the adapted child reflected in its relationship to its parents in terms of compliance or rebellion.

These elements determine much of the pattern of our lives which Berne has analysed in the form of 'life scripts'. It is when the doctor lapses into the child ego state that there can be difficulties: at times he will feel affronted, aggrieved, frustrated, or angry. An experienced doctor will recognize these states, and shift the transaction back as far as he is concerned to the 'adult' or 'parent' state. He can do this by cultivating a sense of reality, a sense of proportion, and a sense of humour. The latter can be very important and if difficult patients can be 'humoured', the transaction can be restored to the 'adult' level and if the transaction is successful both can stand back from it and enjoy the joke together. This is often a successful ploy with children. If a yelling child is paradoxically asked to yell much louder, he will often quieten down immediately, just to show who is the boss. He may also enjoy the situation while the doctor can get on with dealing with the problem. Berne gives examples of 'crossed transactions' which are rich sources of unsatisfactory communication or of incomplete information. A patient might complain of a 'pain in the neck'. At the literal adult level the doctor might discover evidence of tension and tender areas in the neck muscles and prescribe appropriate treatment with analgesics: but the patient may remain unsatisfied and will probably respond badly to the treatment. At another level the cause of the tension in the neck muscles can be suppressed emotional states of frustration, anger or irritation deriving from some unsatisfactory personal relationship in the patient's home or social milieu. The cliché 'pain in the neck' is correct both physically and psychologically. This sort of thing is behind much of what is termed psychosomatic disorder and the crossed transactions in the doctor–patient relationship can reduce the doctor's ego state to that of the negative or rebellious child. In general, transactions need to be parallel and complementary with the doctor acting the 'adult' or when necessary the 'parent'. If he acts the 'child' any communication is likely at the best to be silly or useless, and at the worst disastrous to any positive relationship.

The doctor is an interpreter of fairy-stories and myths. He is the seeker for 'the truth of the matter'. Patients hide behind them for various reasons including:

Times when they find that ordinary language has become an inadequate tool for expressing their real feelings of unease.

When fear makes it impossible to speak the truth.

When there is an ulterior purpose in being ill. Examples of this would be the need to be considered to be ill in order to manipulate a spouse into some desired reaction or to evade some situation which cannot be faced: the child wanting to avoid going to school at the beginning of term, or perhaps bed-wetting to get the attention of worried parents.

Lastly, we must consider the role of the doctor as a teacher. Patients with medical problems require not only treatment and advice, but information and understanding in the sort of language with which they are familiar. Analogies can be used. Consider for example the motor car; it may fail to function if there is a fault in the mechanism, or it may be 'out of tune' when there is a breakdown of the integration of the functioning of various parts of its mechanism. Further, things are not improved if the vehicle is driven hard while 'out of tune'. In these days of prolonged high arousal due to unresolved anxiety tension leading to fatigue, and from repeated stimuli leading to adrenaline flow without adequate physical outlet, faulty functioning is commonplace. No treatment is likely to be successful if the patient does not provide the right conditions for it to be effective. Heavy smokers with bronchitis or diseases of the arteries are unlikely to improve very much. It still happens that many people lack any basic knowledge of anatomy or physiology. They want medical magic, and can be quite prepared to have major operations or complex medical treatment with little idea of what it seeks to achieve.

Some are still afraid to ask questions of supposedly busy doctors, and may fear to hear things they wish to avoid. Nevertheless, these fears must be recognized; any impression of assumed omniscience on the part of the doctor is to be deplored. It is not a sign of weakness to admit that medical knowledge is a limited, if expanding field of learning, and there is no excuse for the doctor when he attempts to hide his ignorance behind a lot of medical jargon which will be misunderstood. Patients, in general, resent any reassurance based on illusions which subsequent events will shatter. Words need to be used with care: they may not be taken down and used against the doctor, but they can certainly be remembered by the patient long after the doctor has forgotten the occasion.

What transpires in the doctor's surgery can be seen in terms of drama; sometimes the play is a tragedy, sometimes a comedy, sometimes it is trivial and ephemeral, and sometimes of classic proportions. The general practitioner sees his actors play different roles as the years pass and the generations come and go; they make their entrances and their exits, while he himself is something of an actor manager. This may be compared to the life of the hospital doctor who deals with a large number of patients over short periods of time in a setting divorced from their natural home, work, and social milieu (see Chapter 5).

NON-VERBAL COMMUNICATION

Pietroni (1976) has examined the question of non-verbal communication between general practitioners and patients. He divides the subject into four areas which he describes as:

(1) *Proxemics*. The study of space, time, position and artifacts as part of a dynamic communication process.

(2) *Kinesics*. The study of facial expression, body posture, hand gestures.

(3) *Paralanguage*. The study of vocal emphasis and intonation as communication.

(4) *Touch*. The study of how, when and why touch is employed as part of the communication process.

These cues can be picked up by the doctor if he has the art of attentive listening. He can, for instance, study the kinesics of the situation in the patient and himself. He may note a lot of displacement activity which denotes a high degree of arousal usually, but not always, due to anxiety. The patient may screw his or her finger tightly round a handkerchief, or smooth his or her hair, or twiddle the fingers while crossing and uncrossing the legs: meanwhile the doctor wipes his spectacles unnecessarily, or plays around with pens and other bric-a-brac on his desk, or he may just doodle.

While on this subject it has been noted that many children find a heavily bearded bespectacled doctor to be an alarming figure. Finally, an amusing observation has been made when video tapes of consultations are played at a much slower rate than they should be run. 'An almost dance-like pattern can be observed between the therapist and the patient, such as can be observed in courting couples.' The implications of this interpretation of events need further research and elucidation.

Communication begins before the patient sees the doctor. The reception area and the skills of the receptionist will make an immediate impact for better or for worse increasing reassurance or tension as the case may be. The arrangements of the consulting room and its decor, and even the doctor's clothes will affect confidence. It is usual now for the patient to be seated at the side of the desk instead of opposite to the doctor with its implication of there being a barrier. A display of scalpels, syringes with hypodermic needles and other paraphernalia can be upsetting to the sensitive. Finally, and importantly, the art of physical examination and touch needs to be cultivated if the patient is to be confident and the physical signs of disease elicited. This very personal part of the medical transaction is paramount.

The experienced doctor will pick up a variety of useful signals from just watching and listening to non-verbal activity; the tone of voice, the gesture, the posture, or the facial expression. These can declare whether something the patient is hiding is the real reason for his fears and anxieties, or perhaps he hopes that ill health would form an acceptable excuse for personal difficulties and failures. Sometimes non-verbal communication can have a special interest as when an artist is asked to depict his feelings or experiences in pictures, or a musician is asked to express his mood on his instrument.

THE PATIENT

The patient confronts his doctor in the surgery because of feelings of disease, and he brings with him an assortment of fears, hopes and expectations. These to the doctor can be rational or non-rational as he approaches the problem from a different angle conditioned and determined by his own specialized education, his idea of his social standing, and his self-confidence. Society which provides the means and facilities which enable medicine to be practised is always present to a greater or lesser extent, and such things as the political climate and the views on medical matters expressed by the media will form a large portion of it. The patient will have heard much talk about medicine and doctors in pub, office, factory or drawing-room, and these anecdotes will have been exchanged with an eye on the interest and emotional impact on the audience rather than for their factual content.

In the past, village and small town life had many years in which to evolve into ways of mutual understanding and ease of communication; people could accept their own particular role and respect the roles of others. With industrialization and the advent of high-rise flats with the comparatively sudden influx of people from abroad of various ethnic origins with very different mother tongues and traditions, communication and the proper exercise of medical skills has become much more complicated, making considerable demands on all parties. The big towns have seen a deterioration in the communication and relationships between different age groups, different working groups and different ethnic groups both at the verbal and intuitive levels. This gives rise to resulting tensions which can manifest themselves in ill health.

The patient may overplay or underplay his part in the drama; often he prefers to say what he feels about his problem in emotional terms which can confuse the real issue. He is probably hoping for easy reassurance or to be given some pill or medicine which will bring him relief. He does not understand always that most treatment means that he will have to provide the right conditions for the treatment to be effective. Many people are taking regular doses of tranquillizers while refusing to take measures to reduce tension and strain. In this sense they are fighting their tranquillizers and will be asking for bigger doses and prescriptions.

Not only are the patients' and doctors' thought processes different but there are also differences in the way language and individual words are understood. For instance, the word 'cancer' is to many people virtually a death sentence, while to a doctor it will denote a whole range of illnesses having in common a disorder of cell growth and proliferation. Some types are controllable or curable, and some not so. Much the same could have been said about the class of disorder coming under the heading of 'infection', until the advent of antibiotics reduced the threat implicit in this word: nevertheless, some infections remain a serious threat. The choice of words in the consultation needs thought and care. Careless words certainly cause distress and misunderstanding.

THE DOCTOR

Ideally the GP, like the priest or vicar, should live in and be a part of his community. If he is a family man he will have learned much about the cares and worries which may confront the young parents of the children in his practice; and he himself should be free from domestic tensions which can undermine his confidence and colour his outlook on life.

The doctor–patient relationship is usually easy and pleasant in a village or small town setting, if the GP is reasonably extrovert and can share the pleasures and sorrows of his community. He is seldom off duty from the point of view of measuring his words as he will meet his patients in shop, pub, church or sports club, and light chat is apt to take on a medical tinge. He learns to cope with this with forbearance, patience, and a sense of humour. He also needs to have his escape routes to where he can be himself and not 'the doctor'.

Doctors' personalities, backgrounds and life experiences can vary as much as those of their patients, and in group practices it will be found that a certain type of person will seek out a particular doctor and a different sort of person will prefer another doctor. What determines these choices is not always obvious, but the freedom of choice of doctor is something precious and it is to be encouraged. A mature and understanding doctor will recognize this, and be ready to suggest a change if it is likely to help in solving the patients' medical problems.

SOCIAL AND CULTURAL ASPECTS

This can be discussed in terms of supply and demand, both of which are determined by social attitudes acting through numerous pressure groups, the media, and finally through the prevailing political climate. In these days of highly developed medical technology it is impossible for there to be the simple doctor–patient relationship divorced from any overt or covert outside influences. This may not apply in some of the realms of fringe medicine which is becoming increasingly popular as both doctors and patients come to resent the inevitable intrusion of what they believe to be bureaucratic or political considerations.

There is a fear of these amorphous and little-understood influences, largely based on a lack of understanding and information in regard to them. However, if advanced and expensive medical resources are to be available to meet the patients' needs the organization and finance of them must be taken into account by the doctor, who must be able to discuss these things, when necessary, with patients in a dispassionate way based on factual knowledge, rather than on hypotheses which are easily refutable to the consequent chagrin of all concerned.

An extreme example of cultural problems was highlighted by the Prince of Wales in his presidential address to the BMA. He pointed out that Sikh women cannot go to male doctors and that there are no Sikh women doctors. They require the services of women doctors who have learned something about their way of life and traditions. Even attending hospitals and surgeries can be a traumatic ordeal for them.

In some societies it is the height of bad manners to come directly to the point in a conversation. Mutual enquiries and well-wishing about each other and their families must precede the real business of the day. Then there can be difficulties in non-verbal communication. There are people who feel ill at ease if there is too much looking directly at the face, while European people expect a close eye-ball mutual regard. The experienced doctor will pick up his cues and improve his reactions accordingly. But, as Prince Charles indicated, there must be much more understanding and appreciation of the cultures and customs of other races than one's own.

TRAINING

Until recently, the GP was not prepared for the part he is called upon to play by the medical schools, which inevitably are hospital orientated, and he must learn about the complex technology of diagnosis and treatment. Quite properly he has to acquire an understanding of the scientific method and the place of statistics and probability theory. There is no formal instruction in the philosophy or history of medicine and he has to make up his own mind on the importance of purpose, meaning and value. His views in these areas may be very different to those of his patients, particularly if science has given him a reductionist outlook on people and their problems. It is only to the extent that he is aware of his own prejudices that he can begin to be conscious of those of his patients, and to make allowance for them so that he will be able to communicate and to exercise his skills in a constructive and useful manner.

More attention to the training in skills of communication has been paid by GPs than by any other speciality in medicine. This rather provocative statement could only be applied to the field of postgraduate education but more recently the advent of Departments of General Practice within the medical school has led to their becoming the nidus of applied behavioural science in clinical medical studies.

The undergraduate stage of medical training lasts five years and has recently undergone a major scrutiny in terms of both aims and content (HMSO, 1968). Prior to 1968 it was concerned with the production of a 'safe doctor' and had remained so for over a hundred years. Upon graduation the new doctor was supposed to be competent for unsupervised practice in a number of fields, including general practice. The standards of general practice were thus the standards set by the qualifying examination. The wide recognition of the inadequacy of this has led to the necessity for a further four years of training before a doctor can be appointed as a principal in general practice in the National Health Service. That is, a doctor with whom patients register and who provides responsible care. The first year of this period is general graduate training and the remaining three years for general practice are speciality training, for two years within approved and appropriate hospital posts and for one year in an approved and supervised training practice.

Since 1968, the object of undergraduate training has been to produce on graduation a doctor who has such a firm grounding of general medicine that a further period of training will turn him into a specialist in whatever field he decides to practise. In the undergraduate phase, although the communication exemplars chosen may be from general practice, the models must then be applicable to clinicians working in any field of patient care. There are, of course, many examples of communication in which the doctor–patient relationship is not central. For example, in communication with other doctors or other colleagues, but in teaching about communication with patients it has always to be placed in the setting of the development of this very personal relationship.

There are, broadly speaking, two types of interview: one that is for the benefit of the interviewer, such as the potential employer, and one that is for the benefit of the interviewee. The medical consultation falls clearly into the latter group, it is designed to take information and to give information. It is also designed to try to modify action or behaviour as a result of this exchange and this is why the relationship is so important to the student and the trainee general practitioner. The teaching of communication skills can be divided into three categories: the technique of 'taking a history', that is obtaining information; the techniques required in order to give information so that recall is possible; and the techniques and background required to achieve 'compliance' with a set of goals agreed between doctor and patient.

During 'history taking' sessions the student is taught how to establish rapport with a patient. The importance of the greeting, the introduction of the doctor to the patient, the use of names is stressed as well as the setting in which it takes place. The stereotype of a group of 'white-coated' doctors gazing down at the near-naked and recumbent body of the patient as the setting for an exchange of information is too well known to deserve comment but regrettably still occurs. Today's student is taught the importance of eye contact, facial expression, body position and seating arrangement as a way of making people comfortable and enhancing communication. Once the setting has been agreed, the influences of the 'third party' upon the consultation have to be understood. In undergraduate teaching he is nearly always present, and often the fourth and fifth party as well. It is recognized that this not only alters the behaviour of participants but changes the nature of the information that is communicated. In a bid to minimize this effect and allow the 'true' consultation to be used as a teaching tool teachers have begun to use two techniques, sometimes separately and sometimes combined. The modern video-camera is small and unobtrusive. The resulting film can be played back to participants and to others for critical discussion. Teaching suites now frequently have a two-way mirror with sound-conveying systems built into one wall allowing others to watch and hear what transpires during a consultation.

The overriding principle of confidentiality has to be borne in mind and patients are always asked for their consent before either of these techniques is used and, if a film is made, asked to view the film and consent before any wider showing is made. These two techniques have allowed young doctors and their seniors to become much more sensitive about what is said and done in the interview. The techniques are now beginning to be used in vocational training with trainees and even in continuing education.

Both students and trainees are being taught systems to improve the ability of the patient to recall information that is given to them during the consultation. It is known that it is a highly stressful situation and that information recall is selective and distorted. Doctors are becoming aware that the actual words used, the number of ideas presented and their order are important. Memory aids are more frequently used.

Compliance, that is persuading a patient to follow the advice that is given, is an extremely complex subject meriting its own section in *Index Medicus* and the publication of several thousand studies. Certain 'ground rules' have become clear as a result of these and can be taught. Most attention has been paid to the compliance of patients in relationship to medication, though it is obviously important to think about compliance in terms of other advice, such as losing weight, stopping smoking, wearing seat-belts and so on. It has, for example, become clear that complicated regimes of drug taking produce low compliance, that drugs with unpleasant side-effects have low compliance rates and that the age, sex and social class of the patient and the sort of illness that they suffer from also makes differences. But even when all these factors in the drugs or in the patients are corrected there still remain major differences produced by the way in which different doctors relate to different patients.

Communication between doctors and patients has, in summary, become an increasingly important area of education and the time and effort expended on it is likely to continue to increase for some time to come.

ABILITIES AND SKILLS

Before the last war there were GPs, particularly in rural areas, who had to be medical jacks-of-all-trades, and who were able to do routine operations in cottage hospitals. But, the increasing complexity of medical technology and treatment has brought about many changes, and made it necessary for doctors to develop new skills to meet new situations and challenges. Even if no longer a jack-of-all-trades in the old sense the modern practitioner has to be master of much wider fields of knowledge and to be able to apply his learning and skills with confidence.

These abilities can be grouped under the following headings:

A sound understanding of modern medical science which is taught in the medical schools and on which he has to pass qualifying examinations.

Experience in hospital as a junior qualified doctor learning the practical applications of medical science in a clinical setting under consultants.

Experience as a trainee in general practice learning the arts of primary care. One of the main problems is in deciding what complaint is of a trivial or transient nature, and what physical signs can be considered to be within normal limits. This can be difficult as potentially serious illness may present in the early stages only minimal symptoms and signs.

The art of listening to and talking to patients and their relations. The object is to gain as clear as possible an understanding of the true problem or problems being presented.

The art of decision making and knowing what action is likely to be correct in the circumstances. This is essentially a matter of devising the proper strategy and tactics for success.

Communicating the proposed strategy and tactics to the patient in language which he can understand, this means avoiding medical jargon and current trendy expressions, the latter being usually misunderstood when used by doctors.

Acting as the patient's agent when it is necessary to use hospitals or public health facilities like the district nurse service or geriatric day centres. A knowledge of the bureaucratic and committee structure of the NHS is essential, and it is usually necessary for the individual practitioner to make himself personally acquainted with medical and lay administrators, or the problems of facelessness can arise.

The doctor's role as a business man. As a private contractor he is responsible for the structure and day-to-day running of his business. He must meet his partners in formal minuted practice business meetings to make decisions and to define policy. Informal meetings take place on most days. There are responsibilities for buildings, staff, finance, and general maintenance. These things are taken care of in hospitals by administrators, but the general practitioner needs to learn these skills in his trainee period.

A knowledge of the local environment. This means that he should be familiar with the main industries in his area and should get to know the industrial medical officers and personnel officers of the local factories. Through them he can often form a good working liaison with the industrial nurses who often are able to be helpful in such matters as fitness to return to work or in getting light work for those of limited fitness.

The general practitioner's field of operations embraces his surgery, the patients' homes, and the local working environment all of which are important for the understanding and management of medical problems both in the short and long terms. Finally at the end of the road he must do what is possible to see that death is dignified, an undignified death such as suicide will adversely affect the family's well-being for many years to come.

FUTURE DEVELOPMENTS

The question needs to be asked as to whether current trends in General Practice are moving in the right direction; this is to say towards the better provision of health as defined above, through the use of more developed skills and technical aids. The latter would include the growing use of computers for record keeping, making appointments, and for research. The value of the General Practitioner service in the NHS will be assessed by various methods of professional audit now being tried out in several places.

The GP service accounts for about six per cent of the Health Service expenditure, and some years ago it was estimated that each GP was responsible for costs of £36 000 per annum as compared to £25 000 for each consultant in time and services. However, as much of the GP's routine work is in preventive medicine and the control of chronic disorders it is impossible to estimate the 'value for money'. What is prevented does not happen and cannot appear in the credit sheet.

By the nature of his work the General Practitioner is closely involved in the family structure of the patients and in local industries and working conditions. To do this adequately he has to fill a special if ill-defined social role in the community. He needs to know about farming practices if he is working in the country and what toxic chemicals can cause health problems. At times he will co-operate with the veterinary services over animal diseases which can also affect humans. In industrial areas he will need to know about the use of industrial chemicals and working conditions when they carry special risks. Without such knowledge he cannot give adequate advice on whether a patient is fit to work or whether he may require light duties on a temporary or permanent basis. It is unfortunate that very few general practitioners have visited their local factories and got to know the industrial doctors, industrial nurses or personnel officers, all of whom would benefit, when working conditions are important factors in ill health (see Chapter 8). This is an area where communication skills need to be used so as to avoid misunderstandings. The Trade Unions are now interested in health problems. Through all these labyrinthine mazes the GP has to tread warily, remembering that his first duty is to his patient and not to the employer or union representative. In practice, difficulties need seldom arise and patients can be helped to manage to work within their limitations.

In all the transactions between the patient and the doctor, it is important that the latter should retain his own autonomy. Sympathy, understanding and empathy are useful and necessary concepts, but there is a danger of doctors becoming too emotionally engaged in patients' problems and reverting to one of the child-ego states as defined by Berne. Some rapid psycho-analytic procedures popular in certain practices can result in perilous transference reactions which may be difficult to handle. Professional detachment and expertise in both medical and social matters are essential if problems are to be solved, and patients helped to stand on their own two feet without having to be too dependent on the medical profession.

All this is uncertain territory and it will not be adequately explored until the history and philosophy of medicine becomes an academic and research discipline taught to students at some stage of their careers. The appointment of professors in General Practice in most medical schools is a hopeful if belated sign of progress for the future (Drury, 1981).

Acknowledgements

The author is grateful to Professor M. D. Drury of the General Practice Teaching and Research Unit of Birmingham Medical School for many discussions of these issues and in particular for the section of this chapter on general practitioner training which he contributed.

References

Berne, E. (1969). *The Games People Play*. (Harmondsworth: Penguin)

Berne, E. (1975). *What do you say after you say Hello?* (London: Corgi Books)

Byrne, P. S. and Long, E. L. (1976). *Doctors Talking to Patients*. (London: HMSO)

Drury, M. (1981). *Whole Person Medicine*. Inaugural Lecture published by the University of Birmingham

HMSO. (1968). *Royal Commission on Medical Education*. (London: HMSO)

HRH Prince Charles (1982). Presidential address to the British Medical Association. *Br. Med. J.*, **285**, 185

Pietroni, P. (1976). Non-verbal communication in General Practice. In B. A. Tanner (ed.) *Language and Communication in General Practice*. (London: Hodder and Stoughton)

Zygmond, D. (1981a). Transactional analysis in medical practice, part 1. *Update*, **24** (2), 181

Zygmond, D. (1981b). Transactional analysis in medical practice, part 2. *Update*, **24** (2), 281

5
The Hospital Doctor

S. J. SINGLETON

INTRODUCTION

The limits of acceptable practice within which any doctor acts are very wide; the quality of his work may vary from indifference to excellence, yet be included within competence. This chapter is not concerned with the quality of technical work in detecting and treating illnesses but rather the difference between negligence and minimum competence in the less technically able, and the factors that put the excellent above the very competent in those who are technically very able. These latter factors are in the social skills domain. We can assume that in providing specialist or secondary care (a distinction which will be described in detail later) the hospital doctor is fully equipped with particular technical and individual skills in medicine; it is attitudes and social skills which set the excellent apart. The differences that make a hospital doctor unacceptable or satisfactory are determined by knowledge and experience. It is in the grey area above satisfactoriness that the effect of attitude appears, here there is scope for a study of social skills.

There are, of course, other problems. An adverse environment will tend to diminish performance, it will be the doctor who works with congenial colleagues, the co-operation of allied professions, an adequate supply of technical services and in pleasant surroundings, who will be inspired to give a better service. The style and extent of education and training equip different personalities to varying degrees, and the remuneration involved in taking responsibility and devoting effort, motivates different individuals to a greater or lesser extent. These factors will be discussed, but it is how attitudes and social skills operate in hospital doctors that is the primary concern. Thomas Percival (1803) wrote 'Hospital physicians and surgeons should minister to the sick . . ., reflecting that the ease, the health, and the lives of those committed to their care depend on their skill, attention and fidelity'. This chapter aims to discover how attention and fidelity are brought to bear.

However, what exactly is a hospital doctor, and which particular sample best represents the group as a whole? Broadly, there are two major groups into which hospital doctors conveniently fall; they are either physicians or they are surgeons. In Table 5.1 the two groups are broken down and a third section of medically qualified people who work in hospitals is also listed.

Table 5.1　Hospital medical staff, showing numbers of consultants in post on 30 September, 1980 (DHSS 1981)

Medical		Surgical	
General medicine	1045	General surgery	954
Mental illness (adult)	1083	Gynaecology and obstetrics	703
Paediatrics	519	Orthopaedic surgery	648
Geriatric medicine	405	Ophthalmology	398
Child/adolescent psychiatry	297	Ear, nose and throat	372
Diseases of the chest	222	Urology	146
Rheumatology/rehabilitation	217	Accident and emergency	131
Dermatology	207	Cardiothoracic surgery	112
Radiotherapy	188	Neurosurgery	88
Neurology	157	Plastic surgery	82
Mental handicap	152	Paediatric surgery	40
Cardiology	115		
Genito-urinary medicine	108		
Nephrology	63		
Clinical neurophysiology	46	Others	
Gastroenterology	40		
Clinical pharmacology	39	Anaesthetics*	1625
Clinical physiology	31	Radiology	825
Medical oncology	24	Histopathology	556
Nuclear medicine	22	Haematology†	335
Infectious diseases	27	Medical microbiology	293
Endocrinology	21	Chemical pathology	174
Others	45	Others	106

*Skills are mainly 'medical' but interactions are surgical.　　　† Many have clinical responsibility and are 'medical'.

It is immediately apparent that the hospital doctor is a member of a highly heterogeneous group. Even amongst those who are generally thought of as surgeons one finds both the generalist and the practitioners with highly specialized expertise, for instance, eye surgeons.

Many teaching hospitals and large district general hospitals will provide separate departments for these different doctors, but other smaller hospitals look more to the general physicians or surgeons who may also have a special interest. Furthermore, within any single group of doctors sharing the same speciality there is a wide gap between the most junior member, only recently qualified and possibly only passing through the speciality as part of an overall training, and the senior consultant, a practitioner in a particular field for more than 20 years.

Against this spectrum of knowledge, experience and expertise it is difficult to look at and try to measure the social skill of a hospital doctor. Many generalizations are worthless and do not warrant further study. This chapter will attempt not to be comprehensive but instead will demonstrate how for any specialist, at any stage of his or her career, social skills will set them apart. Whatever service or assistance they provide, they usually interact with people.

THE HOSPITAL DOCTOR

During the Second World War a coalition government took the decision to introduce a National Health Service, following the publication of the Beveridge report. It was announced in a government white paper in 1944, legislation followed in 1946 and in 1948 the Act came into force.

Part of the new National Health Service was formed by a combination of the voluntary and the Local Authority hospitals. Medical staffing followed the voluntary hospital pattern of specialists or consultants, as opposed to the former local authority Medical Superintendent model. Over the years since then, the most dramatic change in 'the hospital doctor' has been the increasing numbers of junior staff who have been appointed to assist the consultants.

Table 5.2   Hospital doctors in posts 1980 (DHSS 1981)

	Consultants	Senior registrars	Registrars	Senior house officers
General medicine	1045	216	660	1026
Mental illness (adult)	1083	288	691	738
Paediatrics	519	133	242	855
General surgery	954	212	673	663
Gynaecology and obstetrics	703	128	499	1203
Orthopaedics	648	134	360	655
Total	4952	1111	3125	5140

The consumer of a service would normally expect to play a considerable role in the choice of where, and from whom, that service is sought. Not so the patient requiring the services of a hospital doctor in the United Kingdom.

Unlike many countries which have a well developed and sophisticated system for the provision of medical care, there is in the United Kingdom a major distinction between the hospital and the non-hospital based doctor. The primary care of the community is undertaken by the General Practitioner or family doctor and the hospital provides quite separate, specialist or secondary, medical care.

There are special circumstances where clinics in hospitals are available to the general public without prior referral by their family doctor, for example those organized for the treatment of sexually transmitted disease and many patients will take themselves, or be taken by others, to a casualty department. Overall, however, the hospital practice a patient is exposed to is outside his personal control. So, the consumer of hospital practice does not choose a particular doctor and he will know nothing of that doctor's merits. The family doctor usually makes the choice.

The health service has another fundamental difference from any other kind of consumer service. The hospital doctor (and his co-workers, the nurses and other health care professionals) has a sense of personal responsibility for individual patients which affects his relationship with the managers of the service. The key decisions in clinical care are taken by the doctor but the consequent actions must be supported by administrative services. The hospital doctor is perhaps unique in being a professional who neither chooses his clients nor directly administers his business.

EDUCATION AND CAREERS

The hospital doctor starts his career in common with all aspirant doctors, by passing his 'A' level examinations to a sufficiently high standard such that he can gain entrance to a medical school. Once there he completes a preclinical course of two years (or sometimes three years, leading to a Bachelor of Science degree) studying the basic sciences of medicine, acquiring the background knowledge that enables him to practise. A clinical course then ensues, usually lasting three years, during which time the basic skills of medical practice are acquired so that he has the expertise to enable safe diagnosis and treatment of illness to be undertaken. A variety of specialist subjects such as psychiatry, obstetrics and gynaecology and paediatrics are introduced.

Following final examinations for the degrees of Bachelor of Medicine and of Surgery the newly qualified doctor undertakes his 'pre-registration' year. During this time he or she will do six months of surgery and six months of medicine as a 'houseman' in hospital practice. Only on the successful completion of this experience is the doctor fully registered on the General Medical Council list as a medical practitioner. For those doctors intent on becoming hospital consultants of whatever speciality, there is a longer period of postgraduate training varying between five and fifteen years.

Table 5.3 Timing of a doctor's speciality decision (Hutt *et al.*, 1981)

Time	Men	Women	Total
Before or during medical school	33%	14%	28%
0–5 y after qualifying	47%	47%	47%
6–10 y after qualifying	13%	16%	14%
10+ y	6%	19%	9%
Not yet	1%	4%	2%

Seventy-five per cent of all doctors have decided what they are going to do within five years of qualifying. Before moving on to discuss what a skilled doctor is, in the social context, it is worth noting how doctors feel they make the decision about what they should be doing. When asked what attributes of their career choice they found attractive the top two were the diagnosis of illness (92%) and the treatment of illness (91%). Women, taken separately, had as their second choice 'improving patients' quality of life' (93%). At the bottom of the list were attributes like 'treating old people only' (3%) or 'dealing with basically healthy people' (14%). Only 31% of doctors regarded 'dealing with social problems' as an attractive attribute of their job. On being asked about factors influencing career decision, top of the list 'of great importance' were a positive interest in work (91%), fitting in with family circumstances (41%) and job security (40%). Doctors' view of themselves is best seen in the factors which scored highest as those which were 'of no importance', for example, possibility of private practice (73%), status of speciality in profession (56%), regular working hours (50%) (Hutt *et al.*, 1981).

It would seem that the image then is of an unselfish, interested practitioner diligently setting about the diagnosis and treatment of illness. If this is really true it can be appreciated how important social skills are in distinguishing 'good doctors'.

DOCTOR–PATIENT INTERACTION

At first sight, it would seem that the ability to communicate with people is a central skill for any doctor let alone a hospital doctor. However, many achieve status and success with little obvious ability of this kind. The reasons are twofold: A number of jobs undertaken by hospital doctors keep them apart from the sick population. A much broader group have technical skills or specialist knowledge which allows them to complete their work although their philosophy or lack of 'bedside manner' (an often quoted but poorly defined skill which will be returned to later) keeps them apart from the patient.

A good example of the first category might be the histopathologist. The details he needs of a particular patient can easily be read off the request form sent to him with each specimen. His conclusions can be reached without involving others and his report is more often than not communicated to the clinician in written form. Of course, the pathologist who excels will always be a good communicator with his surgical colleagues, his co-workers, his technicians, etc., but there is no direct relationship with the patient. In the second group, there is the surgeon, immortalized in fiction but who often exists in real life, who marches through his routine with hardly a word to his patients.

The vast majority of hospital doctors do interact with patients. The spectrum ranges from the radiologist, who may only have a few directions and comforting words to say as he undertakes a special X-ray examination, through to the psychiatrist, who bases nearly everything he finds out, and can do, on the relationship he achieves with his patient.

From the patient's point of view, the interaction is achieved through a relatively simple process (see Figure 5.1). He changes from being a 'well person' to the perception (in himself or by others) that he needs medical aid. A great proportion see their family doctor, get the aid they need, and one way or another, return to being well. Some will perceive a greater or more urgent need than they know their family doctor can provide. They either 'dial 999', walk or are taken by friends into the nearest casualty department. Or, as previously mentioned attend the hospital doctor directly in a 'special clinic'. The majority of hospital patients are those that the primary care doctors refer to specialists in the hospital or to casualty because they cannot give them all the attention they perceive that the patient needs. Each interaction usually goes through three phases (see Figure 5.1); the initial encounter, continued relationship and the disposal.

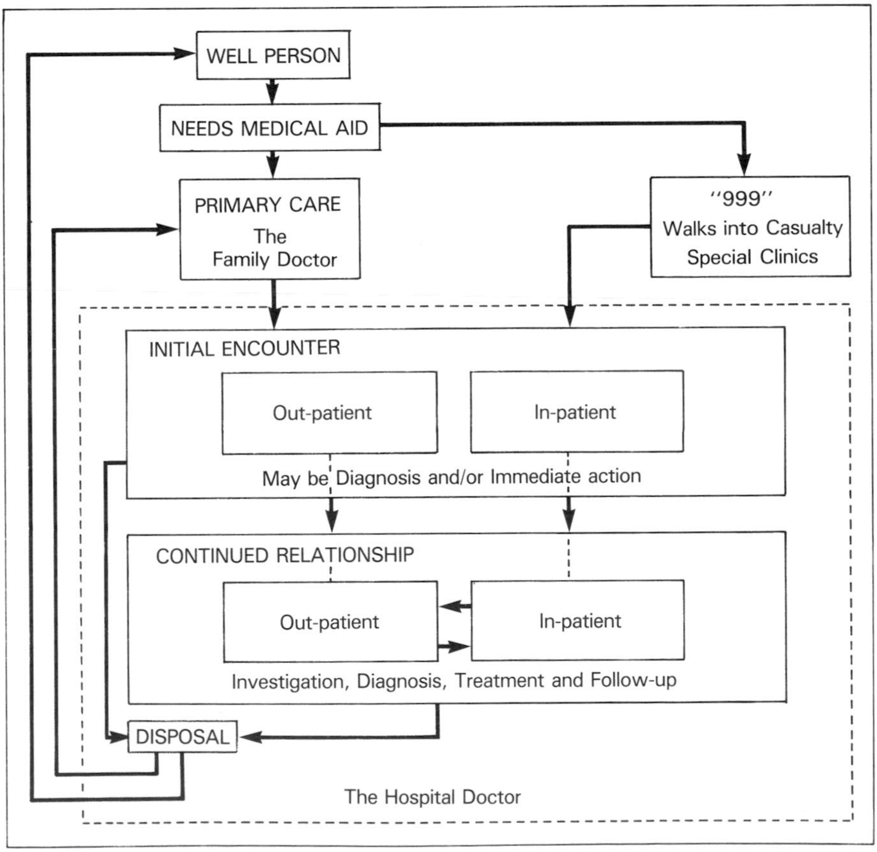

Figure 5.1   The patient interaction

The disposal is simple. The patient is either returned to being a 'well person', returned to the care of his own family doctor, or he is passed on to another hospital doctor and another initial encounter takes place (sometimes the patient dies). In each case the hospital doctor ends his responsibility for the patient, terminating the interaction. The second phase may be missed out completely if the patient's problem is easily solved. Usually it is not so cut and dried and some relationship, no matter how brief, must be entered into. It may be continued at 'intervals' in the out-patient clinic.

The initial encounter

Many factors govern the initial encounter with the hospital doctor (Wulff, 1980), two, however, are dominant. *Patient distress:* whatever causes him to be in hospital, whether it be a referral by his family doctor weeks before, or a sudden and shocking accident, the patient will have and exhibit a certain degree of distress and anxiety. *Doctor urgency:* in his initial encounter, there is always a degree of urgency with which the doctor feels he needs to make a decision, take action and proceed to solve the patient's problem. (The distinction between the doctor's need to solve the patient's problem, and his desire and/or ability to relieve the patient's distress is important and will be enlarged upon.)

In Figure 5.2 a plot of these two factors has been made. The vertical axis covers an imaginary scale of patient distress, from minimal to extreme; and the horizontal axis a scale of urgency on the part of the doctor from none to that of dire emergency. This simple plot produces four zones into which a number of examples can be fitted.

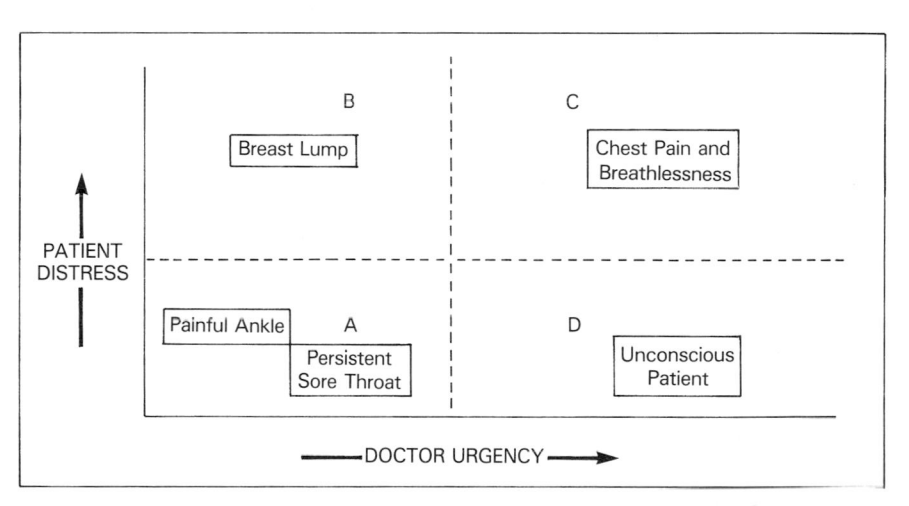

Figure 5.2   The initial encounter. Zones: A—The encounter can be relaxed; B—The patient may feel that the approach of the doctor is not appropriate; C—Medical emergency and urgent treatment is required to relieve anxiety; D—The doctor is under pressure from the problem rather than the patient

Zone A: Here the encounter can be relaxed. The patient is not distressed and the doctor feels no urgency to proceed at speed. The most benign example is of a painful ankle. The patient clearly wants something doing about it and the doctor aims to achieve relief of pain. Neither of them initially sees anything sinister in the problem and the relationship can continue unimpeded. More interesting is the example of a patient presenting, perhaps at casualty, with a persistent sore throat. He is neither particularly distressed nor anxious (assuming the discomfort is relatively slight). As the problem is rarely more than a virus infection and only sometimes a bacterial infection that truly needs intervention, the doctor feels no particular urgency. However, the interaction is different from the sprained ankle in that the doctor does perceive the possibility of something sinister; he may wonder for instance, about the possibility of acute leukaemia. If the patient had any inkling of this possible diagnosis he would be in a completely different state of mind and the interaction would take place in the next 'zone'.

Zone B: Here the patient may feel that the approach of the doctor is not appropriate. There exists extreme anxiety on the part of the patient but little urgency in the doctor. A good example is the unfortunate lady who finds a lump in her breast. Her fear of cancer, if it is overt, will produce huge anxieties. Firstly she will wonder why her GP's request for a consultation is not dealt with by return of post. When she does get to out-patients, she will search every phrase and every word the surgeon utters for a hint of sinister news. For the surgeon there is no such urgency. The problem is common enough, it may or may not turn out to be cancer, but only in the fullness of time when he has completed his investigation—even if the wait takes until the lump is excised and is under the pathologist's microscope.

Zone C: When the patient's distress is intense and the doctor feels a great urgency to solve the problem, a medical emergency is in progress. Paradoxically, the patient may be relieved of some anxiety if the doctor does not display any sense of urgency, for instance in dealing with a patient suffering an acute asthmatic attack which will be worsened by anxiety. However, in most circumstances the patient's distress is physical as well as mental and is only relieved by the prompt action of his medical attendant. For example, severe chest pain associated with breathlessness requires urgent treatment to solve the problem.

Zone D: Here the doctor is usually under pressure from the problem rather than the patient. Being presented with an unconscious victim of a road traffic accident certainly concentrates the mind of an admitting casualty officer; little or no social interaction takes place. Another separate example, related to the problem of a persistent sore throat seen in Zone A, might be included in Zone D. If, through a certain set of symptoms and signs, a doctor recognizes an emergency of which the patient is unaware, special problems ensue. A good example is polymyalgia rheumatica. The presentation is often classical, with pains and stiffness around the shoulders. The doctor's urgency in trying to clarify his diagnosis arises because it is associated, when untreated, with the sudden onset of blindness. It is not difficult to imagine the anxiety of a patient who realizes this possibility, or the remorse of a physician should he fail to make the diagnosis in time.

A number of factors other than the possible diagnosis are bound to affect both patient and doctor.

Physical surroundings—A great many initial encounters will take place in the Out-patients department. Such consultation almost always takes place after a considerable wait, in inhospitable surroundings, for the normal patient. The doctor is under pressure because of the limited time he can allocate to each patient. When, however, the patient lies in bed on a ward, time may not play any role but the alien nature of the patient's surroundings may subject him or her to as many pressures.

State of undress—Although essential for thorough examination, both the doctor and the patient may be inhibited, pressured or otherwise compromised by the patient's enforced nakedness. The necessity for the doctor to touch his patient when examining can create other difficulties.

Being out-numbered—If the patient can, he is expected to speak for himself. However, this often takes place in the presence of two, three or more doctors and/or nurses. As if that were not off-putting enough, the doctors may (and sadly often do) talk amongst themselves, about the patient and about things the patient does not understand, as if the patient were not there.

Any number of other contributing factors can be recognized, in their most distilled form, each contributes to the patient's distress and anxiety, and to the doctor's need to make a decision. To negotiate the initial encounter skilfully the good doctor must be able to:

Recognize the degree of distress and anxiety in the patient, however inappropriate he may feel it is.

Contain or conceal his urgency when it may damage the relationship with his patient, and channel it to good effect when it is a medical necessity.

Take his cue from the patient, because he can be certain that the patient will take his cue from the doctor.

The continued relationship

The relationship a doctor has with his patient can be viewed as an extension of the initial encounter. Rather than being static, the degree of distress and anxiety exhibited by the patient, and the attitude of the doctor to that patient with his particular problem, change progressively as the interaction proceeds.

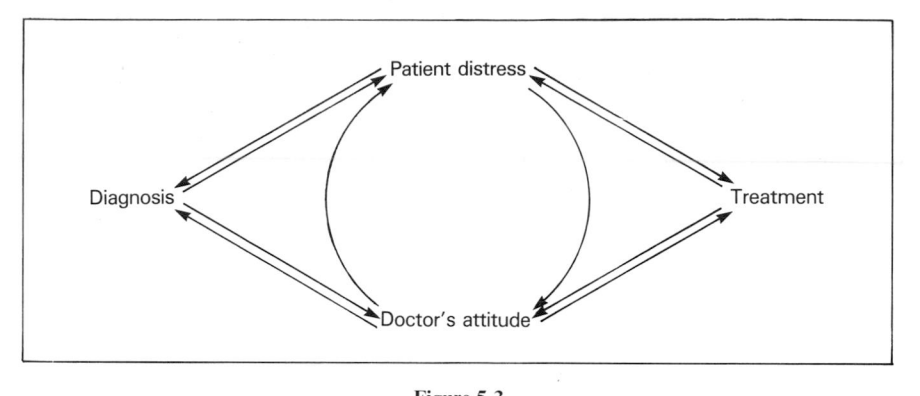

Figure 5.3

The relationship rolls along in the following fashion:

The patient has entered the initial encounter with a degree of distress and anxiety dependent on what he thinks is wrong with him. Immediately, he adjusts this level according to the way in which the doctor reacts. If the patient thinks there is nothing to worry about and then is suddenly confronted with a disturbed doctor he is going to worry more, conversely an extremely anxious patient may be calmed by a relaxed doctor.

The sensitive doctor assesses the reactions of the patient and adjusts his response according to the degree of distress exhibited by the patient and the inherent urgency of the medical situation.

Having seen the way the doctor reacts, the patient adopts a different attitude, either of lessened or of heightened anxiety.

The doctor adjusts his response, etc.

Somewhere in this progression, the actual diagnosis and then the treatment required, interferes with the relationship. In Figure 5.3 this is illustrated as a two-way effect:

The diagnosis (when it is reached) will clearly affect the doctor's attitude. When it is explained to the patient, a concomitant alteration in his mental state also occurs.

Both the attitude of the doctor and the patient can alter the diagnosis or treatment. For example, after making a judgement about how his patient may react to the diagnosis a doctor can lie or disguise the truth. Equally, the degree of distress that a patient has, might be given a label of its own by the doctor, creating a new diagnosis. In choosing the way a patient is treated, the doctor may well make alterations based on judgements about how he thinks the patient will 'cope'.

The treatment itself may change the patient fundamentally. Intensive chemotherapy given over a long period for leukaemia, for instance, often has a dramatic effect on a patient's morale. As they often feel things are getting considerably worse their anxiety (for them appropriately, but often in the doctor's eyes, inappropriately as they are getting medically 'better') increases.

In the continuing relationship, once more, the physical surroundings, numbers and changes of doctors, etc., all contribute, but again it can be argued that the degree of distress in the patient and the sense of urgency and attitude of the doctor, are paramount.

The 'good' doctor

Using this simple model, more observations about what makes a 'good' hospital doctor can be made:

The doctor must be sensitive to the patient's mental state and realize that the patient will adjust it, not only in response to his medical state, but in response to the attitude of the doctor.

The doctor must be flexible enough to adjust his attitude, not just to the requirements of putting the medical problem right, but to allow the patient to be relieved of as much anxiety as possible.

The doctor must be able to communicate the meaning and the implications of a diagnosis so as to avoid provoking unnecessary anxiety.

Any treatment given must also be explained in a way that makes it as acceptable as possible.

Much of this is true for all doctors. The reason for discussing what happens between the hospital doctor and patient in such detail, is because the patient is that much more vulnerable, due to the seriousness of his condition combined with the different status of a 'specialist' as distinct from the familiar family doctor. Few patients will not feel that the hospital doctor and his opinions carry more weight than the reaction of his family doctor, if only because the family doctor has sought the referral on the patient's behalf.

What are the characteristics of a good 'bedside manner' which a patient may look for in a hospital doctor?

Understanding—Successful rapport can only be achieved if the patient is sure that the doctor understands what he is saying to him. This is not just an expression of shared cultural characteristics. Many patients are inarticulate, through shyness, low intelligence or a combination of these and other reasons, but this does not necessarily mean they have no insight into their own inability to be comprehended. Even the dullest of people know, or at least think they know, when the doctor has got the wrong end of the stick. The problems are just as acute if the patient, perhaps of very high intelligence, or using excessive dialect or jargon, thinks he is being understood when in reality he is not. Nothing dampens confidence more than having to explain yourself for the third or fourth time. Finally, of course, the patient will only truly co-operate if he thinks he is being allowed to be understood. Too much assumption and interruption by the doctor can be alienating.

Having a successful relationship—All that has been described previously about the 'rolling' relationship of doctor and patient can work in two ways. Only if the patient has his anxiety and distress relieved will he attribute 'a good manner' to the doctor. A medical cure can be achieved by anyone with the relevant technical knowledge and skills, but far from everyone is a 'good doctor' as far as patients are concerned.

Being understood—Following on from feeling that the doctor understands what he is saying, a patient must understand what the doctor is telling him. A good doctor has to be able to use his appreciation of the patient in the way he explains what he wants the patient to say, to do and to know.

Being in hospital

It must be emphasized again that the patient is only in contact with a hospital doctor because of the relative seriousness of his plight. The doctor must be able to identify any block to communication between him and the patient. He must proceed to create an atmosphere for acceptance of investigation and of treatment, many facets of which may be disturbing and unpleasant. He must find a way of breaking bad news and of supporting dying patients, always avoiding too much emotional involvement. A lot of this is achieved by being a member of a team who are all involved in caring for the patient.

TEAM SKILLS

Inevitably each hospital doctor is part of a team or group whose specific aim is to look after the patient. Much of the real skill of a good and successful doctor is his or her ability to be a useful team member. A hospital, as indicated earlier, can be divided up into a variety of different groups, autonomous yet interdependent. To most patients, the most obvious division is that of separate wards. To the doctor, however, often the most important division is that of separate departments, or even more specifically, separate so-called 'firms' whose medical staff all work for one specific consultant (to the consultant, the most important division is clearly his 'firm'). Administratively, the hospital divides into medical and non-medical, the difference between providing medical aid and providing 'hotel' type facilities.

The main members of the team to which any doctor belongs are:

Colleagues

Colleagues can be either junior, peer or senior, and they can either be from the same department or from a different department. They may have similar aims and interests or they may have conflicting aims and interests—as is true of any large organization. The catch with hospital doctors is that the service provided is for the person in need. Maintaining this objective in the face of personal ambition, peer-group rivalry, political infighting (currently almost always motivated by the division of dwindling funds) and professional jealousy is no simple task. The good hospital doctor has to be able to cope with all of these demands to be maximally useful to his patient.

Nursing staff

Nurses are in charge of wards and care for the needs of the patients. It sounds simple and it is. However, an atmosphere of co-operation must exist between the nurses and the doctor if anything is to be achieved for their patients. The good doctor recognizes that many patients will improve to an extent such that he is no longer needed, despite him rather than because of him. Good nursing care is where patient wellbeing and recovery begins and ends. The nurses also carry out the administration of many drugs, perform many technical and medical procedures and assist the doctor in many tasks, all of which require understanding of what the doctor wants. This extension of the 'nursing role' is not viewed by all nurses (or all doctors) as a good thing, but done in the right spirit the patient is bound to benefit.

Administrators

As with any large and complicated organization, the more senior a member (in this case doctor) becomes, the more he must be responsible for the decisions about how the organization is funded and administered. In the National Health Service this is a moot point, but all senior hospital doctors need the diplomatic, political and committee skills of a good manager.

Other services

Most special skills in a hospital are available to any doctor in the investigation and treatment of his patient. Judicious use of them is a practical skill derived of medical knowledge and experience and is outside the scope of this chapter.

It is clear that how the hospital doctor becomes a successful team member is a complicated business. It does not necessarily depend upon the hierarchical system described earlier, but the authority vested in the seniors, over the juniors, is the basis for it. The juniors in any 'firm', for example the houseman and registrar of a consultant surgeon, may deliberately modify their medical practice to suit 'the boss'. It isn't enough just to close a surgical incision in the way most favoured by the consultant, such that he will approve on the ward round the next morning. All juniors are 'in training' and therefore are expected to learn and use the methods of their superiors. Junior medical staff may often change their boss every six months or a year, so one can appreciate some of the conflicts that may arise. 'Junior' is also a relative term. The new houseman, only a week into medical practice, expects and needs to be guided and to be covered in all of his decisions and actions. But a Senior Registrar, maybe ten years into his training, may feel distinctly unhappy at altering a decision he feels is sound (based on his previous extensive experience of a problem) because he knows that his current 'boss' would disapprove.

The ward round is the hospital vehicle of these problems, conflicts and ultimately, the expression of good teamwork when it exists. The consultant surgeon may choose to see all of his hospital patients every day, usually less often but hardly ever as infrequently as only once a week. He will usually expect his junior staff to accompany him and they do. Around each bed the consultant and his retinue gather, together with the nurse in charge of the ward that day, and make their decisions. Or do they?

The spectrum ranges from the autocratic boss who simply imposes his view—a situation frequently needed when the junior staff are unreliable, inexperienced or just not there—to the team approach, where the whole problem may have been discussed extensively (perhaps over coffee or at an informal 'round table' session) before the doctors appear at the bedside, putting their collective decision into action. For the surgeon, the best decisions may well depend on the bedside visit. The timing of an operation may depend on up-to-the-minute examination findings, a change in the patient signalling dramatic action. The surgeon also has to believe that he personally is right, if you plan to do an operation on someone, believing you are right is crucial. Equally, for the consultant psychiatrist, for instance, the best decisions will depend on a lengthy discussion with the members of his staff most acquainted with the patient, with the views of the nursing staff, psychologists, social workers, etc., all considered in the plan for the care of the patient.

The good hospital doctor appreciates his position, knows what is required for the care of his patient, and can take decisions that are appropriate. I well remember being a medical student in my first clinical year; the whole set (over a hundred students) were gathered together to hear the Professor of Medicine extol the need to be able to take decisions. 'If you can't take difficult decisions you might as well leave now'; the message was clear, we would not make 'good' doctors if we were poor decision takers. Of course no one actually took the decision to leave so we all remained in our seats. The minority of this group of students who have pursued a career in hospital medicine must have been relieved to discover that decision taking can often be shared, particularly while the skills are being acquired. The essence of being a good hospital doctor as a member of a team of doctors is to participate appropriately in decision taking such that although the responsibility remains with the individual at the head of the group, some decisions are made at each level and the medicine that is practised is good medicine.

The nature of taking responsibility is also brought into focus when considering the relationship between the doctor and the nurse. On the ward round, with the consultant present, there is no doubt as to who has the responsibility, similarly when the registrar is conducting a round it will be he who makes the final decision and has the final word. Equally, in the middle of the night, when a nurse sends for the houseman to see someone he or she is worried about the houseman will be expected to be able to take decisions, plan management and initiate action. Very much the first part of a nurse's appreciation of the good doctor is his ability to take unlaboured decisions, be clear in the requests he makes of them, and his ability to carry out any action that is needed.

Close behind those requirements, however, comes the essential requirement that the nurse thinks the action is appropriate (and therefore is based on a correct decision). The good nurse doesn't himself or herself try to be a doctor and judge the true medical correctness of a decision, but is in a unique position to judge action based on knowing the patient. Doctors do not spend their time with patients in the way the nurses inevitably do; good nurses know their patients very well indeed. The conflicts that arise when nurses are sure that patients have 'had enough' or should 'be left in peace' are often very traumatic. The doctor would be very insensitive about his patient not to realize the atmosphere and consider the nurse's conclusion himself, either in discussion with the nursing staff, or from his own appreciation of the plight of the patient. Equally, for medical reasons alone, the nurses might be wrong.

The treatment of patients with relapsed haematological malignancy may provide such cases. Often they are young, appear to be in considerable discomfort and distress and the treatment may require them to go through many more problems. Often the day is lost, and the fight has to change direction and cope with the patients' discomforts rather than their disease; but, almost as often, something can be salvaged and should be. This can be very controversial, many doctors and nurses disapprove of the treatment some dying patients receive, often only in an attempt to give them 'a few more weeks'; but equally it is often the patient who is most ambitious to have those weeks.

SPECIFIC PROBLEMS

Amongst the more common general problems are coping with relatives, bad news and dying patients, coping with expectations versus available resources and the issue of mistakes.

Coping with relatives, bad news and dying patients

The hospital doctor gives a second line of medical care in support of the general practitioner; he is inherently a specialist or in specialist training. To a very large extent, therefore, the very good hospital doctor is simply one who knows his speciality well, is well trained, thorough and practises his art intelligently. In addition, however, it has already been argued that the relevant social skills are the feature that distinguish the excellent from the good and the average from the very poor performer. The requirements of communicating with patients have been discussed; in dealing with relatives there are a number of common pitfalls where the otherwise good hospital doctor can get into difficulties.

Firstly, in not providing enough information; too often the nursing staff are left to discuss patients and distribute news to the relatives.

Secondly, in assuming the wrong attitude. Just as the patient who doesn't understand what he is being told feels he cannot quiz the doctor too closely, so the relative can feel he or she has 'spoken to the doctor' but remains none the wiser. People often need to be told things in simple terms, although through television and other media coverage general medical knowledge is reaching a higher standard in the general public. Even though the words heard may be totally unintelligible people can none the less identify a condescending or dismissive attitude.

Thirdly, in creating friction between patient and relative. This will be discussed in detail shortly, in connection with dying patients, but unnecessary stress is sometimes unintentionally created when a different story is told to the patient and to the relatives. Ill people and their nearest and dearest can well do without the pressure of thinking they each have things to hide from each other. Tact and common sense are also needed when trying to get information out of relatives that may be medically relevant, but which the patient is hiding from the doctor. The quantity of alcohol consumed is a classic example. A man with liver disease may not be trusted to give an accurate answer about his alcohol intake, but his wife might be upset to be asked. Equally, deceit can pile on deceit when it emerges that the wife also is an alcoholic.

Breaking bad news and dealing with dying patients are areas where the socially skilled doctor is so much more useful to the care of his patient than the socially unskilled (but perhaps otherwise accomplished) doctor. The first crucial step that any doctor takes in breaking bad news is actually to decide to do it. Considerable debate exists within any group of otherwise harmonious medical staff about the wisdom or otherwise of informing patients, relatives or friends about bad news. If we take the most obvious, for example, a man who is investigated for a persistent cough and perhaps a little weight loss, who may turn out to have lung cancer: regardless of whether or not any treatment is anticipated or planned, many doctors would argue about the need to tell the patient of the diagnosis.

This author feels that unless there are really exceptional circumstances the patient and his relatives should be told, no matter how bad the news. There are a variety of reasons. The many specialist terminal care hospices almost universally require knowledge of the diagnosis to be a prerequisite of entry for the patient and their extensive experience must be respected. Too often wives or husbands have to look after their loved ones with one or other pretending that all will be well. This conflict often continues despite obvious indications that both partners in fact do know what is going on and secretly wish they could be frank.

Trust and confidence in the doctor can be shattered by a failure to communicate the truth. Bad news sometimes comes as a complete surprise, and more often the implications of a certain diagnosis may have been totally unanticipated. Rarely, however, does the patient mistake evasion by the doctor, or the relative miss the fact that he or she is not being told the whole truth. Having made the decision to tell a patient of their diagnosis and its implications, communication has to be maintained. Again, too often, because a patient is dying, he or she is left with too little information, support and help from the socially inept doctor.

Sudden death is a different problem from bad news. Seen principally in the accident and emergency department, the sudden death of a previously well person is not an uncommon event. There is no easy way to tell anyone about their loved one's death and it is outside the brief of this essay to discuss the way people react to it. All of the doctor's communication skills, tact, common sense and experience are needed most when dealing with death and the despair of losing loved ones. Socially competent doctors communicate bad news themselves and try to avoid delegating either to more junior doctors or to the nurses.

Coping with expectations versus available resources

There are two facets to this problem. Firstly not all hospitals are equipped, either physically or in terms of expertise, with all the necessary facilities for complete medical practice. Very often a doctor may recognize what has to be done but be unable to do it himself. He needs to refer the patient away from his hospital to a centre where the necessary skills or technical services exist. Often this will involve some facet of treatment which the doctor would not necessarily wish to undertake even if he could, but nonetheless, herein is a source of frustration and discontent. It is not practical or necessary for every District General Hospital to be like a large teaching centre. The second conflict, between the doctor's expectations and what he is actually able to do for financial reasons, cuts across all hospitals (Black, 1979). This frustration that doctors must cope with can lead to bitterness, and consequently poorer practice than is feasible.

The other side of the coin, the practical limitations that probably improve medical practice, are best exemplified by the way junior staff often proceed towards a diagnosis. Always keen to be conversant with the most modern diagnostic aids and investigations, the less experienced doctor is tempted to apply a 'blunderbuss' approach to arriving at the correct diagnosis. If given a completely free hand he might even perform every investigation even remotely applicable and try to derive the correct diagnosis only when as many results are available as is possible. The more experienced clinician may disapprove of this approach and himself be able to use more acumen and discretion when reaching a diagnosis. However, only in an atmosphere of true restraint of resources does the proper training become essential so that every hospital doctor spends money with discretion. The feeling that investigations and treatments represent 'spending money' is essential for this atmosphere. The habits developed by such constraint are almost universally better than in the 'blunderbuss' technique.

Mistakes

The doctor who attempts something outside his experience or makes a decision outside his responsibility courts disaster. But mistakes inevitably occur even when the best circumstances prevail—perhaps because of over-tiredness or shortage of time to consider a decision. The good doctor is aware of the pitfalls wherein mistakes are made and in this atmosphere mistakes also will be recognized early. It is difficult to generalize about what can be done once a mistake is made, as far as the patient is concerned, but what about the doctor? The hospital doctor is under considerable pressure, if there has been an error. There are the pressures of personal failure to meet responsibility to the patient and of peer-group respect or trust consequent upon that failure. In judging the circumstances and cause of the mistake the avoidance of repetition is usually achieved. It is worth noting also that in medical practice, dealing with ill people, a mistake might be relative to other observers' opinions and might well have occurred in circumstances clearly unavoidable.

CONCLUSION

The analysis of the 'skilled hospital doctor' has been made based on one major assumption. Excellent and indifferent doctors in hospital practice are differentiated primarily by the depth of their knowledge, the level of their technical skills and the extent of their experience of particular medical problems. Sickness and accident occur in certain forms; the ease with which they can be managed depends primarily on how efficiently the problems are identified and on skill in taking the appropriate action. Experienced doctors will have usually met the problem before and therefore are 'better' at dealing with it.

The difference between doctors and other professional problem solvers does not depend on either medical knowledge or experience. They all have two funds of information on which their ability depends—firstly a knowledge of the manifestations (the symptoms, signs and investigatory findings) of different problems—in the doctors' case, of the diseases. Secondly they have knowledge and experience of the ways in which the problem can be solved— the treatments. Applying these, firstly to the data collected about the problem (the information from taking a history, examining a patient and doing any tests on him) to make a diagnosis and then, secondly, to solve the problem, is exactly what a car mechanic or a plumber, as well as a doctor, does. The doctor is unusual because his problem solving involves individuals. There will always be some expression of that individuality on the disease but in essence the diagnostic and therapeutic problem—for example a chest infection—is not different in different patients. It is the social interactions, the communication skills, the emotional responses of the patient and their family which differ and make every problem in medicine unique.

No matter how good or extensive his purely medical knowledge, there is a set of special abilities a hospital doctor must have, namely:

He must be a good communicator, recognizing his position as 'the doctor' and using everything both he and the patient says as a tool in arriving at the true nature of the problem.

He must be a responsible team member. Although individual skills need to be used and applied in caring for the patient, there is always a collective responsibility for solving the problem. He has to be able to take appropriate decisions, recognizing in himself the need to rely on other members of the team to make them when it is appropriate.

There are a number of purely social encounters, like the necessity to break bad news, where the skilled hospital doctor stands out from his less socially able peers, whose medical knowledge may be equal or superior.

Modification of his expected or desired practice, because of economic and organizational pressures outside his control, can make him sometimes a better, sometimes a worse practitioner.

In common with everyone else, doctors need to be able to cope with failures and mistakes, without it interfering with the practice of their skills.

Without the necessity to resort to reason or justification, most patients, most relatives, most doctors and most nurses identify 'good doctors'. They often do this without any evidence that problems can be efficiently solved or that everything attempted or carried out will be successful. The judgement is made, often on the briefest of encounters, without reference to reputation, examination of qualifications or study of research and innovative achievement. It is made because the relationship the doctor has with his patient or colleague 'feels' right. It is not outside the scope of the good hospital doctor to see the needs of any relationship and adjust his temperament, language, approach and attitude such that all his encounters will 'feel right'.

References

Black, Sir Douglas (1979). The paradox of medical care. *J. R. Coll. Physician Lond.*, **13**, 2, 57–65
DHSS Medical Manpower Division (1981). Medical statistics and prospects in the N.H.S. in England and Wales 1980. *Health Trends*, **13**, 2, 57–60
Hutt, R., Parsons, D. and Pearson, R. (1981). The timing of and reasons for doctors' career decisions. *Health Trends*, **13**, 1, 17–20
Percival, T. (1803). *Medical Ethics, or a Code of Institutes and Precepts, adapted to the Professorial Conduct of Physicians and Surgeons*
Wulff, H. R. (1980). *Regional Diagnosis and Treatment*. (Oxford: Blackwell)

6
The Occupational Physician

D. SLATTERY

THE OCCUPATIONAL HEALTH TEAM

The responsibilities of the practitioner in the occupational health field fall into two broad categories. The first is concerned with the effect of health or rather ill health on ability to work. This involves the assessment of fitness of individuals for various occupations and advice to those individuals and their employers of the constraints involved and the best way that these may be overcome. The second category is concerned with the effect of work on individuals and groups. This field covers a wide range of problems including the treatment of acute injury at work, the effects of physical and chemical environmental conditions and the psychological stresses inherent in any organized social activity.

To be effective in these roles the occupational physician will need the assistance of a wide variety of other professionals, medical colleagues, nurses, engineers, chemists, etc. In larger industrial undertakings involving over, say 10 000 employees the occupational physician may have a number of these staff directly responsible to him in his own unit and in this respect he becomes a manager in his own right. This situation is not unique to doctors in industrial practice. Although in hospital practice managerial skills are now almost entirely confined to leading a small team of colleagues, the development of larger group general practices has meant that some doctors in practice have had to become involved in the management of more complex teams consisting of nurses, welfare visitors and other paramedical staff.

In general the role of the manager does not come easily to the doctor, his selection, training and early experience has been based on a caring, one-to-one, relationship with his patients. Moreover, the role is essentially advisory rather than executive. The conflict that necessarily arises from time to time between the needs or desires of the individual and the needs of the unit, is one that recurs in a large number of activities but as we shall see the importance of retaining the correct image is particularly important to the occupational physician.

The relationship between the doctor and the nurse in industry is interesting because of overlap of roles. The traditional tasks of doctors are to diagnose and to prescribe treatment, that of nurses is to carry out that prescribed treatment in the light of their own training and experience in the care of patients. In industry, however, the nurse is often operating in geographical isolation from direct doctor control and has therefore to develop skills of diagnosis and judgement akin to those normally exercised by the doctor. The control of this situation by the doctor requires a considerable degree of sensitivity as the potential for mutual resentment is that much greater than in most other forms of medical practice. This problem is less significant in the relationship with other paramedical staff in the team such as physiotherapists, radiologists, laboratory technicians where the specific skills and technologies are more clearly defined. The lead role of the doctor is seldom resented here as the respect of the doctor for the individual's expertise in his or her own field leads to a positive relationship.

The concern of occupational physicians for the environment giving rise to accidents and ill health has led to a close association with two other groups of professional staff, namely safety officers and occupational or environmental hygienists. In a number of organizations the environmental health and, perhaps less often, safety teams have been brought together with the medical department administratively, and the doctor may find himself having to manage staff whose primary discipline is not medically based. Under these circumstances the doctor has to develop his leadership without the support of a traditional role or relying on the expertise gained by broader training and experience.

This broader direct managerial skill is mainly confined to larger organizations and occupational health units. A great deal of occupational health practice is carried out by very small teams consisting of the doctor, a secretary and one or two nurses. The doctor will still require the use of the resources discussed but in this case he controls these in a purely functional manner, the direct management being in other hands be it internal or external to the organization in which he is working. This in itself may present problems particularly in the field of availability and maintenance of standards.

THE INDUSTRIAL ENVIRONMENT

To a certain extent the doctor in industry works in an alien environment. Unlike the hospital or general practice the purpose of the organization quite clearly does not exist primarily for the care of individuals but to produce goods and services for its customers. To a manager the top priority is the continued existence or expansion of the organization and this is achieved by providing the appropriate product or service at a price that will show sufficient profit to justify the resources being employed. In his eyes the employees, including himself, are just part of that resource. That industry has a wider social role in providing employment which in itself is a necessary element in the health of individuals or of society as a whole comes comparatively low in the list of the manager's concerns. Although at Board level the development of medical departments within industry may have a considerable altruistic element, and this was certainly so in the early days in such companies as Rowntree's, Lever Bros, etc., at the operating level the major place of the doctor and his team is seen to be the maintenance of this resource at the most effective level. In saying this it is not suggesting that there is no humanity in the way in which managers handle individual cases but only that this humanity is tempered by the concern for profitability. This is seen clearly in the attitude of managers in varying economic climates. When industry is prospering there is little difficulty in finding a niche for those employees having a disability but when the economic wind blows cold the effectiveness of such employees is judged more harshly. Similarly when the doctor is concerned with specific health hazards affecting the workforce there is a strong feeling by most managers that his advice is likely to cause trouble, reduction in output and expense.

Traditionally doctors are used to their patients accepting their assessments and advice without significant question. When dealing with management, however, this situation does not hold good. The success of a doctor coming into industry is dependent on his ability to sell both himself and the service that he is offering as a benefit to the undertaking. This is particularly important in the development phase of a new medical service to an industry. In doing this he has the advantage of the standing afforded to the profession as a whole by society. The doctor in industry, however, must be prepared to spend a considerable amount of time with individual managers justifying the work that he is trying to do and its value not only to individuals but to the organization and its objectives. In order to do this effectively he must have sufficient understanding of the attitudes and objectives of those managers and to explain his own objectives in terms that they understand. When talking to a production manager he needs to understand the importance of attendance, work output and skills; to an engineer it may be a matter more of intellectual performance; to an accountant a matter of wasted resources. Unless the doctor can achieve this rapport with the different types of management with whom he has to deal he can only rely for support in his actions on welfare and humanitarian grounds and as we have seen this may be a flimsy foundation on which to build in adverse economic situations.

Most managers are professionals in their own right and recognize professionalism in their colleagues. In order to gain acceptance and credibility and thus support from the managers with whom he comes in contact he must demonstrate a high degree of professionalism within his own sphere. This professionalism is not only a question of clinical competence as a doctor but because of the influence he and his team wish to bring to bear on the broader aspects of employment he must be able to present evidence derived from other disciplines such as chemistry, engineering, occupational hygiene in an objective and logical manner. Most generalizations and emotionally-based judgements are not acceptable in today's industrial scene.

It is unlikely that a doctor working within industry can avoid becoming involved with trade union organization at some level. Unlike the management, trade union officials' and shop stewards' primary concern is for the employees, both as individuals and as groups. One might therefore assume the doctor in industry would be immediately welcomed by the trade unions and have their full support and co-operation. Unfortunately for a number of reasons, some of which need not concern us here, this is not so. In the trade union mind the doctor is equated with the management team and the distrust by the unions of any management action, particularly those that are altruistic, transfer across to the role of the doctor. The doctor and also the members associated with his team such as safety officers are often seen by trade union officials and shop stewards as being employed by the management to cover up their actions insofar as these may give rise to ill health among the employees that they represent. It is unfortunate that there are a number of well publicized situations where the development of knowledge from a medical point of view of the ill effects of certain materials has lagged behind their general use within industry; often quoted is the example of the incidence of cancer associated with the use of blue asbestos and also of vinyl chloride monomer. These subjects are extremely emotive and it is very difficult to get a balanced judgement in terms of acceptable risk.

Another cause of distrust is in association with claims for compensation in cases of accident and ill health related to work. Before the last war a number of doctors were employed by industry to help defend them in cases of common law compensation and the image of the so-called 'compo' doctor still lingers with us. Unfortunately in many cases when a doctor in industry advises an individual employee that he should undertake alternative work, the work available is of a less skilled nature and such a change of employment will therefore inevitably involve a loss of wages. The trade unions representative's concern to defend the individual employee's income may well lead him into conflict with the doctor.

THE INDIVIDUAL EMPLOYEE

Although the occupational physician must, to be totally effective, interface with the management and with the trade unions, it is important that he does not lose touch with the basic traditional role of the doctor as the adviser to individuals in a direct doctor–patient relationship. To do so presents two major hazards, one to himself and the other to his image in the society in which he operates. One of the most important influences the doctor can bring to industry is to champion the individual human being, be he employer or employee, against the growing mechanistic classifications. An individual may be a manager or a worker, blue or white collar, he may be a turner or a clerk, a coppersmith or a salesman, a clock number or a grade five executive, but to himself and to the doctor he remains a person.

It is only by the continued contact with individuals and the direct handling of their problems that the doctor in industry can prevent himself from sliding first into the language and later the attitudes of generalization inherent in complex organizations. Fortunately the nature of the tasks and his early training makes this fairly easy. The examination of individuals for assessment for work is a routine procedure requiring individual judgement but even here the danger of systemization can be found. The paperwork found in many industrial organizations is so structured as to encourage classification. Moreover, the introduction of computerization in medical records encourages a black and white style. Pain becomes a tick in the appropriate box and anxiety another.

The constraints of employment such as job availability lead to difficult and painful decisions and because of this the temptation to hide behind impersonal systems may be very strong. The doctor who falls to this temptation may rapidly lose touch with his professional ethic. If he cannot give his recommendation directly to the individual he should not make a recommendation at all. There is no more telling situation than recommending early retirement on grounds of ill health to an employee who is unwilling to accept that his career has ended.

In the preventive field similar opportunities and dangers exist. Statutory regulations lay down the levels of exposure to toxic substances and to other pollutants. It is the occupational physician's duty to monitor the health of those exposed to such noxious agents. These regulations and other standards are based on group studies and although they incorporate considerable safety margins are unable to take account of individual human variation. It is comparatively easy, safe and publicly defensible to apply these standards in rigid and absolute terms. The doctor who does so and does not take into account not only the physical individuality of an employee but also his psychological and social background is not fulfilling his task. At the end of the day the slide rule is no substitute for the stethoscope.

As the physical environment comes under control in employment doctors working in industry have become increasingly involved in the psychological upsets which impinge upon work. Not only such gross manifestations of breakdown such as alcoholism, depression and chronic anxiety states but also those minor disturbances which lead to poor judgement, poor performance and absenteeism are a major concern to both management and employee alike.

In this area the doctor works at several levels. In the first place he is the informed listener to the individual's fears, doubts and worries. Psychological distress is still considered not wholly acceptable in society, and a considerable number of employees come to the works surgery to consult on physical symptoms of a trivial nature and it is important not to dismiss these without allowing the opportunity for the individual to bring out the real concern. Time, patience and some skill is necessary for this communication to develop but in this he does not differ from others who take on such a counselling role.

The doctor in industry does have a specially important place as on the one hand he has the aura of his profession and on the other he has a particular understanding of the working environment and the relations that develop within it. It is in this field that the image of objectivity and the integrity of the doctor is vitally important. He must be seen to have knowledge of and influence with the management and if necessary the trade unions but equally he must be seen to stand apart and be able to handle the situation with all the confidentiality of the normal doctor–patient relationship. Frequently the employee can be led to take the appropriate actions on his own behalf with such support as is necessary from the doctor. On other occasions the doctor may have to take a lead role but he must always be sure that he has the employee's understanding and acceptance. However tempting it may be, the doctor must tread extremely warily in trying to manipulate a situation for the individual's own benefit behind that individual's back.

Having said this, however, the management have a right to expect the medical adviser to give them the same help in the sensible handling of employees suffering from psychological disturbance as they receive in the case of those suffering from physical illness. Such cases, where the judgement of the employee is clearly impaired, provide some of the most difficult situations of ethical judgement.

A considerable number of stress-related disorders are exacerbated by faults within the organization. By highlighting the incidence of these conditions in certain areas of a working unit the faults may be identified and to a greater or lesser extent may be relieved. To help in this process the doctor must have some basic understanding of management and organizational theory.

Many stressful situations develop within a unit, however, from the personal management style of individual managers. In some ways these may be easier for the doctor to recognize and to understand but again the conflict may arise between that individual, the needs of his peers and subordinates, and even the needs of the organization as a whole. From time to time the doctor may have the opportunity to play a key role in finding a satisfactory adjustment to improve the situation.

THE MEDICAL PROFESSION

The organization of medical services in this country is based on the individual medical practitioner servicing a discrete population essentially that of the pre-national health service panel. The general practitioner is contracted to supply all forms of medical advice and treatment to his patients (Chapter 4). Should he decide that a specialist opinion is required he will refer the patient to a consultant normally based in the local hospital. In this case the consultant will investigate, advise and treat the specific condition either medically or surgically and then return the patient to the care of his general practitioner (Chapter 5).

In this simple organizational model there is no clear place for the industrial doctor. He has no prime responsibility for the medical care of the employees, all of whom have their own general practitioners, nor is he an ordinary hospital based consultant working in one of the recognized specialities. It is true that some occupational physicians are general physicians in the hospital service who have specialized in the diseases of occupation, but these are few and far between and are not, in the sense we have discussed, industrially based doctors.

Under these circumstances it is not surprising that the role and aspirations of the doctor in industry are often not clearly understood by his colleagues and may easily be resented. Since the last war a knowledge and acceptance of the speciality has developed within the profession but the average doctor in industry still needs to be careful in his relations with his medical colleagues.

Whether dealing with an individual employee's general practitioner or with a consultant handling a specific condition, it is essential to establish the aims of the industrial doctor to be the same as that of his colleagues, that is the earliest recovery of health and function of the patient. Because the most frequent cause of contact between the industrial doctor and his medical colleagues is in association with absence from work and because he is more acutely aware of the importance of return to work in the restoration of full function, this interest may be misconstrued as hustling patients to their disadvantage on behalf of the management. Tact has therefore to be exercised in explaining to the general practitioner or the consultant the positive objectives of supervised rehabilitation and resettlement and the part that can be played in this by the industrially based medical unit. Similarly the routine surveillance and care afforded to employees who are vulnerable either from the nature of their disability or the nature of their work may also have to be justified in certain cases. Having said this, however, with a little care and trouble, co-operation is easily achieved and a team approach to individual problems can be developed.

A more difficult area is when employees approach the industrial doctor with problems which have little or no relation to their work. Sometimes they come because of the convenience of getting medical advice during working hours and these are comparatively easily dealt with. Sometimes they come because they are unhappy with the advice they are receiving from their own general practitioner or some consultant. Under these circumstances considerable care may have to be taken so that on the one hand the relationship between employee and his general practitioner is not undermined and on the other that he gets fair and sensible advice. In this type of situation it is essential that the general practitioner is not by-passed but is kept informed of all the relevant details. Even in doing this latter, however, it is still necessary to make sure that the employee himself is aware of any communication.

As the speciality of occupational medicine has developed, so the role of the occupational physician and the industrial doctor has become more widely accepted within the profession as a whole. Moreover with increasing specialization in medicine a team approach to the care of patients has become more commonplace, and medical care is now provided in a more complex way than that described in our original model.

ESTABLISHING CONFIDENCE

It must be recognized that the doctor in industry has very little fundamental authority and therefore, to be effective he must first define his role and establish his credibility. This situation is in contrast to doctors working in the National Health Service where the responsibilities of the family practitioner and specialist are reasonably clearly defined and accepted both by the employing agency and by the public it serves.

It goes without saying that the industrial physician must first demonstrate his clinical skills as a doctor in diagnosis and therapy but because of the complex nature of the relationships his success also depends to a great extent on his attitudes and style. A not uncommon failing is a certain lack of humility in assessing his own position in society. Health, as indeed life itself, is held by individuals and society as a whole to be of great importance and naturally the medical profession is therefore held in high regard. Doctors from an early period of their training are used to having their advice taken without much or any question. This almost invariably leads to some degree of intellectual arrogance in relation to their work. The occupational physician whose work impinges on so many disciplines outside medicine and where other priorities may hold sway, such as the success of the business, continuity of employment and personal advancement, finds his advice judged in the context of other technical and social considerations. Under these circumstances he may have to make a positive effort to be seen to be open-minded and ready to debate the solution to any problem, including those which he might under other circumstances have considered to be within his exclusive authority.

This does not mean, however, that he can allow himself to be unduly swayed by business considerations or personal and political aspirations of the individuals he is dealing with as it is essential that he retains his integrity in relation to the health of those for whom he is responsible. The occupational physician must have, and be seen to have, a sound basis of humanitarian ethic and must have the courage to state it and stand by it when necessary. His credibility, however, requires that in the practical application of this ethic he shows an understanding of personal aspirations and economic constraints. He must not fall into the trap of confusing integrity with inflexibility. For example in considering the fitness of an individual, such as a diabetic, for a job he must consider what risks may be involved. If the risk is confined to the individual alone he must ensure that it is clearly defined and understood by the employee, but accept that the final decision may rest with the individual. If, however, others may be involved as, for instance, in the case of a driver, the responsibility of the occupational physician for other workers or the public becomes overriding and the decision will have to rest with himself.

PROFESSIONAL JUDGEMENT

As we have seen the major role of the occupational physician is in the field of preventive medicine and, therefore, professional judgement goes beyond the diagnosis and treatment of disease. One of the major difficulties facing a doctor in his work is the amount of information, much of it highly technical, that has been generated over the last few decades with which he must be familiar. In spite of this, the amount of hard fact, and indeed, understanding of the causal relationships in the development of disease is still remarkably poor. We know that exposure to certain chemicals is associated with an increased risk of developing specific cancers such as β-naphthylamine induced bladder cancers in the dye industry. It is still a matter of considerable controversy, however, as to whether there is a safe dose of this and similar chemicals that an individual can receive which does not carry this risk. With chemicals as potent in their action as β-naphthylamine there is perhaps little difficulty in deciding the level of control that is justified and indeed in the case of this particular chemical, it is now totally banned within industry. More and more chemicals are now being studied for their cancer-inducing potential and as waiting for evidence of disease in humans is totally unacceptable, tests on animals and other biological systems are used. As a result the number of chemicals being added to the list of those having properties which make them suspect increases monthly and impinges on nearly every activity within industry. The interpretation of these studies to industrial safety requires some form of cost–benefit analysis relating the potential risk to those who handle the materials to the benefits that may accrue to society from their use. This debate is of course of wide and general interest but to the occupational physician it presents a real and practical problem requiring his personal judgement in each particular situation in which it arises. He must be seen to make such judgements and be able to justify his position.

Various forms of cancer are diseases which are fairly easily defined and their effects on mortality and ill health are well accepted. The effect of other toxic materials on the body are not so well defined. We are now able to detect minute quantities of elements such as lead within the body and can also measure changes of function of various organs associated with such levels. The question that arises is whether such changes or abnormalities are the first sign of disease producing ill health or a reduced expectation of life, or whether they are part of the natural adaption mechanism of the body. It might be judged wise to consider all such changes as harmful but to do so is likely to have an unacceptable effect, both on individuals' livelihood and on the economics of industry. Such judgements cannot, therefore, be made lightly or without adequate consultation with those directly involved.

COMMUNICATION

Consultation is an essential part of decision making but that very consultation presents problems of its own. Most of the matters with which the occupational physician is involved are extremely emotive whether they are concerned with an individual's health and fitness for his work or with the hazards within industry. It is essential, therefore, before starting any discussion of this nature to be aware of the pitfalls that may arise, so that they may be either avoided or at least handled with discretion.

To bring out into the open by discussion the restrictions imposed by disease or disability is an essential part of rehabilitation, but the ability of an individual to accept and come to terms with the situation varies very widely. The endeavour must be to carry the patient with one in understanding not only in terms of the physical elements of the problem but also of the emotional reactions involved. Any background information that can be gained may be of value in understanding the personality and motivational aspects. Reluctance to accept the real state of affairs or fear of the consequences may make the patient reluctant to co-operate in open discussion but every effort must be made to retain the patient's confidence both in himself and in the doctor.

Consultation with the workforce of potential hazards may be equally difficult. Quite apart from any opportunity that such a discussion may be seen to provide to those of the workforce representatives with political aspirations, there is an underlying emotional fear among the workers themselves of dangers, particularly those that are unseen such as radioactivity. Paradoxically because the symptoms of exposure to many agents are not immediately obvious or involve a long latent period, for example exposure to asbestos and the onset of asbestosis, in contrast to injury from mechanical accidents, there is reluctance to take the trouble to carry out the safety precautions or wear protective equipment. In an attempt to overcome this reluctance there is a temptation to work on the emotional aspects resulting in unproductive conflict. A more constructive approach is to give a clearly understood explanation of the facts supported by a disciplined style on the part of the management. This particular problem has been exacerbated by the tendency to over-dramatize in the popular press and on the television. The resulting increase in knowledge but not necessarily of understanding in the population is liable to engender distrust when attempting to communicate a balanced judgement to groups of employees. To overcome this the occupational physician must take the trouble to research the subject well and to learn the skills of clear and simple presentation avoiding the use of unnecessary technical jargon.

LEADERSHIP

It is common experience that people show considerable reluctance to accept the constraint associated with the prevention of accidents and disease as instanced by the attempts to reduce road traffic accidents. This resistance is to be found no less in management, groups of workers and individuals within industry. To overcome this inertia a very positive drive is required of the occupational physician. He must be convinced of the rightness of his task and to communicate his enthusiasm firstly to his own team. Regular face-to-face contact with all those directly concerned with the work, whether directly responsible to him or not, is essential. Personal commitment is extremely difficult to generate through indirect communication whether this is by writing or through a third party. Similarly patience and perseverance are required to push forward the task when dealing with those with authority for action, be they workers' representatives or members of management. Again personal contact is an essential ingredient and both the occupational physician himself and the members of his team must go out and take their point of view and aspirations to those who have the power and not wait to respond when asked to do so. The interest and concern that may be generated following an accident or some other dramatic event very rapidly fades in the light of other pressures and the art is to keep this interest alive in the absence of any dramatic event. The ability to give to what is generally seen as a negative and constraining subject a feeling of progressive urgency is difficult, but an extremely valuable aid to success.

SENSITIVITY

Determination to achieve clearly perceived objectives must not cloud the sensitivity to other views. Too direct and forceful a style will inhibit many individuals from expressing what is on their minds. Most individuals have an inherent desire to treat doctors in a polite and respectful manner and there is, therefore, a tendency to give lip service to his suggestions in the absence of the conviction required for action. In dealing with matters of policy this may lead to constraints and frustrations in achieving the objectives.

The need for this sensitivity in communication is of course even more essential when dealing with the individual patient. There are a number of good reasons for an employee to feel inhibited when first approaching the occupational physician. In the first place the role of the doctor in this context may not be clear and in particular the question of confidentiality may be in doubt. The patient may also be unsure of the relevance or significance of the real problem especially where this is of a psychosomatic nature. For some or all of these reasons the patient may present symptoms unrelated or only partially related to the underlying problem. Of course this is not always so and it requires some skill and experience to recognize those cases which justify the time and trouble to unravel the often complex problems underlying the presenting symptoms.

Problems arising from stress are some of the most important and difficult that come into this category. Stress is seldom generated purely within the working environment, but is commonly presented to the occupational physician partly because it is popularly associated with work and partly because the effects are most clearly seen at work. Discussions with a patient are often obscured by his or her reluctance to discuss with the occupational physician affairs outside work and it may take considerable patience to persuade the employee that all his relationships are likely to be relevant, not only those in the working environment. It is not uncommon to find that a manager feels unable to cope with his work, which he puts down to a quantitative overload. In practice that overload is exacerbated by his often subconscious commitment to his family and other outside activities. The delicate adjustment between work and social involvement may be upset by any change of circumstances, either a new job or a new boss on the one hand, or an ill mother-in-law or the arrival of a new child on the other, but to solve the work end of the situation the occupational physician must unravel the whole.

CONCLUSION

We have seen how the doctor in industry has a double role of advising individuals with problems within that environment and also of attempting to modify the environment itself to reduce the morbidity which it may engender. In order to play these roles effectively he must first understand the organization within which he is working, not only from an administrative point of view, but also the ethic within which it operates. Although one can make generalizations about industry, every firm and unit differs significantly depending on its history, its geographical background, its product, and the people who work in it. The doctor is not in a position of direct authority except within his own department and he must, therefore, influence decisions about people for whom he is responsible with a full understanding of the culture in which he is working.

Furthermore in dealing with employees he has two modes of operation, one directly advising individuals or groups of employees on matters of health, but also by interfacing with management or outside medical advisers to act on the employee's behalf in achieving any appropriate change.

The complexity of the interacting elements of the total task means inevitably that the development of skills in the occupational physician is a comparatively slow process. Not only must he learn about a range of new technologies often involving academic disciplines unrelated to his training as a doctor, but he must also absorb the cultural elements that go with the many facets of industrial activity. He must develop a sympathetic appreciation of the values of the different groups within the organization such as managers, engineers, trade union officials and the shop floor workers themselves. And finally he must weave all these together with his own medical experience and ethic into a working model against which to make his judgements without the loss of his own identity.

The occupational physician with his double responsibility for the individual employee and for the company interest may well find himself in the position of arbitrator when dealing with problems involving employees, their work and the medical profession outside industry. In these situations he will require all the skills associated with arbitration, understanding, clarity of thought, a reputation for good judgement, the ability to communicate simply and with conviction and capacity to accept compromise without losing sight of principles.

The field of occupational medicine is wide and many faceted and as a result has drawn to itself medical practitioners of widely different experience and interest. There are doctors with a special interest in the surgical treatment of accidents, there are chest physicians, toxicologists, epidemiologists and those with a concern for rehabilitation. This primary interest may be changed or modified by the needs of the particular job but often remains as the cornerstone on which the developing skills are built. The elements of the task are acquired because of the necessity to broaden the base of influence to achieve the prime objective. These objectives may seem to vary depending on the major interest of the particular doctor or the specific environment in which he is working, but in practice, viewed from the outside, there is a consistency in style and method of operating common to nearly all occupational physicians.

7
The Physiotherapist

D. CANEY

INTRODUCTION

The word physiotherapy is of Greek origin and has two roots, 'phusis' which relates to the physical or natural and 'therapeia' which means 'treatment'. Originally the word was used to explain 'natural' treatments in contra-distinction to drug treatments. The term now subsumes a spectrum of treatments including such diverse methods as electrical stimulation and radiation, tissue mobilization and manipulation and resisted free and passive exercise. These have developed in the last 80 years from an initial scope of practice which was limited to massage and remedial gymnastics. After the granting of the Royal Charter in 1920 the professional body became known as the Chartered Society but the word physiotherapy was adopted as recently as 1945, thus replacing the more cumbersome and less inclusive 'Chartered Society of Massage and Medical Gymnastics'.

The early history of the profession is relevant because it illustrates the importance which was placed by the emerging profession on social approval. In 1895 nine practitioners of massage formed the first professional group known as The Society of Trained Masseuses. Sixty-five years later, by act of Parliament, physiotherapists with other paramedical groups were given public recognition by the creation of a state register of practitioners. There are currently approximately 15 000 physiotherapists on the state register. Over 6000 'whole time equivalents' are employed in England in hospitals within the National Health Service. In the directory of private practitioners 750 physiotherapists are listed, while others work within health clinics, or in industrial medicine. About 93% of practitioners are female. A recent development has been the expansion of physiotherapy into community medicine to work alongside general medical practitioners in order to assess, advise and treat patients in their own homes, thus diminishing the need for costly or time-consuming visits to hospital; and improving the speed with which patients can receive relevant advice. This development has proved to be valuable in the treatment of a wide variety of conditions such as chronic chest disorders and strokes.

EDUCATION AND TRAINING

The education of a student physiotherapist is full-time over a period of three years. There are currently 32 schools of physiotherapy in the United Kingdom which prepare candidates for the examinations of the professional body. The standard of entry is comparable with that of a university, but for obvious reasons it is an additional requirement that all candidates are physically fit. Individual schools set their own detailed criteria for admission. One criterion which is frequently demanded is evidence of an active interest in social welfare, such as community service or other voluntary participation in benevolent activity.

Thus the initial selection of candidates produces a group of people (prior to any physiotherapy educational influence) who are socially aware and who have experience of situations where social skill is important.

The educational programme places emphasis on the detailed study of anatomy and physiology and relates these to knowledge of the body's function in health and disease. Physiotherapists are particularly concerned with re-habilitation methods for those who have locomotor impairment (i.e. impaired function of joints, muscles or nerves) and this requires a knowledge of biomechanics as well as an understanding of a wide range of skills. The physiotherapist is required to work as a member of a team in the treatment of many respiratory and cardiovascular conditions, as well as in the pre- and post-operative care of patients undergoing surgery. Her role in these cases may be more specialized requiring the ability to use appropriate ventilatory apparatus, such as that which will assist breathing or the evacuation of unwanted secretions from the lung, in addition to more routine measures. The student is required to learn the most effective means of handling the patient, so that however little the patient can co-operate, the aims of treatment are achieved with as little physical strain to the operator as possible. These and all other practical skills are practised on fellow students so that a degree of competence is achieved before the skill is transposed into the clinical situation.

Student clinical practice in physiotherapy departments is closely supervised by qualified and experienced practitioners who advise and correct the learner.

The student is required to have a minimum of 1000 hours clinical experience before qualification. This amounts to approximately one-third of the total educational time available. This experience is gained in a wide range of situations including wards and outpatient departments of general and specialized hospitals, clinics and special schools, and with a variety of age groups from babies to the elderly. The student must also gain experience in the appropriate approach to those who have widely differing needs for treatment. The spectrum of care is extensive, varying from the young expectant mother who receives postural advice and relaxation training but who is a healthy fit person, to the paralysed semi-conscious brain-damaged patient after a road accident. Not only must the therapist be able to treat the patient and communicate effectively with him, but it may also be necessary to explain the importance and method of treatment to relatives or others who will assist the patient, so that all can function as one team without the counter-productive effect of conflicting methods. Not only must the student develop competence in different environments, with different age groups and types of patients and their supporters, but she must also learn to communicate effectively with members of her own and other disciplines. Although much of the initial instruction in these skills is given in the classroom of the training institution, there remains much 'on the job' learning where appropriate attitudes and values are acquired through observation and discussion. They are 'caught' rather than taught.

Assessment of effective learning is rigorous by both formal and informal methods. Written and practical examinations test the theoretical aspects of the course and continuous assessment of all practical skills is conducted in both the classroom and the clinical situations. The professional body is the arbiter of professional standard and at the present time controls the curriculum content and method of examination and assessment. Through appointed senior professionals who act as a central committee, it determines who shall act as regional examiners and monitors and co-ordinates their standards. The professional body, therefore, acts not only as a representative body for the qualified, but also strongly influences through examination method and personnel, the emphasis of the educational programme.

THE TASKS

Advances in medicine and paramedicine have been rapid in this century. Physiotherapy typifies this advance. From the limited effectiveness of massage and remedial exercise which was the original scope of the techniques offered by the profession's pioneers at the turn of the century, physiotherapists now offer a wide range of treatment modalities. These include the use of movement techniques suitably modified to individual need in order to achieve the aim of mobilizing joints, strengthening muscles or improving co-ordination or endurance. Such techniques may be applied to individuals or groups of patients, within the medium of air or water, with or without apparatus. Passive mobilizing techniques may be applied to soft tissues by massage or to joints by specialized manipulation.

Electrical treatments include stimulation of muscle or nerve by long or short pulses for treatment or diagnostic purposes, the use of specialized emitters of defined spectra (infra-red and ultra-violet) and the use of high-frequency (short-wave diathermy for thermal effect) and ultrasonic apparatus. The use of heat or cold is frequently coupled with other treatments.

In order to determine appropriate treatment the physiotherapist must first extract relevant information from the patient's past medical records and review any factors which may be germane to the patient's presenting condition. The patient is then examined by the physiotherapist. This examination will probably include pertinent questioning, as well as observation, palpation and various tests of function. The findings of the examination will be analysed so that objectives can be determined and a suitable treatment programme can be drawn up. The patient's progress will be monitored and the effectiveness of treatment determined by repeated reassessment. When treatment objectives have been achieved the patient will be discharged, or reviewed after a suitable interval.

How then can the tasks of such a professional be analysed? There are several possible approaches. One could consider the physiotherapist as a member of a health team, responsible for the rehabilitation of those who have been afflicted by different types of illness or injury. Thus, the tasks of the orthopaedic physiotherapist which are essentially concerned with the maintenance or restoration of movement or muscle power, will differ from those of the community physiotherapist where greater emphasis is placed on advice and health education. An alternative approach would be to identify the differing tasks of treatment (analytical, manual, electrical, kinesiological). Both of these approaches assume but do not make explicit the importance of the social interaction between the physiotherapist and the patient, for unless the professional authority of the therapist is accepted by the patient it is unlikely that effective examination or treatment can occur. The importance of this social interaction will be explained subsequently in greater detail. At this point it is sufficient to emphasize that each patient represents a unique combination of problems which the therapist must analyse in order to determine appropriate remedial methods.

SKILLS AND ATTITUDES

In order to carry out these tasks the therapist must have cognitive, motor and affective skills. Cognitive skills (Bloom, 1956) refers to the knowledge of theory and method inherent in the job. They are classified in a hierarchical order from the concrete to the abstract in six levels starting from simple knowledge, ending with evaluation. Gonnella (1966) related Bloom's general educational objectives to physiotherapy educational objectives. She identified skills which were required by physiotherapists at all six levels of the taxonomy.

A simple clinical example of the use of cognitive skills will illustrate the point. A patient with a limp is referred to the physiotherapist for re-education in walking. There appears to be no relevant medical history. The physiotherapist must draw on her knowledge of anatomy and kinesiology to assess muscle power and joint range, interpret her findings, analyse the results in order to determine the appropriate method and stage of treatment, and synthesize a unique treatment programme. The final stage of evaluation would be required in order to determine the effectiveness of treatment.

Motor skills are required by the physiotherapist in handling the patient, demonstration of exercise, or control of apparatus, but this skill is not confined to situations where the physiotherapist performs acts to or for the patient, for it is also her job to educate or re-educate the patient who for some reason has diminished or lost motor skills. Motor skill demands accurate perception, the ability to interpret and respond correctly to perceptual cues, and to grade the response appropriately. The skilled practitioner must be able to discern which of these components of motor skill is deficient in order to teach the patient how to regain lost motor ability.

Affective skills appear in the interaction between the patient and the physiotherapist which is an essential part of all treatment and assessment. In most cases the patient is able to respond verbally without difficulty to the physiotherapist, but the degree and type of response will be determined by the physiotherapist's approach. If the patient is to derive maximum benefit from treatment it is important that the social relationship between patient and therapist is one of trust and that it is established quickly, yet trust is normally only achieved in long-established relationships. How is this paradox accomplished?

The first essential appears to be the development of professional attitudes. The term 'professional' implies a degree of commitment to shared values within the professional group, with an agreed set of ethical principles. These values and principles are recognized in the setting up of professional associations to safeguard the standards of the profession, and ultimately by the establishment of a statutory body to safeguard the interests of the patient against any professional who transgresses the code or who falls short of the standard of competence. The student from the beginning of training is educated in the professional attitudes which will be required. The need for confidentiality is stressed when patients' records are read, and students are instructed in the requirement of impartiality irrespective of the patient's class, colour or creed. The personal appearance of the student is required to conform to certain professional standards when uniform is worn, so for example, hair must be 'off the collar' and finger nails short. These requirements are not dogma, they are in the interests of hygiene and safety, and have the effect of developing a uniformity among this group of health service staff which the patient is aware of but finds difficult to define. The very nature of the type of treatments which the physiotherapist carries out are such that touch must play an essential part. In modern medicine where machines and monitors have displaced many of the skills of the 'caring professions', physiotherapists probably retain more treatment and assessment skills where manual touch is required than any other health care group. It is important, therefore, that the hands of such professionals must be acceptable to all patients; long fingernails and potentially damaging adornments such as rings are inappropriate.

Becker *et al.* (1961) investigated the development of professional attitudes amongst medical students. He found that much of this was achieved by observation and imitation of senior professionals. The same is true of physio-therapists where students and young staff learn the social skills appropriate to different professional situations by observing their clinical superiors. The fact that most physiotherapy departments in which junior staff are employed have a fairly large staff facilitates this learning process. Although different treat-ment situations require some modification of approach, the physiotherapist is required to maintain a certain degree of social distance from the patient. Over-familiarity is regarded as an abuse of the professional role and could seriously undermine the fragile relationship with the patient. The fact that all the practitioners share common professional attitudes helps to create a situation in which the patient is able to trust the individual therapist who treats him.

SOCIAL SKILLS

Communication with peers

The social skills of the physiotherapist are not limited to her interaction with the patient, but extend to a large number of other groups. It is often necessary, for example, to explain aspects of treatment to the patient's relatives or friends, so that they can assist the patient's recovery. This requires the ability to interpret technical terms into lay language, to determine the level of understanding of the 'assistants' and to ensure sufficient understanding so that dangers resulting from over enthusiasm or misunderstanding are avoided. The physiotherapist learns to interpret cues such as voice intonation to determine what is meant by the well-meaning relative who says 'I'll see he does his exercises', which can mean anything from a threat to a promise.

Similarly, the physiotherapist has to communicate with other health care professionals, not all of whom will understand the particular jargon which is in common use among physiotherapists. It is in the patient's interests that all members of the health care team understand the aims and methods of treatment which are used in a particular patient's treatment regime, so that their work is co-ordinated. Explanation of method may, therefore, be necessary between the professionals, but must be done in such a way that the status of each group is not diminished. Such explanation requires considerable skill. In order to elaborate this point, reference may be made to the importance of the position of the patient's limbs during the early stages of recovery following a stroke. All those who handle the patient should be made aware of the importance of correct positioning and this obviously involves a wide variety of health care staff. Many of these staff are experts in patient care in their own field, yet in the particular case described, the positioning advised by the physiotherapist should be the one adopted by all.

Social interactions within the profession are just as important as those between the professions. The National Health Service which is the main employing authority of physiotherapists has a hierarchical structure for its clinical staff; each level being broadly accountable to the next. The art of encouraging those more junior in experience to develop expertise, while at the same time ensuring that the client's interests are preserved is the difficulty encountered by seniors at all levels and in all specialisms. This requires special sensitivity to emerging potential and the ability to determine the right timing for increasing the responsibilities placed on junior subordinates; not all of whom develop at the same rate or have an equal potential for doing so. Juniors, on the other hand, are required to differentiate between those situations which are within their competence, and those for which they need help. The junior staff member must determine whether the essential aspects of the condition are sufficiently similar to one which the therapist has treated before, or whether the significant features need more experienced advice. Such decisions are often influenced by the degree of confidence which the junior has in the senior and the degree of social interaction which exists between them. The amount of development of the junior and the quality of treatment which will be received by the patient may be strongly influenced by the degree of social skill of senior colleagues in training their juniors.

Communication with patients

Before examining the social skill requirement of the physiotherapist's interaction with the patient, it will be appropriate to describe the broad spectrum of people who are referred to the physiotherapist's care. Treatment may be carried out on groups of patients with a similar disability, or (more frequently) individually. Groups may vary in size from two or three to 20 or more, the larger groups obviously requiring more formality in their organization. The age of those referred for treatment will also vary, from the newborn to the elderly. The condition for which the patient is sent for treatment may be local, affecting only a small part of the body, or general, affecting one whole system or group of systems with or without associated personality change. The condition may be acute or chronic, the onset sudden or insidious. Disease and accident are respectors neither of culture, class, colour nor sex. Patients are therefore a microcosm of society. Physiotherapists on the other hand are recruited primarily from middle-class backgrounds and must be academically able to cope with a demanding course of training. The majority are female who work before and after the child-rearing period.

Nearly all patients are referred to the physiotherapist by a medical practitioner and most have been through the hospital outpatient clinic system or casualty department. During this process, the individual concerned has acquired the 'identity' of 'patient' and has come to accept the code of behaviour which is expected of that role (Goffman, 1959). The patient accepts implicitly that the professionals know what is best for him and most patients unquestioningly obey all those whose professional role is accepted as legitimate.

If such a person is referred to a specialist department such as physiotherapy, the status of the staff of that unit are already perceived as expert simply because of the doctor's referral. Very few patients question the expertise of staff or the validity of the treatment carried out. This degree of blind confidence in the 'expert' conditions the initial interaction between therapist and patient. However, different patients demonstrate different attitudes to their disability—some are unwilling to admit that there is anything wrong 'Doctor's sent me here, but I don't know what for—I'm alright'—the 'deviance disavowal' described by Davis (1961), some are totally obsessed by their problems so that they ignore even those things which they can still do—most are apprehensive and anxious. Fear may demonstrate itself as aggression or submission. The physiotherapist will meet all these attitudes in her first encounter with different patients and must be able to understand and interpret them so that she can establish a relationship with the patient which will create the right environment for that patient's treatment. Just as the patient perceives the physiotherapist as an expert (irrespective of her years of experience—or the lack of them), the physiotherapist seeks to establish an identity for the patient by key questions which will be asked at the initial examination or treatment session. Such key questions relate to the patient's social background (age, occupation, marital status, hobbies) and medical history. Although these questions are asked as part of the analysis necessary to determine appropriate treatment, inevitably the therapist gains a reasonably detailed picture of the individual concerned, which will influence her interaction with him.

A more spontaneous rapport is likely to be effected with patients who evoke sympathy (e.g. the elderly person living alone) or who are directly compatible with the age, social class, sex or personality type of the therapist. However, professional education has taught the 'expert' that impartiality is essential in administering patient care and such natural reactions are guarded against, greater effort being made to establish adequate communication with those patients who are more 'difficult'. In putting a patient at ease, the onus for directing the social encounter lies on the physiotherapist. It is her responsibility to ensure that the patient understands the need for treatment sufficiently so that the patient will be motivated to carry it out. Although he may initially perceive the therapist as an 'expert' his confidence in this status will be undermined if he fails to understand the relevance of the treatment which is given; especially if such treatment is painful or difficult as many rehabilitation procedures may be. The physiotherapist must therefore ensure that effective communication with the patient is established. Several factors may militate against this. The first is the patient's attitude to his illness. If for some reason the patient wishes to adopt his sickness role permanently (perhaps because of the extra attention which it gives him) his willingness to co-operate with treatment may be at a very superficial level. Although he may 'listen' to the therapist and appear to understand, successive treatments indicate the lack of improvement which would normally be expected. The second factor which may impair communication is the patient's lack of understanding of the therapist's language. All physiotherapists are encouraged as part of their training to use non-technical language in their communication with patients, nevertheless the inadvertent use of technical terms may baffle the patient. In a multiracial society, there will also be those who are referred for treatment whose native language is not English. Substitution of signs and demonstrations may be inadequate means of communication. If the patient is not from the physiotherapist's social class there may also be defective communication or different interpretation of the meanings of words. The skill of the physiotherapist as a communicator is to determine how well the patient has understood and to 'translate' her communication if necessary until her message has been received effectively. Equally important is the physiotherapist's responsibility to receive the information which the patient should impart about his physical condition.

Non-verbal communication

Verbal communication is obviously important in both directions but, as Argyle (1978) has demonstrated, non-verbal communication is also used extensively during interpersonal interactions. The use of non-verbal communication in the paramedical field has not been investigated to any great degree. Nevertheless, observation of interactions between patients and physiotherapists indicates that non-verbal communication is used extensively. Eye contact with the patient is deliberately sought by the physiotherapist in order to determine, for example, the degree of pain which the patient is experiencing. Stress of this nature can be interpreted from facial cues such as the degree of dilation of the pupil and contraction of specific facial muscles. Frequent eye contact also serves the function of reassuring the patient. For the same effect, physiotherapists use touch which is also an essential component of palpation. Thus an investigative technique is readily extended to serve a communicatory function. Patient's verbal responses are reinforced and encouraged by head nodding; and the patient is made to feel secure by the position and posture of the therapist in relation to him; she will deliberately sit down beside the patient if she wants to encourage him to talk. This contrasts with the usual treatment posture of the physiotherapist which is standing, whereas the treatment posture of the patient is lying or sitting. It is interesting to note that the professional role of the therapist allows her to violate many of the accepted codes of non-verbal communication without fear of misunderstanding on the part of the patient or others. Jourard (1971) conducted an interesting experiment on the areas of the body which could acceptably be touched by specific others (e.g. same sex friend, opposite sex friend, etc.). The role of the physiotherapist (like the doctor) allows individual practitioners to violate the touch taboo if the need of the patient requires it. Touch is obviously a particularly important means of communication with the very young and the very old. Frazer (1981) investigated the non-verbal behaviour of five qualified physiotherapists and five physiotherapy aides in a simulated treatment situation. He found that 'this experiment confirms that the approach of the qualified staff is significantly different from that of the unqualified aides. With the physiotherapists the level of interaction is increased in terms of touching, eye contact and verbal exchange. . . . The three physiotherapists scoring highest in clinical competence also looked more at the patient, touched him more often and for longer periods and had the shortest periods of silence during the course of their treatments'. Although it is unwise to generalize from such a limited experiment, observation and experience would support these findings. It is also interesting to note that the physical distance of the physiotherapist from the patient is usually least when the patient's condition is most acute. Mehrabian (1972) in a role-playing experiment involving a hatstand found that proximity was governed by perceived liking; for physiotherapists it is possible that proximity is governed by perceived need. For example a therapist who treats a postoperative chest patient will support such a patient for coughing using her hands and trunk, and the arm of a patient who has dislocated the shoulder is supported on a pillow placed across the therapist's knees. Such physical proximity would be open to serious misinterpretation under other circumstances. As the acuteness of the patient's condition diminishes, so the physiotherapist's proximity decreases. When verbal communication methods fail, the physiotherapist may substitute demonstration, using passive movement of the part to indicate the required exercise. This is a conscious use of a type of non-verbal communication, whereas most forms of NVC are 'unconscious'.

There are, therefore, many verbal and non-verbal means through which patient and therapist interact. Both patient and therapist are playing their respective roles throughout the interaction but it is impossible for either of the interactors to conceal completely their own personalities. The 'patient' may be fearful, dependent and in pain, but his essential personality characteristics of extraversion, or introversion, neuroticism or stability will assert themselves. Similarly the essential characteristics of the therapist will also be obvious. The personality types of patient and therapist will to some extent determine the outcome of the interaction. In Frazer's experiment already referred to, the physiotherapist who was rated as the best by the patient in terms of professional competence was ranked as eighth out of ten in terms of humour, friendliness, attractiveness and poise. However, it is important to note that the patient was suffering from relatively minor 'conditions', where effective treatment required a fairly authoritarian approach. The personality characteristics which would predispose to liking in ordinary social interactions do not, therefore, necessarily predispose to liking in clinical interactions. It is possible that what the patient appreciates most is a confident, organized yet caring approach, which the physiotherapist communicates through verbal and non-verbal means.

One of the non-verbal methods of communication is the effect of uniform and the 'setting' of the physiotherapy department. Uniform is an immediately recognizable means of establishing status and authority. White uniform is associated with hospital staff. Special insignia such as badges and shoulder flashes indicate particular categories or status of staff. Patients recognize such uniforms and assume that all wearers of similar uniform have similar expertise. Strangely they rarely seem to differentiate between student physiotherapists and qualified staff. In order not to undermine the patient's confidence, the student supervisor adopts the role of 'colleague' rather than tutor and this deception is rarely detected or commented on by the patient. However, if the student wears a different uniform from her qualified superiors the difference in status is more readily detected by patients. Haney et al. (1973) investigated the effect of uniform and role on the behaviour of volunteer subjects. Their results indicated that subjects rapidly adopted the role which the uniform required. The wearing of a recognizable physiotherapy uniform is one of the conforming influences in establishing 'professional' behaviour.

The environment of the physiotherapy department also imparts information to the patient. The type of equipment, departmental organization, the degree of privacy accorded to the patient, his proximity to other patients, even the typical hospital 'smell' all form an important part of the background to the interaction between patient and therapist. Whereas these form part of a familiar setting to the therapist, they are all new and perhaps frightening to the patient. The patient's perceptions may have been preconditioned by well-meaning friends who may refer to physiotherapy departments as 'torture chambers'. The first encounter of such a patient with the physiotherapist may therefore be biased.

The initial interaction of the physiotherapist with the patient is of prime importance in establishing the right background to treatment. Although there is no experimental evidence it is probably true that what the physiotherapist is, is of equal importance with what she does, for without an effective social interaction, the outcome of treatment may be vitiated. This is particularly true in those conditions where stress and increased muscle tension are present, for each of these will in turn heighten pain perceptions. Confidence in the therapist will induce relaxation, thus improving the response to treatment modalities aimed at pain relief. The degree of interaction between mind and body is still only vaguely understood. Many of today's so-called psychosomatic disorders were 'cured' in past centuries by priests, or more recently by family doctors, who acted as counsellors. Today the patient's problems are more likely to be referred to the psychiatrist if the 'mental' element is dominant or to the physiotherapist if the 'physical' element is paramount.

Where patients are treated in groups, the skill of the physiotherapist lies in fostering a group response among those who are total strangers, but who share a common physical problem. A strong group identity can encourage a degree of commitment and dedication towards recovery, which may be difficult for the individual to achieve alone. For example, patients who have suffered a heart attack may be encouraged to join a cardiac rehabilitation class, where they will carry out graded exercise to regain full physical fitness. The success or failure of such a group depends largely on the confidence and positive attitude of the physiotherapist who leads it. If she shows apprehension this will quickly spread to the whole group and undermine the effectiveness of the treatment.

It might be assumed that no social skills would be required in the treatment of the unconscious patient. The patient cannot be interviewed and cannot respond verbally. However, such an assumption would be false. The method of handling of the patient forms a means of non-verbal communication which determines to a certain extent the patient's physical response. It is also apparent that long before the patient can respond verbally, he is able to receive and understand sensory input. Indeed his sensory awareness may be heightened, and sounds may be amplified. Under these circumstances the physiotherapist requires even greater social skill, for she must communicate without the advantage of feedback. Such communication in vacuo is difficult to sustain, and appears foolish to those who are uninformed. While the patient appears unconscious it seems useless to tell him 'I'm going to bend your knee now'—or 'We're going to turn you over'. Yet without such information the patient who is marginally aware but unable to communicate is being treated as an object not a person.

COMPETENCE AND EXCELLENCE

It has now been demonstrated that the physiotherapist requires skill in three main domains or areas; cognitive, psychomotor and affective. Most of these skills are centred on the treatment of patients, though some interpersonal skills are necessary in order to communicate effectively within and between professions. Because physiotherapists have responsibility for patients a minimum level of competence has to be established. This minimum level is taken as that which is the pass mark in the external written and practical examinations which occur at the end of the third academic year and in the continuous assessment of practical skills which occur throughout training. There are no further obligatory examinations which must be taken after qualifying, though a recent publication has suggested that these may be introduced (CPSM 1980).

Figure 7.1 illustrates the relationship of skills which a student physiotherapist may demonstrate towards the completion of her education.

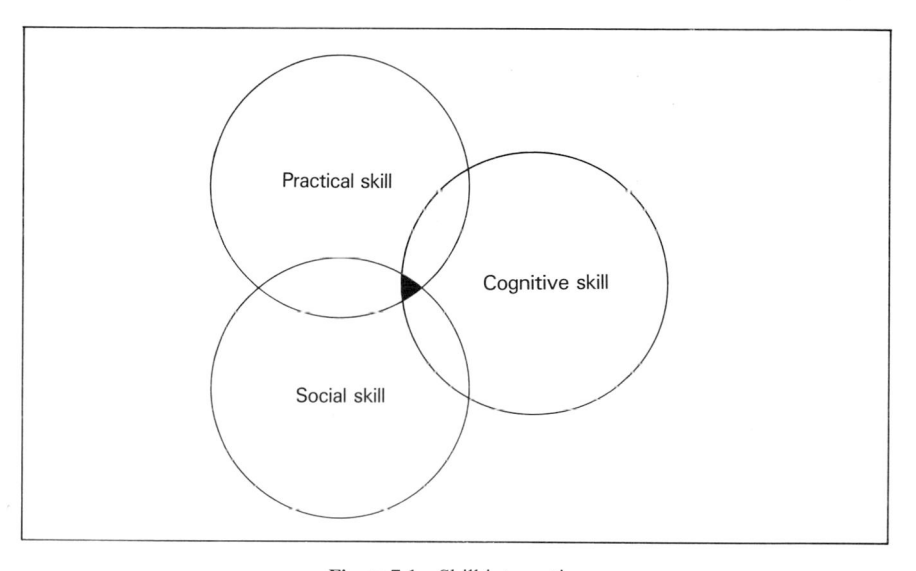

Figure 7.1   Skill integration

In this diagram the three skill areas are shown overlapping each other. The area where all three intersect is solid. This represents the part of the student's skill which is adequately integrated, that is, where her clinical experience is sufficient for her to have a reasonably co-ordinated grasp of her skills and is able to apply them appropriately. The aim of student education is to maximize the degree of overlap of the three skill areas, but in view of the diversity of clinical fields in which physiotherapists operate, it is unlikely that the student will have gained sufficient experience to have achieved adequate integration in all clinical areas before qualifying. This is recognized within the profession, and supervision and help is given to the newly qualified until adequate standards of skill integration have been achieved. This raises the question of what is adequate. Whereas cognitive skills can be assessed by written and oral examination, and practical skills can be assessed by practical tests, interpersonal skills can only be judged subjectively within the context of the situation within which they occur. Each patient presents a unique interactive experience for the physiotherapist which the presence of an assessor will to some extent modify.

Although the knowledge and practice base of physiotherapy is constantly being expanded, at any one moment this base in finite. The social skill requirement can be regarded as infinite. Experience enlarges the physiotherapist's awareness of different reactions to illness and disease, but it will never allow her to predict accurately the particular response of an individual patient or her own reaction to that response. The importance of the social skill component is recognized within the examination system when the student is assessed on 'his ability to establish rapport with the patient' and on 'his ability to communicate effectively'. However, as this relates to the student's performance on one occasion, with one patient, under observed conditions, it is hardly a fair assessment of the student's social skill. It is likely that a student who lacked such skill would have been advised to withdraw at an earlier stage of training; or would have done so on her own initiative. The student who lacks social skills quickly realizes her inadequacy and feels uncomfortable in situations where she is like the proverbial square peg in a round hole.

Within any experienced professional group there are those who have above average ability, who stand out amongst their peers. These are the experts, who in physiotherapy are the exponents of skills required within a particular field of clinical experience. By concentrating on a narrow field they are able to expand the boundaries of knowledge and practical skill and teach others. The term expert, however, is not necessarily synonymous with the concept of excellence, 'expert' having connotations of worth and virtue. In any professional group all may aspire to excellence whereas only a relatively small group will become experts. If all may aspire to excellence it is worthwhile attempting an analysis of its components, for relatively few seem to achieve such a standard.

It has previously been stated that the minimum level acceptable for professional qualification and registration is that which is deemed 'competent'. It therefore follows that those who wish to be excellent must first of all be competent. Competence can be described as the ability to perceive, understand and respond to cues appropriately. The cues which are referred to may be the obvious ones contained in the patient's history or those which may be elicited during examination or treatment, or they may be the less obvious ones which may easily be missed. Such concealed cues may give the therapist who finds them a more accurate picture of the patient's need, thus allowing more effective treatment to be undertaken. However, simply finding cues is not all that is required, for unless the physiotherapist can perceive that widely separated symptoms, for instance, may be related, the significance of the findings will be lost. Perception depends on past experience. The expert's perception tends to be limited to one field, whereas the therapist of excellence can interpret the cues within a broad framework of experience. Understanding the perception implies more than merely relating information to a textbook model. It requires the ability to see the patient as a whole person, to comprehend his physical and emotional response to his condition and to understand this within the social context in which it has occurred. Having perceived and understood the cues, the physiotherapist must respond appropriately by selecting treatment and carrying it out. It is clear that perception, understanding and making the appropriate response all require good interpersonal skills as well as cognitive and practical skills.

That which marks out the person of excellence would appear to be, first of all, *experience*. Experience increases the possibility that cues will be perceived, and having been perceived will be understood as significant. The relative importance of cues must also be appreciated so that priority can be given to particular treatment objectives. This requires the ability to *select* that which is significant from the data available. The person of excellence appears to have greater *facility in the ordering of data* and to be able to do so more speedily than the merely competent. The real hallmark of excellence, however, appears to lie in the therapist's ability to 'get on the same wavelength' as the patient, to *adapt* quickly to different personalities, to create a situation in which the patient develops confidence in the interest and ability of the therapist. Clearly such confidence must be founded on knowledge and skill. The therapist who has integrated her social, cognitive and practical skills is more likely to be esteemed excellent by peers and patients.

Figure 7.2 illustrates such a person.

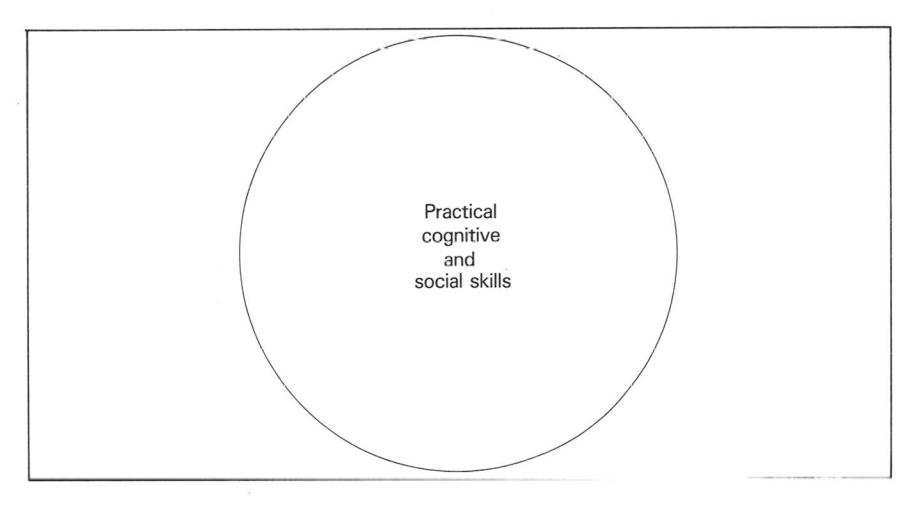

Figure 7.2   Total skill integration model of excellence

DISCUSSION

There are few health care professions in which the practitioner requires to have actual physical contact with the patient. Some medical investigations obviously require such contact, but a large number of manual procedures have been obviated by tests and treatments in which physical contact has been replaced by medical apparatus. Decreasing reliance on physical proximity and personal contact between patient and professional has also diminished the opportunity which the patient has to communicate his fears. Within this situation, the physiotherapist has a unique role. By virtue of the nature of the task she can establish verbal and non-verbal communication with the patient. Most assessment and treatment tasks in physiotherapy require physical contact with the patient by a practitioner who has been educated to 'see through her hands'. Such is the strength of the legitimizing force of the therapist's role that a patient who is a total stranger will accept such physical contact without question. The skill of the therapist lies in knowing when and how to use such physical contact. Sudden or careless handling of a painful limb can destroy the patient's confidence not only in the therapist as a person, but also in the treatment which she may wish to carry out. Conversely if manual skills are used appropriately, effective non-verbal communication will facilitate future therapeutic interactions and in this context the patient frequently feels able to give verbal expression to fears which would otherwise be repressed. Particular emphasis is given to non-verbal communication when the patient is very ill or dependent, when extensive use is made of manual skill, and social distance between the therapist and the patient is consequently diminished (e.g. in the treatment of a patient with acute respiratory disease). The therapist's position in relation to the patient sometimes contrasts strongly with that of the close relative who is frightened by the illness and unfamiliar situation of his loved one. The therapist tends to move closer to the very ill patient, but fear drives the relative farther away.

As the patient recovers, the situation is reversed and 'normal' social distances are resumed. Sickness and dependency seem to change the perceptions of acceptable social distance for patients, relatives and health care professionals. Diminishing incidence of touching by the physiotherapist signals an improvement in the patient's condition and his increasing independence. Both parties seem to understand the meaning of this specialized form of non-verbal communication. Although such illness or accidents which necessitate referral of a patient for physiotherapy are relatively infrequent occurrences in the lives of most individuals, yet there is spontaneous ability in all patients to interpret and respond to the specialized forms of communication required by the patient–therapist interaction. The social skill of the therapist guides and determines the effectiveness of that interaction. On the rare occasions where the patient takes advantage of the familiarity occasioned by therapy, the physiotherapist immediately increases social distance beyond that which would be normal for a purely social interaction.

There is a scarcity of research to support these intuitive statements and that which does exist relates to American physical therapists. However, emphasis is placed on the importance of social skills by Leopold (1954), Ramsden (1968), Goldin et al. (1974) and others. It is also clear that where the therapist is thought by the patient to understand his need, the patient will be more likely to respond positively to the therapist conditioning a self-reinforcing interactive response. (The patient feels better, the therapist is pleased with the improvement . . . and so on.) One piece of research which supports some of the intuitive statements of this chapter was carried out by Grannis (1981) in America. Her investigations into the characteristics of the ideal physiotherapist involved in geriatric care compared the perceptions of therapists and patients. She found that there was agreement among both groups on the following:

(1) Has a good sense of humour which uplifts the moods of others.

(2) Presents instructions to the patient in a clear and concise manner.

(3) Carefully and thoroughly evaluates the patient's condition.

(4) Appears to have care and concern for the individual with whom he or she is working.

Items 1, 2 and 4 are obvious interpersonal skills and 3 requires interpersonal skill. It would, therefore, appear that in a remedial profession, such as physiotherapy, the social skills of the practitioner are one of the determinants of excellence.

References and further reading

Argyle, M. (1978). *The Psychology of Interpersonal Behaviour*. (Harmondsworth: Penguin)

Becker, H., Geer, B., Hughes, E. and Strauss, A. (1961). *Boys in White*. (Chicago University Press)

Bloom, B. (1956) (ed.). *Taxonomy of Educational Objectives: Cognitive Domain*. (New York: David McKay Co. Inc.)

Council for Professions Supplementary to Medicine (1980). *Future Requirements and Opportunities*

Davis, F. (1961). 'Deviance disavowal: the management of strained interaction by the visibly handicapped'. *Social Problems*, 9 (2), 120–32

Frazer, F. (1981). *Unpublished Ph.D. Thesis*. Appendix 9. Exploration of a Physiotherapy Treatment. The University of Aston in Birmingham

Goffman, E. (1959). *Presentation of Self in Everyday Life*. (New York: Doubleday and Co. Inc.)

Goldin, G. J., Leventhal, N. A. and Luzzi, M. H. (1974). The physical therapist as 'therapist'. *Phys. Ther.*, 54, 484–9

Gonnella, C. (1966). Referred to in *Handbook for Physical Therapy Teachers*. (New York: APTA)

Grannis, C. J. (1981). The ideal physical therapist as perceived by the elderly patient. *Phys. Ther.*, 61, 479–86

Haney, C., Banks, C. and Zimbardo, P. (1973). Interpersonal dynamics in a simulated prison. *Int. J. Criminol. Penol.*

Jourard, S. M. (1971). *Self Disclosure*. (New York: Wiley Interscience)

Leopold, R. L. (1954). Patient–therapist relationship: psychological consideration. *Phys. Ther.*, 34, 8–13

Mehrabian, A. (1972). *Non-verbal Communication*. (New York: Aldine–Atherton)

Ramsden, E. L. (1968). Interpersonal communication in physical therapy. *Phys. Ther.*, 48, 1130–2

8
The Psychotherapist

C. BARKER

INTRODUCTION

There is nothing new about the activity of psychotherapy. Attempts to solve personal problems through conversation can be traced back to biblical times, and in many tribal societies the shaman or medicine man has the role of helping to resolve psychological disorder (Frank, 1973). However, the way that psychotherapy is currently practised, organized, researched and theorized about make it a peculiarly twentieth-century phenomenon.

Modern day psychotherapy can be traced back to Breuer and Freud's (1895) famous case of the patient 'Anna O.' Breuer, a senior colleague of Freud's, discovered that when his patient recalled, under hypnosis, memories associated with the onset of her distressing symptoms, her symptoms were alleviated. Anna herself christened this method the 'talking cure'. Breuer, feeling that he was becoming over-involved with the patient, later withdrew, leaving Freud to pursue the implications of the method. He replaced hypnosis by the technique of free association, introduced the analysis of dreams and transference, and developed the 'talking cure' into what soon became known as psychoanalysis.

The psychoanalytic movement has continued to grow steadily throughout the century. It has become increasingly fragmented, as different schools—e.g. Jungian, Adlerian, Sullivanian—developed and split off from the main body. It has also become increasingly ossified, as yesterday's revolutionary ideas have become today's orthodoxy.

From quite another quarter in psychology came the second important development. Work by the Russian physiologist, Pavlov, on the conditioned reflex was taken up by American psychologists and developed into the doctrine of behaviourism. In the famous (and ethically dubious) case of 'little Albert', Watson and Rayner (1920) were able to demonstrate how little eleven-month old Albert could, by the process of conditioning, be made to fear a small furry animal that he had previously liked. This experimentally induced phobia later generalized to other furry objects, including a fur coat. This process of maladaptive conditioning was taken by the behaviourists as a paradigm for how psychological problems develop. Its corollary, that problems could be 'unlearnt' by other kinds of conditioning methods, was developed in the 1950s by Wolpe, Skinner and Eysenck, among others, into what became known as behaviour therapy or behaviour modification.

The last two major developments in the history of psychotherapy were both in different ways reactions to psychoanalysis and behaviourism. Humanistic psychology, the so-called 'third force', was a reaction to the reductionism and determinism of these two approaches. Humanistic psychologists place great emphasis on individuals' wholeness, uniqueness and capacity to make conscious and healthy choices. Rogers' (1951) Client-Centred Therapy embodies these beliefs. Client-centred therapists attempt to create trusting relationships in which clients are able to explore their deeper feelings and resolve their own problems for themselves, without the explicit guidance of their therapist.

Cognitive therapists take their text from Epictetus: 'Men are disturbed not by things, but by the view which they take of them'. They focus attention on their clients' maladaptive or irrational thought processes. In Ellis's (1962) Rational Emotive Therapy, for example, the therapist attempts to elucidate clients' irrational thought patterns and challenges them to replace their irrational thoughts by more rational ones.

Thus a major difficulty in analysing the social skills of the psychotherapist can be seen. Therapists from different orientations appear to operate according to radically different precepts. The psychoanalyst has been likened to a 'psychic detective', a Sherlock Holmes who tracks down the causes of the patient's problems in the deep layers of the unconscious mind. Behaviourists, on the other hand, often liken themselves to engineers or technicians, who adjust the rewards and punishments in their client's environment so that problem behaviours are reduced or eliminated. Humanistic therapists see themselves as 'facilitators' who set up the psychological conditions under which their clients can work out their own salvation. And cognitive therapists often resemble a lawyer cross-examining a witness, as they attempt to get their clients to admit to and correct their errors in reasoning.

Nor is this all. A recent compilation, the *Psychotherapy Handbook* (Herink, 1980), lists over 300 kinds of psychotherapy from Active Analytic Psychotherapy to Zaraleya Psychoenergetic Technique! At this point, most skills analysts are probably tempted to pack their bags and leave. However, on closer investigation the picture is less bleak than it seems. Although there is undoubtedly a great diversity of approaches, underneath they share substantial common ground. Also, it appears that therapists who operate exclusively in terms of one particular theoretical model are more the exception than the rule. Garfield and Kurtz's (1974) survey of 855 American Clinical Psychologists found that 55% labelled themselves as 'eclectic' (i.e. drawing from several orientations), compared with only 11% for the next most popular label, psychoanalytic.

What is psychotherapy?

Psychotherapy can be formally defined as 'the informed and planful application of techniques derived from established psychological principles, by persons qualified through training and experience to understand these principles and to apply these techniques with the intention of assisting individuals to modify such personal characteristics as feelings, values, attitudes and behaviours which are judged by the therapist to be maladaptive or maladjustive' (Meltzoff and Kornreich, 1970 p. 6). This definition perhaps overemphasizes the planfulness and technicality of what is often a spontaneous interaction between client and therapist. No distinction will be made here between psychotherapy and counselling: use of these terms tends more to denote differences in training and professional allegiance than differences in procedure.

Psychotherapy may be conducted by any of the 'helping professionals'—psychiatrists, psychologists, social workers, nurses and counsellors—and other professionals such as teachers and clergy. It may also be conducted by trained non-professionals such as helpline workers or volunteer counsellors. The term 'psychotherapist' will be used here as a generic label covering all of these trained helpers. The term 'psychoanalyst' refers to a practitioner who has trained at a recognized psychoanalytic institute and who conducts therapy along orthodox psychoanalytic (though not necessarily Freudian) lines.

Although the focus here will be on trained helpers, it should be noted that they do not have a monopoly on the activity of therapy. Anyone who has tried to help a friend, family member, student or colleague with a personal problem can be described as conducting informal psychotherapy. An important and not yet fully explored question is to what extent the skills of trained psychotherapists differ from those of able natural helpers (Durlak, 1979).

Psychological therapy is appropriate for a wide range of clients or patients (the terms will be used here interchangeably). It can be used to help them deal with 'problems in living', i.e. those situations that cause people stress or which they find difficult to cope with. Examples are family discord, bereavement, career decisions, and adjusting to illness or disability. It can also be used to help individuals resolve problems which stem from their own personality or behaviour patterns, such as phobias, obsessions or addictions. It can also be used with psychotic conditions, such as schizophrenia, in which the individual loses contact with reality. However, in the psychotic conditions psychological treatment is usually secondary to pharmacological methods.

The goal of psychotherapy is for the therapist to help the client resolve the presenting problems, and possibly also to help the client find more adaptive modes of living in general. The presenting problem may be one of troubled feelings, such as anxiety or depression; maladaptive thoughts, such as lack of self-confidence or lack of trust in other people; or unacceptable behaviour, such as aggression or kleptomania. Many problems involve all three of these elements. Clients often come into therapy to work on a specific problem, but during the course of therapy find that other issues also emerge as problematic. Sometimes limited goals have to be established in order to prevent the therapy from continuing indefinitely.

Therapy can be conducted in a number of different modalities. The most usual is individual therapy, in which the client and therapist meet together for weekly sessions lasting about an hour. The duration of therapy may be anything from short-term, around six sessions, to long-term, lasting several months or years. Some therapists, notably psychoanalysts, see their clients several times per week. Therapy may also be conducted in groups, with a more or less stable membership of about seven to ten patients. In family and marital therapy, the therapist sees a married couple and possibly one or more of their children together as a unit. In group, marital and family therapy, it is common for therapists to work in co-therapy pairs (usually consisting of a man and a woman therapist). Here, attention will be restricted to individual therapy only.

Finally, there is the question of what does psychotherapy actually achieve. Research evaluating the outcome of psychotherapy has had a long and tortuous history, sparked off by Eysenck's (1952) claim that there was no evidence that psychotherapy helped people recover from neurotic problems. Eysenck claimed that approximately two-thirds of clients who had psycho-therapy improved, but so also did two-thirds of people with similar problems who had not had treatment. Hundreds of additional studies have since been conducted, as research methods have become increasingly refined. Although the issues are still far from resolved, recent reviews of the literature point to two broad conclusions: that psychotherapy does produce a measurable gain compared to untreated control groups and that different therapeutic orientations produce approximately the same degree of benefit (Bergin and Lambert, 1978; Shapiro and Shapiro, 1983; Smith, Glass and Miller, 1980).

WAYS OF ANALYSING THE THERAPIST'S SKILL

There has been no shortage of attempts to analyse the skill of the psycho-therapist. The volume edited by Gurman and Razin (1977) cites hundreds of studies on what makes psychotherapy effective. However, despite this mountain of research, the field is still in a primitive state of development. There are few solid, reliable results and no agreed-upon research paradigms.

Each researcher examines the psychotherapeutic process from a different angle, focusing on a different variable.

Even to analyse the therapist's behaviour as a 'skill' raises contentious issues. Many practitioners regard psychotherapy as a science, an activity that has regularities that can be analysed and predicted. However, others regard it as an art, an essentially unpredictable and ineffable personal encounter. These practitioners feel that the therapeutic relationship is vitiated by any attempt to dissect it into components and are wary of the mechanization and false sense of certainty resulting from the application of science to human relationships (Lomas, 1981; Smail, 1978).

My own position lies somewhere between these two. I believe that there do exist lawful relationships in psychotherapy, that certain activities of the therapist are likely to produce predictable effects on the client. But these relationships are necessarily probabilistic rather than deterministic. The best therapist in the world cannot *make* someone get better. The task of the scientist is thus first to describe what occurs in therapeutic interactions and then to predict the likely consequences of certain important classes of behaviour.

However, I believe that certain aspects of the therapeutic relationship will remain beyond analysis. Experienced therapists often report that it is not their carefully planned interventions from which the client benefits, but the spontaneous, often unnoticed aspects of the interaction (Yalom, 1980). In this respect psychotherapy is much like friendship or love. Although it is possible to predict on the basis of similarities in backgrounds or values that certain people are likely to become close with each other, there is still a very large unknown in the equation—the kind of 'chemistry' that occurs between any two people. I recently had the experience of transferring a client with whom I had been making painfully slow progress over to a trainee whom I was supervising. The therapy then took off like a rocket: the client made enormous gains in just a few weeks. Various explanations are of course possible for this different reaction (including the explanation that my own skills need improvement), but it is likely that there was some subtle matching of personalities between the client and the trainee that did not occur between the client and me.

Furthermore, techniques cannot be divorced from the person of the therapist. Two therapists may have trained at the same institution, followed the same textbooks and been supervised by the same supervisors, yet their therapy styles may still be quite distinctive. Likewise, some trainee therapists seem to have natural talent and quickly grasp what they are supposed to be doing, while other trainees develop their skills very slowly. Thus, techniques and personality are complementary factors.

Despite this, much is to be gained from analysing the therapist's skill. As therapy training becomes more eclectic, therapists will have a variety of techniques at their disposal, and they need to know which are likely to be effective with given clients in given situations. Psychotherapy training is still rather haphazard (British Psychological Society, 1980; Shiffman, 1981) and careful analysis of the therapist's skill can help clarify training goals and procedures. Finally, there is the issue of registration or licensing of psychotherapists, which is conducted, if at all, on criteria only marginally relevant to interpersonal ability. Analysis of skilled performance can help clarify the grounds on which professionals are accredited. However, the time when training and accreditation will be based on empirically-derived criteria still seems very far off.

The skill of the psychotherapist can be analysed at different levels of analysis (Goodman and Dooley, 1976). The psychotherapeutic relationship, like any other personal relationship, may endure over a period of weeks, months or years. Yet it can be broken down into a number of meetings (referred to as sessions), which can themselves be broken down into short 5–10-minute episodes, which consist of individual talking turns, which consist of sentences, and so on down.

The present chapter will consider both a small and a large unit of analysis. The small unit will be the individual therapist response or talking turn. This is usually the smallest unit of interaction considered by psychotherapy researchers (although an interesting exception is the linguistic analysis of Labov and Fanshel, 1977). Analysis of therapy at the level of the individual response aims to predict what impact different types of responses will have upon the client so that the accomplished therapist can know what is most likely to achieve whatever momentary goal he or she has in the interaction.

The large unit of analysis consists of several consecutive psychotherapy sessions, or possibly the whole therapeutic relationship. Such phenomena as empathy, transference and social influence will be considered at this level.

ANALYSIS OF THERAPIST RESPONSES

A client has been seeing a therapist for three or four weeks, for help with depression. He is telling the therapist how he has been feeling in the previous week:

> 'This is probably the worst that I've ever felt in my whole life. It just seems hopeless . . . like nothing's ever going to change.'

(Before continuing you may wish to consider how you might respond to this statement.) There are clearly many different responses available to the therapist. She* could, for example, say 'When did you first start feeling like this?' or 'I'm sorry to hear that, after you were doing so well last week' or 'Possibly you're feeling depressed because underneath you're really angry' or she could say nothing at all and just wait for her client to continue.

---

* For clarity, the therapist is assumed to be female and the client male.

One of the first problems in analysing psychotherapy is to find a way of classifying the different kinds of responses that a therapist might make. In this as in other areas of the field, different investigators have adopted different procedures: no system has as yet been adopted by the field as a whole. For this section, I will use the framework of Goodman and Dooley (1976), which has the merits of simplicity and applicability to different types of helping relationships. I have also drawn heavily on Goodman's ideas on response mode analysis (Goodman, 1979 and personal communication). Goodman and Dooley's classification consists of six basic response modes: Question, Advisement, Silence, Reflection, Interpretation and Disclosure. It is designed to be a taxonomy of the kinds of verbal responses a therapist might make. Non-verbal behaviour, such as eye contact and body posture, will not be dealt with here (see Scheflen, 1973, for a fascinating discussion of this topic).

Questions are commonly thought of as being solely for gathering information, as in the response 'How long have you been feeling like this?' However, they also have other uses. They can be used to attenuate or soften other types of responses. For example, to say 'Think about pleasant thoughts as well as unpleasant ones' sounds rather abrupt, but it becomes much less so when couched in question form: 'Have you considered thinking about . . .?' Questions may also be used to lead the client towards exploring a particular aspect of the problem: 'How do your current feelings compare with similar episodes in the past?'

One useful distinction is between open and closed questions. Closed questions ask for a specific piece of information that can be given in a word or two, e.g. 'How old are you?', whereas open questions require a more lengthy answer, e.g. 'Why do you think that you're feeling so sad?' The effect of many closed questions is to leave the client little chance to tell his own story, and also to make him feel as though he is being interrogated. For this reason, skilled therapists tend to avoid them except when genuinely seeking specific items of information.

Questions are the most frequently used response modes, comprising between one-quarter and one-third of a therapist's utterances (Elliott, 1979). However, their usage tends to decrease as a therapist becomes more experienced. Experienced therapists avoid them because they often disrupt the flow of the client's self-exploration, and because the question asker is often seen as controlling the interaction, which the therapist usually does not want to do. Also, other responses may be more effective than questions for gathering information.

Advisement refers to any response which attempts to guide the client's thoughts, feelings or behaviour, e.g. 'Think about pleasant thoughts instead of unpleasant ones'. Advisements may take the form of suggestions, prescriptions, advice, or commands.

The naive stereotype of therapists is that they tell people how to solve their problems. This is usually quite false. Patients frequently come to therapy expecting the therapist to tell them what to do, and are often surprised and resentful when the therapist informs them that she cannot or will not do this.

Therapists refrain from giving advice for several reasons. First and foremost, there usually isn't a simple solution to most personal problems, and if there were the person would probably have tried it already. Most people coming to a therapist have already been exposed to all manner of advisement from friends and family, which has failed to be of help. When therapists make suggestions, the client will often respond with 'Yes, but . . .' Second, advisement, unless used with care, makes the client dependent upon the therapist: the therapist becomes a parent figure. This militates against the long-term goal of therapy, which is for the client to be independent and capable of making his own decisions. Third, in everyday interactions advisement is often used as a way of dismissing people's problems. This is especially true of what Goodman and Dooley (1976) call 'chin-up advisement', of the type 'Don't worry, things will be better in the morning'. Finally, advisement is much more effective when it originates from the client rather than the therapist. A skilled therapist will often try to get the client to generate his own solutions to the problem.

This is not to say that therapists never use advisement, although some orientations such as client-centred and psychoanalytic avoid it. Most therapists will use advisement if they believe that they fully understand the client's situation and that the client genuinely has not tried a particular course of action that could be beneficial. The attempt to specify effective uses of advisement has been one of the greatest contributions of behaviour therapy.

Thus, it should not be surprising that research on the frequency of advisement shows the same pattern as for questions. It tends to be used much more frequently by inexperienced or volunteer helpers than by trained therapists (Knowles, 1979; Shiffman, 1981). Elliott (1979) found that the incidence of advisement among trained therapists was about 15%.

Silence. Tapes of psychotherapy sessions often sound quite unlike those of ordinary conversations. One major difference is the pace of the speech. The client is typically talking slowly and painstakingly and the therapist is trying not to intrude upon his introspections. There is often a noticeable pause between the client's finishing a statement and the therapist's responding.

Sometimes the therapist will not say anything at all and convey her attention non-verbally, such as by eye contact. Such silences are used in psychotherapy for two major reasons. One is that they enable the client to direct the interaction, to choose whatever he wishes to talk about. The other is that silence gives the client the freedom to explore his own inner thoughts and feelings without outside disturbance.

An anecdote, probably apocryphal, illustrates these points. A client began his first session with a therapist by talking about his problem for a few minutes. He then fell silent, and the therapist said nothing either. They sat in silence for the remaining 40 minutes of the session. The following week, he came in for his appointment, sat down, and again neither the client nor the therapist spoke: they sat in silence for the whole 50-minute session. The same happened on the next session, and also on the fourth and fifth ones. On the sixth session, the client came in looking much better. He sat down and said 'I won't be needing to come back any more, doctor, you've helped me enormously. Your silence gave me the freedom and support that was just what I needed to work out the problem for myself'. He then thanked the therapist and left. This is an extreme example of non-directive therapy!

Not all clients react so positively to silence. Some become very anxious, as if they are interpreting the therapist's silence as rejection of them or their problems. Part of the therapist's skill lies in creating the kind of relationship where the client feels valued by the therapist, and thus does not feel threatened by silence.

Psychoanalysts also use silence for a more technical reason, to encourage transference. Part of the psychoanalytic philosophy is for the therapist to be a 'blank screen' upon which the client transfers past feelings about significant others in his life. Silence can be part of the technique used to accomplish this.

Reflection. One way that a therapist can help the client to feel safe examining long-suppressed thoughts and feelings is to let the client know that the therapist understands what the client is communicating—not simply the client's words, but more importantly the feelings behind the words. One way this can be done is by the reflection response, in which the therapist paraphrases or 'reflects' the feelings behind what the client is saying. The reflection response was developed within the client-centred school of therapy, in which conveying empathy is a central part of the therapist's activity (Rogers, 1951).

At first sight the reflection seems simple: the therapist parrots back to the client what the client has just said. For this reason it has often been the subject of derisory humour. Yet to use the reflection response well is an extraordinarily skilled endeavour. It requires capturing the heart of a client's often incoherent and discursive message, and to communicate concisely back to him that he has been deeply understood. Even talented trainee therapists may take many months to master this.

Research shows that reflections have their expected effects. Following a therapist's reflection, clients are more likely to discuss feelings, seem to experience themselves more deeply and to become more focused upon what they are exploring about themselves (Ehrlich, D'Augelli and Danish, 1979).

Interpretation. A therapist may use the reflection response to show understanding of the client's inner experience. She would use the interpretation response, on the other hand, to communicate to the client her own perspective on the problem. The distinction is one of frame of reference: the reflection is aimed at the client's frame of reference, the interpretation comes from the therapist's. Interpretations can be explanations, classifications, or diagnoses. For instance, in the example above, in which the client says 'This is probably the worst that I've ever felt in my whole life . . .', the therapist could possibly respond with 'It's probably because you just lost your job that you're feeling so depressed,' or 'You seem to be exaggerating how badly you feel,' or 'You appear to me to be suffering from a manic-depressive illness.' All of these responses would be classified as interpretations.

As is clear from these examples, interpretation is a powerful response which requires considerable skill to be used well. It needs a different kind of skill from that involved in the reflection response. In order to perform good reflections, the therapist must be adept at entering into the inner world of the client; to make good interpretations, she must have a sound grasp of what makes people feel, think and act in the way that they do. This knowledge is gained not only from psychological theory, but also from extensive experience in working with clients' problems, and, just as importantly, from extensive experience in ordinary human relationships. Without it, interpretations become an exercise in amateur psychology.

Interpretation must be used with circumspection, since clients are often unready to hear the immediate truth about themselves or their problems. They may reject these explanations, a phenomenon known as resistance, or possibly become quite upset by them. Inaccurate interpretations will diminish the client's confidence in the therapist, and may be psychologically harmful, as they lead to a client's gaining a distorted view of himself. Interpretations must be used sensitively within the context of a trusting relationship.

Interpretations are intended to help the client by giving him understanding or insight into his problems. They are a cornerstone of psychoanalysis, in which neurotic problems are thought to derive from unconscious conflicts. If the therapist's interpretations can reveal to the patient the reasons for his symptoms, it is thought that he will lose the need for them. In the words of the philosopher Santayana, 'Those who cannot remember the past are condemned to repeat it'. However, it is far from clear that insight alone is sufficient to produce behaviour change: it may be that a patient understands why he is behaving the way that he is, but is still unable (or perhaps unwilling) to change.

Disclosure is the activity of revealing a previously hidden part of oneself to another person. It is the client's predominant response mode in therapy (Stiles and Sultan, 1979). However, it is a relatively rare response by professional therapists; indeed some therapists never use it at all.

The use of disclosure as an important therapeutic response began with the humanistic psychotherapists. The impetus came in large part from Jourard's (1964) *The Transparent Self*, which argued the case for increased disclosure in all types of relationships, including that between client and therapist. The client–therapist relationship can certainly be highly formalized and asymmetric, involving extreme intimacy on behalf of the client, who discloses his deepest problems and conflicts, and extreme guardedness on behalf of the therapist, who discloses nothing at all.

Part of the reluctance that some therapists feel about disclosure comes from the psychoanalytic dictum that the therapist should serve as a 'blank screen'.

Part of it also comes from the therapist's not wanting to burden the client: the belief that the client has enough to worry about with his own problems, without having to worry about the therapist's too. This is a realistic objection, and the therapist using disclosure has to monitor carefully its effects upon the client.

Two types of disclosure are most commonly used. Process disclosures let the client know how the therapist is reacting to him at the moment: whether positively or negatively. For example, the therapist may say to the client 'I feel frustrated with the way that you're always on your guard with me, because I feel I can never get to know what you're really thinking'. In this way the client can gain valuable information about his impact on other people, that can be discussed in the safe therapeutic setting. In 'me-too' disclosures the therapist reveals events in her own life that are similar to those which the client is describing, for example, how the therapist felt about and tried to tackle similar problems of her own. Thus the client may gain insight into how to resolve his own problems, and also will feel less alone with them. The me-too disclosure response is more typical of peer counsellors, for example ex-alcoholics working with problem drinkers, than it is of professional therapists.

Summary of response mode analysis

In sum, response modes provide a convenient tool for analysing what the therapist actually says in the therapeutic interaction (and for analysing what the client says as well). Conceptualizing the therapeutic process in terms of response modes leads to a focus on the different kinds of intentions that a therapist may have, how these intentions translate into responses, and the impact that these responses may have upon the client. For this reason, response mode frameworks are widely used in therapy training programmes.

Response mode analysis also enables psychotherapy researchers to distinguish between different therapeutic approaches. Different schools of therapy make different prescriptions about the appropriate way for therapists to respond. For example, client-centred therapists are enjoined to focus on reflection of feelings and to avoid advisement or questions. Behavioural therapists, on the other hand, tend to rely heavily on those two modes: question and advisement. Research has shown that experienced practitioners representing a particular school tend to adhere to the guidelines of that school (Stiles, 1979). However, it should be remembered that only a minority of therapists strictly adhere to any one school of therapy.

A limitation of response mode analysis is that it tends to focus on form rather than content, i.e. on how things are said rather than what is said. It does not distinguish between a helpful and a hindering question, an empathic and an off-target reflection. Nor does it distinguish between an interpretation informed by psychoanalytic theory and one informed by operant conditioning theory.

A second limitation is that many phenomena in therapy may emerge at a larger level of analysis than the single response. Although single responses can be aggregated to give a global picture of an interaction or even of a relationship, variables at larger levels of analysis are needed to describe fully the therapist's skill. The following section examines some of those variables.

THE THERAPEUTIC RELATIONSHIP

A central question in psychotherapy research is what are the 'active ingredients' of therapy—i.e. what in the complex interaction between therapist and client is responsible for the client's improvement? There is no simple answer to this question. Many variables have been proposed as candidates for active ingredients. Here we will examine three of the major ones: the Rogerian variables of empathy, warmth and genuineness; transference; and social influence. These variables need to be examined at a larger unit of analysis than the single therapist response. Their proper domain is at a level which is sometimes a single session, but more often spans several sessions or the duration of the therapy. For convenience they will be considered here as aspects of the therapeutic relationship.

Empathy, warmth and genuineness

The client-centred group of researchers under Carl Rogers deserve credit for conducting the first systematic investigations into the process of psychotherapy. They used the then newly-developed audio recording methods to conduct some of the first studies of what actually occurred in therapy, leading Rogers to speculate on what made therapy effective. His classic 1957 paper entitled 'The necessary and sufficient conditions of therapeutic personality change' proposed a commendably bold solution. He hypothesized that three conditions need to be present in the therapist and had, at least to a minimal degree, to be communicated to the client. They were empathy, unconditional positive regard, and genuineness.

Empathy refers to the ability of the therapist to understand the client's world from the inside, 'to sense the client's private world as if it were your own, but without ever losing the "as if" quality' (Rogers, 1957, p. 99). Unconditional positive regard (later called acceptance/warmth or just warmth) refers to an attitude of what Rogers calls 'prizing' the client, that is valuing and respecting the client as a person (even though the therapist may at times be critical of the client's behaviour). Genuineness refers to the therapist's being open and accepting her own feelings, or in Rogers' words 'transparent'.

Rogers asserted that these qualities were necessary and sufficient for constructive personality change in the client. In other words, he claimed that the therapist's techniques were of minor importance, and that what matters are the therapist's underlying attitudes. He hypothesized that these conditions would apply to all orientations of therapy, not only client-centred therapy, as is sometimes assumed.

Rogers' paper sparked off an enormous amount of research. Initial findings appeared favourable to his hypotheses, that is they concluded that therapists with greater warmth, empathy and genuineness produced more successful outcomes in their clients than those lower on these qualities. However, recent surveys of the literature have drawn more cautious conclusions (Mitchell, Bozarth and Krauft, 1977; Parloff, Waskow and Wolfe, 1978). Many of the studies that have set out to test Rogers' hypotheses have yielded inconclusive findings, often because they were not designed in such a way as to subject the hypotheses to a stringent test. Thus at present the status of Rogers' three conditions remains open.

There has been much debate about the trainability of the Rogerian conditions. Are they to be regarded as inherent personal attributes, or are they teachable skills capable of being broken down into component parts? Many psychologists have held this latter view and have designed systematic programmes to teach helping skills (e.g. Carkhuff, 1969; Egan, 1982). Others have argued that this is misguided since the skills are an integral part of the person and cannot be taught as discrete entities (Plum, 1981; Smail, 1978). The truth may lie somewhere in between. Some people appear to have the kinds of natural qualities that make them good candidates for interpersonal skills training, whereas with others the training seems like water off a duck's back.

There is also a confusion of correlation and causation. To argue from studies demonstrating that successful therapists are unusually high on quality X, to the conclusion that teaching novice therapists X will make them maestros is patently false. It is similar to arguing that because good tennis players are physically fit, making someone physically fit will then make them a good tennis player. However, while the current empirical status of Rogers' theories is equivocal, his ideas have become part of accepted clinical wisdom. Texts from all therapeutic orientations, such as behavioural (Goldfried and Davison, 1976) and psychodynamic (Weiner, 1975), urge therapists to develop attitudes of empathy, warmth and genuineness. It will probably turn out that the Rogerian variables are necessary but not sufficient, and that effective therapy requires more than simply a safe relationship with the therapist.

Transference

Early in the development of psychoanalysis Freud observed that his patients often acted in strange ways toward him, for example with exaggerated admiration, or with strong negative feelings such as anger, disdain or fear. Freud hypothesized that these emotions were not really directed towards himself, but that he was symbolizing some important figure in the patient's previous relationships. Feelings from these relationships were transferred on to him in the analytic situation. Thus he labelled these strong emotions transference. At first he saw transference as an impediment to therapy, but later realized that it could be used for therapeutic ends, to help the patient re-experience feelings from his early life. Psychodynamic theorists accord trans-ference phenomena a central role in the therapeutic process (Greenson, 1967). They believe that interpreting clients' transference reactions can help them work through the conflicts that underlie their problems.

For example, a patient had been seeing a therapist for several months to deal with her anxiety attacks. In her early life she had been abandoned by her parents and placed in a number of unsatisfactory foster homes. The therapy was going well and the client was making progress. Then the therapist announced that in a few weeks he would be taking a brief summer holiday. The client became furious, and wanted to leave therapy. She said that she knew the therapist 'just wanted to get rid of her'. When at last they discussed these feelings, the therapist drew the parallel between the rejection that the client had received from her parents and her present feelings. She assumed that the therapist (and everyone else) would reject her, just as her parents had. Discussion of these transference feelings helped the client see how she frequently misinterpreted people's behaviour towards her.

As this example shows, handling transference feelings is a delicate exercise. (Even to label them as such is problematic: it could be argued in the case above that the client's anger was perfectly legitimate.) Since transference feelings are often intense, they can arouse comparable feelings in the therapist. Or the opposite can occur and therapists can maintain a cold and aloof attitude in order to avoid dealing with them. There is great potential for damaging the working alliance with the client if the therapist mishandles the transference reactions, e.g. if the therapist tries to interpret them too quickly, or perhaps not at all.

Many therapists do not accord transference phenomena the central import-ance given them by psychodynamic theorists. They may feel, for example, that the client's here and now feelings are of greater importance than past ones, or that what happens within the therapeutic relationship has little bearing on what occurs in the rest of the client's life. However, there is little doubt that these kinds of phenomena do occur in most extended therapeutic relation-ships: it is up to the therapist to decide how, if at all, to deal with them.

Social influence

The client–therapist relationship is one in which there are great inequalities. The client is in a relatively one-down position—he is suffering from emotional problems, must often disclose his most vulnerable feelings and knows little of what to expect in therapy. The therapist, in contrast, discloses little, knows approximately what to expect and in addition often occupies a relatively prestigious social role with the attached expert aura. In this type of unbalanced relationship, the therapist is in a strong position to exert influence over the client. Each therapist must decide how, if at all, to employ this potential influence.

Therapeutic orientations vary radically on how explicitly they use the therapist's social influence to help the client. Behavioural and cognitive therapists represent the pole of greatest explicit influence. They use a number of procedures to modify directly the client's behaviour, thoughts or feelings (Kanfer and Goldstein, 1980). For example, if a man came to a behaviour therapist complaining that he was unable to ask women out for dates, the therapist might attempt to correct the client's irrational beliefs about hetero-sexual relationships, role-play ways of asking women out and actively en-courage him to experiment with different ways of initiating relationships. Or if a client came in complaining of excessive drinking, the therapist might arrange an aversion conditioning programme to make the thought of alcohol repugnant to him.

These direct procedures are unfortunately capable of abuse. The history of behaviour therapy contains some unsavoury examples of methods used by unethical practitioners, often working with institutionalized patients whose powers of informed consent were curtailed. A dramatic fictional treatment of these issues is given in Burgess' (1962) novel *A Clockwork Orange*. A current example is the debate over whether to employ behaviour therapy with homosexuals who wish to change their sexual orientation (Davison, 1978).

The use of direct influence rests on the assumption that the therapist knows what is best for the client, an assumption that many therapists are unwilling to make. They believe that they should not prescribe what is best for the client—that the client must discover this for himself. Often clients may be unclear about what they want to achieve from therapy—indeed this confusion of priorities may be part of what caused them to seek help in the first place—but in the course of therapy they become more aware of their goals and values.

Client-centred therapy carries these ideas to their extreme. Client-centred therapists try to provide a safe environment in which their clients can deeply examine their own feelings and values, and they scrupulously seek to refrain from influencing them during this process. They optimistically assume that given a psychologically safe environment, as defined by Rogers' three con-ditions, people are capable of resolving their own problems in their own way. Psychoanalysts also refrain from exerting influence over their clients. They believe that as a client gains insight into his unconscious conflicts, his need for neurotic symptoms will automatically decrease, without the therapist actively pointing him in the direction of healthier behaviour.

However, even though a therapist may intend not to influence the client, several therapists have argued that influence is actually one of the major mechanisms accounting for psychotherapeutic change. Frank (1973), in his important book *Persuasion and Healing*, compared psychotherapy with such practices as faith healing and Shamanism. Each of these latter employs persuasion on the part of the practitioner and its powers are enhanced if the client believes that it will work. This is true also of psychotherapy. Even quite nugatory treatments often produce change if the client is led to expect they will, a phenomenon known as the placebo effect. Frank argues that the effectiveness of therapy is partly explained by the client's hopeful expectations, which are aroused by the therapeutic situation.

Other investigators have analysed the mechanisms by which the therapist may influence the client. Truax (1966) analysed a case of Rogers', showing that he used empathy and warmth differentially, apparently to reinforce certain types of client statements. However, this may just demonstrate that Rogers was not being a good Rogerian in this particular case. Haley (1963) has provocatively conceptualized therapy as a power struggle between the client and therapist, in which the therapist is subtly attempting to keep the client in a one-down position and the therapy is successful when the client struggles back to a position of equality. From this perspective, the difference between therapeutic orientations does not lie in how directive they are, but rather in how explicit their direction is. Behaviour therapists are seen as being more honest because they are straightforward about how they exert influence.

While these criticisms have some substance, they are overstated. The client-centred and psychodynamic therapies still seem to be less directive than the behavioural orientations, even allowing for subtle influence. The issue is more that their desire to avoid influencing the client may hamper their potential therapeutic effectiveness. Many therapists resolve this dilemma by using a two-stage approach. In early sessions they are more exploratory, helping the client to focus on what they want to achieve from therapy and what conflicts seem to be underlying their problems. For some clients this exploratory phase is sufficient and they seem able to resolve their own problems much in the way described by Rogers. However, others appear to need more explicit guidance, which the therapist may then employ in the second phase. The aim, however, is always to pursue goals that the client wants and that the therapist is comfortable helping him achieve.

DEVELOPMENT OF THE THERAPIST'S SKILL

Most therapists acquire their skills in a formal training course. This may be in a university or polytechnic, a medical school, an independent institute or an in-service training scheme. As discussed above, psychotherapy training is not yet standardized: different institutions conduct it according to their own particular orientations. All courses teach trainees how to conceptualize and assess human behaviour in general and psychological distress in particular (although, again, the theoretical framework used varies from course to course). However, not all give explicit interpersonal skills training. Those that do follow a similar sequence consisting of (1) basic helping skills training, (2) simulated therapeutic interaction, (3) initial client contact, under close supervision, and (4) further client contact, less strictly supervised. Other courses downplay the first two steps, assuming that trainees learn by trial and error during their supervised clinical work.

The first step, basic helping skills training, is frequently accomplished via a standardized programme (such as Egan, 1982; Goodman, 1979; Ivey and Authier, 1978). These programmes aim to broaden the trainee's repertoire of helping responses, focusing on unfamiliar responses such as reflection, and also to teach the basic Rogerian conditions of empathy, warmth and genuineness. However, although derived from the client-centred tradition, they are also action-oriented, teaching trainees when and how to help the client develop new patterns of behaviour. The programmes combine conceptual and experiential components. That is, they not only give information about different kinds of helping responses, but they also include exercises so that trainees can have a direct experience of both giving and receiving different kinds of psychological help. Audiotape or videotape feedback may be used, so that trainees can compare their own performance with each other and with an accomplished practitioner, whether their trainer or another experienced therapist.

After the trainees have assimilated the basic helping skills, they then practise applying them in simulated clinical interactions. This is often done by helping a fellow trainee discuss his or her own personal problems, and then reversing roles. After each interaction, the impact of the trainee's helping style is discussed. Since the 'client' has had the same training as the 'therapist', he or she is able to give detailed feedback on the impact of the 'therapist's' responses. Reversing roles also enables trainees to experience both sides of the helping relationship—client as well as therapist—which gives them added empathy for the client in the actual clinical setting.

Finally, trainees make the transition to supervised experience with actual clients. They work initially with clients who have been carefully screened for suitability, i.e. those without severe problems. Supervisors' methods vary greatly. Some simply meet their trainees after a session to discuss whatever aspects of it the trainee wishes to raise. However, this relies on the trainee's ability to observe fully and recall accurately the events of the session. Unfortunately, distorted perception and selective recall is much more the norm, especially since trainees are often quite anxious during initial sessions. Furthermore, the most important occurrences are often those that the trainee does *not* notice. Thus many supervisors use some form of direct observation. The ideal is to observe the session through a one-way mirror, but if such facilities are unavailable then videotape or audiotape provides an acceptable alternative. Tapes also enable supervisor and trainee to go over the session together response-by-response looking at the effectiveness of the therapist's interventions and considering possible alternatives.

Good courses rotate trainees through several different service agencies and several different supervisors, in order to give them experience of a broad range of client problems and therapeutic methods. It takes the equivalent of about two years' full-time supervised experience plus at least a year's post-qualification experience to acquire a basic competence in psychotherapeutic skills. Clinical psychologists in Great Britain, for example, may take a two-year MSc, of which about half is supervised clinical work, and then work in the National Health Service at Basic Grade for two years before eligibility for unsupervised work as a Senior Clinical Psychologist. (An alternative to the MSc is a three-year in-service training scheme leading to the BPS Diploma in Clinical Psychology). In the United States, the qualification is the PhD, which includes two half years of supervised placements plus a year's pre-doctoral internship. Then a year's post-doctoral work is needed to qualify for licensing.

Following their formal training period, therapists are able to practise without supervision. Unless they arrange voluntary supervision, perhaps with a group of peers, or attend further education workshops, their professional development comes from their own assessment of their successes and failures with clients. Unfortunately, in practice, this feedback is rather one-sided, since usually only the successful clients stay around to provide it. Clients who have had a bad experience with therapy often drop out without telling the therapist why. They may be reluctant to criticize the therapist to his or her face, or may not be capable of articulating their dissatisfactions. Sometimes clients feign improvement when they are unhappy with or frightened by the therapy, a phenomenon known as 'flight into health'. Thus the therapist's feedback is skewed towards the positive: they hear more about what they do well than about what they do badly. Sometimes clients' dissatisfactions are dismissed as part of their problems. For example, one client told her therapist that she wanted to leave therapy because she didn't feel that she was making any progress. The therapist interpreted her feelings as a manifestation of her problems in forming close relationships. While this may have been partly true, the therapist refused to accept the legitimacy of the client's complaints.

Thus therapists must continually regard their work with a self-critical eye. Skilled therapists will encourage their clients to articulate their reactions to the therapy, both positive and negative. However, they must often rely upon themselves to redress the balance of positive and negative feedback. This requires continual vigilance to combat the tendency to settle into a state of self-satisfied complacency.

SUMMARY AND CONCLUSION

Analysing the skill of the therapist is an extraordinarily difficult exercise. There are many theories about what comprises effective therapy—each focusing on a different set of variables—and as yet research has cast little light on how they are to be integrated. Furthermore, therapy is not a homogeneous activity. There is much variability in what may happen, both across different therapists and also with the same therapist across different clients, or even with the same client on different occasions. Finally, some practitioners question whether it is advantageous to analyse the therapeutic relationship as a 'skill' at all.

We have viewed the therapist's skill in a number of different ways, using both the small unit of the individual therapist response and the large unit of the whole therapeutic relationship. These two levels are clearly interrelated, as the whole therapeutic relationship is simply the aggregate of many individual client and therapist responses. However, each unit of analysis allows a different focus. Response mode analysis concentrates on the moment-by-moment interaction and is closely tied to observable behaviour. It enables therapy to be analysed in terms of what actually happens between client and therapist, and this provides a useful framework for both research and training. Relationship level analysis has a broader scope which allows for more general consideration of the complex ingredients of therapy. It enables one to formulate theories about underlying factors that may be responsible for psychotherapeutic change.

The type of training therapists receive varies considerably from institution to institution. Some courses include explicit instruction in helping skills, often using a standardized interpersonal skills training programme. Others rely on supervised clinical experience to provide the training. All courses aim to teach therapists about the various types of therapeutic intervention and what the likely impacts of each may be. Once qualified, therapists tend to work independently, with little opportunity for colleagues to observe their work. Feedback from clients may be distorted towards the positive, thus giving practitioners an unrealistically favourable impression of their own abilities. Therapists must exercise great vigilance in order to gain an accurate impression of the outcome of their work.

I have attempted to give a flavour of how therapists think about their own activity, but there is certainly no shortage of further material for the interested reader. At an elementary level, the volume edited by Corsini (1979) provides brief descriptions and case examples of each of the major therapeutic orientations. At a more advanced level, Garfield and Bergin (1978) and Gurman and Razin (1977) review the empirical literature. Furthermore, many expert therapists have bravely allowed their work to be filmed or taped and thus made available for public scrutiny (e.g. Shostrom, 1965). In this field, there is no substitute for returning to the primary data—the actual interaction between client and therapist—to test other people's theories against one's own direct observation.

References

Bergin, A. E. and Lambert, M. J. (1978). The evaluation of therapeutic outcomes. In S. L. Garfield and A. E. Bergin (eds.) *Handbook of Psychotherapy and Behavior Change* (2nd edn.). (New York: Wiley)

Breuer, J. and Freud, S. (1974) *Studies on Hysteria.* (Harmondsworth, Middx.: Penguin Freud Library. Original edition, 1895)

British Psychological Society (1980). *The Psychological Therapies.* (Report of a working party of the Division of Clinical Psychology)

Burgess, A. (1962). *A Clockwork Orange.* (London: Heinemann)

Carkhuff, R. R. (1969). *Helping and Human Relations* (2 vols.). (New York: Holt, Rinehart and Winston)

Corsini, R. J. (ed.) (1979). *Current Psychotherapies* (2nd edn.). (Itasca, Illinois: Peacock)

Davison, G. C. (1978). Not can but ought: The treatment of homosexuality. *J. Con. Clin. Psychol.*, **46**, 170–2

Durlak, J. A. (1979). Comparative effectiveness of paraprofessional and professional helpers. *Psychol. Bull.*, **86**, 80–92

Egan, G. (1982). *The Skilled Helper: Model, Skills and Methods for Effective Helping* (2nd edn.). (Monterey, California: Brooks/Cole)

Ehrlich, R. P., D'Augelli, A. R. and Danish, S. J. (1979). Comparative effectiveness of six counselor verbal responses. *J. Coun. Psychol.*, **26**, 390–8

Elliott, R. (1979). How clients perceive helper behaviors. *J. Coun. Psychol.*, **26**, 285–94

Ellis, A. (1962). *Reason and Emotion in Psychotherapy.* (New York: Lyle Stuart)

Eysenck, H. J. (1952). The effects of psychotherapy: An evaluation. *J. Con. Psychol.*, **16**, 319–24

Frank, J. D. (1973). *Persuasion and Healing* (revised edn.). (Baltimore, Maryland: Johns Hopkins University Press)

Garfield, S. L. and Bergin, A. E. (eds.) (1978). *Handbook of Psychotherapy and Behavior Change* (2nd edn.). (New York: Wiley)

Garfield, S. L. and Kurtz, R. (1974). A survey of clinical psychologists: characteristics, activities, and orientations. *Clin. Psychol.*, **28**, 7–10

Goldfried, M. R. and Davison, G. C. (1976). *Clinical Behavior Therapy.* (New York: Holt, Rinehart and Winston)

Goodman, G. (1979). *SASHAtapes: Self-led Automated Series on Helping Alternatives.* (Los Angeles: UCLA Extension)

Goodman, G. and Dooley, D. (1976). A framework for help-intended communication. *Psychotherapy: Theory, Research and Practice*, **13**, 106–17

Greenson, R. R. (1967). *The Technique and Practice of Psychoanalysis.* (New York: International Universities Press)

Gurman, A. S. and Razin, A. M. (eds.) (1977). *Effective Psychotherapy: A Handbook of Research.* (Oxford: Pergamon)

Haley, J. (1963). *Strategies of Psychotherapy.* (New York: Grune and Stratton)

Herink, R. (ed.) (1980). *The Psychotherapy Handbook.* (New York: New American Library)

Ivey, A. E. and Authier, J. (1978). *Microcounseling: Innovations in Interviewing, Counseling, Psychotherapy, and Psychoeducation* (2nd edn.). (Springfield, Massachusetts: Charles C. Thomas)

Jourard, S. M. (1964). *The Transparent Self: Self Disclosure and Well-being.* (New York: Van Nostrand)

Kanfer, F. H. and Goldstein, A. P. (eds.) (1980). *Helping People Change: A Textbook of Methods* (2nd edn.). (Oxford: Pergamon)

Knowles, D. (1979). On the tendency for volunteer helpers to give advice. *J. Coun. Psychol.*, **26**, 352–4

Labov, W. and Fanshel, D. (1977). *Therapeutic Discourse: Psychotherapy as Conversation.* (New York: Academic Press)

Lomas, P. (1981). *The Case for a Personal Psychotherapy.* (Oxford: University Press)

Meltzoff, J. and Kornreich, M. (1970). *Research in Psychotherapy.* (New York: Atherton)

Mitchell, K. M., Bozarth, J. D. and Krauft, C. C. (1977). A reappraisal of the therapeutic effectiveness of accurate empathy, non-possessive warmth and genuineness. In A. S. Gurman and A. M. Razin (eds.) *Effective Psychotherapy: A Handbook of Research.* (Oxford: Pergamon)

Parloff, M. B., Waskow, I. E. and Wolfe, B. E. (1978). Research on therapist variables in relation to process and outcome. In S. L. Garfield and A. E. Bergin (eds.) *Handbook of Psychotherapy and Behavior Change: An Empirical Analysis* (2nd edn.). (New York: Wiley)

Plum, A. (1981). Communication as skill: A critique and alternative proposal. *J. Hum. Psychol.,* **21**, 3–19

Rogers, C. R. (1951). *Client-centred Therapy.* (Boston, Massachusetts: Houghton Mifflin)

Rogers, C. R. (1957). The necessary and sufficient conditions of therapeutic personality change. *J. Con. Psychol.,* **21**, 95–103

Scheflen, A. E. (1973). *How Behavior Means.* (New York: Gordon and Breach)

Shapiro, D. A. and Shapiro, D. (1983). Meta-analysis of comparative therapy outcome studies: a replication and refinement. *Psychol. Bull.* (in press)

Shiffman, S. M. (1981). The effects of graduate training in clinical psychology on performance in a psychotherapy analog. (Doctoral dissertation, University of California, Los Angeles, 1981). *Dissertation Abstracts International,* **42**, 2084–5B. (University Microfilms No. 81-22837)

Shostrom, E. (ed.) (1965). *Three Approaches to Psychotherapy.* (Santa Ana, California: Psychological Films Inc.)

Smail, D. A. (1978). *Psychotherapy: A Personal Approach.* (London: Dent)

Smith, M. L., Glass, G. V. and Miller, T. I. (1980). *The Benefits of Psychotherapy.* (Baltimore, Maryland: Johns Hopkins University Press)

Stiles, W. B. (1979). Verbal response modes and psychotherapeutic technique. *Psychiatry,* **42**, 49–62

Stiles, W. B. and Sultan, F. E. (1979). Verbal response mode use by clients in psychotherapy. *J. Con. Clin. Psychol.,* **47**, 611–13

Truax, C. B. (1966). Reinforcement and non-reinforcement in Rogerian psychotherapy. *J. Abnorm. Psychol.,* **71**, 1–9

Watson, J. B. and Rayner, R. (1920). Conditioned emotional reactions. *J. Exp. Psychol.,* **3**, 1–14

Weiner, I. B. (1975). *Principles of Psychotherapy.* (New York: Wiley)

Yalom, I. D. (1980). *Existential Psychotherapy.* (New York: Basic Books)

9
The Police Officer: Myths and Realities

W. G. CUMBERBATCH and J. B. MORGAN

INTRODUCTION

The self-image

'I was called to the King's Arms (a public house). Chummy (the offender) ran out through the back door when I came in. He really legged it! I goes after him down the alley and into the street. He's going like the clappers. Suddenly I sees a taxi coming up. I flag it down and jumps in. Three hundred yards further on round the corner Chummy is still legging it. He sees the taxi, flags it down and—cool as a cucumber—gives his address and climbs in next to me. Oh . . . it was neat that arrest!'

Police Officer answering a question on 'What is real police work?'

It is difficult to avoid romanticizing about police work. The thrill of the chase as described above is quite compelling. Anyone who has spent any time enjoying the intimacy of police officers will have heard such stories and many more dramatic, though probably apocryphal, tales of 'real police work' involving ruthless criminals, overwhelming odds, life and death emergencies, brilliant detective work and the eventual triumph of law and order. Of course, such tales are usually the stuff of fiction and one does not have to watch television for very long to be presented with a police drama which will reaffirm this image of the police as 'avenging blue angels' (Alderson, 1979).

Television fiction

Television drama may seem a curious starting point for a chapter in a book on *real* skills. However, fictional portrayals of the police provide an extremely useful insight into some important aspects of the police culture and its enacted

141

myths. Almost by way of summary, the novels of Joseph Wambaugh (ex-Lieutenant of the Los Angeles police department) have probably provided more insight into policing than any social science textbook to date. The key works *The New Centurions, Choirboys,* and *The Blue Knight* have a cartoon quality in caricaturing in an extremely amusing way some very real truths and very obvious tragedies of policing. The tragedies are very much ones of human and institutional weaknesses and especially the influence of the latter on the former.

Wambaugh, however, offers a rather different image of police to that of our routine TV portrayals. Throughout the 1970s British and American police fiction has presented an image of the 'super cop'. These programmes enjoy a massive audience throughout the world primarily because of the sheer quality of the productions which are worth dubbing into all kinds of unlikely languages. Thus interest in them is not a parochial one. In these programmes, exquisite detective skills tend to feature large—especially in, for example, *Columbo, Ironside* and *Kojak*, while physical prowess, including its extension into the manipulati of firearms or cars, runs a close second, for example in *Starsky and Hutch, Policewoman, The Professionals, The Sweeney.*

This genre of programme will be familiar to all. There are some interesting differences between programmes—especially from an evolutionary point of view. Programmes have reflected quite sensitively our changing conceptions of the police role. Thus, in early police fiction, for example *The Untouchables, Dragnet,* the police were wooden, humourless, almost one-dimensional, law enforcement figures. Although this style continues in occasional programmes, for example, *Hawaii Five-O,* by and large, all modern police drama portrays the police in much more human terms as members of the broader society carrying out a whole range of skilled activities outside that of simple law enforcement/crime fighting. However, while we know that police officers must spend hours on end directing traffic, television showing this kind of work is hardly a recipe for commercial success. At the end of the day the dramatic aspects of police work inevitably dominate and we must return to the popular theme of crime and its detection.

DETECTIVE SKILLS

Fact and fiction

It seems quite curious that a subject as fascinating as detective skills should have so successfully escaped any serious research. The only systematic research has just begun and few conclusions are likely before 1983 (Morgan, ongoing). Of course, many writers have presented quite brilliant analyses of detective skills through works of fiction. The novels of Conan Doyle (Sherlock Holmes), Agatha Christie (Hercule Poirot) and Georges Simenon (Maigret) are obvious classics. Indeed, in many ways such novelists have succeeded in capturing the elements of the detective's skill where research has so far failed.

Partly in preparation for this chapter a number of interviews were carried out with police officers to attempt to elicit police officers' perceptions of detective skills. However, the suggestions offered that good detectives had 'hunches', 'lucky breaks' or 'sheer experience' were not particularly helpful in illuminating the problem. Indeed, such hidden processes are not very compelling or convincing if used in fictional portrayals. More explanation is evidently needed. Novelists and dramatists have quite a serious problem in illuminating the detective process sufficiently to make it credible. The classic Conan Doyle technique of course is to provide a Dr Watson figure to be—as one critic suggested—'the minimal thermometer of the reader's intelligence'. Watson asks the stupid question 'how?' and receives a patient explanation by Sherlock Holmes of his brilliance. Another common technique used to demonstrate the importance of observational powers is to follow the detective's gaze and zoom the camera on to the incriminating cigarette lighter under the table.

The importance of facts especially observed by the acutely perceptive detective is a familiar theme in TV drama. *Dragnet* demonstrated one model of the detection process with the constantly heard sentence 'Just give us the facts Ma'am'. There is little doubt the use of facts and powers of observation to gather facts can be developed to a very impressive level in good detectives. It is quite unnerving to sit opposite a detective in a restaurant and have one's attention directed by the detective to a scenario unfolding before one's eyes when the detective has not noticeably even turned round.

There are books written by and for detectives showing how clues are picked up by the experienced and clever investigator. However, such works, while they offer fascinating reading, do not really offer general rules, for example, Robinson (1978). A good analogy is with the book by Webb *et al.* (1966) on unobtrusive measures for social scientists. This is deservedly a classic presenting a wealth of ideas for non-reactive research using physical artifacts such as the degree of erosion and wear being an indicator of use or popularity of objects (a clue that Sherlock Holmes used too!). Unfortunately the impact of the book on social science research has been minimal. There are probably two reasons for this—one is that the measures recommended are highly specific and, secondly, there is an absence of general theories which would allow the prediction of batteries of useful artifacts.

Conan Doyle described the problem on numerous occasions. For example, in *Silver Blaze* Sherlock Holmes observes that the dog did not bark and therefore the thief must have been known to the dog. This 'fact' was missed by other observers. However, while it is a credit to Sherlock Holmes and his powers of observation, the importance of this example is that Holmes perceives the fact because he has a theory about the nature of dogs (that they do not ordinarily bark at people they know well).

This is an epistemological issue of course. In the sciences, the real goal is not fact finding, but theory generation which allows us to predict, and indeed perceive, facts. Popper explained it well in writing of the 'searchlight theory' of theories—that theories cast a searchlight beam into the dark unknown and allow us to perceive things we did not know were there (Popper, 1959; Kuhn, 1962, 1970). Thus relativity theory is still generating new predictions of facts like black holes in the universe.

The analogy between the role of the creative scientist and the brilliant detective is worth pursuing. In both cases the solution/discovery/theory can be logically explained by hindsight but such logic remains a retrospective interpretation which has only marginal validity as an account of the thought processes which gave rise to that discovery (Bastick, 1982). This subject has received some attention from writers such as Arthur Koestler (e.g. *The Ghost in the Machine* and *The Sleepwalkers*), Liam Hudson (e.g. *Contrary Imaginations*) and Nobel Prize winning scientists like Sir Peter Medawar especially in his *Induction and Intuition in Scientific Thought* (1969). In brief they suggest that our formal accounts of how research is done—as reported in journals—is fraudulent in the sense that these accounts deny the creative element in science. Watson (1970) in *The Double Helix* presents an entertaining account of this creative process while Siegel and Zeigler (1976) in their book cover some of the mysterious dynamics of what is, essentially, detective work. It must be concluded that while various novelists have touched more closely on the subject than formal research to date definition of the skills remains elusive.

Using information

In many ways, though, definition of such skills is quite unnecessary for an analysis of policing. It is really most unlikely that the average police officer will ever in his career perform or even witness those exquisite detective skills that he has enjoyed in countless TV productions. The reason for this is simply that the vast majority of crimes are usually either very likely to be solved by routine investigation or they are very unlikely to be solved at all. Fortunately, the clear-up rate for serious crimes tends to be very high. Zander (1979) has shown why. In his study of Old Bailey cases, the identity of the defendant seems to have been reasonably clear on or near the outset of the enquiry in 87% of cases. Morgan (1980 and ongoing) has shown that well over 92% of crimes known to the police are discovered by the public who provide the majority of crucial information. Other studies, for example Reiss (1971), Coleman and Bottomley (1976), McCabe and Sutcliffe (1978), yield similar figures of public detection of around 86%. In Morgan's study, crimes that were 'solved' contained in their crime files over twice the amount of quantitative information and six times the amount of qualitative information as crimes that were not 'solved'. The various bits of information in the crime files were each rated by experienced police investigators on a Likert scale of value in terms of probability of detection, 'solving' of the crime. In this, where information was provided by the public during a police interview, the information was credited to the police 'since it was felt that in an interview genuine police skills are involved in the extraction of information'. Morgan (1980, p. 74). Evidently this method can be justified thus, but will necessarily overestimate the police role. In particular it will ignore the role of informants (an issue that will be returned to). Nevertheless, in this analysis of crime files it was shown that in cases where crimes were solved, the public still provided nearly twice the amount of information as the police.

Interrogation

The available evidence suggests that police officers consider the social skills of interrogation to be vital to their role. For example, Witt (1973) asked a large number of veteran detectives whether there were any other ways that crime could be solved apart from interrogation. In the two cities studied 65% and 71% replied 'No'. More than this, only 7% and 10% respectively in the two cities thought that interrogation could be eliminated without loss to law enforcement.

Mass media portrayals of the police role would tend to reinforce this belief. A common theme in police drama is that of the unco-operative criminal who is finally 'tricked' into confession. Occasionally, considerable dramatic success is obtained from the tension induced when information must be obtained urgently, for example from a terrorist on where a bomb has been planted. In such productions a variety of skills are demonstrated. *Columbo* needles; he goes back time and time again with requests for clarification on something that 'bothers' him. Superintendent Barlow in *Softly Softly* is at his best when playing the dual role of hard man/soft man, alternatively frightening then befriending his suspect. In the real world, Deeley (1971), Driver (1968) and Zimbardo (1967) describe some of these tactics used in police interrogation.

An important distinction must be made, however, between an interview and an interrogation. A useful one is that made by Mettler (1977) who suggests that an interrogation involves 'the questioning of a suspect or a reluctant witness, the nature of which is more adversarial than that used in a non-adversarial interview'. Thus 'the basic purpose of an interrogation is to attempt to secure a confession' (Milte and Weber, 1977). There is little convincing evidence to suggest how difficult confessions are to elicit. Those who have written on the subject, for example Reik (1959), Driver (1968), Williams (1960), seem to suggest that there is something of a compulsion in offenders to confess. Whether or not this is the case, very few citizens seem to decline invitations made by police officers to accompany them to the police station (Ashworth, 1976). Moreover, both in the USA and Britain, concern has often been expressed at the validity of confessions with the suggestion that too many innocent people may admit to offences that they have not committed. In the USA this led to an important case *Miranda v Arizona* which was erroneously believed for some time to disqualify confessions as evidence in court (see Pepinsky, 1970).

Perhaps another perspective on interrogations is to examine how important they are to the solution of crimes. Witt (1973) examined 478 police files and concluded that interrogation was 'unimportant' or 'unnecessary' in between 76% and 86% of cases. Sobel (1966) examined 1000 cases and suggested interrogation as vital in only 10% of these!

There are good reasons, however, why confessions should be so assiduously desired by police officers. For one thing, successful prosecutions are never certain—as McCabe and Purves (1972) have shown 'the acquittal of a defendant was attributable to a single cause—the failure of the prosecution (normally the police) to provide enough information or to present it in court in a way that would convince both judge and jury'. Confessions provide the additional information and/or save time. Also they demonstrate contrition in the offender which is important in justice. Moreover, they are psychologically important for police officers in confirming their judgement of guilt and in highlighting the detective's skill (Laurie, 1970).

This need to demonstrate skill is in many ways more important than the existence of it. Before discussing this notion further, two other skills may be noted in our television 'supercops': (1) physical prowess and its extension into the manipulation of firearms and cars and (2) forensic skills/technological expertise.

Physical prowess

Although at first sight physical fitness and strength would seem essential for police work, there is a lot of myth attached to this. This is well illustrated by an interview with one very senior officer recollecting his early experience as a police constable:

> 'Gypsy fights were always the worst. Ears got bitten off and God knows what else. Anyway one day a call came through. "Gypo fight at the *Black Horse*". Sarge (the senior officer) turns to me and says "come on lad" and we ran out of the station, me with my heart in my mouth. We turned left and went at a steady jog down the road. After 20 yards I suddenly realize the *Black Horse* is the other way and say "Hey, Sarge, isn't the *Black Horse* the other way?" "That's right lad", he says—and we keep running all the way round the block! By the time we get there, 10 minutes later, they're all knocked out—on their backs. If we'd got there earlier, *we'd* have been on *our* backs.'
>
> *Interview on 'real police work'.*

This case is interesting because of the emphasis which modern police forces have given to fast response times since motorized vehicles and personal radios became generally available. Police officers are more likely to arrive quickly at incidents which still contain considerable amounts of energy and violence potential. Of course, the television supercops are not only prize-fighting pugilists but also expert fast-draw marksmen so that they usually handle such situations in their stride. The reality for police officers is rather different. Many get seriously injured or even killed in attempting to effect an arrest.

Concern with the numbers of police officers assaulted by offenders resisting arrest has led to a number of interesting action research programmes. Hans Toch for example, showed, not surprisingly, that 'busy' police officers were more likely to be involved in physical conflict. However, certain officers had unusually high numbers of physical conflict with citizens. These officers were subjected to a 'violence reduction' programme which seems to have been very successful (Toch et al., 1975; Grant et al., 1982). Somewhat similar experiments have been run by Bard (1970, 1973), Goldstein et al. (1979), and Treger et al. (1974) using crisis intervention training techniques. In essence the skills taught were of de-escalating situations before arrest was attempted. Actions such as removing the helmet, unbuttoning the jacket and sitting down are obvious non-threatening ploys that a police officer might use in dealing with excited people.

Aggression is an unusually contagious emotion (Berkovitz, 1972; Bandura, 1973) which may when demonstrated by a police officer reduce villains to fear and surrender, but more than likely will not.

Forensic skills

Perhaps an even greater myth surrounds the issue of forensics. In the early days of Conan Doyle this was not a specialized function. Sherlock Holmes could recognize almost every cigar ash he came across. Today detectives rely on 'forensics'. The achievements of forensics are extremely impressive. TV programmes such as *The Expert* have romanticized this role. Again, unfortunately, the reality of police work is rather different. Peterson (1978) has shown that in a nationwide American survey of crime laboratory proficiency reports, 'unacceptable' responses were as high as 68% for hair type, 71% for blood and 34% for paint. It is hardly surprising therefore (although the above unfortunately had nothing to do with it) that the famous Rand Study on criminal investigation concluded that in only about 3% of crimes examined were the arrests a result of special investigative efforts by CID and forensics (Greenwood et al., 1977).

POLICE TASKS

Solving crimes

While the media portrayals of police officers show them as supercops, the reality of criminal investigation is rather different. In most countries of the world the probability of a crime being solved is fairly predictable given the nature of the crime. Offences against the person still usually involve assailants known to the victim and have a high clear-up rate. Property offences (e.g. burglary) rarely allow the public to identify the offender and are thus rarely solved except by 'taken into consideration' admissions. *TICs*, as they are known in the trade, are offences for which a person has not been arrested but which are admitted whilst a person is in custody. They are the subject of some humour among police and offenders alike. TIC admissions probably account for nearly half of all crimes cleared up. Mawby (1979) in his study of Sheffield crime found 40% of all offences examined were cleared in this way, while Lambert (1970) found that, in a sample of 2000 offences in Birmingham, 44% of these were cleared by TIC admissions.

The thrust of the argument so far is that crimes are very rarely indeed solved in the way TV drama would have us believe. Police TV drama is misleading. However, it would be equally misleading to conclude that police officers neither possess nor need sophisticated skills. But let us first examine 'real' police work.

Real police work

Particularly over the last decade and a half, understanding of police work has increased rapidly and now amounts to a knowledge almost equivalent to the 'heresies' put forward by Bronowski (1967). Bronowski suggested that our heresies now are: that we no longer believe the world is unique, that man is unique or that life is unique. In this we go against the established wisdom of our elders. Police research has rather similarly destroyed virtually all our cherished beliefs about policing and shown them to be myths.

Perhaps the most important discovery in police work has been that the police ordinarily *fail* to enforce the law. The term 'discretion' is now widely used to cover this phenomenon, for example Goldstein (1960), Banton (1964), La Fave and Wayne (1965) and Davis (1969). In various large, comprehensive observational studies it has been shown that arrest takes place in less than 25% of cases where the law has been violated (Reiss, 1971; Black, 1968). Evidently much depends on the seriousness of the offence. However, this is hardly the point. Traditionally the judiciary had been seen as the discretionary element in the criminal justice system. Recognizing that the police have discretion is something of import and is still not fully appreciated in the police literature. After all, the judiciary is a highly esteemed profession. High Court judges are assumed to be of the highest educational level, morality, and so on and receive salaries commensurate with this. Yet, evidence shows that a judge's discretion is less in terms of offences discharged (around 40%) than those dealt with by police officers (around 75%). It is also important to note that in discussing police discretion, researchers write of the lowest echelon of policing—i.e. the police constable/patrol officer. More than this, in countries where firearms are routinely carried, this discretion also includes the discretion to enforce or to fail to enforce the death penalty.

The second discovery was one that increased appreciation of the role of police discretion but clouded issues considerably. This was the discovery that probably less than 25% of police work has anything to do with crime (Reiss, 1971; Clark and Sykes, 1974; Rubinstein, 1973; Cain, 1973; Manning, 1977). Banton (1964) discussed the 'peacekeeping' role of the police as distinct from the law enforcement role. By the end of the decade it had become obvious that by the nature of their work, few police officers have much opportunity to become involved in activities which could lead to a challenging detection and arrest.

The third discovery was that, in a sense, police work is defined not by the police but by the public. Thus over 80% of police mobilizations are *reactive* in that the public demand a police response and this determines the nature of police work (Reiss, 1971; Morgan, 1980).

Finally, the fourth discovery was that the remaining assumptions of the police role—for example that the police detect crime and that police patrols prevent crime—were just not supported by any convincing evidence (Kelling *et al.*, 1974; Chaiken *et al.*, 1975, 1977; O'Connor and Gilman, 1978). Indeed, even in the occasional cases of police strikes, ordinarily there has not been very much increase in serious crime (Whitaker, 1982) although, of course, such phenomena are a little misleading.

Curiously, the above literature has had little effect on policing. It is true that since the 1970s more and more published attention has been put on the skills required in police–community relations. However, the major impetus for reforms in British police training were as a consequence of the riots in Britain and particularly Lord Scarman's report on the Brixton riots (HMSO, 1981; Scarman, 1982).

DEVELOPING RESOURCES

Training

The reform in police training has been followed from emphasis on the service role of the police. In the past most police training in most countries has been concerned with legalistic and procedural issues. The rote learning demands of this on probationer police officers has and remains considerable. In Britain even for promotion exams they must learn four volumes of Baker and Wilkies *Police Promotion Handbooks (Criminal Law, Criminal Evidence and Procedure, General Police Duties* and *Road Traffic)* and in addition need to know the *General Orders*. In the Metropolitan Police these general orders offered by the Chief of Police run to 10 000 paragraphs covering all admitted mistakes and advice on police discretion such as the speed at which speeding offences may be deemed to have occurred (e.g. 77 mph in a 70 mph limit). Little time is allowed for such learning. In Britain probationer training is approximately 400 hours whereas in the USA only 19 states required more than 200 hours compared with 9000 hours for lawyers (IACP 1970).

Not surprisingly, experienced police officers often claim 'you can't police by the book' (Manning, 1977). In saying this they allude to many things—the difficulty of learning the law but more than anything to the fact that police work is learned by experience and that legalistic solutions are merely one way of dealing with situations.

Promotion

What happens backstage when promotion boards sit and consider whether candidates are worthy of higher office? Here is the final irony where one finds a rather different dramatic role being played. Promotion boards remain impressed by police officers who show knowledge of the organization and of the way in which its resources can be used to solve problems of crime. Thus an officer who explains his detective work by reference to information gleaned from the collator's office, crime patterns, other solved or unsolved crimes, discussions with CID, community beat officers and so on, will, in all likelihood, be seen as a sound person for promotion to the administrative ranks responsible for the integration and handling of these various resources. Of course, solving crimes in this way is as much a fiction as is the television supercop. Thus in attempting to go backstage in policing one can easily find oneself merely facing another actor playing another dramatic role.

At the beginning of this chapter we suggested that television fiction provides an insight into the police culture and its enacted myths. The popularity of television fiction lies in part on its ability to avoid the predictable while working within recognized conventions. The conventions of policing are evident for all to see. It is perhaps in the avoidance of the predictable that a police officer survives as a kind of kaleidoscope of popular fiction.

POLICE SKILLS

Identifying 'real police skills' depends, of course, very much on what 'real police work' is. In one study 85% of police officers agreed that 'it is difficult to define the role of the policeman in today's society'. Niederhoffer (1969) described a policeman as 'a Rorschach in uniform'.

In many ways examining how police officers spend their time has led to some misleading if not rather naive recommendations in the literature. No one has so far been foolish enough to recommend more training in those areas which occupy most of police time—drinking tea, general 'easing' behaviour and internal/self-maintaining functions which probably account for over 50% of a police officer's time (Webster, 1973).

It would be possible to list all police functions and note relevant literature to illuminate the skills required—but this would require a good many more pages than possible here and mean a regurgitation of this volume plus sundry others, e.g. Argyle (1981). Evidently police officers, among very many other things, are obliged from time to time to deliver death messages, and, for example, tell unfortunate parents that their only child has been killed in a road accident. Freud (1982) has recently carried out a series of interviews with police officers on how they deal with such cases. While the study is an interesting and indeed a sensitive and useful one, his conclusions are unusual: most police officers are impressed by the uniqueness of each case and do not feel general training would be appropriate or helpful. This unfortunately is a most persistent problem in dealing with police work. Whatever the skills psychologists feel might be needed, police officers quickly counter with impressive accounts of how they have dealt with far more difficult problems than psychologists have ever examined. With our present knowledge of social skills, it would be absurd to suggest to police officers how to interview suspects, deal with violent offenders, cases of sudden death or virtually any other duty which a police officer may be called upon to perform. This is most clearly the case given the short training which police officers currently receive.

Rather than dwell on the range of skills which police officers routinely, if irregularly, need, it is more instructive to ask of police officers—'what makes a good copper?' There is a high degree of consensus on what the essence of good police work is: being able to cope with situations in a decisive and quick-witted way and an ability to communicate effectively. Egon Bittner (1974) for example, suggests:

'A policeman is always poised to move on any contingency whatever, not knowing what it might be, but knowing far more often than not he will be expected to do something . . . he literally sees things in the light of the expectation that he somehow has to handle the situation'.

The whole ethos of policing encourages a resourcefulness in dealing with novel situations. This is perhaps one of the few skills which is unique to this occupational group. However, police work is very situational, practical and experiential. Few incidents dealt with by police officers will be immediately observed by colleagues so that, ironically, media myths of policing are quite readily absorbed into the police culture.

The experienced detective often becomes a novelist bent on perpetuating the mystique of detective work. Almost inevitably he will be reluctant to negate that image. The media images of the detective necessarily focus on personalities rather than the slow tedious methodological fact collection of the organization—for fairly obvious dramatic reasons. Similarly, the police officer in order to demonstrate his *special* skills will be strongly encouraged by the peer culture to produce a script of dramatic success. The shopkeeper who provides crucial information may necessarily become 'my informant' who must be protected by anonymity and possibly rewarded financially from the appropriate police funds!

There is, of course, an important element of truth in this fiction, especially with experienced police officers. Street training as much as anything provides the knowledge of how to develop and *use* informants. The process by which this is done remains shrouded in secrecy but bargaining and negotiation are obvious elements. Plea bargaining within the courts has emerged as a new phenomenon (Baldwin and McConville, 1980). Possibly a much greater amount of bargaining takes place before this where the experienced detective may take a longer-term view of offenders and use his discretion in the enforcement of the law in exchange for information. Thus prostitutes and barrow boys may trade with some impunity, other offenders may be charged with more petty offences than would normally be expected and so on.

This area of police discretion is not one which the novice or 'rookie' can know much of from formal training. Indeed the novice will tend to see all situations from a fairly simple legalistic position. The experienced police officer will develop more 'practical' working relationships with his clients and being more confident in his ability to solve problems, will use the law as an *aid* to solving them. For the novice the law may be his only term of reference.

Police training must inevitably ignore such issues and concentrate on the problems which may arise from discretionary behaviour. Training for detectives in England and Wales will emphasize policing by the book and cover evidential skills, procedural rules and so on, partly because such skills are necessary for his role as prosecutor but also because if the permissible legal framework under which investigations are conducted is violated at any stage, then cases may be dismissed in the courts.

Behind the image of legalistic certainties, policing is an uncertain and indeed largely ineffective business (Wilson, 1968). Despite police work, crime rates rise, recidivists continue their criminal careers, the public can be truculent and unco-operative and so on. More than anything there is a general feeling that the police are 'Damned if they do, damned if they don't' (Klein, 1968). This is only part of the reason for the frustration and disillusionment so often noted in police officers. Thus, it is arguable that the real skills of policing lie in offering an image of effectiveness rather than providing the reality of it. So long as the public believe that police officers possess very special skills of detection, forensics, interrogation and so on then policing remains comparatively easy. Potential criminals may be deterred and offenders 'come clean' with instant confessions in the hope of leniency.

CONCLUSIONS

In this chapter, we have attempted to convey something of the elusive essence of police work. Reference has been made to both empirical research on policing and to fictional media accounts. We have suggested that while the emphasis of many fictional accounts is misplaced, they nonetheless offer some important insights into the police culture and its enacted myths.

The problem in generalizing about the skills of a police officer stems from the very situational, practical and experiential nature of police work which covers a very wide variety of tasks. More than this, partly because little police work is immediately observable by an officer's peers, media myths of policing seem to be readily absorbed into the police culture to amplify its dramatic elements. In television drama for example much dramatic emphasis is placed on the skills of observation and interrogation. Detectives will be encouraged to emphasize these skills in accounts of their work whereas in reality such skills will be rarely demonstrated nor indeed important for the day-to-day activities. Crime detection accounts for a small proportion of police work and is relatively predictable given the information which the public provide. Usually, few demands will be made on the police interviewer since witnesses and victims willingly provide the crucial information. Experience and skill will be needed by detectives to develop working relationships with informants. Hence the use of discretion not to enforce the law may be the most sophisticated skill demonstrated. Police discretion can be compared to the skill of a judge or magistrate. While experienced police officers probably usually fail to enforce the law (which is seen as just one tool for dealing with situations encountered), they nonetheless may face the risk of disciplinary action as a consequence.

In view of the importance of the public in detecting crime, an ability to communicate effectively with the public is a necessary skill for police officers to develop. Additionally, knowing how to defuse potentially violent situations through verbal and non-verbal communication would seem a prerequisite for the police if they are to retain community consent in their work.

Finally, while the ethos of policing encourages police officers to cope with situations in a decisive and quick-witted way, they are far from being the supercops of most television fiction. Fortunately, the mass media have tended to reflect quite sensitively our changing conceptions of the police role and we now see the police in much more human terms carrying out a very wide range of skilled activities beyond that of the simple law enforcement so beloved of early drama.

References

Alderson, J. (1979). *Policing Freedom*. (Plymouth: Macdonald and Evans)
Argyle, M. (ed.) (1981). *Social Skills and Work*. (London: Methuen)
Ashworth, A. J. (1976). Some blueprints for criminal investigation. *Crim. Law Rev.*, 594–609

Baker, E. R. (1978). *Baker and Wilkies Police Promotion Handbooks.* (London: Butterworths)
Baldwin, J. and McConville, M. (1977). *Negotiated Justice.* (London: Martin Robertson)
Bandura, A. (1977). *Aggression: a Social Learning Analysis.* (London: Prentice Hall)
Banton, M. (1964). *The Policeman in the Community.* (New York: Basic Books Inc.)
Bard, M. (1970). *Training Police as Specialists in Family Crisis Intervention.* (Washington DC: US Government Printing Office)
Bard, M. (1973). *Family Crisis Intervention: from Concept to Implementation.* (National Institute of Law Enforcement and Criminal Justice, Washington DC: US Government Printing Office)
Bastick, T. (1982). *Intuition. How We Think and Act.* (Chichester: J. Wiley)
Berkovitz, L. (1972). Words and symbols as stimuli to aggressive responses. In J. F. Knutson (ed.) *Control of Aggression: Implications from Basic Research.* (Chicago: Aldine-Atherton)
Bittner, E. (1974). A theory of the police. In H. Jacob (ed.) *Potential for Reform of Criminal Justice.* (Beverly Hills: Sage)
Black, D. J. (1968). Police encounters and social organizations. *PhD Thesis:* University of Michigan
Bronowski, J. (1967). *The Identity of Man.* (Harmondsworth: Penguin)
Cain, M. (1973). *Society and the Policeman's Role.* (London: Routledge and Kegan Paul)
Chaiken, J. M. (1977). *What's Known about Deterrent Effects of Police Activities.* (Santa Monica, California: Rand Corporation)
Clark, J. P. and Sykes, R. (1974). Some determinants of police organization and practice. In D. Glaser (ed.) *Handbook of Criminology.* (Chicago: Rand McNally)
Coleman, C. A. and Bottomley, A. K. (1976). Police conceptions of crime and 'no crime'. *Crim. Law Rev.,* 344–60
Davis, K. C. (1969). *Discretionary Justice.* (Baton Rouge: Louisiana State University Press)
Deeley, P. (1971). *Beyond Breaking Point: a Study of Techniques of Interrogation.* (London: Arthur Barker Ltd.)
Driver, E. (1968). Confessions and the social psychology of coercion. *Harvard Law Rev.,* **82**, 42–61
Freud, N. (1982). Death messages: the police officer as bringer of bad news. Paper given at International Conference on Psychology and The Law. Swansea, July 1982
Goldstein, J. (1960). Police discretion not to invoke the criminal process. *Yale Law J.,* **69**, 543–88
Goldstein, A. P., Monti, P. J., Sardino, T. J. and Green, D. J. (1979). *Police Crisis Intervention.* (New York: Pergamon Press)
Grant, J. D., Grant, J. and Toch, H. H. (1982). Police–citizen conflict and decision to arrest. In V. J. Konecni and E. E. Ebbesen (eds.) *The Criminal Justice System.* (San Francisco: W. H. Freeman)
Greenwood, P. W., Chaiken, J. M. and Petersilia, J. (1977). *The Criminal Investigation Process.* (Lexington, Massachusetts: D. C. Heath)
HMSO (1981). *The Scarman Report.* (London: HMSO)
Hudson, L. (1968). *Contrary Imaginations.* (Harmondsworth: Penguin)
IACP (1970). International Association of Chiefs of Police: Police Training. The Police Staff College, Branshill
Kelling, G. L., Pate, A., Dieckman, D. and Brown, C. E. (1974). *The Kansas City Preventive Patrol Experiment: A Summary Report.* (Washington DC: Police Foundation)
Klein, H. T. (1968). *The Police: Damned if They Do, Damned if They Don't.* (New York: Crown)
Koestler, A. (1959). *The Sleepwalkers.* (New York: Macmillan)
Koestler, A. (1967). *The Ghost in the Machine.* (London: Hutchinson)
Kuhn, T. S. (1962, 1970). *The Structure of Scientific Revolutions.* (Chicago: Chicago University Press)
La Fave and Wayne, R. (1965). *Arrest: the Decision to Take a Suspect into Custody.* (Boston: Little Brown and Co.)
Lambert, J. R. (1970). *Crime, Police and Race Relations.* (London: Oxford University Press)
Laurie, P. (1970). *Scotland Yard: A Study of Metropolitan Police.* (Chicago: Holt)

Manning, P. K. (1977). *Police Work: The Social Organization of Policing*. (Cambridge, Massachusetts: MIT Press)

Mawby, R. I. (1979). *Policing the City*. (Farnborough: Saxon House)

McCabe, S. and Purves, R. (1972). *The Jury at Work*. (Oxford: Blackwell)

McCabe, S. and Sutcliffe, F. (1978). *Defining Crime: a Study of Police Decisions*. (Oxford: Blackwell)

Medawar, P. B. (1969). *Induction and Intuition in Scientific Thought*. (London: Methuen)

Mettler, G. B. (1977). *Criminal Investigation*. (Oxford, Massachusetts: Holbrook Press)

Milte, K. L. and Weber, T. (1977). *Police in Australia*. (London: Butterworth)

Morgan, J. G. (1980). The public as detection of crime. *MSc Thesis*: Cranfield Institute of Technology

Niederhoffer, A. (1969). *Behind the Shield: Police in Urban Society*. (New York: Doubleday)

O'Connor, R. J. and Gilman, B. (1978). The police role in deterring crime. In J. A. Cramer (ed.) *Preventing Crime*. (Beverly Hills, California: Sage)

Pepinsky, H. (1970). A theory of police reaction to Miranda v. Arizona. *Crime and Delinquency*, **16**, 379–92

Peterson, J. (1978). *Crime Laboratory Proficiency Study*. (Washington DC: US Government Printing Office)

Popper, K. (1959, 1968). *The Logic of Scientific Discovery*. (London: Hutchinson)

Reik, T. (1959). *The Compulsion to Confess*. (New York: Farrer, Strauss and Codaly)

Reiss, A. J. (1971). *The Police and the Public*. (New Haven: Yale University Press)

Robinson, G. F. (1978). *Catching Criminals: Some Basic Skills*. (London: Police Review Publication)

Rubinstein, J. (1973). *City Police*. (New York: Farrar, Strauss and Giroux)

Scarman, Lord (1982). *The Scarman Report: The Brixton Disorders 10–12 April, 1981*. (Harmondsworth, Middlesex: Penguin)

Siegel, M. H. and Zeigler, H. P. (eds.) (1976). *Psychological Research: The Inside Story*. (New York: Harper and Row)

Sobel, N. R. (1966). *The New Confession Standards*. (New York: Gould Publications)

Toch, H., Grant, J. D. and Grant, R. T. (1975). *Agents of Change: A Study in Police Reform*. (New York: J. Wiley)

Treger, H., Thomson, D. and Jaeck, G. S. (1974). A police–social work team model: some preliminary findings and implications for system change. *Crime and Delinquency*, **20** (3), 281–90

Wambaugh, J. (1970). *The New Centurions*. (Boston: Little Brown and Co.)

Wambaugh, J. (1971). *The Choirboys*. (Boston: Little Brown and Co.)

Wambaugh, J. (1972). *The Blue Knight*. (Boston: Little Brown and Co.)

Watson, J. D. (1970). *The Double Helix*. (Harmondsworth: Penguin)

Webb, E., Campbell, D. T., Schwartz, R. D. and Sechrest, L. (1966). *Unobtrusive Measures: Non-reactive Research in the Social Sciences*. (Stokie, Illinois: Rand McNally)

Webster, J. (1973). *The Realities of Police Work*. (Dubique, Iowa: Brown)

Whitaker, B. (1982). *The Police in Society*. (London: Sinclair Browne)

Williams, G. (1960). Questioning by the police. *Crim. Law Rev.*, **1**, 325–46

Wilson, J. Q. (1968). *Varieties of Police Behaviour*. (Cambridge: Harvard University Press)

Witt, J. W. (1973). Non-coercive interrogation. *J. Crim. Law C. & P.*, **64** (3), 320–32

Zander, M. (1979). The investigation of crime: a study of cases tried at the Old Bailey. *Crim. Law Rev.*, 203–19

Zimbardo, P. (1967). The psychology of police confessions. *Psychol. Today, June*, 17–20, 25–7

10
The Judge

W. A. N. WELLS

INTRODUCTION

In this paper, I am speaking for myself alone. No other judge could be expected to agree with everything I say, although I should be surprised if every judge did not agree with much of what I say. Having lodged this caveat, it will be possible to be briefer, and to speak with less qualification than might otherwise have been expected.

When reading this paper it is essential to bear steadily in mind that what a judge must do in law is considerably less than what he may, and, generally speaking, should, do in practice; and what he may and should do is often the product, not of legal precept or principle, but of practical experience and human understanding that have been developed and are put to use to achieve justice. By justice I mean here (to borrow from Justinian) 'the set and constant purpose to give to every man his due'. What is there denoted manifestly travels well beyond justice according to law. In the definition, what is of supreme importance is the purpose; mankind, the laws of mankind, and the adminis-tration of those laws, are all imperfect; but judges can, as human beings, reconcile the ideal and the practical by constantly demonstrating that they have adopted that purpose as their own.

In short, a judge's endeavours must be directed to achieving this practical goal: that every person who emerges from his court after a case is over—parties, counsel, witnesses, listening public—will say, without reservation, 'That was justice in action'. Of all those persons, the most important is, of course, the party who loses; but, in varying ways, justice must be done to, and in relation to, all concerned, and it is essential to realize that the formal result of a hearing—verdict, order, decree, sentence—may be unappealable, and yet justice, in the fullest sense of the word, may not have been done to all concerned.

The question whether justice has been done must be judged against the background of the system of trial obtaining in our courts, which is the adversary system. That system is founded on two principles: first, that great truths emerge from strong challenge and argument; and second, that counsel who represent the parties owe a duty to their respective clients, to present their cases in the most forceful manner and in their best light, and an equally compelling duty to the court, to join with it in the search for justice.

The role of a judge in the administration of the adversary system is often misunderstood. He is sometimes spoken of as if he were no more than an umpire: his only function, it is supposed, is to give a ruling or to make a finding when asked to do so, but otherwise to remain silent and aloof, and to refrain from intruding or taking the initiative at any stage. Such a description is misleading. A much better analogy than that of the umpire is the catalytic agent. A judge's task, according to his oath of office, is to do right to all manner of men, without fear or favour, affection or ill will; and if he is to be true to his oath he must be prepared to act of his own motion again and again in the course of a trial. The purpose of this paper is to discuss what he may be obliged to do if he is to do justice, or (as the oath puts it) to do right, to all manner of men. How is he, axiomatically an imperfect creation, administering an imperfect system, to do right or justice to and in relation to the extraordinary variety of imperfect men, women, and children, who appear before him? It will be convenient to examine his responsibilities under five separate heads:

Judge and counsel;

Judge and witness;

Judge and prisoner;

Judge and jury;

Judge as conciliator.

It need hardly be added that it is impossible to be exhaustive.

JUDGE AND COUNSEL

The precious and delicate relationship between judge and counsel rests on trust, and nothing can be allowed to impair that trust. The judge will best maintain that trust if his constant purpose is to ensure that the adversary system operates at its best. He must be courteous, and eschew sarcasm and mockery. He must learn the arts of listening, and of patience; 'an overspeaking judge is no well-tuned cymbal' (Bacon 'Of Judicature'). But it is possible to do all these things, and yet to be firm; a judge may be polite as well as forthright and strong. In particular, he must do what he can to facilitate and encourage the formulation of each counsel's case. If he interrupts, it must be in order to clear his mind, and to ensure that he is understanding fully what is being placed before him. If he identifies difficulties in what is being advanced in argument or evidence, it must be in order to invite or encourage counsel to resolve those difficulties, if that is possible.

If one counsel is plainly less able, skilled, or experienced than his opponent, he should interpose, as he thinks best, in order to prevent the better counsel of the two from snatching at an error or omission of the other, or from otherwise taking advantage of his superiority as counsel as distinct from the superiority of his case, and should, where and to the extent practicable, restore the balance. If a mistake has been or is being made, he should correct it—if correction is legally open; if obstacles to the smooth and effective presentation of a case loom up, he should warn those affected.

In all his dealings with counsel, he should use such skills as he has retained from his experience at the bar, in order to expedite proceedings (where possible), not to disrupt them. When in colloquy with counsel, he ought to ask questions in order to elucidate, not to confound or confuse—especially if he has junior counsel before him; he ought to probe in order to discover, not to display superior skill or scholarship; if he sees difficulties in what counsel is asking or advancing, he ought to identify and formulate the difficulties as things to be overcome together, if the law allows it, but without relish. An error may be perceived and pointed out, but there is rarely need to castigate the perpetrator of it.

On the very rare occasions when a judge must deal with intellectual dishonesty or dereliction of duty, he does so most effectively by identifying and drawing attention to the failing displayed so that counsel may simply see it as his own shortcoming, and not as something by the use of which the judge has got the better of him.

When a witness is under examination by counsel, a judge must exercise and demonstrate restraint in many ways. In the nature of things, a judge is likely to be at least the equal of counsel in his proficiency in the art of examining witnesses, but he should never ask questions in order to indulge his own skill as a barrister. He should do counsel the courtesy of assuming that they know what they are about, and he should not, unless the interests of justice imperatively demand it, open up new topics or adopt fresh approaches in cross-examination, except at the close of cross-examination, and then only if the topic is apparently of real significance in the case. A judge may, of course, interpose questions at any stage—indeed, often—if he is seeking to make sure of something, or to test his understanding of an answer, or to clarify something that has been obscurely expressed. But the distinction is both clear and wide between questions asked in order to resolve some doubt or ambiguity, or otherwise to assist, and questions by which, for a time, the judge takes over the role of counsel.

It is probable that, on the whole, counsel will contribute most to the administration of justice if the judge, by his manner towards them, his expression, and his choice of words, conveys the impression that he believes counsel are doing their best; that they have thoroughly prepared their work; that they are actuated by the highest and purest motives; and that they are anxious to help in the administration of justice as well as to present their cases effectively.

It should not be supposed for a moment that the foregoing precepts and standards are commended because they conform to the image of what may be supposed to be the community's, or the profession's, idea of a good judge. The suggestions or recommendations are here advanced because, in various ways, they promote or strengthen the trust that must exist between bench and bar if the adversary system is to work efficiently, and enables that system to produce its best results. Every precept and standard commended is derived from a social skill in action, the test of which is to be found in its capacity to have effect as a catalytic agent in the personal inter-reaction of judge and counsel.

JUDGE AND WITNESS

In his relations with witnesses, the judge should regard this purpose as predominant: namely, to ensure that the witness does himself justice, more especially where, as is common, the witness finds himself in an unfamiliar setting.

What follows is, in truth, a description of little more than courtesy and consideration, backed up by commonsense and imagination. Once again, the importance of exhibiting these virtues does not depend on popular hope or expectation, but upon the realization that witnesses are more likely to reveal the truth if they are treated well than if they are ill treated.

Two simple examples make the point. Most witnesses, immediately after they have taken the oath, find themselves at a loss; they do not know whether to sit down, remain standing where they are (which is usually back a yard or so from the front partition of the witness box), or to advance a step but remain standing. The witness who is addressed courteously by the judge, 'Mr X, please sit down if you would prefer to do so' finds this slight but significant, cause of embarrassment removed, and is helped to feel more at ease.

Then again, the question how the witness is to be addressed arises. There are countless different ways of addressing a person, which vary with the age, sex, profession or calling, and social background, of the witness. The judge who takes the trouble to address the witness correctly or, if he does not know, takes the trouble to find out, helps further to restore the witness's confidence and self-esteem, which may have been impaired by being subjected to the ordeal he is then undergoing. Witnesses may also suffer from physical ailments or deformities, nervousness, or embarrassment caused by the subject matter of their testimony or from their position with respect to the parties. The list of causes for a witness's discomfort, physical or emotional, is endless. A judge must be continually on the alert to ensure that a witness is kept as free as is humanly possible from extraneous interferences with his capacity or willingness to speak fully, freely, and frankly. Every cause of discomfort or inhibition that is removed by the judge's intervention, if counsel has failed to remove the cause himself, is another positive step towards ensuring that the witness before him does not conceal or misrepresent the truth.

After the examination has begun there are many other ways in which the judge may fulfil the role of a human catalytic agent: he may help a witness who finds himself at a loss for words; he may interpose questions to clear up ambiguities or uncertainties that may lead the witness to be faced with apparent, but perhaps not real, inconsistencies or contradictions; he may suspect that a witness has misunderstood a question and yet be afraid to admit that he has, and he may, accordingly, save the witness from error; he may divine that counsel and witness are at cross-purposes, and intervene in order to bring them back to common ground. He will ensure that a witness is not unkindly mocked and that jokes are not made at his expense.

Where counsel is finding difficulty in extracting information, and his witness is becoming frustrated and perplexed, the judge may use his own skills and tact, and develop other and effective means for eliciting what is wanted. Occasionally, where a judge finds himself presented with a contumacious prevaricator or someone who wilfully refuses to assist the court, or with a self-appointed court jester, he may intervene sternly; but such interventions are more effective when they spring from the judge's manner and temperament, and less effective when they are based upon straight threats of imposing a legal sanction.

Again, a judge may interpose with great effect when he suspects that a witness is being threatened by fear of reprisals at the hands of persons outside the court; a word from him is likely to restore the witness to calm.

The situations in which the way of a witness can be eased are endless. I have discussed many of them at some length in a paper on 'Examination in Chief', but there are many more. I am referring not to professional arts based on legal rules, but to social skills whose exercise is prompted by the need to put and to keep a witness in a frame of mind in which he will lose the many inhibitions that inevitably and naturally hinder his understanding of questions, the free flow of his recollection, and the expression of his thoughts in clear and unambiguous language. A judge's interventions are rendered effective by his direct personal experiences of hundreds of witnesses whom he has examined while at the bar and on the bench.

JUDGE AND PRISONER

During trial

Where the prisoner is unrepresented—Now that legal aid is readily available in most jurisdictions, prisoners are usually represented, but sometimes they are not—for example, if legal aid is justifiably refused, or the prisoner declines it. From the outset, the judge's role must be made clear to the prisoner: the judge is not a do-gooder, nor will he display draconian severity; he is there to assist the prisoner in the presentation of his defence, so far as an outsider is capable of doing so, and within the limits of his responsibility to safeguard the due process of the trial.

The judge should ensure that the prisoner is kept aware of what is happening at every stage of the trial and, so far as it is practicable, that he understands the reason for each step in the trial process. In particular, the prisoner must be left in no doubt about what are the decisions that he must make, what are the circumstances he must consider to arrive at those decisions, and what will be the consequences of each decision.

Although the prisoner is called on to examine witnesses, the judge must not hesitate to assist him in framing questions, and to develop what appear to be his intentions. In particular, he must take care to explain, wherever an explanation seems to be called for, all rulings on evidence, practice, and procedure. Although the professional standards of Crown counsel are usually high, the judge should keep an eye on the presentation of the Crown case, and should do what is necessary to keep that presentation strictly within the bounds of the law.

Throughout, it behoves the judge to eschew the technical language of the law, and to use the ordinary language of the man in the street. He must not, however, patronize or appear to do so. His approach to the prisoner must at all times be direct, simple, polite, and commonsense, while maintaining a modicum of aloofness to make it clear to all that he is not abandoning his judicial role.

The judge should not hesitate to interrupt the prisoner if by the manner and conduct of his defence he is moving into legal danger, and take such steps as are necessary, in the presence or absence of the jury, to explain to him what the danger is, and what must be done to avoid it.

An adherence to the foregoing principles will, of course, help to ensure that no miscarriage of justice according to law occurs, but the reason for urging their adoption is that by it the judge will, it is to be hoped, convince the prisoner that 'the law' is not trying to take advantage of him, and give him the confidence necessary to advance everything available that may reasonably make for a defence. By these means, right may be done to the unrepresented prisoner.

Where the prisoner is represented—The judge here must not only bear in mind what should be done to maintain the efficacy of the adversary process and mutual trust between bench and bar; he must also remember the prisoner as the man most obviously and immediately affected by his rulings.

Accordingly, the judge, in giving rulings and joining in a colloquy with counsel on matters under debate, must at all times be careful to express himself in terms of principle and commonsense, and not confine himself to abbreviated rulings in purely technical terms. By these means, the prisoner will be led to appreciate that the judge is actuated by a sense of fairness as well as by technical rules of law. For the same reason, the rulings and directions should be given in language that the prisoner will understand.

After conviction

Where the prisoner is not represented—The judge must be careful to avoid even the remotest suspicion that he is moved by vindictiveness or glee. It is not that judges feel these emotions, but there are some in the community who think that they do, and the prisoner may well be one of them. The judge must be careful to impress on the prisoner that he wants, and will seek, all information that is relevant to the question of sentence, including the prisoner's background, history, and future.

When the prisoner is addressing the court in mitigation, the judge should, amongst other things, assist him to express himself clearly, encourage him to amplify what he is saying, particularly where he seems to have jumped over something that could, if developed, be of assistance. The judge should not hesitate to point out to the prisoner those circumstances in the case adverse to him that call for explanation or further explanation.

The judge must show himself willing to follow up enquiries by all the means at his disposal—police, probation officers, medical experts (including psychiatrists), psychologists, social workers and the like—and make sure the prisoner is made fully aware of what is to be done, why the further enquiry is being pursued, and the substance and implications of the further information when it is received. In short, the judge must make sure the prisoner realizes that, whatever else the judge must weigh and determine, he wants to see the prisoner's case in mitigation as fully developed as circumstances permit.

Where the prisoner is represented—Virtually the same precepts apply as are mentioned in the sub-paragraph above, except that much more help for the judge can be expected to be given by defence counsel without any prompting by the judge. But once again, a judge may keep himself well within the law by saying and suggesting virtually nothing, whereas he ought, if he is to do right, express himself in such a manner as demonstrates to the prisoner what his attitude is to the case in mitigation. Questions, suggestions, and comments, coming from the judge, and formulated with the foregoing precepts in mind, will keep the prisoner aware that justice in the widest sense is the purpose of judge and counsel.

Remarks on sentencing—When the judge is actually sentencing the prisoner, whether represented or not, the judge should ensure that the prisoner realizes that he, the judge, has mastered all the circumstances of the case, and that the prisoner understands why the judge is making the order he intends to make.

It is important here to emphasize that a judge's remarks on sentence are fundamentally different from formal reasons for judgement. Remarks on sentence are personal to the prisoner; they represent the judge's personal assessment of the prisoner as a human being whom the judge must punish or otherwise deal with, his understanding of the prisoner's weaknesses and strength, and his appreciation of the circumstances of the crime in the widest sense of that expression. Remarks on sentence are made person to person, viewing sentencer and sentenced as human beings; they do not represent an essay on criminal jurisprudence, or a monograph on moral delinquency.

On how a man is treated by the judge when remarks on sentencing are uttered may well depend the whole future shape of the prisoner's attitude to society and the law. There is a vast difference, so far as the prisoner is concerned, between being talked at and being talked to, notwithstanding that both modes of address may be within the boundaries of the law. The following are remarks on sentence made by a judge when sentencing a prisoner who had pleaded guilty to an unusual form of bank robbery; the facts sufficiently appear from the remarks. When reading them it should be borne in mind that legally all that was required was the pronouncement of the order.

You realize that in sentencing you there are many more facts and circumstances to be considered than just you and your future. As your counsel frankly conceded, your case is one in which it would be out of the question to do other than impose a sentence of imprisonment. Before, however, turning to that sentence, I intend to record certain conclusions about you and your background, and to invite the Parole Board to consider what I say. Nothing a sentencing judge says binds the Parole Board, but I have no doubt that the Board will have regard to my remarks:

(1) I have deliberately refrained from imposing a non-parole period. This leaves the Board free to appraise your progress and to grant parole when, in its judgement, the time has come to do so.

(2) I am satisfied that you are contrite, and have come to understand what a frenetic and unhappy life you have been leading, more especially when you were in the grip of your obsession with gambling. You see, I am sure, that your way of life was bound to bring you to disaster.

(3) I am satisfied that you have received, are now receiving, and will receive, the support and encouragement of your two sisters and of the woman with whom you have lived, and whom you wish to marry. My firm impression of your two sisters, who gave evidence, is that they are persons and citizens of the highest calibre who are devoted to you and who are entirely dependable. The third of the above-mentioned women did not give evidence, but it sounds to me that marriage with her would help greatly to stabilize your life.

(4) I am satisfied that the two principal factors that led you into this tragic affair were your obsession with gambling and your urge to maintain a life style well beyond your means.

(5) I am satisfied that you have both natural and educated ability and skills well above the average, and that there is no justification for the lowness of your self-esteem,

the origins of which have been described so thoroughly and vividly by your sisters. Your father may have done you much harm in your adolescent years, though one would wish to have both sides of the story before reaching firm conclusions on this matter.

(6) I am satisfied that there are good grounds for hoping that your life will ultimately be stabilized. All these things may particularly be said in your favour as well as the other facts and circumstances canvassed by your counsel in his persuasive and helpful address and described in the evidence. But other facts and circumstances must be borne in mind which more particularly concern the community and its interest in the maintenance of internal peace.

This was a deliberate and planned crime. It was not perpetrated in a moment of mad impulse. A choice was made. There was ample opportunity to draw back. Its essential features were worked out by you in Melbourne. The basic strategy was to make a rapid sortie from interstate, rob a bank, and escape to your home state before the hue and cry was thoroughly organized. You took precautions to create confusion over your physical appearance. You bought for the operation a replica firearm which you effectively used—without actually presenting it—to frighten the bank officer into doing what you wanted. You escaped with something over $5000. Much of this sum has been recovered; there is some uncertainty over what is still missing, but it is certain that the amount is over $300.

You used no actual violence, no actual firearm, no ammunition real or unreal. You used no aggravated means for inculcating terror. You only were involved. Once apprehended, you were frank and helpful to the police. You were, apart from the other features of your life and personality already referred to, under some pressure from your ex-wife who was seeking payments of alimony; I have no doubt of this because immediately you reached a place of safety you sent to her in WA $650.

I must think, however, not only of this crime, but of other similar crimes that may be planned; not only of this bank officer, but of other bank officers; not only of this bank, but of other banks and places where large sums of money are kept and that are vulnerable to rapine and violence; not only of you, but of others who may be financially insecure and who may be minded to follow your example. I must bear steadily in mind that this sort of crime is disturbingly prevalent.

I do not overlook Mr Johnson's point to me that the execution of your plan displayed some of the marks of the amateur; but I cannot overlook either that recent cases in these courts reveal that some people without experience of such a crime take to robbery under arms with an almost careless nonchalance which is quite horrifying. This tendency, in my opinion, must be severely discouraged.

I do not pay much regard to your previous convictions, which are different from the present one. I pause only to observe that you must at least have learnt through them that breaches of the criminal law are likely to attract punishment.

I must now discharge the two-fold duty of protecting the public and of showing such mercy as is consistent with the discharge of that duty. As part of your sentence I require you to enter into a bond pursuant to s. 313 of the Criminal Law Consolidation Act the terms of which are as follows:

(1) It will be for a period of three years which will commence upon the termination, in due course of law, of the sentence that I am about to impose.

(2) It will be in your own recognizance of $500 with one surety in the like sum, or two sureties of $250 each.

(3) The conditions are:
   (a) That you be of good behaviour and keep the peace.
   (b) That you be under the supervision of a probation officer and that you will obey his directions generally, and in particular as to employment and residence and as to your associates.
   (c) That you abstain from all forms of betting, gaming, and wagering whether, in the circumstances, lawful or not.

I declare that your probation officer may authorize your residence in another state subject to such directions as he deems expedient and as are consistent with the terms of this bond. The other part of your sentence is that you be imprisoned and kept to hard labour for a term of $3\frac{1}{2}$ years. I fix no non-parole period.

JUDGE AND JURY

A satisfactory working relationship between a judge and the trial jury is essential to the conduct of a fair trial. Such a relationship is unlikely to come into being naturally; a positive and conscious effort must be made by the judge to establish and maintain it. A jury that has been allowed to become perplexed, suspicious, affronted, or fearful, poses a threat to the due administration of the law, and is almost certain to lead to a miscarriage of justice, even though, upon review, it appears that the prisoner was given a fair trial according to law.

What has just been said should not be misunderstood. The last thing intended to be suggested is that a judge should work himself into a position of ascendancy over a jury. What is intended is that the judge should labour to ensure that the jury are not inhibited or frustrated, or prevented in any way from doing the best they can with the material provided. The judge should, therefore, I suggest, adopt these aims:

(1) To dispel the sense of unfamiliarity and apprehension that afflicts all but that comparatively rare species—the juror who has had useful previous jury service.

(2) To make the jury appreciate that they are part of a court team, of which the other members are counsel and the judge, and that the team should work together to give a fair trial.

(3) To convince the jury that they are not, for some unaccountable reason, viewed by the community, in general, and the courts, in particular, as poor cousins of judge and counsel in the trial process; that, on the contrary, they bring to that process just the qualities and experience that are needed to complement the work of judge and counsel.

(4) To give to the jury belief in their ability to arrive at verdicts with confidence and without releasing the spectre that remorse or agonies of doubt will assail them in the future over what they did as jurors.

Dispelling the sense of unfamiliarity and apprehension

As soon as possible after jurors appear in court to begin their tour of duty, the entire panel should be brought together before a single judge, and given a short talk on what may conveniently be labelled 'domestic administration'. This talk should attempt to allay or resolve as many as possible of the apprehensions and misconceptions that worry most jurors before they start their work. It may deal with such purely practical subjects as: the usual periods during which the court will sit and will adjourn; the provision of meals; morning and afternoon breaks; the parking of jurors' cars; arrangements that are made to inform families or dependants if a jury finds itself deliberating late into the afternoon or evening; arrangements to transport jurors home if they are kept late in the evening; the organization undertaken if a jury is kept together overnight because they have not arrived at a verdict after many hours of retirement, and are tired. The jurors should also be informed that they are summoned to assist in the administration of justice because they are what they are, namely, a cross-section of the adult men and women in the community, who are accordingly asked to bring with them and to use, for the understanding of those concerned in a case and the interpretation of the evidence, their knowledge and experience of the ways of the world, and of how the ordinary members of the community may, therefore, be expected to behave and to react. The jurors should be reminded that they are brought from the same community as that from which accused persons come, and as that which trusts them, as far as their responsibility goes, with the upholding of the law.

By an address of this kind the jurors will, it is to be hoped, lose much of their unfamiliarity with their place of work, and their apprehension about the nature of their duties. But as trials proceed before working juries of twelve, the judge should go further. At every convenient and appropriate opportunity while the trial is in progress, the judge should ensure that the jury knows what is being done, and why. He may do this either by turning to the jury and offering them an explanation of some particular event, or special practice; or he may, when giving directions or rulings, express himself in such a way that the jury is carried with him by ensuring that they understand both the direction or ruling, and the reasons for it.

Making jurors aware that in a trial they will act as part of a team

A judge should satisfy himself that, either before the trial begins, or in its early stages, an explanation has been, or will be, given to the jury of the several functions of judge, jury, and counsel. He may become so satisfied by addressing the jurors himself, or by listening to Crown counsel give the necessary explanation, but however it is achieved, the jury should be made aware from the outset that the roles of judge, jury, and counsel (who constitute the three principal divisions of the court) are interdependent and complement one another. In short, they form part of a team, and if any one division fails to perform his part the whole team effort fails.

At every point in the trial where it is appropriate to do so, the judge should attempt to reinforce the jury's realization that they have an important duty to perform, and what that duty is. For example, when the jury is asked to retire in order to allow counsel freely to debate the admissibility of a challenged item of evidence, the judge would be wise to use the first of such occasions to explain to the jury that, as they know, their duty is to reach a verdict 'on the evidence', which means 'on the evidence properly before them'; that an argument over the admissibility of evidence can hardly take place without first knowing what the disputed item of evidence is; that if the evidence was revealed in argument before them, and then disallowed, they would find themselves in some embarrassment in consequence of their knowledge. The judge should, at the same time, explain that each of the divisions of the court is likely to be ignorant of knowledge possessed by either or both of the other two; that, for example, neither he nor the jury is aware of the contents of counsel's brief; that neither he nor counsel become aware of what jurors say to one another in the jury room while they are deliberating (except in the few cases when it becomes necessary for judge and counsel to learn the state of the voting in support of a returnable verdict); that neither jury nor counsel are made aware, generally speaking, of what a judge has recorded in his note book; and that the trial system works the better by reason of all those states of ignorance.

Jurors are not the poor cousins of the trial process

Throughout the trial, whenever the judge is addressing the jury, or speaking to counsel, witness, or court staff, with the jury present and in earshot, it is imperative that the judge, by his attitude and manner of speech, should treat the jury as intelligent and responsible men and women and as possessing an ordinary grasp of English; they should never be allowed to think, or to have grounds for suspecting, that they are regarded as a lesser breed within the law.

Situations in a trial when a judge is faced with the absolute necessity of abiding by that precept abound; I mention now two as illustrations. One of the primary responsibilities of a judge towards his jury is to give them directions on so much of the law as is to be applied to the case. Broadly speaking, there are two ways of discharging this responsibility; the judge may state the law in legal terms and in not many more words than is necessary to constitute the statement; or he may explain the relevant law and give them an understanding of the principles behind the law.

It should not be supposed that a judge would avoid reversal by an appeal court if he literally did no more than state the law in a compact series of legal propositions, without any discussion of the ways and means by which those propositions could be applied to the evidence. But there is the world of difference between simply stating the law and stating how, as stated, it can be applied, on the one hand, and stating the law, imparting to the jury a grasp of the principles on which the law is founded and the reasons for its operation, and explaining how, consistently with those principles and reasons, the law may be intelligently applied to the facts.

By the first method of exposition, the judge may do his duty under the law, but the jury are likely to receive the impression that they are being told, 'Yours not to reason why, yours but to obey'. By the second method of exposition, the jury are brought to an intelligent understanding, not just of a legal proposition, but of a principle, and their confidence in their own ability to perform the functions of finding the primary facts, and of applying the law to those findings, will be greatly strengthened.

The validity of the foregoing distinction and precept may in a measure be regarded as confirmed by the intelligence (which I can tender from my own experience) that juries who receive a direction that is little better than the mouthing of a formula, frequently return and ask for further directions on the law after they have been deliberating for a time, but juries who are taught to grasp a principle almost never do.

It may be also reported with confidence that juries can best be given a grasp of principle by illustrating its operation through a series of homely examples drawn from imagined facts outside the case before them; in this way, the principle is shown in action, and can be made to spring to life in their minds. The second example of a situation in which the jury are treated with respect in an important part of the trial, comes from those parts of the summing-up in which the judge is discussing the facts. In those circumstances, the jury is given the best understanding of its responsibility as finders of fact by presenting the factual issues so that they come to realize how their particular experience, knowledge of the world, discernment, understanding of mankind, or logic and reasoning (as the case may require), can be used to resolve them.

It is one thing to identify the issues, and pass them on to the jury without further comment or assistance. It is entirely another to show how the sort of experience and mental equipment that a jury can bring to the court can be used to arrive at a decision with confidence.

Giving the jury confidence in their ability and freeing them from the spectre of future doubt and remorse

It should be impressed on the jurors that after the evidence is complete, the addresses of counsel delivered, the summing-up given, and the jury's deliberations concluded, no persons in the world (including themselves in the future) will ever be in a better position to assess the validity of the verdict they are about to return than they are themselves. In particular, no person will ever have received, as they did, the material then before them or the assistance by then given to them appraising that material, and they will never have the same concentrated focus on the case as a whole as they then will have. It would be pointless, therefore, for them to have doubts or misgivings later about the justice of their verdict, or to allow the uninformed remarks of armchair critics to worry them. Observations to this effect by the judge will help to convince the jurors that he understands, as a human being, how their responsibilities are likely to weigh on them; they will be heartened and relieved by his assurances, which are obviously born of experience.

It may be of interest to append some general observations about the sort of language that should be used when addressing juries. It is of no small importance to arrive at a right decision on this topic.

Men and women who come for the first time to jury service are likely to bring with them a suspicion of the law and her ways; it is unnecessary to debate whether that suspicion is well- or ill-founded—it is there. It is danger-ously easy, when addressing juries, to use language that will be judged, through the barrier of suspicion, to be patronizing. It is just as easy, if the language used is too flowery, to create the impression that the speaker is showing off, or, if the language exhibits too pronounced a tendency to emulate basic English, to leave the jury with the belief that the speaker is resorting to baby-talk. If the speaker is too solemn, he finds it hard to retain the jury's attention, and may be regarded as pompous; if he has recourse too often to humour, he is likely to be regarded with the same distaste as the man who jokes at a funeral. If the speaker descends to slang too obviously he may well be regarded as undignified.

On the whole, the best style seems to be to adopt, as nearly as may be, the simplicity of the language of the man and woman in the street, relieved of its ungrammatical features, and given form and cogency by imparting rhythm and balance. What is said may be relieved by occasional humour—but not any humour. What seems to be wholly acceptable—and no attempt is here made to offer an explanation for this phenomenon—is the humour that is created by using a well-known cliché slightly out of its usual context, the whole being set about with a border of irony. Sarcasm, facetiousness, funny jokes, should all be avoided like the plague. Very occasionally a line or two of poetry will be received well, and will drive home a point; so also will one of the obscurer proverbs; but in each case, once is enough.

All these suggestions or admonitions should be regarded not as instruction in the art of oratory, but as offering means for communicating in such a way as to obviate any propensity on the part of the jury to find material for feeding their suspicion of the law, thus enabling them to appraise soundly and fairly what is being put to them.

JUDGE AS CONCILIATOR

In South Australia, a judge in a civil case is given statutory power to initiate a conciliation process if he is of opinion that a settlement may be achieved; if his move is unsuccessful, he is empowered to continue the hearing. In other jurisdictions, judges exercise similar powers, with or without statutory authority; where that authority is lacking, however, a judge may regard himself as disqualified by an attempted conciliation that fails.

The art of the conciliator draws on many of the judge's human faculties; he must show tact, discernment, sympathy, and imagination, and exercise to the full his skill in exposition and reasoning. The art is personal to the man, but there are certain goals to be sought, though not necessarily in the order in which they are now set forth.

(1) The conciliator must usually attempt to disengage the motives of the parties for embarking on, or continuing, the litigation from their beliefs in the intrinsic merits of their respective cases; those motives may vary markedly from the natural and ordinary desire of a person wronged to vindicate his rights. Once those motives are identified and rehearsed before the parties, the way is often open, by taking account of those motives, to work out a settlement.

(2) It will clear the air if the judge points out trenchantly and frankly the apparent strengths and weaknesses of the parties' cases at the stage then reached in the hearing. A judge knows, from experience at the bar and on the bench, that the parties have probably been told very much the same sort of thing by their own legal advisers, but have obstinately refused to accept what they have been told because they have been, and are, prompted by extraneous motives to continue. When the judge tells them the same sorts of things as their legal advisers have told them they face a moment of truth, and are likely to be moved to consider settlement.

(3) The judge may also instil a sense of reality, if he informs the parties what each may be expected to suffer if he loses. Again, the parties have probably been given the same information but have stubbornly pushed it aside.

(4) The judge will probably try to avoid, as far as possible, thinking aloud and being heard by the parties to be in the process of working out a proposal for settlement. It is much more effective, if it can be done, to have a proposal for settlement ready. The proposal should not be cut and dried, but contain within its structure a degree of flexibility so that it may be varied to accommodate points made in subsequent discussion. A take-it-or-leave-it attitude in the conciliator is likely to annoy the parties, but a willingness to be flexible, within reasonable limits, may allow either or both to save face on less important issues.

Because of the unique relationship of trust existing between bench and bar it is often possible, in a preliminary discussion with counsel held in the absence of the parties, to learn from them what they would, as professional advisers, jointly regard as a reasonable compromise. This information is capable of making a vital contribution to the foregoing proposal laid before the parties by the judge.

There are no principles of law that are capable of making a contribution to how the conciliator sets about his task. What he says, and his manner of saying it, is dictated by his ability to talk to and with people, without talking at them; his understanding of human character and temperament; and his empathy. The best conciliators display some of the most advanced social skills that are to be found in our community.

CONCLUSION

Before parting with the subject of this paper, I desire to emphasize again, that, though the precepts commended by this paper take effect in a legal setting, they are not legal rules or legal practices; they are suggestions for the exercise of social skills that may be thought apt to assist in the administration of the law, and that tend to promote results that are not only results according to law, but results that do right, or justice, in the widest sense, to all manner of men.

11
The Referee

J. J. THORNHILL

INTRODUCTION

In the world of the Ancient Greeks the Olympic Games were a deep religious cult. The Greeks could not divorce intellect from muscle—both were necessary parts of *arete*, the quality of a perfect man. Although the formal games of Ancient Greece were individual in nature, excavations have shown that there may have been some form of team games. During the demolition of an ancient wall in Athens in 1922, a sculptured column base was found which depicts a scene reminiscent of the modern game of football. Team games have long been a part of English sporting heritage and their place in the spectrum of sport is vital. Sport has always been an integral part of school curricula and children have been and still are encouraged to play games for the pleasure derived from them, the physical activity they afford the body, the skills which they develop.

This chapter will examine two different codes of ball game—Association Football and Rugby League Football. Both these games are played on a rectangular field between two teams. Each team has a half of the field of play and it is responsible for protecting the line at the rear of that half. Both codes are based on the principle of ball possession and progression to the other team's line. In these two games the competitive element is foremost and this is exemplified by writers on the games who frequently use the terms 'attacker' and 'defender'. Both codes involve games in which two teams of at least eleven players should have an equal and fair opportunity to obtain possession of the ball. A team in possession should have a reasonable chance of progressing to 'make an attack' on its opponents' line. However, the defending team should have an equitable chance of dispossessing the attacker. By nature each game has its individual skills and differing degrees of physical contact. Rugby League has a much higher level of physical interaction than Association Football.

These are all ingredients for a very tense situation, in which human emotions can become highly aroused. If we then add yet other ingredients peculiar to the professional game such as supporters, promotion and demotion, winning bonuses, sponsorship, directors, we now have a recipe for a very volatile situation. To ensure fair play, sets of rules have been defined, by which the participants are given an equal opportunity for possession and progression. In any contest played according to a set of rules, it has become necessary for there to be someone who can ensure that the game is played in accordance with that set of rules.

In both the modern games of Football and Rugby League, there is a single arbitrator of rule contravention. This person is called the Referee and it is his responsibility to ensure that the game in which he officiates is played in accordance with the set of rules. Each current code has a set of seventeen laws which include the duties, responsibilities and powers of these match arbitrators. As the two codes and their respective laws have developed over the years so the role of referee has changed since it was first thought necessary to have external match control.

REFEREE STRUCTURE

It is the ambition of every referee in both codes to officiate at England's national stadium, Wembley, in the final match of a cup competition. Both codes have competitions for the senior teams culminating in the final match played at Wembley. The honour of controlling this final match is given to only a few referees and the actual official is chosen from those referees on the lists of the senior leagues. These leagues are the Football League and the Rugby Football League. To reach these lists a referee must follow through a process of training and examination, grading and classification, practical field assessments and written reports.

A referee's promotion depends on his knowledge of the laws and his ability in the practical application of those laws in a match situation. His knowledge of the laws can be tested in a written examination, but his practical skill is assessed in two ways. Both codes use retired referees and officials to act as assessors. They attend matches and provide written reports on the referee's performance. Secondly, in most matches, also, each of the two competing clubs give the referee a mark.

Under both codes a referee is appointed to officiate in every match and in senior matches he is assisted by two colleagues—called linesmen in Football and touch judges in Rugby League. These assistants are usually less experienced, but nevertheless, in their own right, refereeing in less senior matches and aspiring equally to the cup final. In every referee's career development he must act as one of these assistants.

Association Football

In English Association Football, there are nearly 20 000 referees divided into three classes as shown in Figure 11.1. In this pyramidal structure, the senior league is the Football League. Beneath this there are a number of leagues called Contributory Leagues, which are organized regionally to serve those senior professional clubs which are not members of the Football League. Beneath these Contributory Leagues there are many senior local amateur leagues in each County Football Association called Feeder Leagues. All the other leagues are called Junior Leagues. Each of the leagues in this structure chooses its own referees independently of the Football Association and other leagues.

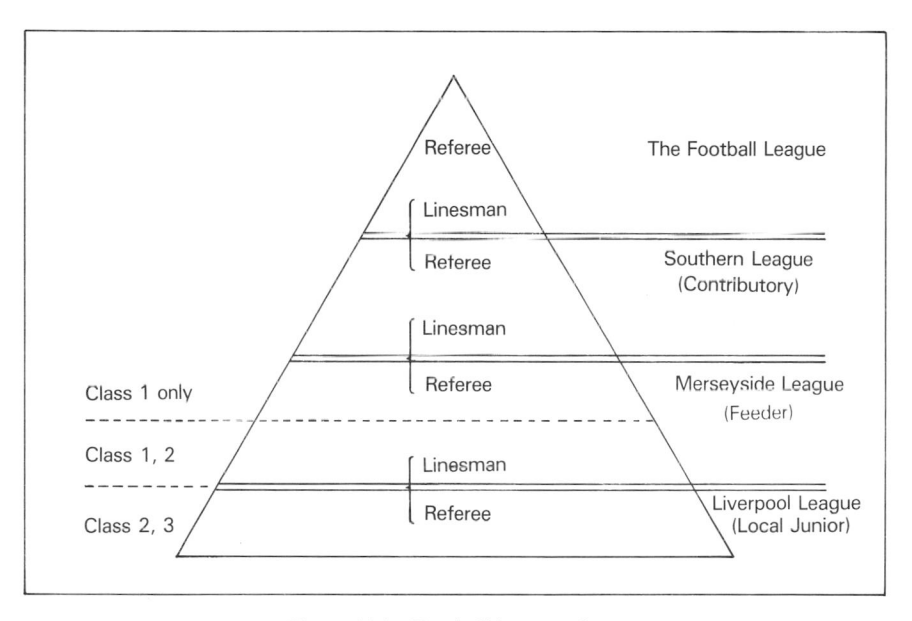

Figure 11.1 Football league referee

In the assessment as a Class 3 referee, most County Associations use short courses followed by an eyesight test and a written examination. After at least two years as a Class 3, promotion to Class 2 may be based on club marks or a practical field assessment made by a senior referee or assessor. In some associations it is based on club markings, written papers and practical field assessments. After at least another two years as a Class 2, a referee may apply for promotion. The basis for this promotion again varies. Most County Associations use the club markings as a filter to identify referees suitable for field assessment. In some associations club markings, written examination and field assessments are all used.

Once a referee has attained Class 1 status, his progress through the pyramidal structure of leagues is based on club markings and assessors' reports. These assessors are appointed by the contributory leagues and they assess linesmen on their lists who have achieved high marks as referees in their feeder league. A linesman may then be promoted to the referees list of his contributory league. After a year on this list, he is usually placed on the linesmen's list of the Football League and in the 1982–3 season this list contained 160 linesmen. The Football League arranges for one of its own assessors to watch each contributory league referee in at least two games. Any referee considered satisfactory will be invited for an interview at the end of the season. As a result of that interview, he may be promoted to the referees list of the Football League.

A referee appointed to the Football League list will cease to act as a linesman except in international and senior cup matches. In the 1982–3 season the referees' list contained 88 referees. In each season approximately 10% of the referees are replaced for one of two main reasons—they may have reached the retiral age of 48 or they may have received consistently poor markings. A referee is usually appointed to four matches in a five-week period. Each match will involve considerable travelling and the referee is paid suitable expenses in addition to his fee of £40. In each game he is assessed by a league assessor who sends a written report and marks to the league. The referee is sent a copy of the written report but not the marks. These assessors are recruited from retired referees and linesmen. The Football League decides who shall be included on its lists of referees and linesmen and is, in effect, the referee's employer. Each year every referee must pass a fitness test. From the Football League referees the Football Association may nominate up to seven for the International Panel.

Rugby League Football

In Rugby League the system is different in a number of ways. Firstly, there is only one controlling body in the professional game—the Rugby Football League, which administers the professional game and leagues. This body is also responsible for the testing, grading and promotion of referees. Secondly, the grading system is related to the structure of leagues and is based upon the referee's practical experience. There is also the British Amateur Rugby League Association (BARLA) which, at the time of writing, is considering its own grading system. An outline of the structure of Rugby League will explain the somewhat curious grading system. The Rugby Football League, established in 1895, administers the senior league—the Rugby Football League comprising mainly northern clubs and Fulham and Cardiff. The reserve or 'A' teams are formed into two regional leagues— Lancashire and Cumbria, and Yorkshire. There is also a national Colts League. BARLA controls eight regional amateur leagues and several other local amateur leagues. There are four grades of referee but no Grade 3 (see Figure 11.2).

When a person wishes to become a referee he usually joins a referees' society. The society will arrange for him to referee matches in under-age leagues. Dependent on his progress he may be given games in open age, local or regional amateur leagues. A referee between the ages of 16 and 35 may sit a written examination of 100 questions in an hour on the laws of the game set and marked by the Rugby League. If he passes this examination with at least 80% and is recommended by the amateur league in which he is officiating he

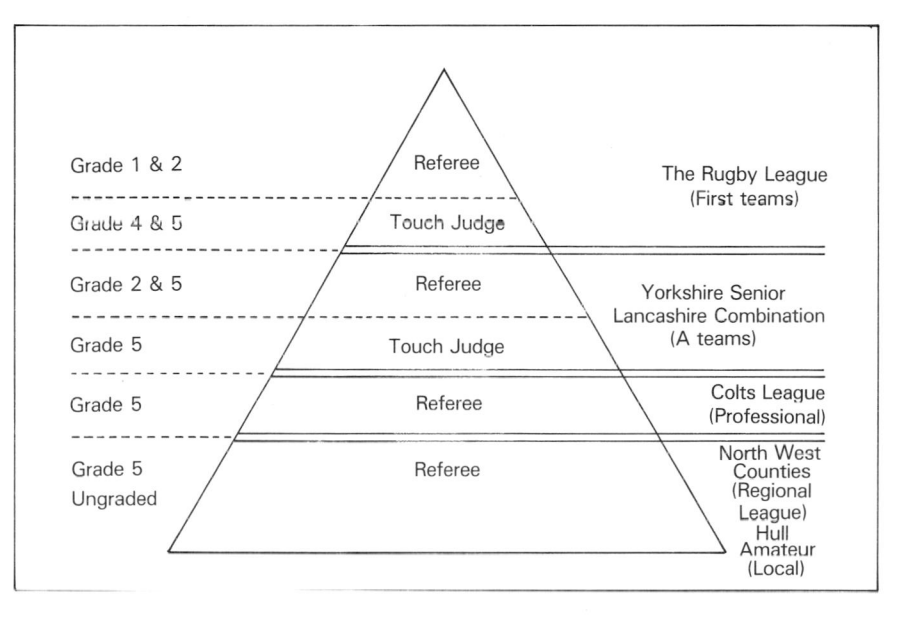

Figure 11.2   Rugby league referee

will be appointed as a Grade 5 referee. Then he will be given appointments as a touch judge in 'A' team matches and also one or two appointments as a referee in Colts matches. After at least six months, a Grade 5 can expect to be appointed as a touch judge in the senior Rugby League. During this time he will be refereeing in the senior amateur leagues and dependent on marks and advice he may be offered appointment as a referee in 'A' team matches. In these matches he will be assessed by the assessors who may then recommend his appointment to Grade 2. If a Grade 5 referee has not been promoted to Grade 2 by the time he has reached the age of 40 he will be regraded as a Grade 4. As a Grade 4, he will be given three matches in five weeks as a touch judge in the Rugby League. Three times a season each Grade 1 and 2 referee receives a written report from the assessors detailing his progress with advice and suggestions where appropriate. Every senior referee must undertake health screening each year and also a fitness assessment at least twice a season.

REFEREEING TASKS

The laws of each game indicate the duties and powers of the referees. It is the application of those duties and powers that make a good referee. In specific terms the job of a referee is to apply 17 laws formulated by others. In that sense he is more of a policeman than a legislator. But he is more than that even, for within the framework of the laws he has judiciary powers which allow him to impose sanctions and penalties. He has to give instant and correct decisions and adjudicate on a variety of different problems that arise in every game. Some of these problems may not have specific written solutions and the referee must solve them by using experience and commonsense based on a thorough knowledge of the laws. A referee can demonstrate his knowledge of the laws in quizzes and competitions, but his ability to interpret and apply them can only be shown in match situations. To referee effectively he has to gain the respect of players and to this end, physical fitness, mental alertness, man management and thorough knowledge of the laws are the ingredients.

A match is played for the players and the spectators, not for the referee. It is an art to officiate at a match in which two teams are striving to win. The referee's presence causes the participants to avoid rule violations. This presence must be unobtrusive, but strong enough to have that effect. A referee is constantly under assessment from players, team coaches and managers, club directors, assessors, fellow referees, spectators, press and himself. Each of these individuals use different criteria upon which to base the assessment. The factors influencing a referee's performance are many and varied. The role of a referee is a social one—in which he interacts with the players and his assistants, in a managerial, disciplinary, judiciary capacity—a very complex character. The components need to be finely tuned to ensure that the match is without conflict. A referee can actually create conflict in a number of ways: incompetence in laws and mechanics; inability to create rapport; dramatic or officious control; antagonism to players; indecision and slow reactions. A football or rugby match is a social event involving at least 25 people with one person in control. There has been considerable discussion on types of power and Weber (1947) distinguishes between power and authority, stating that power involves force or coercion. He specifies three types of authority: legal, charismatic and traditional. The referee by the nature of his office has legal authority bordering on power. He hopes that by experience and reputation he will gain charismatic authority, but he does not have traditional authority. Another relevant way of differentiating power is the structure advanced by French and Raven (1968). Their typology is based on the nature of the relationship between the power holder and the power recipient. There are five types of power: reward, coercive, legitimate, referent and expert. A referee can be said to have coercive and legitimate power—the power and legal authority of Weber. The exercise of his authority and powers requires the referee to perform certain tasks. We can classify the tasks of a referee under four headings, which though separate are interrelated with each other.

Physical

Both codes have games in which physical strength is important. They are based on skill and movement at speed. A referee must always be in close contact with the centre of action and this may require swift movement around the field of play. The two codes are different in this respect that in football the referee is physically active for much more of the match. The following comparative table shows the differences in the percentage time spent on specific activities.

Table 11.1   Percentage distributions of time

Activity	Football	Rugby
Standing	9	38
Walking	37	27
Jogging	33	20
Running	17	12
Utility	4	3

Mental

This is the cardinal task of the referee. As the laws show, his main duty is to ensure that the players comply with these laws. He has to make objective and subjective assessments on contraventions of the laws. Every match has a number of incidents to which a referee must react. This reaction may be to stop the game for a penalty or free kick, to talk to a player or players, to administer the official caution or dismissal, or to play on. Even though he allows play to continue he has had to make an assessment of an incident. The comparative table shows the frequency of types of incidents upon which the referee has to make an assessment in an average game.

Table 11.2   Distribution of incidents

Football		Rugby	
Fouls	34	Penalties	23
Advantages	12	Tackles	242
Corners	9	Scrums	25
Goalkicks	13	Tries	6
Throw-ins	12	Conversions	4
Goals	3	Goals	3
TOTAL	83	TOTAL	303
	secs		*secs*
Reaction every	65	Reaction every	16

Management

A referee manages a complex social event with emphasis placed on enjoyment, skill, entertainment, and winning. However, each match is a unique event with two opposing teams striving to win. This inherent opposition provides opportunity for aggression and conflict. A referee has to control this event in such a way that every participant can contribute and display his own personality and individual skill within the laws. In the fulfilment of this task the referee should gain the respect of the players, each of whom is an individual with his own personality. Studies have shown that a player is an intricate personality with all the common traits and an adequate supply of determination and aggression. The referee can by an appropriate approach to the management of this involved event prevent areas of conflict. He may need the wisdom of a Solomon to differentiate between transgressor and transgressed. He must be able to curb the over-enthusiasm of a player without impeding that player's natural skill and ability. Management of a match is a complex and difficult task.

Communication

In the management of a match, a referee has to communicate with the players and his colleagues to indicate his reaction to each incident. He must communicate displeasure at unfair play, indicate decisions and their strength. He uses the whistle to transmit these reactions. He may have to communicate verbally a state of warning to the player whether it is unofficial or official—called a caution—or eventually his ultimate power of dismissal. If he needs to use these ultimate powers written concise reports need to be made.

SPECIFIC SKILLS

Physical

The physical demands of both codes are high. A referee needs the abilities to walk, jog, run, sprint in any direction and where necessary to vary pace and intensity of the physical activity. A referee may need to sprint 50 metres and then decide upon a try or separate a scuffle. For this he needs to have good powers of recovery. The varying pitch and weather conditions will also affect his physical performance and he needs the skill to cope with such conditions as hard grounds, deep mud, heavy snow. In such unfavourable conditions a

Table 11.3   Referee heart rate (b.p.m.)

Subject	1	2	3	4
First half	120	144	126	130
Second half	120	120	132	132

referee needs the stamina to maintain his physical capacities for the whole of the match. Studies have also shown that referees are subjected to intense psychological pressure, in addition to these physical pressures. This results in high average heart rates during the match situation. Table 11.3 shows the results of a study by the author which measured the referee's heart rate immediately following each period of play.

In a later study a detailed record was made of heart beats during the game, each match incident and referee activity. From this analysis it was possible to derive a Game Intensity Factor for each minute of the match. Figure 11.3 is a plot of the heart rate against the derived GIF for each game unit in the first half of a match. There is a 0·91 correlation between the two plots and the peaks

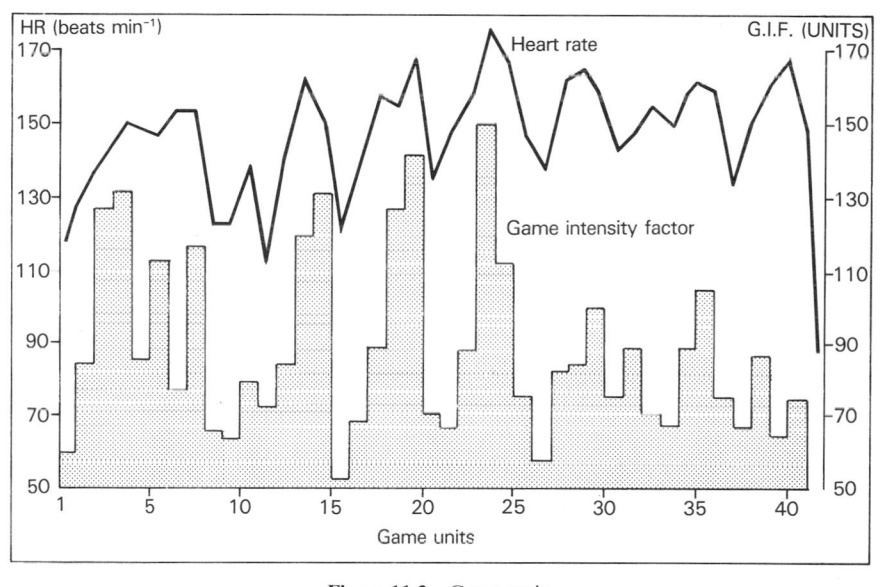

Figure 11.3   Game units

and troughs are related. In Game Unit 15, the heart rate is 150, the GIF is 130. In this unit the referee sprinted 60 metres to adjudicate a points scoring situation. Unit 24 shows a heart rate of 172 and a GIF of 150. In the three minutes prior to this unit the referee had been standing still—but he had to control three difficult scrums in a position where the visiting team was within five metres of the home team's try scoring line. At the end of the unit, the visiting team broke through and scored the try. A psychological pressure creating a high heart rate.

Mental

Both codes differentiate between intentional and accidental breaches of the laws. A referee needs to be acutely aware at every incident so that he can recognize any intent in the player's action. He must be able to interpret the laws in any given situation. Although the laws are comparatively explicit they do not cover every incident, and a referee has to be able to categorize the incident before he can impose the appropriate penalty. He needs to understand the concept and purpose of the game and the part that is played by 'the spirit of the law'. Law 12 in football specifies that a goalkeeper may take only four steps before he has to release the ball for it to be played by another player. This law was so framed to ensure that goalkeepers bring the ball back into general play as quickly as possible. That is the 'spirit' of the law. A referee should only penalize when the goalkeeper is transgressing both the letter and spirit of the law. There can be considerable variation in intensity of game and incident conflict. A good referee can adjust his attitude and the strength of his control. The semi-final of a cup match between two aggressive teams will present a harder test of a referee's powers of observation and control than a match between two clubs in the middle of the league table. The former has more potential for quick flare-ups and high conflict. In addition to the pressures from the match, the laws and the players, there are the added pressures from working with his two assistants. He is conducting a continuous co-operative dialogue with them and if there is conflict here, from a personality clash or promotion competition, that dialogue may be jeopardized.

Management

Everybody who has a management role must have some power or authority. In the French and Raven typology, a referee's power is coercive rather than reward. The player, who is the recipient, recognizes that the referee has the ability to distribute punishments, but not to give meaningful rewards. The effect of the punishment may be to give a resultant reward—e.g. a goal or two points for a goal. The referee does not reward good behaviour or skill, he punishes breaches of law. He also has legitimate power—which is akin to the implication of the Weber distinction between power and authority. Under this power, the recipient, the player, acknowledges the right of the holder, the referee, to influence him and he has an obligation to follow the directions of the holder. Referent and expert power do not apply to the referee in his situation. A referee is at the same time an authority and in authority. The referee's ability to use his power and authority with confidence and control is central to a successful performance. He must show that he is the authority on the laws by his perfect application of the specific laws and sensible interpretation of those areas where there is room for interpretation. Another skill in management is to use commonsense to temper justice with mercy. Each individual player must be approached in a manner which will not alienate co-operation from that player. A positive referee will identify the factors creating tension and conflict and effect punishment relative to the intensity and the unique personalities of the participants in any incident.

Communication

In any social activity such as a match in which there are over 25 participants, various levels and types of communication take place. A referee has the whistle and with it he can communicate his feelings—a sharp strident blast must surely indicate the seriousness of the offence. The hand signals a referee employs must be clear and precise. The rugby code specifies exactly how the signals should be given. He must have the ability to talk to, with or at players as incidents may require. He must also be able to modulate and control his voice. A fiery confrontation can often be de-fused with a touch of humour and firmness. The referee's control is more positive if it is based on his legitimate power rather than his coercive power. A rapport developed with the players or at least some of them can help to enforce this type of power. He can encourage the player's confidence in himself and respect by his manner, voice, facial expressions, reactions. He cannot hope to communicate if he himself loses his temper, whatever the provocation.

SKILL DEVELOPMENT

The skills required to make a good referee are many and varied and it is often said that a good manager or referee is born not made. Nevertheless, much training and instruction can be given to assist potential senior referees to develop the skills applicable to their particular needs.

Physical

Training patterns and schedules have been developed by the Football and Rugby Leagues for their senior officials. The Referees' Association has prepared a Manual for Referees which includes sections on physical training. These schedules include strength, flexibility, mobility and stamina exercises. Circuit training is advised and sprint and stamina work is also included as is the use of weight training. Advice about diet and health is also given. Both codes require the senior referees to undergo a physical fitness test each season.

The football referee test

Referees are required to sprint a distance of 25 metres within 5 seconds and to repeat this eight times with a 25-second rest period after each 25-metre run.
  Total test time = 4 minutes (5 seconds + 25 seconds) × 8.
  A 15-minute recovery/rest period is allowed before the second test.
  The number of metres run on level ground by each referee in the course of 12 minutes will be recorded but anything less than 2300 metres will be considered a failure. Candidates must run for the full 12 minutes and *not* stop when reaching the minimum distance which applies irrespective of age.

The Rugby League referee test

The referee undergoes the test twice in a season. Data is obtained for the following variables:

> age; height; body weight; percentage body fat; body type (somatotype); lung function; haematology (blood structure); cardio-respiratory indices before, during and after exhaustive exercise on a treadmill; motor performance via a power jump test and an agility run; psychological profiles.

> A report is produced which shows the referee's level of fitness based upon these data items. A referee will not be offered appointment if his weight is outside desired limits or if he has an unsatisfactory fitness report.

Emphasis has also been placed upon the relationship of health to fitness and the Rugby Football League requires its referees to undergo an electro-cardiogram stress test under the control of a cardiac specialist. As a result of this three referees have been removed from the list since 1979. Once a referee is declared healthy then he may attempt his fitness test again.

Mental

Referees are firstly encouraged to regularly read and understand the laws of the game. It is difficult to train a referee in recognition of intent, though he can develop his own skill by watching other referees. He must be prepared to analyse every match that he controls. The Football Association has developed a self-analysis sheet with 47 questions which any referee can use. In his analysis, he should examine areas of conflict in a match. If confrontation has arisen in the scrums, a referee must examine his own control over this tense situation. He can ask himself if he applied the laws correctly at every scrum. He can spend time listening to other referees, players, managers, coaches and others concerned with the game. The Football Association has also produced four training films. These show real match incidents and can be used by referee societies and County Football Associations.

Management

An attribute of the good manager is a calm and prepared approach to his task. Routines for kit preparation, travel, attitudes to club officials should be developed. If a referee has to travel a distance then he should set out in plenty of time to allow for car or train delays. Arrival less than an hour prior to the commencement of the match will create an added stress for the referee and upset the natural balance required. On the field a referee must learn to appreciate the individual characteristics of each player. Recognition of how a player reacts to a pass from the wing can assist in assessment of his character.

The facial expressions of players will often belie their feelings and intentions. Knowledge of laws can be tested in quizzes but a referee should learn to succinctly interpret the laws by setting up different situations for himself. Attendance at coaching classes, referees' society meetings, quizzes and matches can only increase ability to control and manage. A match is a micro-reflection of the world at large. Consideration of the referee's own life and occupation will help to develop an understanding of the factors creating tension and conflict. A referee's reaction to a supervisor who thrusts aside a job upon which he has lavished time and energy should give some indication of how a player feels when fouled after an attacking 60-metre run with the ball. It is really only the time scale that is different.

Communication

Practice at the approved signals should be done in front of a mirror or with a colleague. Society meetings often have sessions in which referees can learn to administer cautions and dismissals in a reasonably calm atmosphere. Some societies have augmented their training with practical demonstration teams. These teams can present very realistic situations, building in as many stress factors as possible. The realism of these actors can be very strong. Humour can be an asset as can a strong voice, but each referee must recognize his own ability to use such aspects of his personality. In the rugby code a continual verbal rapport is a central component in a controlled game. With help from senior colleagues standard letters for reporting a variety of incidents can be prepared. Prompt response to all communications whether on or off the field will impress and create respect.

REFEREEING STRATEGIES

The purpose of training and education programmes is to improve the practical application of a referee's skills.

Physical

Movement around the field should be used to best advantage. Sprinting where necessary, using correct breathing techniques will bring an official into close contact with a decision-making situation. After a fast 50-metre sprint a referee will be better able to adjudicate on a try or a corner/goalkick if he has controlled his breathing and is not completely out of breath. Positive anticipation of the play by moving during dead-ball time will place a referee in good positions. At set pieces it is wise to stand in slightly different places. In the rugby code at a play-the-ball a referee must stand five yards from the ball on the defensive side. If he always stands to the right of the action, players will become aware of this and take advantage. Variation can assist the referee to see incidents as they occur. Quick movement to an area of friction can often reduce it, and players will be less likely to dissent from a decision if the referee is in close proximity when he makes it. The referee's pattern of movement should give a side-on view to an incident involving two players. To see the slight push in the back when two players are tackling for the ball requires that side-on wide angle viewpoint. If the referee is assisted by two colleagues he must also keep them well in view so that he may promptly react to any signal they give.

Mental

It is paramount that every decision is given swiftly and confidently. Sharp, clear signals will demonstrate the referee's knowledge of the laws and aid his authority. In recognizing the distinction between those technical offences which are breaches of the laws, such as a foul throw-in, and those which break down the pattern and flow of play, such as continued use of off-side, a referee will show to players his appreciation of the game. Deliberate offences against an opponent must always be recognized and penalized relative to their intensity. During the whole of the game, a positive referee will maintain a consistent interpretation of the laws. One of the most serious threats to a referee's authority is dissent. A player can show dissent by word or action, such as throwing the ball away or waving the fists. Every such action should always be promptly dealt with—a stern word can often suffice.

Management

In the senior matches, there is a management team of three officials. The referee can encourage co-operation from his assistants by treating them as assistants and not juniors. Precise instructions must be clearly given to them and the use of a smile can often smooth a tense situation prior to a clash between the two top clubs. The first impression players, spectators and other participants in this social event have of a referee is his appearance and entry to the field of play. If he looks smart and walks or runs with confidence he has overcome the first hurdle. Attitude to players will bring the respect required. Each participant is an individual and a referee must temper his approach to each individual. Observation of the players from the time of reaching the ground and during the early part of the match will help identify their personalities and attitudes. The field of play is often considered a battlefield, and in times of stress and crisis individuals can exhibit traits of personality not seen in non-conflict situations. The eyes are an indicator of mood and passion and observation of the players' eyes can act as a good barometer of tension that is building up. When a player is fouled by a deliberate trip from behind or an elbow tackle, a quick word of understanding may moderate the offender's reaction and subsequent behaviour. In one aspect of management the codes differ. In rugby a referee must give a clear indication of his decision and if required an explanation. In football, it is felt that explanations can give occasion for dissent. This is perhaps because the structure of the game of football is such that the referee is far more remote from the players than his counterpart in rugby.

Communication

The repertoire of a referee for communication is full. Use of the whistle to indicate authority is vital but it must be remembered that it is a game of sport and not a musical event in which a referee is participating. Signals, modulation of the pitch of the voice, facial expression, eyes can all indicate mood. In the rugby code the tackle and scrum situations are potential areas of law contravention with nearly fifteen offences that can be committed at each. Gentle encouragement will assist in the correct functioning of these situations. If there is a tendency towards friction then the stern, sharp, loud command comes as a sudden surprise—and a controlling influence. Although the players may be without self-control, a referee must never lose his control, no matter how much provocation there may be. Communication through temper can never be productive in match situations. A player who is willing to talk should be encouraged and a rapport can be developed such that later in the match that player may help to cool and control tension in other players. Talking to, not at, a player, by looking at him, after he has been fouled can help alleviate his feelings. Reports must be precise with only, but all, the relevant details. A referee must remember that he is the eyes of any committee which has to act upon that report. In cases of player misconduct, the referee is effectively the prosecutor.

CONCLUSION

Although the job of a referee has been subdivided into four separate modes, it must be clear that there is considerable overlap. In the management of a match a referee must use all his skills of communication, his knowledge and interpretation of law, his physical ability to move around the field to be in positive positions. The good referee in either code is able to manage the tense situations which occur in the arena. In a match he is an important participant, whose power and authority well used can contribute to the enjoyment of the game for participants and spectators alike. His presence should be felt rather than seen and it is preferable if he uses legitimate power and authority.

The tasks of a referee in either code are very wide ranging and complex. The skills required to perform those tasks are similarly disparate and the efforts to train and educate future referees are developing all the time. Officiating is an art, which can be learnt by a number of people. Just as every player is a unique individual, so each referee is unique. Amongst the senior referees of both codes are a variety of different characters and personalities. Previous studies by the author have shown that there is no specific personality profile for senior referees of either code. It must be remembered that although the referees in both codes are paid a fee for their services, it is nevertheless, a part-time activity. When a man puts on the referee's black or red shirt—his badge of office—he also puts on the mantle of supervisor, manager, policeman, judge, adviser. In this role, he is attempting to discharge different types of duties. In his own employment he may not experience any of those types of duties. The senior referees come from a very wide range of employments. There are manual workers: carpenters, bricklayers; semi-skilled: machinists, lorry drivers; self-employed: butchers, off-licence owners; professional: teachers, lecturers; middle-managers: salesmen and many others. Refereeing breaks down the normal socio-economic barriers and all referees meet together on an equal plane to discuss mutual problems. Whether a person is a worker or manager, he is able to cull valuable assistance from his employment. In many ways the workers make more efficient referees as they have an empathy with the hard-working players whom they are controlling. There are some ex-players amongst the senior referees, but they are a small minority compared to the total of ex-players.

The tasks of a referee have been defined and the appropriate skills explained. No one referee can have an equal abundance of all those skills—indeed one of the skills is to recognize shortcomings and to take advantage of positive points. Beside specific skills a referee needs certain qualities.

At all times a referee must be himself, he cannot imitate another.
Quick reactions will ensure good split-second decisions.
Confidence to take decisive action promptly is vital.
Calmness at all times will see referees through difficult situations.
Firmness tempered with warmth and a smile can often have a disarming effect on players.
Fairness and consistency will win respect.
Integrity is an important quality in any arbiter.
Judgement must be fine, fair, firm, and precise.
Leadership will make for a co-operative management team and co-operation from the players.

These qualities if used positively will enhance a referee's performance and improve his chance of promotion. It is often a thankless task but can be a very rewarding and enjoyable one. The perfect referee is not yet born. Every referee should, however, strive for perfection. The gamesmanship era means that decision making is now more difficult. He must not only get the normal decisions correct, but also distinguish the fake from the real. A good referee is like a conductor orchestrating the smooth flow of the match. To withstand the broad compass of pressures the referee must use all his qualities, abilities, training and experience. In this way, the words of the Earl of Warwick will not be echoed.

> *I have perhaps some shallow spirit of judgement;*
> *but in these nice sharp quillets of the law*
> *good faith, I am no wiser than a daw.*

Henry VI Part I

Bibliography

Boot, R. L., Cowling, A. G. and Stanworth, M. J. K. (1977). *Behavioural Sciences for Managers.* (London: Edward Arnold)

Bunn, J. W. (1950). *The Art of Officiating.* (New York: Prentice Hall)

Fabian, A. H. and Green, G. (1960). *Association Football.* (London: Caxton)

French, J. R. P. and Raven, B. (1968). *The Bases of Social Power in Group Dynamics.* (London: Harper and Row)

Godwin, T. and Rhys, C. (1981). *The Guinness Book of Rugby Facts.* (London: Guinness)

Hall, R. H. (1972). *Organizations: Structure and Process.* (New York: Prentice Hall)

Taylor, J. (1977). *Soccer Refereeing.* (London: Faber and Faber)

Thornhill, J. J., Quinn, G. and White, J. *The Effect of Stress and Physical Activity on Heart Rate, Blood Pressure and Rate Pressure Product in Rugby League Referees.* (Unpublished)

Thornhill, J. (1981). Developmental techniques for assessment of the psycho-physiological demands of match officiating with reference to Rugby Football League senior referees. *Proceedings Sport and Science*, **1**, 50–7

Weber, M. (1947). *Theory of Social and Economic Organization.* (New York: The Free Press)

12
The Professional Negotiator: Roles, Resources and the Run of the Cards

R. J. LOVERIDGE

INTRODUCTION

Negotiating and bargaining are daily activities for everybody. We are constantly testing our needs and objectives against those of other people. Through exchanges of information, suggestion, proposition and instruction we discover what are feasible objectives within a given situation and the price we should have to pay to achieve them. These transactions are more often conducted on an inter-personal basis, than in an inter-organizational context. Often, the needs we attempt to satisfy in our daily negotiations are those of self-respect, recognition, affection and personal security—rather than cash: the price that is often exacted is in similarly non-pecuniary terms.

The market for management literature has recently been flooded with guides to negotiating techniques. This flood is in itself an interesting phenomenon ranging from the more conceptual work of Strauss (1978) to pragmatic guides to tactics such as those of Atkinson (1975). From a concern with logic of systems and with technical planning, managers are apparently turning to the development of personal influence in conditions of operational uncertainty and contested authority. How far can such guidance be found in the techniques and tactics of professional negotiators?

This paper sets out to examine behavioural strategies pursued in such formal negotiating arenas as the diplomatic summit meeting, the court-room or the smoke-filled rooms in which collective bargaining is supposedly played out. It aims to relate the skills and techniques utilized by full-time negotiators to the context and outcomes of the transaction including the type and form of contract or agreement emerging from the process and flow of their personal interaction with others.

THE MANAGERIAL ROLE

In carrying out their day-to-day responsibilities, managers start from a basis of formal authority derived from their position in an organizational hierarchy. But experience shows that their decisions are rarely made on the basis of this narrow ledge of legitimacy. A Canadian observer has suggested that executives spend around 40% of their time in creating and maintaining purely personal relationships and much of the rest of their time in monitoring and disseminating information in a purely informal manner (Mintzberg, 1975). It is through these relationships that managers generate a personal credibility which extends beyond that acquired by rank or qualification. The information they seek will indicate more accurately than any computer output could what will be the likely outcomes of their decisions within the political arena of the office or factory floor.

Other observers have described the manager's role as that of constantly meeting the needs of those holding a stake in maintaining his or her situation (Strauss, 1978). Whatever the technically feasible outcomes of managerial decisions, without a minimum degree of commitment from colleagues, sub-ordinates, and the concentric web of others affected by their actions, managers can have no certainty that decisions will be carried out in the manner required. Even the technical expert whose influence within organizations depends on formal qualification has to spend time on generating personal credibility with others. It might be possible to classify organizational roles by the degree to which they are based on the performance of technically definable tasks. Clearly such a classification would tend to relate to one's position in the organizational hierarchy; roles generally become more programmed at the point of task implementation and more diffuse and open-ended in matters of strategic moment. By and large the designers of organizations appear to standardize and to routinize as much of their internal workings as possible. In maintaining external relationships however, managers often have to rely on the judgement and skills of the professional negotiator.

THE NEGOTIATORS' ROLE

Professional negotiators exist on the boundaries of organizations—they are, in this sense, marginal people. At the same time they are usually crucial to the creation and maintenance of the system of authority they represent. This is so whether the negotiator is a sales representative, a company buyer, an inter-national diplomat or a lawyer arguing a client's case before a judge. In each case they are ultimately responsible to a principal or client and normally to a wider collective interest. Through their actions negotiators consciously or unconsciously claim a field of jurisdiction for their principals. Their successes and failures reinforce or diminish the political influence of their parent organization *vis-à-vis* other organizations with whom they deal.

Perhaps for this reason, like other boundary keepers, their personal identity is usually disguised behind a uniform. In the extreme cases like that of barrister's periwig and gown, it is accompanied by a great deal of formal ritual. Even when apparently informal, the negotiator's behaviour is surrounded by a decorum that allows the negotiator to act out a well-recognized stereotype. In this way the risks which might come through allowing personal foibles to stand between the content of the negotiator's argument and its impact on the receiver are minimized.

Their dress and mannerisms may in fact positively identify them as negotiators. This is particularly true of lawyers and stockbrokers, for instance. Generally these are not employees of their principals but self-employed agents. Such go-betweens are of great importance where the field of negotiation is defined in terms of a socially endorsed network of informed buyers and sellers such as the law courts and financial and commodity exchanges. Even where the role is defined as internal to an organization it is often filled by someone who knows the external terrain. Until recently it was quite usual to find ex-shop-stewards occupying senior industrial relations posts in management, for example. Like salesmen, industrial relations managers often appear as emissaries bearing news of the battle. In the time-honoured tradition, their neck is often forfeit for bad tidings.

In most circumstances encounters with adversaries are scheduled and regulated by agendas that are agreed well in advance. The skills of the negotiator therefore become most evident in his or her use of the rules of the game during the course of a negotiation and in the preparation for each new episode in a continuing and recognized ritual. In other words the defence of bureaucratic order is itself heavily bureaucratized. Of course this may be equally true of the role of line manager. He or she may work in a stable environment and be responsible for an even and predictable work flow. On the other hand, day-to-day operations may be such as to present a range of problems and opportunities for decision making, any one of which can test the basis for his or her authority. But the line manager produces rules as a by-product of producing widgets.

The modes of day-to-day social control adopted by line managers tend to be shaped by the technical contingencies surrounding the production of goods and services and by the immediacy of feedback derived from attempts to implement operational decisions. Of course the outcomes of formal agreements have to have regard for the conditions in which they are to be implemented but the part played by the professional negotiator in the production of an agreement is often far removed and socially isolated from that of the line manager. The procedural and relational links between the arenas in which contracts are composed and concluded and the situations in which they are to be implemented may sometimes be close and direct but are more likely to be far removed and ambivalent.

The social isolation of the professional negotiator can therefore make it difficult for him or her to relate the terms and conditions that he or she achieves in the negotiating chamber to the conditions under which control has eventually to be exercised and rules implemented—whether this be in the workplace or in the streets. For example, a reason given by British industrialists for eschewing courts of law in the enforcement of business contracts, or by British trade unionists for not using arbitrators in the manner of their American counterparts, is the lack of understanding shown by the British judiciary for the practical implications of their pronouncements. For the negotiator it may appear that the lack of understanding emanates from his client's unwillingness to accept the logic of the situation, a logic which can only be seen from his or her professional standpoint. Professional negotiators are likely to see their remoteness and lack of involvement in the outcomes as a positive asset in making an objective assessment of the negotiating terrain (see for example the case of *John Bland and Co.* v. *National Dock Labour Board*, 1969, described in Jackson 1975, 53–9).

Yet there is obviously a danger that success in a negotiation might be counted in terms of the contest itself rather than in the light of its long-term effect on the constituents of the negotiator. Not only does the professional's self-identity within his or her role often tend to breed a desire for personal victory but so does the context in which it is acted out. Reportage of both collective bargaining and corporate financing by the mass-media tends to present a scenario reminiscent of a medieval joust in which, inevitably, there is a Black Knight and a White Champion.

The adversarial system of administering justice in British courts acts in a similar way to advance jurisprudence through a series of situationally related victories rather than through the considered interpretation of a civil or criminal code in the manner of Continental Europe. The immediate arena in which the negotiator performs clearly affects his or her style and strategies. Bearing in mind that the contractual outcomes can be presented as a system of governance or control over the parties to the agreement, we may perhaps ask how far formal negotiations as 'happenings' can take on a significance that is quite dysfunctional to the day-to-day operations of organizations that are party to them?

Three dimensions of bargaining

If this displacement of roles and purpose is to be avoided the relationship of the negotiator to the client or constituent must be managed at least as carefully as relationships within groups and organizations. This intra-organizational, or 'back-home' bargaining as Walton and McKersie (1965) describe it, has to be geared to the sequential development of relationships in negotiations with external groups. It involves more than the simple communication of information about how things are going 'at the front'. Expectations of the outcomes have to be shaped and maintained within realistic levels. Negotiating agendas have to be amended to take in new areas of possible advantage or to give way on those that are no longer defensible or attainable. Much of the skill of the negotiator is to be seen in his or her ability to maintain a position along all of these differing dimensions of interaction with others. For the sake of simplicity these might be combined in just three—a vertical one, and a latitudinal and a longitudinal one.

The vertical dimension describes the handling of communications with the negotiators' principals or constituents: it is shaped by the essential bridging nature of the role and extends to the development of the negotiators' authority within the negotiating chamber. It is highly dependent upon the ability to communicate within and across differing levels of social status and social meaning. In formal settings it not only involves a personal ability to interpret events to an audience in the most effective terms but also to set up and to maintain a negotiating team. The existence of a stable group of specialist negotiators allows a division of labour and enables the process of interaction during the course of negotiations to be orchestrated and conducted in relation to the contingencies thrown up during the process itself. To be most effective the base of the negotiating team must rest in the heart of the parent organization from which it can gather all necessary resources when required by the front man or conductor. He or she thus obtains immediate access to strategic data and to authority to commit the full resources of the client when required to test the nature of the relationship with the other party.

The latitudinal dimension describes the knowledge of the terrain held by the negotiator and his or her ability to move across it in a creative manner: the composition of a package of offers and counter-offers which is attractive enough to obtain a settlement at the lowest cost to one's principal can entail an intimate knowledge of the other party's potential needs and the use of some imagination in developing new ways of meeting them, or indeed in creating them. In British industrial relations, as in British marketing, attempts to draft imaginative agendas have tended to go unrewarded. This may be due to the basic conservatism of British buyers and sellers. More fundamentally perhaps it could be attributed to the failure to build trust between the parties.

Even the most conservative representatives have to negotiate around the separate dimensions of price and how it is to be paid, the length of the contract period, the timing, location and manner of delivery, the quality, quantity and packaging of the goods or services to be exchanged, etc. Yet reaching an unintended impasse can be the result of an insufficient appreciation of the room for manoeuvre provided by these dimensions and the opportunities for opening up the mind of the other party to new possibilities for exchange. This apparent tunnel vision may be the outcome of the socio-emotional impacts of the negotiating process itself. Contest or conflict may reduce the ability of the contestants to perceive anything other than victory defined in the most narrow terms (Swingle, 1967).

While being capable of generating emotion in others, one of the essential attitudes of a professional negotiator is the ability to remain completely dispassionate in his or her own approach to negotiating goals and outcomes. That is not to say that emotional displays are not important. A display of controlled anger in the intimacy of the negotiating chamber may be far less costly to one's client or principal than withdrawal from the prevailing contract. An expression of dedication to a principle can be used to give the other party an early warning of a possible confrontation if he or she presses a forthcoming item on the agenda. The use of emotive language is also important in gaining a commitment from one's principals, especially if they are, as in many instances of collective or organizational negotiations, also one's constituents (that is to say that they have some voice in the reappointment of the negotiator). But, like a surgeon operating on a human body, the professional negotiator has to be aware that his or her assessment of the situation, the agenda and its context, and the stance and strategy to be adopted within that situation, must be carefully insulated from his or her personal hopes, aspirations and value commitments. To do other- wise might very well betray the very outcomes to which their services are dedicated.

The third, longitudinal, dimension of negotiation describes the flow and process of activities from preparation of case to agreement on final outcomes. This includes a knowledge of or 'feel for' the sequential development of interpersonal roles and relationships during the course of the shared activity. It is this interactive process that provides the focus for most texts on negotiating techniques, particularly the manipulation of others' feelings and opinions through the process of what Walton and McKersie (1965) describe as 'attitudinal structuring'.

Much of the conceptual framework used in the teaching and analysis of negotiating techniques derives from applications of social psychology to group dynamics. In particular the work of consistency theorists such as Sherif and Sherif (1953); Newcomb (1956) and Festinger (1962). The sequential development of group roles is seen as being directed towards one of two outcomes. These are usually described as being on one hand 'problem solu- tions' or 'integrative' goals and on the other 'issue resolutions' or 'distributive' goals. The stances appropriate to each required outcome are seen to be either co-operative or contestual and the strategies and styles adopted by the parties are seen to derive from one of these two dichotomous perceptual and attitudinal stances.

While most of the recent literature has been based on empirical observation or the involvement of the authors in professional marketing, labour relations and other specialist negotiation roles, the complexity of movement required in mixed-mode bargaining escapes such simple dichotomies as those generally used in prescriptive texts. As these pieces of jargon suggest, movement between the polar modal types is regarded as being either conciliatory or provocative. This movement is seen to take place along all three dimensions. Conciliatory gestures have to be pursued in the language of pragmatism and technical application rather than that of principle and value commitments. At the same time both the willingness and the imagination to develop a wide range of items and to tap an even wider range of stake-holder perspectives must be present or able to be developed. It is to this latter aspect that most social psychologists have addressed themselves in prescribing appropriate behavioural mannerisms and styles of verbal and non-verbal communication (for example Walton and McKersie, 1965; Dutton and Walton, 1966).

One of the problems involved in translating this literature into operational technique is the assumption that the negotiator is operating in a totally congruent and directly complementary manner along each dimension of social interaction. In practice transactions along the vertical or authority dimension may be taking place with totally disparate agendas and almost always arrayed according to different role configurations and relationships. Strauss (1978) has criticized interactionists such as Goffman (1959) for ignoring these aspects of the wider social contexts in his analysis of 'impression management'.

Perhaps it may also be said with some justification that the timing and importance of technical knowledge and information in relation to the substantive agenda is discounted somewhat by all varieties of social scientist in their anxiety to draw attention to the importance of behavioural process and self-perceived status. The manner which social and technical, or task-related knowledge and skills combine in the presentation of argument and 'impression management' remains relatively unclassified and, perhaps, unclassifiable. One might perhaps compare attempts to use such classificatory schema for training purposes with the use of the *Highway Code* in learning to drive (Egan, 1975). Ultimately, the use of clutch, steering and brake has to be combined with an ability to 'read the road' in a manner that can only be learnt by long practice. In the case of the professional negotiations, each of these separate activities is socially and cognitively disparate. Learning to let the clutch out is somewhat simpler!

A second problem involved in the interpretation of the literature is that movement from a confrontational stance and the accompanying mode of operations, to a co-operative or even consensual one is usually assumed to be unidirectional, along all dimensions. In practice, the commitments of all the parties to any transaction have to be worked out in a manner that often requires the application of negative sanctions even when the party applying the punishment wishes for a collaborative outcome. The relationships that shape the stance of the negotiator and, more importantly, of the principal, are not only those involved in the present interaction but also those that will create a suitable context for the future operation of the agreement or contract emerging from it.

NEGOTIATORS' MODES AS A FUNCTION OF OUTPUT

Logically one might expect these positions and strategies adopted by negotiators to be related in some part at least to their perception of the obligations
being undertaken within a transaction. In particular the (vertical) involvement of their principals (clients or constituents) might be seen to relate to
the scope of the agenda (latitude allowed) and the length of time over which
the agreement is to operate (longitudinally maintained relationships with
the other party). Transactionist economics describe two main kinds of outcomes from negotiation. The first is spot dealing and the second is contingency contracting: both terms are derived from the analysis of Williamson
(1975).

Dealing involves a sequence of discrete exchanges at an agreed price, time
and quantity in which the procedural obligations of the parties are transitory
and involve neither side in ongoing responsibilities toward the other (legally
defined in the phrase 'let buyer beware'). Contracting, by contrast, results in
an agreement to supply goods or services over a period of time at stated
intervals and to given quantities and qualities subject only to changes brought
about by specified contingencies. It implies a degree of interdependency
between the parties that is not acknowledged in spot transactions. The benefits
to be derived from joining the respective futures of the parties for a given
period of time are seen to be greater than the risks involved in the increased
interdependency for either party. On the other hand either their trust in each
other is not sufficient for them to rely on an informal and personal contract
or, more likely in the modern world, their statutory obligations cause them
to insure against exigencies that may bring their contract to an end or lead
them to modify it. Generally the exchange is a relatively narrow one cir-
cumscribed by conditions that allow either side to withdraw in a variety of
circumstances.

Rationally it might appear unwise to undertake spot dealing unless the
market conditions are what are described by economists as perfect. This is a
situation where both parties have to accept a going rate because the market is
too competitive and the flow of information too open for either side to gain an
advantage by misrepresentation or the manipulation of sentiments. Only in
these circumstances can both buyer and seller be assured that the exchange is
taking place at the best available price.

In practice spot markets tend to grow up wherever there is a possibility of
very large short-term gains to be made from anticipated shifts in trading
conditions, matched by short-term losses by those too faint-hearted to take
part in what is usually a fairly frenetic process. Profits are generally made from
speculation on futures, anticipated crops of sugar cane or cocoa beans or in
the movement of scarce commodities, such as oil, between remote markets.
Paradoxically the existence of an established spot market is wholly dependent
upon the trust that each buyer has in each seller ultimately to deliver a parcel

of oil, minerals or financial stocks at the agreed price at some agreed future date. Underlying the apparent hysterical interaction between members of exchange markets are long-existing social ties between dealers. The ground rules for the operating of spot markets, whether taking place between stall holders in Petticoat Lane or between brokers operating around the corner in Throgmorton Street, are carefully policed and enforced by the participants.

Since rules cannot be used opportunistically the manipulation of sentiments in the intercourse of spot dealing is focused upon shaping the other's confidence in the future state of the market. This may be done remotely through, for example, the buying and selling of blocks of stocks or more directly through the timing of one's exits or entrances to the market (i.e. the price level at which one starts or stops bidding) or through the direct expression of confidence or doubt in daily social interaction with rivals. The time available for decision making within the actual transaction is minimal, especially when the spot market takes the form of an auction. Yet opportunism is a key element so that pattern recognition and timing become important characteristics of a spot dealer.

Clearly patterns and sequences can be discerned in the operation of spot markets and the rational management of portfolios has brought considerable routinization to their operations. They remain, however, obdurately capricious and subject to the effects of 'animal spirits' as the late John Maynard Keynes described the basis of Stock Exchange dealings. The explanation might be that when the short-term risks are so high, and when the ego-involvement of the dealers is so great, most of them will prefer their own judgement above that of a probability curve. So long as a market remains based on sequential spot bargaining it may therefore be considered inherently unstable.

The formal elements in spot dealing, both substantive and procedural, are relatively simple. In spite of the esotericism attributed to the process by the use of dealers' jargon both the knowledge of the product specification and the techniques of buying and selling employed are much less complex than the management of even the simplest drop forge or screw factory. In the multi-faceted situations created by the division of labour within manufacture and administration, relationships and roles become segmented. Personal trust between the actors gives way to an instrumental commitment to formal contract. At the same time the costs of opportunism are magnified by the interdependency of roles created by the work flow of manufacturing organizations.

Long-term relationships such as these tend to become routinized by repetition and habit even when the desire for efficiency is not present. Opportunism, outside agreed limits, may indeed be costly beyond the price of a single failure since it destroys the established expectations that one partner has of the other. For all of these reasons organizations tend to protect their relationship with others in a manner that anticipates the effects of all major contingencies. Such contingency contracts cover most areas of intra-organizational and inter-organizational activity and are the stuff of life for professional negotiators.

The most significant feature of long-term contracts is that by their very implementation they become modes of governance. Even when the procedural aspects of an agreement are relatively simple the substantive exchange affects the work flow within the involved organizations over a stipulated period of time. From this effect there flows a need for consistency within all aspects of the agreement and with other agreements that impact upon similar areas of internal administration. This is of course especially so when buying and selling labour services or when fixing the conditions upon which they are bought and sold through collective bargaining. This has led some observers to describe the process as the creation and maintenance of 'a system of rules' (Dunlop, 1958).

Consistency with client needs is therefore a major constraint on the actions of a negotiator. As mentioned earlier differing perceptions of those needs are a continuing problem to be handled by the client and his or her professional representative and are therefore weaknesses to be exploited by their rivals. Indeed a problem for the negotiator may be to decide how far to take advantage of the weakness of his or her opponent's bargaining position without destroying the confidence of the rival's principals in their representative's ability. In the longer term the misrepresentation or opportunistic use of market or legalistic contingencies can damage the established expectations built up over a period between the client and his or her trading partner. For example 'pulling a smart deal' through the sale of a deficient component to a final assembler may destroy a long-established relationship between a supplier and customer. Yet the use of power in adversarial bargaining demands just such a manipulation of the other's view of risky elements in his or her client's operating environment.

The timing of a renegotiation of a contract can be as crucial in contract bargaining as it is in spot dealing. Just as a spot dealer times his or her movements in and out of the market by reference to past and anticipated trends in prices so contractors may attempt to utilize contingency clauses in modifying or terminating contracts. When negotiating with unions in a tight labour market it may be very difficult for an employer to substitute out of the use of services provided by a group of employees crucial to the manufacture of products in high demand. If that group can precipitate negotiations, for example through disagreeing a piece-rate payment, then they can take immediate advantage of their market strength. If, on the other hand, they await the termination of existing wage agreement to submit their claim the employer may have been able to so arrange his or her stocks of finished goods in relation to distribution requirements as to be able to take a long strike without serious loss of profit. Needless to say both tactics are typical of the style of negotiation adopted in the motor vehicle labour relations over the last 30 years. It does not take a weight of evidence to suggest that such instrumental approaches to contractual obligation have fed and reinforced the lack of trust already existing between the parties in their day-to-day work environment.

THE RESOURCES AVAILABLE TO THE NEGOTIATOR

Rationally speaking, the ultimate objective of a transaction is to place an exchange value on a defined parcel of goods or services delivered at a particular time and place and discounted against foregone opportunities for other transactions known to be open to the parties. The power of one party relative to the other stems ultimately from their relative dependency on the outcomes of the deal. This is often expressed in the form of a simple equation expressing what an economist would describe as the cross-elasticities of supply and demand (Chamberlain, 1951). It appears with great regularity in text-books and its calculation is part of the recommended preparation for formal negotiations. It is doubtful whether the construction of such equations has great utility when considered in isolation from the process of influence generation contained within the negotiating process itself. Each of the three dimensions along which negotiating activity proceeds to a final outcome has a varying effect on a dynamic balance of power existing between the parties.

Power testing tactics are therefore quite usual at various stages of a negotiating relationship along one or all dimensions. At the extreme these involve a temporary withdrawal from an agreement or a refusal to renew a culminating contract. Evidently this involves a risk for both parties and not only acts as a test of the market situation of each principal, but also of the latters' commitment to their respective representatives in the negotiating arena. Consequently boundaries are rarely tested in an explicit manner in the early stages of a negotiation unless the transaction has been defined as a confrontation by one or both parties. For example, the party who considers him or herself to be the stronger in one area of the transaction may seek to constrain the width of the agenda in order to reduce the potential area of interdependency. He or she may 'go over the head' of the other representative in order to test his or her authority to deploy resources. More generally influence is generated through relational interactions of an opportunistic nature in which the timing and style of presentation are at least as important as substantive content. Examples now constitute an armoury of gambits and ploys designed to elicit information, commitment or mere compliance from the other party. (See, for example, Walton and McKersie, 1965 *op. cit.*; Atkinson, 1975; Winkler, 1981.)

By and large the opportunistic use of market position is not as evident in contract negotiation as the strategic use of procedures. Contract negotiation not only produces rules but, as described earlier, is played within a highly bureaucratized, and often ritualized, setting. Legal opportunism is, of course, the normal mode of operating in law courts but it is also the most common form of negotiating in everyday work roles. Experienced negotiators not only act within the rules but make creative use of them. Grieving against the action of the rival principal or disputing his or her use of the agreement is commonly used in a strategic manner to increase the jurisdiction and status of the aggrieved party. The best-known example is, of course, the widespread increase in status gained for their role by shop stewards in the British manufacturing industry through the expression of work place grievance during the 1950s in spite of the limited bases of their formal recognition by employers. It is quite normal, however, to find contractual terms being disputed in all kinds of organizational situations by superordinate members as well as by junior employees simply in order to advance their own status and authority. A similar selective use of the rules of procedure during the course of a negotiation for new or renewed contracts is usually attempted by experienced negotiators.

The limits to the use of opportunism are presented by the relative market or constitutional strength of the parties in the long term. The stronger party will assert their superior power to bring about a change in the structure of the bargaining arena. For example, several multi-national corporations have blamed the opportunistic use made of market and procedural advantages by British shop stewards for their withdrawal of capital investment from this country (*Sunday Times*, April 1981). In practice the radical restructuring of a relationship is usually seen to involve such risks for both parties that each recognizes a limit to the opportunistic use of power long before it is necessary to demonstrate its costs so explicitly.

However, for these limits to be realized, both parties must be in the position to assess the relative risks involved in their stratagems. This entails not only a statement of intent to take action but a demonstration that the intention will be carried out. The realization of one's intentions is best obtained either when the other party has previous examples with which to compare the present threat or has sufficient information upon which to judge the likelihood of its fulfilment.

Misrepresentation of one's position is commonplace in negotiation not so much through the use of deliberate falsehoods as through ambiguity in the expression of intent and the use of rhetoric in argument. In most cases the intention is not usually deliberately to deceive but simply to keep one's options open to the last possible moment in order to close on a better deal in the light of a constantly changing trading environment. The result of this prevarication is often that the parties stumble into power-testing confrontations as the only means of obtaining true information on their mutually shared market situations.

NORMATIVE BOUNDARIES TO CONFLICT

The transactionist school of economists such as Williamson (1975) suggests that the risks of buying and selling in this way cause parties eventually to establish long-term non-contractual relationships. Other political economists such as Olson (1965) suggest that alliances are formed because of a realization of the existence of 'common goods' between the two parties: that is the existence of interests best served by a common approach to the problem. The dependency of each upon the other becomes such that they are both monopoly suppliers of a service to the other. Knowing the limits to the sanctions that one can apply to the other helps both parties to determine a scale of rewards and punishments within those limits. The longevity of the relationship tends to bring about a sensitivity to the other's behaviour which makes it increasingly unlikely that market or legal deterrents will be deployed. Thus personal rather than collective behaviour becomes strategic to a successful long-term relationship.

Even before this degree of interdependency is achieved, however, a successful negotiator is often being adjudged by his or her ability to improve the rewards derived from a transaction by his or her constituents without directly involving them in the contest during its course. The boundaries to the arena are set by the social and organizational division between spectators and gladiators. Once the audiences are asked to join the contest the negotiator has usually either suffered a defeat or is in danger of doing so. In either case he or she is in danger of losing control of the audience to some former non-combatant brought into the contest through the mobilization of the spectators.

The same may be said of the opportunistic use of alliances or coalitions with other principals or the representatives of other interests in the transaction. Like Machiavelli's Prince, the negotiator has to assess his or her dependency on potential allies with the same assiduousness that is applied to the assessment of competitors in the fray (usually allies are competitors in some other sphere of activity anyway). The introduction of allies into the process of negotiation is best timed to relate to agenda items allowing the greatest coincidence of interest with the principal but also their greatest dependency on their host. Should the outcomes of the negotiation be such as to increase the dependency of the principal on an erstwhile ally, then a short-term gain from the official opposition can turn into a pyrrhic victory. The rise of some of Britain's most successful merchant banks can be seen as related to their 'loyalty' to successful bidders in take-over contests. Their clients have subsequently fallen victim to their former allies in the aftermath of conflict when effective control within their companies has passed to the appointees of the bank.

The direct involvement of members of the organization on a collective basis in the manner of, say, a shop steward, is clearly different from the strategic engagement of organizational resources through normal bureaucratic channels in the manner of, say, a company salesman or even the regional officer of the trade union. In Olson's (1965) terms organizational members may not even be aware of the existence of goods held in common with fellow employees or, more probably, may not be prepared to bear the personal costs of the collective action required to obtain or to defend such common possessions. Thus the presentation of the negotiation as a defence or advancement of the personal status of each constituent may be part of an educative process initiated and sustained by the negotiator as a means to creating a collective identity among his or her constituents. Only by creating such a unity of purpose can the bargainer set objectives which have a reasonable chance of fulfilling the expressed needs of all constituents. More importantly perhaps, only by creating a unity of action among constituents can the same bargainer create a monopoly control over the supply of goods or services required in order to be able to bargain about their price with the would-be consumer.

The shop steward's role is evidently the best example of this educative process outside the more esoteric fields of international diplomacy and armed revolution. In more mundane contests employers often seek to mobilize worker commitment behind export sales drives, or nowadays, in simply keeping the firm open, by appeals to group solidarity and cohesion around a common cause. Whatever the ultimate objective the language used is the rhetoric of patriotism or group loyalty in the face of a hypothesized contest or a threat stemming from outside the group or of grievance stemming from some morally just cause (Sherif, 1967). Arguments referring to unfairness and inequity rank with those of chauvinism in their ability to generate, as well as to derive from, feelings of moral indignation (Hyman and Brough, 1975). The response they invoke is an emotional one.

This emotion can become the lubricant of social engineering just as logic can provide its cutting edge. Emotion helps formerly conforming individuals to accept arguments for radical action that might have otherwise been considered 'irrational' (Smelser, 1962). Grievances originating from specific issues or substantive objectives focused upon narrow concerns can be raised to the broader terrain of the group or collective purpose through the invocation of social values or, more prosaically, through their expression in monetary values. Either or both are means to providing the negotiator with the solidarity of support and flexibility of brief required for him or her to obtain the greatest bargaining leverage. Even in the most routinized negotiation the portrayal of the transaction as a contest rather than as a collaboration with the other party is more likely to invoke a group response from constituents and therefore to facilitate the negotiator's use of his or her bargaining power. Images of Sir Galahad or St Joan are more likely to prevail over those of Albert Schweitzer or Florence Nightingale in the symbolism of the successful negotiator!

At the same time the generation of emotion through the use of principled argument may lead to changes in the normative context of negotiation and as suggested above, lead to the displacement, and possible replacement of the negotiator (perhaps through burning at the stake!). There is little danger and often a great deal to be gained by engaging an audience of constituents in a little mass singing or the shouting of slogans: even the employment of cheer leaders may be allowed. On balance the more distant the audience involvement, the more effective their occasional expression of support for the performer. Ratification of the outcomes during the culminating stages of bargaining sequences may be necessary in order to sustain the support of constituents and stake owners outside one's own organization. Their wishes will have been anticipated by an experienced negotiator, so that the process should be no more than an endorsement of the strategy being pursued.

The normative limits to conflict—and to audience involvement—are not only maintained but reinforced in the tactics employed by negotiators. Yet we are faced with a good deal of evidence from mythology, history and contemporary experience that negotiators from different institutional contexts regard their arenas in quite a different way. For example, the need for French envoys to international negotiations to return to their principals at every new agenda item, is often contrasted with the autonomy and apparent informality of the British while the openness of American styles of negotiating behaviour contrasts with the expressionless giving and receiving of information by Japanese and Russian representatives. This remains true even when the short-term role of envoy is transformed into that of permanent delegate to the United Nations Organization or the European Community Directorate. (For more rigorous evidence see Harnett and Cummings, 1980.)

Clearly the manner in which negotiators operate is affected both by their cultural context as well as by their own personalities insofar as these affect the style and stance adopted within the negotiating arena. The boundaries to this arena or to audience involvement vary immensely across different types of negotiation, different institutional and industrial contexts and different countries. Evidently much depends upon the nature of the negotiator's role within the prevailing structure of governance and the manner in which he or she has formally to justify his or her strategies and positions. The more stable the bureaucratic structure within which negotiations take place, and the more closed-end and long-term the agreements that emerge, the more tightly one might expect the limits to audience involvement to be drawn and the less room for emotional rhetoric as a vehicle for their involvement.

GRIEVANCE AND GRIEVANCE HANDLING

One of the characteristics of the leadership models presented by social psychologists is that line managers are usually seen to have a choice of style ranging from the 'instructional' use of formal authority to the 'participative', in much the same way as bargaining theorists see negotiators as moving from

distributive to integrative modes (Tannenbaum and Schmidt, 1958). In practice it might appear that industrial managers spend much of their time
arbitrating and conciliating between other parties and in the handling of
grievances generated by one individual or group of subordinates against
another. In situations of social change aggrieved groups become more numerous as statuses change and occupations and departments are threatened.
Much can be done to avoid grievances by tracing the manner in which
decisions are made and engaging stake owners in problem defining exercises
rather than instructional directives (Walton, 1969). But grievances will continue to occur because people's moods, aspirations and fantasies are more
fleeting and complex than any organizational structure so far designed by
managers or by their would-be advisers in academe.

By its very nature spontaneous grieving expresses frustration and an
inability on the part of the grievant to alleviate a source of threat or hurt. It
usually contains elements of relative deprivation and unfairness. This is
particularly so if the issue is seen as central to the grievant's view of his or
her self-image or personally held values. If nothing is done to alleviate the
distress felt by the grievant over a long period then subsequent events might,
according to consistency theorists at least, become realigned by the grievant to
a newly acquired, oppositional, frame of reference (Festinger, 1954).

Grievance handling, whether performed badly or well, thus becomes an
important educational technique—perhaps the most important educational
technique available to line management (or for that matter the diplomat,
salesman or lawyer). If performed well it will reinforce a 'moral' commitment
to the existing framework of governance or more specifically of the employee
to his or her management. If performed badly it will reinforce the existing
sense of injustice and, ultimately, of alienation from prevailing structures of
authority.

Grievance processing often engages all three dimensions of bargaining.
Latitudinally it involves moving from a narrow agenda focused only upon the
incident that triggered the grievance to a broader consideration of the context
in which the grievance arose. Walton (1969) and other students of conflict
advance the notion that structural contradictions are endemic to complex
social situations. Grievances are no more than fragmented evidence of an
underlying cycle of conflict and occur when the cycle surfaces at a level which
triggers emotive outbursts among organizational participants. Therefore the
longitudinal process of grievance processing must move from an immediate
concern with the narrow substance of the incident to an exploration and
handling of its socio-emotional significance.

Putting these dimensions together in the manner illustrated below provides
the would-be grievance processor with a sequence of objectives to be adopted
at each stage of the negotiation. It indicates the nature and width of agenda to
be adopted and the style and context within which the transaction might be
taking place if it is to have greatest effect on the grievant. Its use as a

heuristic device may be further expanded by applying it to the management of organizational changes. By reversing the likely flow of events the innovator can attempt to anticipate the responses and likely sources of opposition to any proposed restructuring of relationships before they actually occur and attempt to handle each individually and separately before the event.

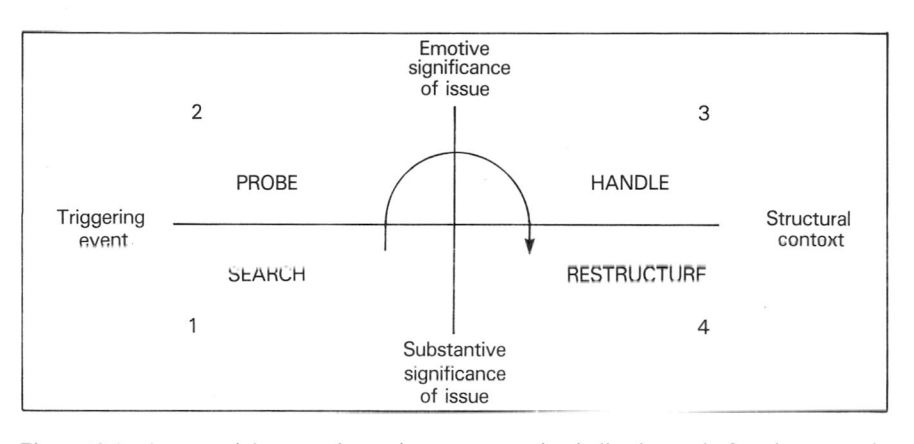

Figure 12.1 A sequential approach to grievance processing indicating main functions at each stage of negotiation

Clearly the most important choices have to be made in regard to the third quadrant — namely how to 'handle' a grievance. As was indicated earlier in this chapter, most grievances have what might be described as 'spontaneous' elements and 'calculative' elements. The former occur out of the individual's sense of loss, threat and frustration, the latter in the use of the conflictful incident to advance his or her strategic importance and control in the market or workplace. The opportunistic use of grievance ultimately can only be controlled by bringing it within the confines of a routinized and consistent usage of procedures. This implies the even-handed application of sanctions to unauthorized activity in an overt and neutral manner. At the same time sensitivity to the ego-related needs of the other party must in the modern world go beyond a concern for temporary effective rewards received and given in interpersonal transactions. Indeed disjunctures existing between the style adopted in personal encounters and the status of the parties in a wider market or organizational arena may often serve to increase frustration, grievance and the ultimate alienation of the subordinate party in such encounters *vide* the feminist movement!

TRANSACTING NORMS

Contracts which serve to reinforce rather than reduce sources of risk in the normal trading environment of most organizations can generally be taken to be against the long-term best interests of both parties however great the short-term advantages to be gained by one or other. Piece-work wage systems, for example, are often blamed for much of the short-term opportunism in work-place bargaining mentioned above. The constant renegotiation of price to meet prevailing conditions of production enables the development of a mode of spot dealing that feeds off the contingencies in a long-term relationship. The possibility of short-term gain for employees derives not from wide swings in commodity markets but from the opportunistic use of the medium-term dependency of the employer on their services and the ambiguity of the rules surrounding the operation of piece-work schemes (Brown, 1972).

More widely the incremental nature of decision making in the United Kingdom has been associated with a preference for open-ended commitments often based on ambiguous precedent or custom and practice. Domestically the English mode of bargaining is described as pragmatic but abroad it is more generally described as perfidious and opportunistic. Historically based on the assumption of a trust existing between closed communities of 'gentlemen' it once ensured the ultimate dominance of the largest land-owners within the well-understood order of a feudal system (Perkin, 1969). To acknowledge dominance in a written contract would have entailed loss of face for the subordinate party and would have precipitated a confrontation. In an island community conflict was avoided by surrounding socially divisive contra-dictions with a certain ambiguity in meaning, perhaps best represented in the catholicism of the Church of England or in its modern political equivalent, the SDP–Liberal Alliance!

More to the point the use of open-ended informality first in a mercantile and later in an industrial setting served two purposes. Firstly it appeared to avoid the overt imposition of control of one party, the employer, over the other—often a sub-contracted tradesman. Secondly it enabled what British industrialists still refer to as 'flexibility' in their arrangements, particularly with suppliers of components and services. Unfortunately this euphemism only applies when the buyer is in a dominant market or legal position. Once the situation is reversed, as it was in employment relationships during the period of prolonged economic growth following the last war, then the 'open-endedness' of the arrangement is an invitation to opportunism on the part of the formerly subordinate party. This could often take place with little recognition of the contextual contingencies that might eventually force a restructuring of the employment relationship.

By contrast the contractual framework of business transactions in the United States has always been relatively overt and became increasingly so in the years of massive immigration and economic growth that followed the Civil War (Maine, 1886; Larson, 1977). Not only did minority groups such as trade unions seek to ensure their status by legal means but throughout the nineteenth century Government legislated against cartels and monopolies in a manner that ensured the continuation of independent contracting—and the need to seek professional guidance through the body of corporate law created in this way. Grievances and disputes within contracts came to be registered systematically and to form the basis for the renewal of contracts. Arbitration in disputes of rights became normal so that even when there had been no resort to the courts the necessity for recording and presenting argument clearly and logically in terms of legal precedent became central to the role of negotiator. In many areas of industrial relations and business negotiation it is now accepted practice only to employ lawyers (Beal and Wickersham, 1959).

In countries such as Germany and Japan the movement from feudal militarism in government to a centralized corporate state was accomplished in a manner that reinforced an existing status hierarchy within their respective societies. More importantly the deference for authority and moral adherence to a civil code of conduct displayed by members of these societies is such that in many areas of civil and commercial activity relational bargaining proceeds with little attempt to test its normative limits (Barrington Moore, 1978; Dore, 1973). Perhaps the most ritualized demonstrations of market strength are those that take place regularly in Japanese labour relations. Each spring union members parade with banners and sashes in support of their wage claim— with their company's consent.

By contrast to this ritualized activity, spontaneous protest in later developing countries is often violent and expresses a more fundamental frustration than is to be found in the more instrumental withdrawal of labour practised in Anglo-Saxon countries. The deaths of demonstrators during protests over the building of the new Tokyo airport brought no demand for the Japanese equivalent to a 'Home Office enquiry': the violent ejection of steel workers from Ruhr mills at the time of their closure contrasts with the queues for redundancy payments at the time of the British Steel closures. Much of this emotion stems from the value-oriented nature of conflict in countries with a long tradition of centrally concentrated authority. While the economist sees such a concentration of power as bringing greater efficiency, the social psychologist points to the greater likelihood of alienation from the objectives of the state or from company leadership experienced by citizens and workers.

The history of conflict resolution and the modes of grievance handling adopted by politicians and managers also varies from one state to another and has contributed to an ideology within each country which is more or less divisive in its effects on communal solidarity. Grievances are more likely to be articulated as part of the regular mode of social negotiation when the cognitive model of the transaction shared by citizens is that of a long-term contract between parties of roughly equal strength rather than one where one party can 'call the shots' by moving in and out of the market at his or her own choosing. Where, as in the United States, the rights of both parties are underwritten by the constitution and where a tradition of 'countervailing power' has been followed by legislatures, this model of their world is perhaps more likely to be held by professional negotiators (Galbraith, 1952).

Institutionalized systems of this kind provide a basis for conflict that can be handled within recognized limits without involving all constituents all of the time. Where, because of habitually open-ended modes of bargaining adopted by negotiators, those limits are not clear and when even the intentions and purposes of the parties remain ill-defined, then the 'flexibility' of movement provided by the system can simply reproduce an ongoing opportunism in the strategies of negotiators. In this case either so much time is taken in handling strategic grievances as to detract from any other objectives held within the system or any one of these latter grievances can regularly engage everyone's attention. This can be particularly disturbing if, as in Britain, the style of open-ended informality adopted by negotiators is related to an abhorrence of overt conflict reflected in most areas of normative behaviour.

By contrast social systems in which constituents' orientation to negotiation is based on a normative commitment to moral authority and in which control is frequently centralized and remote there is often little facility or opportunity for the expression of grievance. There was, for example, no explicit grievance procedure in the National Health Service or Civil Service prior to the 1970s: like the industrial relations system in Germany, collective relations at plant level in these sectors of employment were based on an assumed unity of purpose between employer and the representatives of collective labour. One of the difficulties in coping with radical social change in such unitary structures of governance is that negotiators' styles become so geared to the drawn-out discussion of long-term problems and objectives that they are ill-equipped to deal with personal grievances. They often appear excessively insensitive in dealing with them and naive in responding to the emotional protest that can follow from their initial blunders (Loveridge, 1971).

DISCUSSION AND CONCLUSIONS

The role of the professional negotiator is socially and organizationally both a marginal and an insulated one. Yet it is crucial both for his or her client as for the other parties involved that an awareness of the long-term implications of an agreement should be maintained at all stages of the negotiating process. This is difficult because of the emotional involvement and identity of negotiators with the process and outcomes of the transaction and the manner in which it is treated as a test of strength and ability by others, most particularly by their clients or constituents.

Opportunism is practised in a variety of interpersonal and interorganizational stratagems making use of cues, signals and sanctions across a range of media. The skills of a professional negotiator are therefore normally seen to be more judgemental than simply computational. In judging the timing and form of an offer or acceptance in terms of the mood and disposition of the other negotiator or of his or her constituents, the skilful negotiator is seen to be able to bring about a settlement on terms significantly better than those expected by his or her constituents.

However, in the context of an industrial organization it may be more valuable for his or her principals that the outcomes of the negotiation should be predictable and that the idiosyncratic sequence of bids and offers should be directed towards this end rather than that of short-term gains. In this case some knowledge of the likely difficulties in carrying out the substantive and procedural elements of an agreement may be desirable in its negotiation. By and large the longer the term over which the contract is to operate and the wider its substantive coverage or latitude, the greater the technical knowledge required of the negotiator.

On the other hand the more strategically central the issue for one or both parties the more likely the principal will wish to be directly involved with its negotiation and vice versa. In either case the skills of the negotiator may be displayed in negotiating along the vertical dimension of intra-organizational authority that joins his or her role to that of the client or constituents. In the long-run his or her authority and autonomy becomes strengthened not so much by successes in *ad hoc* transactions as in the durability of the agreements that are produced. The more strategically important the contract for the operations of the client organization the more all of its activities will be enhanced by the predictable terms upon which it is able to operate in this core activity. It is likely therefore that to be successful the negotiator will have to attempt to move the negotiating strategy of his or her client away from a sequence of spot deals based upon the opportunistic use of claims or grievances in the key areas of organizational activity. Contingency contracting within understood norms of sanctioning behaviour will therefore be more likely to emerge in areas of strategic importance for the operations of client organizations.

In this paper it has been pointed out that such stable patterns of negotiation have been better accomplished in some institutional contexts than in others. The systematic and consistent manner in which grievance-handling is carried out in the best American practice seems to offer much greater prospects of organizational stability and adaptability than either the open-ended ambivalence present in much of British business life or the potentially repressive unitary regimes of later developing countries. Given the nature and level of individual aspirations in modern industrial societies it seems to this author that a system of governance that is not geared to the handling of individual grievance is unlikely to remain viable in the context of an achieving society. On the other hand if the outcomes of their actions are not fully known to actors with a grievance the results of collective conflict within a highly interdependent social system may be equally self-negating.

Even so, the emotion displayed by constituents in all areas of what economists insist on regarding as a purely rationally calculated activity belies the suggestion that bargaining resources are only used opportunistically.

Strikes are undertaken, contracts are withdrawn, deliveries are delayed, on points of 'principle' involving perceived inequities, untruths or simple retribution against the other party. Fear and insecurity of status are as present in most audience responses as greed and hedonism. Weakness rather than strength can drive either the negotiators or their constituents to acts of violence against each other. The boundaries to conflict are therefore better seen to derive from the respect and dignity offered by one party to the other in the daily management of organizational activity.

On the other hand formal agreements create and legitimate a hierarchical order. Persuading the weaker party that it is necessary for him or her to accept a subordinate status and to engage in relational bargaining from this position, however 'rational' it might appear, may be quite difficult. The role of the professional negotiator may often be that of educator, with all of the moral responsibility that that role involves for the incumbent. Through his or her handling of the scope and timing of negotiations and the recognition and status earned by the parties, professional negotiators play a vital role in maintaining the fabric of industry and society.

References

Atkinson, G. G. M. (1975). *The Effective Negotiator*. (London: Quest Research Publications)

Beal, E. F. and Wickersham, E. D. (1959). *The Practice of Collective Bargaining*. (Homewood, Illinois: Irwin) (1967 edition)

Brown, W. (1972). A consideration of custom and practice. *Br. J. Indust. Relat.*, **10** (1), 42–61

Chamberlain, N. W. (1951). *Collective Bargaining*. (New York: McGraw Hill)

Dore, R. (1973). *British Factory—Japanese Factory: the Origins of National Diversity in Industrial Relations*. (London: Allen and Unwin)

Dunlop, J. T. (1958). *Industrial Relations Systems*. (New York: Holt Rinehart and Winston)

Dutton, J. E. and Walton, R. E. (1966). Interdepartmental conflict and co-operation: two contrasting studies. *Hum. Org.*, **25**, 207–20

Egan, W. (1975). Towards a theory of action. *Personnel Rev.*, **4** (4), 5–23

Festinger, L. (1954). A theory of social comparison process. *Hum. Relat.*, **7** (2), 117–40

Festinger, L. (1962). Cognitive dissonance. *Sci. Am.*, **207**, 93–106

Galbraith, J. R. (1952). *American Capitalism: the Concept of Countervailing Power*. (London: Penguin) (1963 edition)

Goffman, E. (1959). *The Presentation of Self in Everyday Life*. (New York: Anchor)

Harnett, D. L. and Cummings, L. L. (1980). *Bargaining Behaviour: an International Study*. (Houston: Dame Publications)

House, R. J. and Baetze, M. L. (1979). Leadership: some empirical generalizations and new research directions. In B. M. Staw *Research in Organizational Behaviour*, pp. 341–423. (New York: JAI Press)

Hyman, R. and Brough, I. (1975). *Social Values and Industrial Relations—a Study of Fairness and Inequality*. (Oxford: Blackwell)

Jackson, D. (1975). *Unfair Dismissal: How and Why the Law Works*, pp. 53–9. (Cambridge: Cambridge University Press)

Larson, M. D. (1977). *The Rise of Professionalism—a Sociological Analysis*. (Berkeley: University of California)

Loveridge, R. (1971). *Collective Bargaining by National Employees in the United Kingdom*. (Ann Arbor: University of Michigan Institute of Labor and Industrial Relations)

Machiavelli, N. (1532). *The Prince.* (New York: Mentor) (1955 edition)

Maine, H. S. (1886). *Popular Government.* (London: Murray)

Mintzberg, H. (1975). The manager's job: folklore and fact. *Harvard Bus. Rev.*, **53** (4), 49–61

Moore, B. (1978). *Injustice—the Social Bases of Obedience and Revolt.* (London: Macmillan)

Newcomb, T. M. (1956). The prediction of interpersonal attraction. *Am. Psychol.*, **11**, 404–575

Olson, M. (1965). *The Logic of Collective Action—Public Goods and the Theory of Groups.* (New York: Schocken Books) (1968 edition)

Perkin, H. (1969). *The Origins of Modern English Society, 1780–1880.* (London: Routledge and Kegan Paul)

Sherif, M. (1967). *Group Conflict and Cooperation.* (London: Routledge and Kegan Paul)

Sherif, M. and Sherif, C. W. (1953). *Group Conflict and Cooperation.* (London: Routledge and Kegan Paul)

Smelser, N. J. (1962). *Theory of Collective Behaviour.* (London: Routledge and Kegan Paul) (1976 edition)

Strauss, A. (1978). *Negotiations: Varieties, Contexts, Processes and Social Order.* (San Francisco: Jossey Bass)

Swingle, P. G. (1967). The effects of the win–lose difference upon cooperative responding in a 'dangerous' game. *J. Confl. Resol.*, **11**, 214–22

Tannenbaum, R. and Schmidt, W. H. (1958). How to choose a leadership pattern. *Harvard Bus. Rev.*, **36** (2), 95–101

Walton, R. E. (1969). *Interpersonal Peace-making: Confrontations and Third Party Consultation.* (Reading, Massachusetts: Addison Wesley)

Walton, R. E. and McKersie, R. B. (1965). *A Behavioural Theory of Labor Negotiations.* (New York: McGraw Hill)

Williamson, O. E. (1975). *Market and Hierarchies.* (New York: Glencoe Free Press)

Winkler, J. (1981). *Bargaining for Results.* (London: Heinemann)

13
The Salesman

R. M. C. POTTER

INTRODUCTION

The question we have to answer in this chapter is: 'What social skills are needed by salesmen?' The historical reply is almost caricature. It creates the image of the quick-fire, fast-talking, foot-in-the-door butt of the musical halls of the 1920s—the 'commercial traveller'. The current answer is totally different—in the competitive commercial world of the 1980s many companies can only guarantee one plus factor over their competitors—the professionalism of their sales function. In any one market, differences between products are diminishing—even price ranges and trading terms are similar between competing companies, themselves becoming fewer and bigger. Hence the emergence of the sales function as the cutting edge of the company, and the resultant training in 'customer awareness' inculcated in everyone from the Managing Director downwards.

The change in the image of the salesman is not fortuitous—there have been changes in environment, job and skills requirement which have brought it about, and it is from the base of this change that the skills, particularly the social skills of the salesman, need to be examined. As his job has changed, so has there been a change in the type of individual best fitted to do the job, and a change in the skills he needs. Today's salesman is a different person from the 'road dog' or 'drummer' personified by Arthur Miller in his (to any salesman) terrifying play *Death of a Salesman*, whose hero works on 100% commission and who goes to work on a 'smile and a shoe-shine'.

THE COMMERCIAL ENVIRONMENT

Since the Industrial Revolution, industry has moved from production-based to demand-based, i.e. the question is no longer 'what can I make?' but 'what do people want?' In production-based conditions the sales function scarcely earned the title; it was more properly a disposal function—disposing of the product to which the combination of managerial inventiveness and newly discovered material resource had given birth. In nineteenth-century Victorian England there was money and interest enough to make this none too onerous a task—especially since so many innovations occurred in such a comparatively short time, and since so many of them at once improved the life of the purchaser or user. The job of 'disposal' became full-time, and the employee entrusted with it toured his customers and potential customers by whatever means he could—horse, pony and trap, or new methods such as the steam train or even the bicycle. He was called a 'traveller', and some 50 years later a 'commercial traveller' to link his function with business rather than globe-trotting.

From both 1918 and 1945 onwards, once war-time backlog was made up, supply eventually outran demand. Industry began to realize that its sales function was essential to increase turnover. Sales organization and other needs were analysed more carefully. Between the wars, both manufacturing and purchasing units were numerous and comparatively small, which meant large sales forces with small territories making many calls in a day. Additionally, sales forces became stratified, or specialized, depending at what point on the line of distribution between manufacturer and customer/consumer they were functioning. On a short line, as in industrial selling, there would be one level of salesman talking over buyers' desks. On the longer line of consumer goods selling, there might be any or all of wholesaler salesman, retailer salesman or doorstep salesman (such as milkman or baker's roundsman).

During the period since 1945 both manufacturing and retailing units in industry have become fewer and bigger. Sales forces have become larger and more complicated. A salesman who 30 years ago might have made 25 calls in a day now makes eight or nine, or even fewer. At the same time, the difference in quality of goods or terms of trading between one manufacturing giant and another has become increasingly narrow, leading to the dependence on the sales function and its professionalism for the 'unique selling point'. Specialization within the sales force has also changed, dependent not so much on where on the line of distribution selling is needed, as on the different aspects of selling which one major outlet may require, firstly to sell in to it successfully, and secondly to service it. Thus in industrial selling the salesman may be the head of a team containing specialists in research, technology, advertising and distribution; and in fast-moving consumer goods selling, a super-store manager may be looked after by a stock supervising senior salesman, a merchandiser arranging displays and women demonstrators on the shop floor. The use of women has in itself been a major change in all types of selling. To the industrial and fast-moving consumer goods categories of selling, there has also been added a third, known as 'service' selling, i.e. intangibles such as package holidays, bank and insurance services, and factory services such as vending machines and laundry changing. The three categories are widely used when sales organization and training theory is discussed, although they indicate more clearly the current nature of the selling environment rather than broad differences in task and skills, particularly social skills, between the categories.

THE JOB OF SELLING

The job of selling has changed over the years against this background of environmental change. We have a picture of rising status, fewer and bigger customers, and more complicated selling interviews. The tasks within the job reflect this picture.

Selling tasks cover the broadest of spectra, systems-relation at one end and people-relation at the other. This has always been so—the 'commercial traveller' had to learn cash collection and banking routines as well as learning how to persuade people to buy. Since 1920 however, this 'task spectrum' has itself advanced on a different plane, one of sophistication, reflecting the changes in the selling environment. The systems-related tasks are now much more complicated than they used to be; the people-related tasks also are now very much more complex than formerly. Systems-related tasks cover what salesmen broadly refer to as 'administration', and have to do with ordering and delivery routines, cash collection and credit control, complaints procedures and recording and reporting on their days', weeks' or months' work. They serve two principal purposes firstly to see that products move one way, and revenue the other, along the line of distribution, and secondly to enable a sales manager to keep control of two factors: the market in which his company is operating (via information on competitors' activities, product popularity, etc.), and of the salesman himself.

Some remarkable systems have appeared over the years, involving salesmen in form-filling, return completion, routine reporting and letter writing until they have often complained that they have spent more time writing than selling. Their attitude towards this side of their job has often given the sales manager an accurate picture of the man himself; e.g. the bad administrator has often made a good 'instinctive' salesman, but not one who can analyse his work as he should, and learn from his own successes and failures; conversely, the good administrator may spend too much time hiding from prospective customers behind mountains of form-filling.

Large strides in making systems-related tasks more time-saving and more simple have recently been made by using micro-electronics; ordering, cash collection and market information can now flow both ways between a central computer and portable terminals used by the salesman, using telephone lines, and even giving the salesman a read-out facility on his home television set. Electronic equipment is also used as a sales aid, i.e. in product presentation to customers on videotape.

People-related tasks have similarly grown in sophistication because it is becoming increasingly difficult to persuade people to buy. The principal reason is that the buyer himself has changed. In industrial selling, buying has advanced from one of the jobs that the boss did (in a small family firm), to a highly specialized function often carried out by a full department headed up by a buyer who himself may have Board status (see Chapter 14). The same has happened in fast-moving consumer goods and services selling—customers are fewer and bigger and buyers are often full-time professionals rather than harassed shop owners or managers serving customers and dealing with salesmen at the same time. Before the nature of the buyer changed in this way, the salesman's task had its roots in systems-relation, i.e. in routine. With perhaps 20 or 30 calls to make in a day, he tended to approach each buyer in the same way: his call followed a pattern (e.g. cash collection, stock-check, order, merchandise) and his 'persuasion', his sales presentation, followed one too. In this way sales sequences grew up, which became drills with little flexibility. Salesmen learned them by rote—some companies even produced a weekly script which was sent to salesmen at weekends for them to learn and use during the following week. This method is still in fact used in selling situations requiring a high number of calls in the day, e.g. door-to-door selling. Generally, the method worked, as buyers with other jobs to do and little time to spare were able to make their decisions quickly—often helped by the decision being a small one requiring a comparatively small financial outlay. For example, an office manager of the 1930s might buy his stationery from one firm, his pens and pencils from another, and his carbon paper from a third. He now makes one big buying decision covering all such items. The salesman's task then, was to 'present'; and he was taught to do it by much the same method as he was taught cash collection procedure, that is by following a drill.

The emergence of the full-time buyer, however, with fewer and bigger decisions to make has made this inflexible type of presentation inadequate. This first happened in industrial selling, when the whole procedure was complicated by tendering and contracting, by other executives being involved in buying apart from the buyer, and by the 'wheeling and dealing' which went on to settle the details of the sale once it had been made in principle. Thus negotiation emerged as a function complementary to selling, and this has since spread to both service and fast-moving consumer goods selling. The salesman now has to think for himself, to use flexibility, and to make decisions within an increasingly broadening authority from his sales management. The level of man employed as a salesman has had to rise to meet the wider job, and he uses his intelligence and initiative to meet an ever more complicated buying/selling situation. This by definition moves the people-related part of his job away from the systems-relation from which it grew to a much clearer person to person base. His job is still to persuade the buyer to buy, but the skills he uses are based not so much on a set sequence as on his own ability to analyse firstly the business situation he finds himself in and secondly what will make the type of man confronting him across the desk buy from him. His need for 'interpersonal' or 'man-handling' skills is greater now than ever before.

THE SKILLS OF SELLING

The range of skills required demonstrates the same spectrum as the job; systems-relation at one end and people-relation at the other. Like the job, their sophistication has advanced as the selling environment has changed. At the same time, the people-relation part of the job depends very much less on the systems, i.e. the formal, end of the spectrum and very much more on the salesman's ability as a human being to interact with other human beings, in short, on his social skills.

There have been many attempts to summarize selling skills as a whole—most of them in the form of sales sequence formulae. One simple version reduces the principal skills to three: plan, communicate and control. They can be linked in parallel to the spectrum already considered:

PLAN—COMMUNICATE—CONTROL

SYSTEMS-RELATED————PEOPLE-RELATED

In this context, the *control* skill is the most people-related; it implies the manipulation and direction of the interview by the salesman. The interview by definition is based on two-way communication which has itself been set up by the salesman using his *communication* skills, working towards an objective decided by him at the *plan* stage. The term 'social skills' can be taken to cover both the *communicate* and *control* areas, since both imply, if successfully executed, the interplay of two or more personalities, hopefully in a constructive fashion. The difference between social skills used in a sales interview compared with their use in a more leisurely context such as a cocktail party is that to one member of the group, at least (the salesman), there is an objective in mind. To examine social skills as a salesman operates them therefore, we should define those related to main headings of *communicate* and *control*. To complete the picture a short description of *plan* is required.

Plan

This function lies behind the way in which the salesman organizes his whole job. It calls for logic, foresight and calculation. Armed with the procedural knowledge which it is hoped his induction training will have given him, he can set up his administration systems, be they simple or sophisticated, so that the appropriate two-way flow of information can take place between himself and his office. This done, he next applies planning to his territory, so that all active and potential outlets are covered in such a way that he spends a minimum of his time in his car and a maximum in front of his customer. Much time is wasted by poor administrative and territorial planning—even down to such details as having the correct literature available at each call and making sure that it is tidily enough arranged in the boot of the car to prevent a sudden gust of wind spreading it evenly over the customer's factory yard.

The third main area of planning is connected with calls to be made. Territory planning puts the salesman in front of the right man at the right time; call planning helps him make best use of that time. Planning is applied to the call in two ways: firstly, by defining a clear objective to the call. Naturally enough, business is the principal objective, but there may be several calls before this is achieved and thus intermediary objectives are needed; secondly, by planning the call itself in terms of its beginning, its middle, and its end. It is at this stage that the *plan* skill impinges on the other two and thus on social skills. Communication is obviously more effective if it is planned first, and control is more easily gained and maintained if, for instance, the customer's reactions are anticipated and answers to them are made ready.

Communicate

Transferring information from one person to another can be achieved mechanically, providing the flow is to be one-way. Early sales presentations appear to have made this assumption, since they scarcely made allowance for any reply by the customer at all—one has only to listen to some presentations still made over the doorstep to see that this still applies. Modern selling, however, depends on two-way communication, and thus there are other important elements apart from talking. All salesmen consequently are taught to observe and to listen. Information is received through both eyes and ears, and sensitivity to it enables the salesman to alter his presentation, or his attitude to suit the customer, his needs and his mood. Linked with this is the ability to memorize and to concentrate, the most difficult of which is the latter. Nobody can concentrate all the time, especially if listening to a long speech; inevitably the listener tends to prepare his reply in his own mind and thus risks missing information, or changes in attitude. In a social situation polite listening is considered 'good manners'. In a commercial situation it is vital if full constructive use is to be made of the other party's contribution to the discussion.

Salesmen are taught two other techniques which must be included in communication skills. The first is how to ask questions, particularly at the outset of an interview in order to set up the required two-way flow. Questions inviting monosyllabic answers such as 'yes' or 'no' or 'sometimes' or 'ten' are fatal—the ball is back in the salesman's court to ask another question, and if he persists in the same strain, then the customer will think he is being 'grilled'. It is better (by careful planning) to ask questions inviting a much longer answer by starting with such words as 'when', 'how', 'what' and so on.

Another important technique of questioning is known as 'check-back'. This is where the salesman seeks agreement as he goes along with such questions as 'don't you agree?' or 'isn't it?' or even 'OK?' This not only breaks up what might turn into a monologue but shows the salesman whether or not the customer is with him in terms of both pace and comprehension. One of the aspects of sensitivity lacking in many salesmen is that they work at their own pace rather than the customer's—this is where their historical reputation for quick-fire patter has sprung from; if they recognize that the customer is the most important participant in the interview then they should speed up or slow down accordingly—to his pace.

The second technique which is taught alongside questioning is the art of summary. This is basically a control technique, enabling the salesman briefly to identify progress made (or otherwise) in the interview. It allows both parties to clarify and gather their thoughts, and above all, gives the salesman the opportunity of bringing the customer on to common ground with him before moving on to the next stage. It is also useful in bringing a garrulous customer back to the proper line of discussion—many deliberately lead salesmen away from it, depriving them thereby of control of the interview.

Finally, under communication skills there is the whole area of non-verbal communication. This covers facial expression, gesture and what has become known and widely developed as 'body language', and applies just as importantly to the customer (to observe and check reaction) as to the salesman (to convey ideas and attitudes). Mood is infectious, the listener tends to catch and reflect the mood of the speaker, which is often transmitted before he opens his mouth. Thus a salesman with a hang-dog appearance and a gloomy expression is unlikely to be listened to receptively by his customer. Sales training therefore includes 'attitude training'; the best historical example is probably the doctrine of 'Right Mental Attitude' taught by the Tack Organization, themselves pioneers and still leaders in the sales training field. This calls for mental preparation of a simple kind, featuring relaxation and the removal of tension. Salesmen are taught the importance of the first impression they make on their customer, even to analyse their hand-shake. 'Smile', say the sales training manuals, implying a relaxed expression on the face reflecting the personality of the salesman rather than that he should go into each call grinning like the Cheshire cat. Gesture is important, though if taken to an extreme as mannerisms, they can be irritating and distracting. Body language has been recognized before its title was invented—salesmen know that to tower standing over a sitting man, tends to dominate him; whether this is desirable or not depends on the selling situation. From the other side, customer reaction can be gauged by observing his attitude to supplement the implication of his verbal replies.

By definition, a salesman, to be successful, must be able to communicate; the traditional outflow from him has been tempered, as the job has changed, by the growing importance of two-way communication, and of sensitivity to reaction in the selling situation. He must be a listener and an observer as well as a talker. In social terms this implies that the requirement for communication skills has matured as the job of selling has evolved.

Control

Communication skills can be put either to positive or to negative use—a man can go through life as a good talker, listener and observer without concrete result; he may make a good philosopher but he will never sell anything! To obtain positive action in a business sense another set of skills needs to be developed. These are the control skills which have already been described as the most people-related, in terms of the systems/people spectrum. Control on top of communication implies guiding the situation to a positive conclusion. In selling terms, this means setting up a business relationship in which the salesman's products or services are bought by the buyer to the benefit of both their companies. The emphasis must be on the word 'both'. It is evident that unless the purchasing company benefits from the transaction then the business relationship will cease. There are 'cowboys' in the selling world who go for the sale regardless, but the greatest proportion of the national selling activity works to the customer's benefit and so preserves the ethics.

Control skills then are those which help the salesman guide the sales interview to a positive conclusion. They are the traditional selling skills which imply maintaining control of the different parts of the interview. At its simplest, the interview has three parts—the beginning, the middle and the end; the salesman must learn how to start an interview, how to guide it through its main course and how to conclude it. The skills concerned have been described in different ways by sales training specialists, usually in the form of a sequence, used as the interview progresses. It is important to recognize, however, that in present day selling more flexibility is needed, and thus the skills which make up a sequence need to be studied separately; nowadays they are much more likely to be used individually rather than as a sequential whole. Thus the three- or five- or seven-step formulae to selling success put forward by sales training specialists over the years need to be broken down before they are taught, and indeed this is how it is now mostly done.

THE SELLING PROCEDURE

A typical definition of selling skills runs as follows:

Opening—Defining need—Selling benefits—Overcoming objections—Closing

Taking these in turn:

Opening

This is an uncomplicated skill, with two objectives—firstly to persuade the customer to stop what he is doing and to listen to the salesman and secondly to start off a two-way conversation. It is the most easily planned, particularly the opening sentences, since until these are delivered there will be no reply anyway. The two principal elements to this skill are those of introduction and of gaining interest. Introduction may be just that, if the customer is a new one, or it may take the form of referring back to the previous call, in order to get down to business as quickly as possible. Gaining interest is obviously a prerequisite to making the customer listen, think and reply; the salesman will plan his 'interest raiser' beforehand and not hope to think of something on the spur of the moment. He will also avoid the common-place—buyers today have no time to discuss weather or football or current affairs before talking business.

Defining need

This is the most sophisticated of all selling skills and one whose importance many salesmen still ignore. It would seem commonsense to find out what a customer's needs are before presenting one's products but too many salesmen, especially in the fast-moving consumer goods and services selling fields, hurry to an account of what their products are and what they will do irrespective of what the customer wants done. This is called 'blunderbuss' selling and clearly has its origins in the one-way presentations of 40 years ago. Industrial salesmen were the first to develop need definition, since there were some industries who from the outset had to tailor their product to the individual need of the customer. There are two aspects to this skill: identifying the need itself and agreeing with the customer firstly that it exists, and secondly what he needs to satisfy it. The salesman must be able to analyse the business situation before him, to see how the use of his product or service will benefit it, and he must be able to persuade the customer to agree with him. This requires another analysis, that of the buyer himself, to estimate what aspect of the product or service will appeal to him, as a person, most. For instance, the product may be cheap, labour-saving and be supported by a good after-sales service. Which factor appeals most to the customer depends on the sort of person he is—if he is profit-conscious or grasping, it will be the price; if he is a worrier or lacks confidence in his own or his company's abilities, it will be the security offered by the after-sales service.

Analysis of the buyer and of his 'buying motive' opens up the whole question of how people are different as individuals, and how they are motivated to buy. It is essential that salesmen should be students of their fellow men, and be interested in the sort of people they are and why they behave as they do. Without turning salesmen into amateur psychologists, it is perfectly possible to show how each of them has a personal 'reflex' filing system, by which they automatically label each person they meet as a 'nice bloke' or a 'difficult so-and-so' or a 'funny man'. It follows that each type would buy for a different reason, depending on his personality type. Buying motives have been variously listed, but the eight most common ones are: profit, pride, status, security, fear, greed, love, hate.

If then, a principal buying motive can be identified through an estimate of the character of the buyer, then the feature of the product to be sold most likely to stimulate that motive can be selected and used, to the exclusion of the other features. In defining need, therefore, the salesman is doing a double job of analysis, firstly of the business, and secondly of the man responsible for buying for it. It can best be described to salesmen as target-definition, with the reason for ordering as the bull's eye, and analysis of the business and of the man as two of the concentric rings. The third ring worth defining is the mood of the man, which may change from call to call and to which the salesman has to adapt. The implication is that if his analysis of the 'rings' is right, then he has identified what is most likely to make this man buy from him, on that particular day, and has so identified the bull's eye. This again has been given different labels by sales trainers, such as the 'Key Issue', or the 'Bell-ringer' or even the 'Hot Button'. If the salesman can be persuaded to look for this before he starts talking about his product, then he will be more likely to sell with accuracy rather than by hit-or-miss. It will be noted that a fair level of analytical ability is expected of him in operating this skill; this is another indication of the gradual change in the job over the years, and the higher level of man needed to do it. He no longer repeats by rote—he thinks, seeks and analyses.

Selling benefits

This is an age-old selling skill reaching right back into the early days of American sales training between the two world wars. Like defining need, it is based on analysis, but this time analysis of the product or service. To continue the analogy of target shooting, benefit selling provides the arrows. One of the main features of a salesman's induction training programme is product knowledge. He learns all about his product or service in terms of a mass of facts, or features, or figures. This done, he sets forth full of enthusiasm to present his product to customers. But a fact to him will mean nothing to the customer until he, the customer, sees how he will benefit from it. And in a selling situation, the customer cannot be left to work out the benefit for himself, obvious though it may be. He is much more likely to be thinking of reasons why he should not buy the product than of how he would benefit were he to do so. The salesman needs to explain the benefit to him, almost like a patient parent explaining to a child that if he goes to bed early he will be nice and fresh to visit the seaside the next day! The first stage is carried out before any call is made by listing the facts or features of the product or service, and opposite each is written the benefits derived from it. It often happens that one benefit can be split into many sub-benefits, as many in fact as there are individual reasons for accepting the main benefit as such. The sub-benefit is the translation of the main benefit to suit the customer's need, i.e. to hit the target. For example, an electric cooker may have a timing device on it *(fact)*. This means that it can be left on its own to switch on a roast (for instance) and switch it off when it is cooked *(benefit)*. If the customer is fond of gardening, it means that she can go and work in the garden without worrying about the dinner *(sub-benefit)*; or if she is a church visitor she can make her afternoon calls without having to hurry home and turn the oven on *(sub-benefit)*; or if she has to collect children from school, she does not have to exhaust herself rushing home to start the evening meal *(sub-benefit)*. Sometimes the main benefit is called an advantage, and the word 'benefit' limited to the sub-benefit, so there is a pattern: *fact—advantage—benefit*. It will be seen that true benefits cannot be identified until the customer's need has been clarified, since they are in fact fairly precise ways of expressing how that need can be met. The true skill lies in translating the main benefit, the advantage, to fit the precise requirement of the customer. Leaving the main benefit hanging in space, as it were, is another example of blunderbuss selling. Having identified the target, it is very much more effective to select and 'shoot' the precise 'arrow' which will hit the target. Another common mistake is to follow the 'precise arrow' with a swarm of others, i.e. having hit the target, to attempt to consolidate by telling the customer of all the other benefits as well. This is usually irrelevant and could lead to 'oversell' which means that the customer begins to lose interest again before the sale is concluded. Accurate identification of sub-benefits is a useful way to overcome one of most salesmen's principal bugbears—price differential. Many elements in a business deal have value to a buyer, i.e. are worth money to him, e.g. quick delivery, exact conformity to specification, advertising to stimulate turnover of stock. If the selected sub-benefit meets the need, then it will have value to the customer, value which might outweigh the lower price of a competitor unable to offer the same sub-benefit.

Overcoming objections

This is a skill which a salesman needs when the customer says 'no'. As in any situation where one person refuses to be persuaded by another, there must be a reason behind the 'no' and it is the salesman's task to discover it. Having done so, an attempt can be made to deal with the objection, to overcome it. Many objections, or refusals, arise through lack of skill earlier in the interview. It may be that the salesman has failed to check back on some of the points he made when trying to define the need; this can result in misunderstanding, or in a question remaining unanswered. Either can cause doubt in the customer's mind and lead him to turn away an attempt to get him to order with phrases like 'I'll think about it' or 'Leave it with me for a month or two'. Again, the salesman may have wrongly defined need, either by failing to assess the business itself or more likely by failing to assess the buyer as a person correctly. Whatever its nature, when an objection occurs the salesman must ask himself, and the customer, 'why?' This again indicates the analytical trend which now runs through the whole range of selling skills. At one time an objection might be accepted and the call abandoned on the assumption that there are plenty more fish in the sea. This is no longer the case.

Closing

Closing is the 'crunch' skill where the salesman brings the interview to a successful conclusion. This will often mean taking an order; sometimes it will mean rounding off positively an intermediate call on the way to an order, which might take several calls to achieve—as often happens in industrial selling. Basically, closing has two principal factors: the first is timing. It is wrong to suppose that the opportunity to ask for an order only occurs at the end of the interview—it could happen at any time, whenever the customer looks ready to do so, or exhibits 'buying signals'. The salesman must be sensitive to such opportunities and having recognized them must use the second factor of closing—courage. It takes just that extra effort to push oneself to ask the all-important question, but there is nothing worse than seeing an opportunity occur and letting it go by to be lost forever, for the want of a bit of courage. Closing an intermediate call likewise calls for timing, and firmness perhaps rather than courage. It is one part of the interview where the salesman *must* be in control, if he is to achieve a positive result.

These then are the five selling skills which help salesmen gain and maintain control of the interview and bring it to a profitable conclusion. As the most people-related of the three main skills listed earlier, *control* requires of the salesman a wide range of interpersonal skills built up from the other two—*plan* and *communicate*. It has been shown that beneath *control* lies *analysis* and perhaps this is the biggest change of all in the present-day salesman—that he is no longer just a performer, but an analyst as well. An analyst of business, of people and of problems. Above all, as he works so much on his own, he must analyse himself and his work, and learn from his own successes and failures.

SELLING SKILLS AS SOCIAL SKILLS

The similarity between selling skills and social skills is clear enough. Where they become people-related rather than systems-related they are in fact synonymous. Looking at it the other way round, selling skills are perpetually in use in social and other situations. Anyone who is persuading someone else to do something he might otherwise not have done, is selling. Teachers sell knowledge, doctors sell health, preachers sell the hereafter. It implies presenting your case to the listener in his terms, not in your terms. Perhaps the clearest way of putting selling skills into context is by defining them as the commercial application of social skills. Certainly our industry is complicated and competitive enough to merit this application. Perhaps, indeed, it needs such skills more than any other.

14
The Industrial Sales Team

P. MOORHOUSE

INTRODUCTION

It would be difficult to estimate the number of persons associated with selling goods and services in the United Kingdom. Wherever there is a need to dispose of output someone will be involved in the selling process. Depending upon the nature of the sale, for either supplier or purchaser, this may involve junior or senior organizational positions and persons with general or specific (sales) responsibilities—perhaps the managing director or the representative. It may also involve groups or individuals. The sales team comprises a number of persons working towards a common end, namely the satisfaction of identified customer needs. Each team member plays a part, particular attention in this chapter being given to the manager, his salesmen and his administrative staff. Following a general introduction the second section considers the team in wider context, focusing upon structure and functions. What the sales team do is discussed in the next section which highlights interpersonal aspects. Social skills are then considered, followed by a discussion, where significant aspects of social skills are identified in relation to mainstream skills theory.

Sales activities

In general the nature of the sales team will depend upon the product to be sold and the markets in which it is sold. More specifically, precisely who is involved will depend on the importance of the sale to the organization and internal constraints. In many organizations the whole selling activity will be the responsibility of someone called the Sales Manager, who will oversee not only in-field salesmen, whose activities centre upon visits to customers, but also in-house personnel (sales administrators), who typically provide support for the salesmen and offer service to customers. This latter group probably maintain sales records, process customer enquiries and orders and may undertake specialist tasks such as credit control or advertising. Whilst spending much of their time within the organization they may have regular contact with customers and conduct the more routine 'maintenance' selling, thus allowing the in-field salesmen to develop new business opportunities.

Types of selling

The degree of importance of business creation in the salesman's job was used by McMurry (1961) to differentiate several types of selling. At one extreme there is little opportunity for creative selling, as in the case of the roundsman delivering products such as coal or milk. At the other extreme are specialist salesmen selling either tangible products (e.g. appliances, cars), where the need is to induce some dissatisfaction with existing products and then present the product as a means of alleviating that dissatisfaction, or intangible products (e.g. insurance), where there is the additional problem of 'dramatizing' the product. Between these extremes the creative ingredient varies through positions of 'inside order taker' at the shop counter, 'outside order taker' typically concerning selling to retail outlets, 'goodwill builder' paving the way for others to take orders through facilitating product awareness (e.g. the medical representative selling to health care teams) and the 'technical salesman' requiring specialist knowledge in what may be regarded as a consultancy role. Lidstone (1975) extends the categorization in the creative direction to include the 'political salesman' selling to large consumers (e.g. flour sales to bakeries) and the 'multiple salesman' who sells to groups such as project teams or boards of directors comprising individuals who may not have similar needs. It may be that one organization is engaged in several types of selling.

The sales subsystem

Although there is a variation in types of selling between organizations dependent upon products and markets, the sales objectives remain consistent, namely to convert products into revenue by securing buying decisions. This is one stage in a perpetual conversion cycle, in which other important stages relate to the procurement of raw materials and bought out parts and their conversion into finished products for sales stock.

The sales department may be described simply by a block diagram of inputs and outputs as shown in Figure 14.1. It is a subsystem generating information transmitted in various forms to the parent system and suprasystem (outside the organization) following the acquisition of different information from similar sources. Prime departmental functions include the acquisition of customer orders, the provision of service to customers, the maintenance of various organizational routines and the implementation of and contribution to organizational objectives.

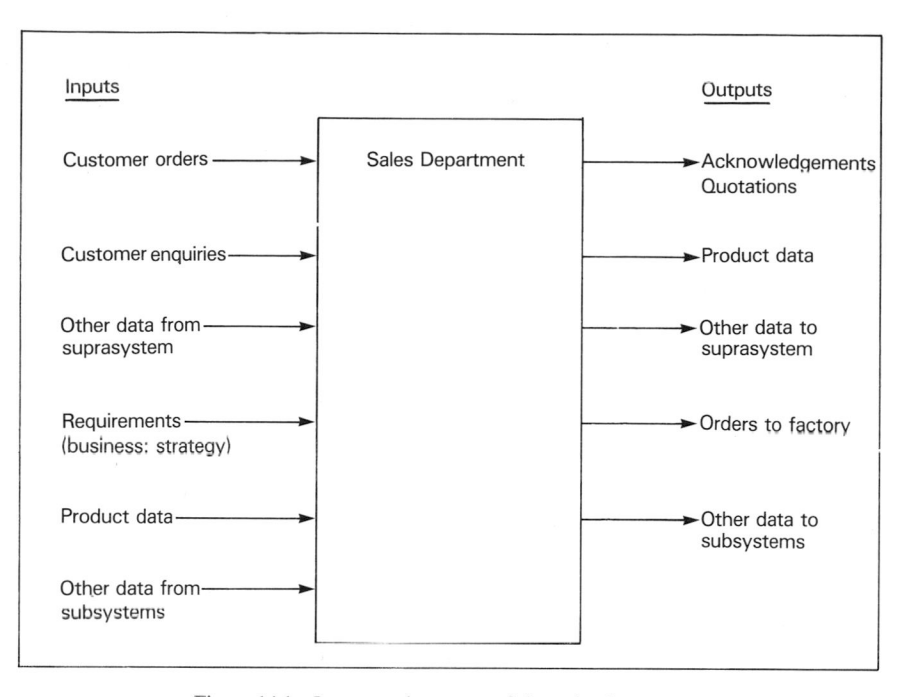

Figure 14.1   Inputs and outputs of the sales department

THE SALES DEPARTMENT

Organization

The sales department is part of a wider organization including other departments such as design, production, finance and personnel. It may be that the
sales department is itself part of a marketing department contingent upon the
nature and development of the organization. In an earlier volume of *Real
Skills*, Burnett (1981) points out that there are several kinds of organizational
structure of varying marketing orientation. At one extreme, where production
is dominant, the sales function serves essentially to allocate and distribute
output (perhaps in circumstances where demand exceeds supply and competition is lacking). At the other extreme, as manufacturers become increasingly
sensitive to customer need and competitor activity (where consumption of
output is a problem), the tendency is towards an 'integrated marketing'
structure comprising marketing services (e.g. product planning, advertising,
etc.) and sales. However, this application of the marketing concept provides
no guarantee of survival. Where there is a similarity between products the
means of attaining a competitive edge rests in the manner in which an organization promotes itself, and in this respect the sales department is likely to play
a prominent role. Indeed a questionnaire survey in the mid-1970s of executives

of top American corporations revealed that personal selling and sales management were rated as increasingly the most important components of promotional strategy (Lusch *et al.*, 1976). As Burnett further remarks the position of the salesman is particularly important in industrial equipment markets where the purchasing decision may prove difficult, since most products are likely to meet the technical specification. Further difficulties relate to differential purchasing criteria of the buying team and the significant financial implications of any major decision. Burnett adds that the salesman is not only involved in persuasion but also in stage managing the technical, commercial and financial aspects of the buyer–supplier relationship. In selling intangible services the salesman's contribution to the purchasing decision is likely to be even more important.

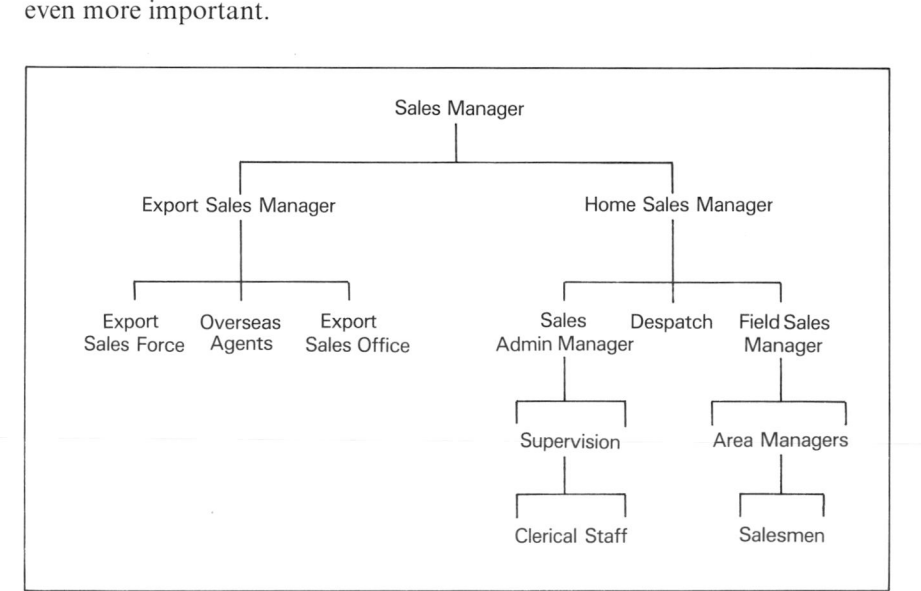

Figure 14.2   Typical sales organization

It may be, then, that the sales department will dominate the organization–market boundary in, say, capital equipment sales, whereas the department will be one of several marketing activities in an organization trading in fast moving consumer goods. Whether or not the head of sales reports to a marketing director or the managing director, the organization for which he is responsible is likely to be divided into home and export sections, with a further division concerning field sales and sales administration personnel. Typically the field sales personnel will be organized by geographical area, as shown in Figure 14.2, although Moss (1982) reports that because of the increasing need for industrial salesmen to acquire specialist customer knowledge, particularly in industries facing technological change and selling systems packages, sales forces are being restructured to distinguish account sales, maintenance sales, individual markets and special product-based teams. Whilst there is no standardization in the organization of administrative personnel, typically sales administration supervision will head clerical staff organized by customer, market, territory or product.

Roles: an overview

The sales team comprises a group of persons of varying responsibility and hierarchical level in a line relationship who are appointed to identify and satisfy customer requirements. An important feature of the team is its orientation to action; the role of team members is not to passively theorize but to actively practise. This devotion to attaining practical results applies equally to inside and outside personnel. Whilst the latter group operate primarily in the field largely aiming to generate business, back at base the administrative staff keep the sales operation tidy through maintaining routines, resolving problems and sometimes expediting procedures. Often the results of the salesmen are displayed in the department and rewards may be offered for improving attainments. This is not the lot of the administrators and Mant (1977) provides an illustration of the problems incurred in an aggressive sales organization where a decision was taken to offer them similar inducements to those of the salesmen. The root of the problem was the administrators' self-perceived inferiority in relation to the salesmen and the problem was resolved when the administrators came to terms with their less risky housekeeping role and recognized their own intrinsic importance.

The securing of essential effort of both salesmen and administrators is the ultimate responsibility of the sales manager. In linking the essentials of formal organization with executive functions, Barnard (1938) suggested that the manager has two further functions, namely to formulate and define purpose and to provide the system of communication. In his purpose-definition or policy-settling role the manager will be constrained by the requirements of the parent system. The communication system is the prime concern of this chapter.

Finally the department as a whole may experience a conflict in roles, since it represents both the parent organization and the customer. The salesman's overriding concern will be to satisfy his customer and in this context it may be that promises are made which the organization is unable to fulfil. Perhaps, for example, goods may be scheduled for delivery that the factory has been unable to manufacture. The problem is the incompatibility between customer requirements and organizational resources neither of which are controlled by the salesman. The sales department thus becomes the centre of an interdepartmental conflict within the organization and a conflict between the organization and its customer.

TASKS OF THE SALES TEAM

It is possible to derive a progressive clarification of what people do in under-taking their specialized activities by means of task analysis. However, there is no reason why task analyses should be universally applicable across salesmen, sales administrators and sales managers. The variation in sales organization and sales activities has already been noted. Nevertheless the general objective is clear, namely to increase product value through transferred ownership. Fundamentally the salesman aims to induce buying, the sales office provides a service to both buyers and salesmen and the sales manager attempts to meet departmental objectives by utilizing his resources which include himself.

The sales manager

The sales manager will provide sales forecasts for the forthcoming period, which involve the acquisition (and assessment) of data from a variety of sources, including front line salesmen. This forecast not only provides guide-lines for future sales but also serves as a yardstick against which organiz-ational performance can be measured. The manager's main resource in meeting the sales plan is the skills of the sales team, but he does have other resources under his control, including money, equipment, time and space. A further task is to budget for his resource requirements. Depending on the organization structure the manager may establish facets of commercial prac-tice, such as rebate schemes, a commission structure, credit facilities, etc. He may also become involved in personnel activities, such as selection and training. In short he will establish department sales practices. He will also co-operate with colleagues in resolving interdepartmental problems and may be part of the committee running the business. Finally it is likely that he will maintain personal contact with some of the principal accounts.

The sales administrator

The purpose of the administration office is to provide a service to customers and salesmen. An important task will be to process orders and enquiries. Processing duties may involve commercial and technical vetting (a skilled person will be sensitive to discrepancies) and the provision of a delivery forecast and price. Quotations will be issued in response to enquiries and firm orders will be placed with the factory, with acknowledgements and delivery letters being sent to customers. Subsequently progressing the order with the factory may become important. The export section will incorporate additional duties, such as raising consignments, issuing and progressing special docu-mentation (e.g. customs declarations, bills of lading, airway bills, etc.), ensur-ing letters of credit are satisfactory, meeting customs and excise requirements, insuring goods and reserving shipping space. It may be that the office has regular contact with customers concerning commercial problems or opportunities and routine sales and may support the salesmen by accompanying them on customer visits and relaying appropriate information. There will be extensive internal communication. Sometimes contacts are of a routine nature, often they concern problem resolution. Other administrative tasks involve the maintenance of various records and data. Finally there is likely to be a miscellany of duties dependent upon the nature of the organization, for example, credit control and market research.

The salesman

The main task of the salesman is to visit customers or prospective customers for the purpose of generating orders. Initially the requirement is to make contact with the customer and, particularly in the case of industrial selling, this may involve identifying members of a purchasing team. A call pattern may be established with existing customers, but in seeking new business the salesman may make 'cold' calls. Secondly the salesman must identify and perhaps shape customer wants and, having acquired various data, he will demonstrate how his product can satisfy these wants. In addition it may be necessary to create a preference for his own product or his total sales package over that of a competitor. It remains to finalize or close the sale, although a post-sale follow-up to ensure satisfaction may also be important. As with all interpersonal communication the process is one of reducing uncertainties at two levels, firstly concerning the issues at hand (e.g. supplies, payments, etc.) and secondly concerning the attributes of the other participants.

Surrounding this core task are several others. For instance the salesman will be expected to plan his sales activities. Perhaps he will establish a longer term call pattern against which a daily requirement of standard and prospect calls may be organized. Furthermore he will be expected to provide information to management concerning the nature and outcome of each call and to maintain up-to-date customer records. (Fenton [1979] provides one such reporting and recording system.) A further task will be to attend meetings where feedback concerning performance may be related, perhaps relatively informally or more formally, for example at a sales conference. Finally, the salesman may undertake a whole miscellany of tasks, such as personally delivering goods and training staff in product use.

Interpersonal aspects

In meeting their task demands it is clear that interaction is important for all the team. Vertical communication with subordinates is important for the manager who also communicates with colleagues and customers. Similarly other team members working both inside and outside the organization communicate both laterally and vertically.

The vertical flow of information is reflected in the manager's leadership role. There is no universally applicable leadership style, the contemporary viewpoint being that style should depend upon the situation that the leader faces (e.g. Vroom and Yetton [1973], Fiedler *et al.* [1975]). Both salesmen and administrators are likely to be affected by the organizational climate and the sales department is similar to other departments in that an important determinant of climate will be the style or attitudes of the departmental head. He will also represent subordinates concerning perceived matters of importance, for example, in securing additional resources or changing procedures. Lateral communication will be important for the manager in joint ventures with colleagues; indeed, relating to peers is significant for all the department. For instance, in computing a forward fixed price, a pricing clerk may require a delivery forecast from provisioning or supplies colleagues. This is an internal liaison role where there is no option of autocratic command.

All who have contact with customers provide an important link in interorganizational communication. The contact role, particularly for the salesman, will be partly ambassadorial in that, irrespective of any selling outcome, the need is to act diplomatically simply because the organization is being represented outside its boundary. The sales team is also involved in transmitting organization-specific data, for instance organizational policies, practices, objectives and difficulties. As an expert concerning his product the salesman may well have an advisory role. Furthermore, Moss (1982) reports that negotiation is becoming increasingly important for the salesman, particularly where the interdependence between buyer and seller was growing. The salesman occupies a good position to yield information concerning the market place. This market intelligence role will involve transmitting general market information and more specific data, such as a customers' grievances and the identity of important persons in the decision-making team. Robertson (1974) reports that, paradoxically enough, a management failure to use the information provided and a failure to stress the importance of information acquisition are two reasons for lack of communication.

The emphasis above rests upon formal organizational communication, but it is worth remarking in passing that information also flows informally (via the grapevine), the importance of informal social groups being discussed by the 'human relations school' (e.g. Roethlisberger and Dixon, 1939).

SOCIAL SKILLS OF THE SALES TEAM

Skills assessment

Since the exercise of skills is a purposeful activity it might be supposed that the attainment of objectives is a clear criterion against which skills may be measured. In the case of the salesman, therefore, a simple criterion of whether or not a sale is made in a sales encounter appears plausible. However, the difficulty is that the salesman's behaviour is not the only contributory factor to the measure of success. Rather, other factors, most generally the selling context, including customer attributes, play a part. To take a simple illustration climatic conditions as well as the salesman are likely to affect umbrella sales. A further objection to this simple criterion is that any short-term gain may, in fact, be offset by long-term difficulties, if say, the salesman has induced overstocking. If the salesman is paid on a commission basis it may be that the sale is regarded as a personal success whilst being organizationally detrimental.

Notwithstanding the difficulties, a variety of measures focusing upon job performance rather than organizational effectiveness have been employed in assessment, including activity indices (e.g. call to order ratios, percentage redundant calls, etc.), remuneration overtime and managerial/peer ratings. The personal judgement, uniquely, is able to take account of the difficulties inherent in the selling situation. It is possible to evaluate the communicative process between buyer and seller in terms of its qualities emphasizing means rather than ends through considering content, structure, clarity and so on. It is also possible to take account of the longer rather than the shorter term, recognizing that a purchase decision may result from several meetings between buyer and seller. Similarly it will be possible to assess the worth of other team members by taking account of contingencies. In sum, assessment is likely to combine different kinds of data, of varying importance, and this is itself a skill.

For the analyst with the purpose of identifying and understanding skills, as Singleton (1979) points out, likely evidence will accrue from three sources, namely the practitioner's performance, his introspections on what he is doing and how he is doing it and the empathy between analyst and practitioner. Using this kind of evidence the objective of this section is to consider the operations that seem necessary for competence in interpersonal relationships.

Skills in intraorganizational communication

The sales manager's task in leading the sales team will be similar to that of anyone concerned with man management. As head of the team the manager's competence (and credibility to his subordinates) will be enhanced through a recognition of the full extent of his responsibility. The competent manager will appreciate the tasks that the team have to undertake and develop a broad knowledge base in order to keep in touch. However, even whilst undertaking his own tasks, he can rarely become divorced from the team perspective. A variety of means may be used to monitor the department, for example following work flow (at what stage is some 'event'?), checking goal attainment (has this event been completed?), or remaining sensitive to discrepancies (why has this stage not been reached or this event not completed?). Feedback as to how the team is performing enables corrective action to be taken and in the context of directing subordinates feedback is also important in checking whether or not any instructions are understood. Whilst data is important to the manager he will be sensitive to his own data processing limitations and his strategies to keep in touch will be balanced against strategies to avoid inessential information. Through limiting inputs ill-considered decisions and ill-presented articulations will be avoided (Welford, 1976)—the manager may, for example, delineate the tasks that he will undertake himself and those that are to be delegated.

Vertical communication upwards tends to be the more difficult in organizations, but the manager must be able and prepared to accept subordinate initiations other than feedback to directives. For instance the sales office may require assistance in progressing orders or require additional resources to meet a peak work load. The manager may also have to protect the sales department from external stresses from both inside and outside the organization. In these circumstances when deciding on a course of action it will be advantageous to know the history and context surrounding the issue at hand. It may be that the manager will need to secure the support of more senior personnel for some decision that extends beyond his span of responsibility. As Sayles (1964) points out, where his seniors are unfavourably disposed to an issue representing subordinates is particularly difficult. The skills in moving forward usually comprise a blend of conceptual and political aspects. Conceptually he must anticipate objections and work out how to overcome them, politically he may introduce the prospect of favours and compromises.

Whilst relating to his subordinates the manager is likely to be sensitive to their personal attributes. He will be aware that their perceptions and actions will be coloured by abilities and attitudes. This is a problem that concerns all the sales team and perhaps most communicators; messages are not usually processed capriciously, rather they are processed habitually. The manager will, therefore, operate an adaptive response strategy. Moreover, the image that he holds of his subordinates, their attributes as individuals, their interrelationships as a group and their access to data will enable him to decide when to dictate, consult or participate in achieving his task objectives (cf. Vroom and Yetton, op. cit.).

The manager also liaises with colleagues in initiating changes or resolving difficulties. He will, therefore, maintain a variety of relationships with persons of similar hierarchical level in either line management or management services. Since there is no authority gradient in these relationships, progress is attained through personal resourcefulness and the relationships also have a strong political flavour. An important feature of any inner representation will be a history of favours given and any shifts in the balance of power through organizational change. This will enable the participant to set a 'price' on some favour—indeed he may operate a discount price structure, the discount being dependent upon the other participant(s). Moreover, as Singleton (1981) remarks, personal interests may intrude upon decision making, in the case of the manager possibly to the detriment of the interests of the system for which he is responsible. This is a reminder that the self is represented internally with varying degrees of strength in any interaction. The skilled communicator will recognize and contain any inclinations that mediate against the successful attainment of objectives. For instance, it may be that the sales manager would be wise to check an impulse to confront a colleague over a shift in power simply because there may be some reason that both participants would find plausible. Self control is likely to comprise affective as well as rational elements, where the requirement is to control feeling states which threaten goal achievement.

Where the need is to liaise with others, it is important to develop good personal relationships. In political exchanges or co-operative ventures it is useful to engender mutual confidence and trust, and most organizational members will be aware of the problems created through not being able to rely on others. If, for instance, the salesman has a query concerning deliveries or product specifications he requires an assurance that an answer will be forthcoming. The skilful communicator will, however, categorize his own initiations in terms of their importance. There is no advantage in repeatedly 'crying wolf', since this will of course merely serve to mask the real crises and fail to elicit an appropriate response. Moreover, the communicator may have to overcome hurdles in securing some action. An illustration was provided by a manager who was required to respond to a customer over deliveries of an item that was subject to modification because of a design fault. It was important to maintain good customer relationships so as to retain supplier status and obtain future orders. The issue reached 'crisis point' near the end of a statistical period when the manager's counterparts in production and related departments were very much concerned with meeting output targets (ironically enough any output being too late for the month's sales). His main problem, therefore, was to overcome conventional thinking and organizational tradition and inculcate a sense of priority regarding the design issue. The communicator must present a clear message and ensure that, despite a welter of other messages, it is received and processed (which is itself a further skill). In the organizational setting it may be that there is information from other sources such as memoranda. Conversations and inspections also serve to orient the receiver to the importance of the message.

Having a well-developed model of another person facilitates being able to predict the other's behaviour (for example, that a particular message will be treated as priority). The model also serves other functions. For example, data interpretation will be enhanced, thereby reducing the risk of a different meaning being ascribed to a message. Choosing an appropriate response may be easier than in a more ambiguous or uncertain situation. The communicator will know with whom he will need to follow up messages, take account of levels of ability and so on. As Welford (1976) points out, when people do get to know each other well they may be able to predict reactions sufficiently accurately to interact 'ballistically' as a group. This means that individual responses become phased and integrated to yield a smooth pattern of initiation and response in line with some jointly held objective. The interaction, although comprising elemental responses, is initiated and enacted as a gestalt, each response relating to not only the present but also the past and future. In this respect it takes time for the behaviour stream to be modified in the light of results.

Skills in interorganizational communication

The salesman has a clear objective to guide any communication, namely to obtain a buying decision in the longer term if not immediately. The significance of an extensive time scale to the individual salesman is that objectives may be modified contingent upon circumstances and the skilled practitioner may be satisfied that his message has been received and understood.

The customer has his own objectives, of course, and the salesman will gain his attention if the message is perceived as being sufficiently important. Supplementary data (for example, advertising in selling to industrial buyers) may be helpful in reducing inattention or immediate rejection and perhaps also salesmen will be discriminating in their calls through the employment of sales 'leads'. Useful ploys in establishing rapport are to focus upon matters of shared interest, topical news of previous discussions. An objective is to avoid antagonizing the prospective buyer, but if for whatever reason salesman and buyer as individuals are unable to interact successfully the tactic is to try and shift attention from any subjective irritation to the more objective content surrounding the sale. The idea is to keep communication channels open to avoid disengagement through carefully screening and selecting information to be presented. This is an important element of the ambassadorial role, and the whole process highlights a hallmark of social skills, namely the development of an inner representation concerning 'what I think you think of me' aspects.

In order to make progress in the encounter, one requirement is to understand the customer's need. In industrial selling particularly the salesman is likely to assist in defining that need. He will allow and encourage the customer to express his requirement, perhaps utilizing other means (e.g. charts, diagrams, inspection) in support of the dialogue. Part of the salesman's skill will concern information pick-up and clearly it is important that he listens to what is said. One of the difficulties with listening is that it is externally paced and the skilful listener must be able to ignore other data competing for his attention.

In developing his understanding of requirements the salesman's strategy is tantamount to imagining himself as the person to whom he is trying to make the sale. Mentally he will place himself in the position of the buyer. His impressions will be formed analytically, determining objectives, whilst also finding out about the buyer as a person; the attitudes, knowledge and abilities that he holds. This understanding will assist the salesman in presenting his product as the fulfilment of the buyer's requirement. Clearly the salesman must know his products, but irrespective of how this knowledge is retained he must be able to make a presentation in terms that the buyer will understand. His objective is to map his own model on to that held by the customer. Comprehensive knowledge is likely to enhance the salesman's credibility, which is important in persuasive communication. Trustworthiness is an important related quality which might be developed over the longer term. As for characteristics of the message rather than the message source, the indications are that the research evidence concerning the effects on the persuasive process is inconclusive (Strongman, 1977).

The salesman should be aware of competitor products and be able to discriminate between them and those that he is offering. To facilitate the persuasive process he is looking for added value in his package. By way of illustration, a salesman who had been unable to secure a distributorship for his product in some region recalled that he finally achieved his objective largely by allowing the last distributor he visited exclusive franchise in the area.

In making the presentation the salesman will neither present too much data nor take communications along too quickly (overselling), rather he will adjust his responses to suit the customer utilizing verbal and non-verbal feedback. He will remain alert for 'buying signals'—experienced salesmen report that they are able to derive a 'feel' over the likely outcome of the encounter. Fundamentally there is some enactive model probably supported by pictorial and symbolic aspects (such as numerical data). At some stage the salesman must close the sale and, as in other parts of the selling process, there are few mandatory drills, rather there is a miscellany of flexible means. Negotiation may be important and hence the salesman or his administrative colleague will require knowledge of transactional elements likely to feature in any compromise, such as credit terms, discounts, deliveries and so on. Thinking will be relatively unconstrained in exploring likely options before converging in making a decision that reflects some flexibility without capitulation such that an organizationally unsatisfactory transaction is agreed.

The sales office contact with the customer may well focus upon problem-solving relating to some facet of commercial practice, such as pricing, payments, terms and conditions or deliveries. Contact may be initiated by either party, for example, the seller may progress payments whilst the supplier requests deliveries. An important requirement is that the administrator is tolerant of uncertainty and this is particularly apposite in the case of exporters. The customer works within his own organizational procedures and systems which will influence his actions. It is through the adaptive approach of all those concerned that problems may be overcome. Fundamentally it is necessary to understand the issue at hand, trying to perceive it from the customer's viewpoint. Like the salesman the administrator must be able to listen and exercise tolerance in the face of criticism and complaint. Often it is a matter of picking out the important signal from what may be a background of noise. Not all requirements are of equal importance and in reality customers come to be categorized reflecting some judgement of the strength of message. It pays to have integrity in these circumstances.

Interaction may prove stressful for the administrator. For instance progress chasing deliveries highlights stresses on the administrators who find themselves located in a buffer between factory and customer. If it is the case that the organization is dilatory in deliveries it is important to know what has happened. The customer may be attuned to bogus feedback and disemblance will not enhance credibility, particularly if the truth emerges later. Providing a credible explanation goes some way towards appeasement. If on the other hand the customer is at fault through failing to consider delivery lead times, part of the response will be educational in trying to prevent the situation recurring. In any event it is important to find a mutually acceptable outcome and this may be derived through negotiation. As mentioned above the process is likely to involve exploration of the problem space *en route* to focusing upon a solution. As in most negotiations one ploy is to reserve the least preferred option. Once more the whole interaction will be facilitated through knowing the individuals concerned, being able to trust the message and being able to compromise with confidence.

Aspirations: a note

The work of the sales team is often demanding. The salesman, for example, may work long hours, spend considerable time driving, devote time outside hours to dealing with paperwork and experience 'rejections' in making calls. The inference is that personal qualities, such as resilience and persistence, will be important. Indeed, turning to the literature, although personality variables appear generally unhelpful, employing tests in the traditional manner Baier and Dugan (1957) and Lamont and Lundstrom (1977), for example, found constructs of 'motivation' and 'endurance', respectively, to be predictive of selling success. For some the sales task may be intrinsically motivating and success usually brings above average extrinsic rewards. For the salesman as well as others in the team the inner motivational representation concerns the reduction of a discrepancy between some ideal state of events and the current state of the same events (cf. Branton [1978] on the aspirations of the train driver). The salesman prescribes his desired outcome, which is to obtain an order, and seeks to close the gap between the goal and the current position of the encounter. Similarly, in resolving some difficulty, the administrator will make the transition from problem definition to problem solution, and the sales manager, in the face of disturbances will aim to keep his subsystem aligned to a prescribed, albeit variable, equilibrium. In this context knowledge of results or feedback is clearly important.

DISCUSSION

Communication breakdown

In understanding health the need is to understand disease. Similarly in skills analysis it is useful to contrast the ineffective with the effective performance state. Drawing together some threads of preceding sections it is possible to identify conditions of a breakdown in skilled performance as follows. Downs *et al.* (1978), less negatively, present several 'vital dimensions' of communication.

Incompatible purposes—As Downs *et al. (op. cit.)* point out, effective inter-action is sometimes determined by the compatibility of participant objectives. If the salesman is determined to sell and the customer is determined not to buy, one of the two will not achieve his objectives.

Restricted performance function—Social incompetence is more likely if partici-pants are not allowed to both send and receive messages. A buyer, himself a former salesman, half seriously mentioned how some salesmen make excellent presentations yet fail to ask for an order.

Feedback deprivation—Feedback is important so that interactive participants can keep a check on understanding and respond to contingencies. Without some response to a message the effects of the message will be more uncertain. If, for instance, the manager makes a proposal to a colleague and receives no response, he will not only be unable to dismiss the matter but also he will remain unsure that the message was received.

Inattention to message—If the communicator operates inappropriate rules in not allowing a message to be processed effective interaction is less likely. It may be, for example, that the salesman ignores a customer complaint.

Semantic confusion—Whilst the syntax of a message may be represented relatively objectively the meaning afforded the message is invariably a subjec-tive phenomenon. In order to make sense of data it is necessary to hold some representation to which that data can relate. If information is not interpreted correctly the attainment of objectives is threatened, for instance if a pricing clerk misinterprets a directive over discount procedures.

Individual difference negligence—Through his prior experiences, current per-ceptions and future objectives each individual is a unique information pro-cessor. The probability of achieving face-to-face social objectives will diminish if there is a failure to adapt to the other person.

Inappropriate response choice—Although it is possible to be sloppy in inter-personal communication, clearly saying the wrong thing may provoke an undesired reaction.

Social skills and other skills

It appears orthodox to point out the similarities between social skills and perceptual or motor skills which lack the complexities of dealing with people. For instance, social skills, in common with other skills, are exercised purposefully. Leaders, liaisers and persuaders all have their objectives which are part of a more comprehensive representation of events. Secondly, social skills are learned, that is social performance improves with experience as new strategies and responses are developed and reproduced in similar situations. The salesman may develop a repartee with customers and other organizational members will learn which approaches work with whom. As a result of learning, subsequent similar encounters may be quickly interpreted and categorized. By contrast the inexperienced person may be unable to comprehend what is happening and hence feel unsure about how to react. This is particularly acute in cross-cultural encounters where purposes and norms may be obscure. Thirdly, social skills are serially organized in that there is some anticipation of the future as well as a reflection upon the past. Competent social discourse is nicely intermeshed, with participants understanding each other well and proceeding smoothly towards a mutually determined conclusion. Fourthly, it appears appropriate to talk of 'skills within skills' in the social context. At an elevated level in the skill hierarchy decisions concern organization of the message. More fundamentally the communicator must not overload the other person with information, but equally he must not provide too little information, since this will create uncertainty and indecision. Clearly a useful tactic is to ask if a message is understood and there is a need to apply other verbal and non-verbal 'techniques'. Following the terminology of Rackham *et al.*, (1971), the communicator must decide when to disagree, provide support, state difficulties, etc., and non-verbal signals, such as looking, smiling and other gestures will facilitate the process. For instance, if the requirement is to maintain communication in the context of making a sale; listening, building, suggesting and questioning will be likely options. In short the process is one of fixing conditional response probabilities upon some verbal or non-verbal initiation and striking a balance between initiation and response. For the salesman the exercise of well-developed drills may be termed 'sales patter' and he may become known as a 'smooth talker'. Within the organization a similar repartee may develop between colleagues inside and outside the team. Next, the decisions over what to say will partly depend upon the context of the interaction, which will also dictate other patterns of behaviour. For instance, *Fortune* magazine of 5 October, 1981, reported that in Japan the best industrial chemicals salesmen behaved in a 'wet' manner, willing to devote a lot of time to cultivating relationships. On the other hand, selling high technology products was best handled with a more 'dry' direct business approach, since buyers were young Japanese with advanced degrees who, apparently, had little time for tea drinking. Finally, feedback is important for regulating social behaviour.

Hallmarks of social skill

Social skills, in common with other skills, involve data processing, including decision making, the distinctive feature being a perceptual reciprocity involving at least two human adaptive systems. Where inputs emanate from another person the additional factor in social skills relates to initiative and attribution (imputing what the other is thinking and feeling). When construing hardware and (non-personal) systems it is not imagined that the hardware and systems construe back and plan accordingly, but mutual construction is the hallmark of social skills. There is not only the opportunity to reflect upon one's own thoughts but also on the likely thoughts of the other about oneself and reflections beyond.

Ordinarily neither participant has exclusive control of the social situation—this is clearly the case for buyer and seller, organizational colleagues, and it also features in supervisory relationships. Each participant has his own objectives which are part of a more intricate model that allows filtering, selection and interpretation of social inputs. Other perceptual processes, such as categorization, will be relevant and the model may be manipulated in working out a strategy to deal with the encounter. Hence the participant looks to the future as well as relating to the present and drawing on the past. More remote information perhaps concerning the other person, the situation or purpose may be important. The context is critical. A further function of the model is decision making, a choice of response, including verbal responses, what to say and how. It is meaningful to talk of adaptive response strategies which operate through taking account of feedback and contingencies. Moreover, there is a need to cope with the inner self.

In short social skills involve modelling (social) reality and mapping the model back into reality, that is issuing a message to the other(s) in a particular context, as shown in Figure 14.3. The term 'options' reflects the choice-making element in responding. Knowing people will facilitate model building and response choice. Consistent with Bruner's more general view of perception, Brown (1965) points out that a recording of data into more economical format within the scope of limited memory and an extrapolation to predict the future are accomplishments of impression formation in interpersonal perception. Encoding is related to categorization—it is convenient to place our dynamic personal expectancies in categories such as 'generous', 'helpful', 'reliable', etc.

In conclusion

Conceptually the interpersonally interactive participant—salesman, manager or administrator—is developing models of the social situation and its participants. Operationally he has to find his way through the interactive process and key factors will guide his route. Such landmarks include objectives,

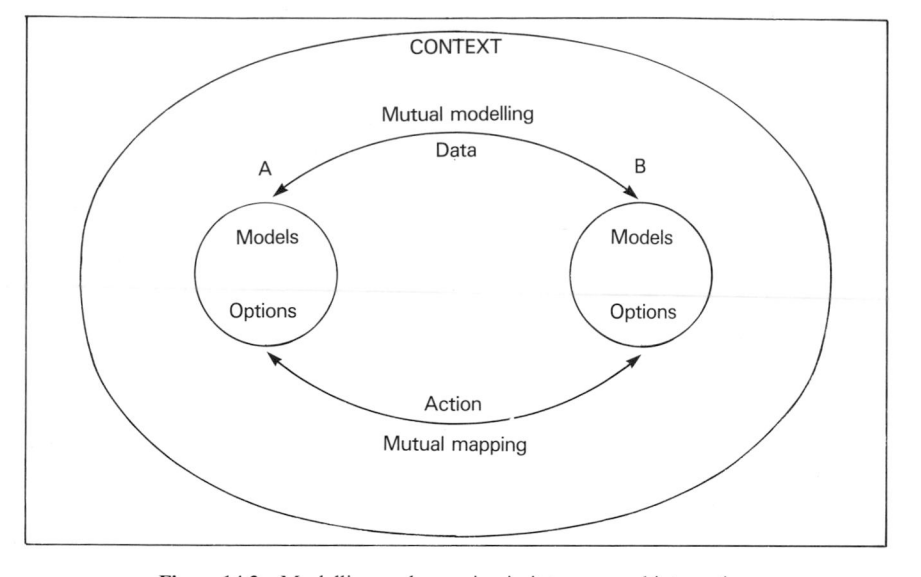

Figure 14.3   Modelling and mapping in interpersonal interaction

process phases, personal attributes and off-line information. For example, the salesman will be guided by customer requirements. Phases in liaising with colleagues may concern 'problem appreciation', 'problem definition', 'solution development' and 'solution implementation'. The leader will be sensitive to individual team members and so on. In this manner the socially skilled person is similar to other skilled persons. Therefore, whilst this volume includes a chapter on individual differences, and whilst it is recognized that differences between individuals are important in interpersonal interactions, the essential features of real skills appear in the generic person and rest not upon variation but upon similarity.

Acknowledgements

I would like to thank Mr B. Joseph and Mr K. D. Pointon for their helpful comments relating to an earlier draft of this chapter.

References

Baier, D. E. and Dugan, R. D. (1957). Factors in sales success. *J. Appl. Psychol.*, **41** (1), 37–40
Barnard, C. (1938). *The Functions of the Executive*. (Cambridge, Massachusetts: Harvard University Press)
Branton, P. (1978). The train driver. In W. T. Singleton (ed.) *The Study of Real Skills, Vol. 1: The Analysis of Practical Skills*. (Lancaster: MTP Press)
Brown, R. (1965). *Social Psychology*. (New York: Macmillan)
Burnett, K. G. (1981). The marketing manager. In W. T. Singleton (ed.) *The Study of Real Skills, Vol. 3: Management Skills*. (Lancaster: MTP Press)

Downs, C. W., Berg, D. M. and Linkugel, W. A. (1978). *The Organisational Communicator*. (New York: Harper and Row)

Fenton, J. (1979). *The A–Z of Sales Management*. (London: Heinemann)

Fiedler, F. E., Bems, P. M. and Hastings, L. L. (1975). New strategies for leadership utilisation. In W. T. Singleton and P. Spurgeon (eds.) *The Measurement of Human Resources*. (London: Taylor and Francis)

Lamont, L. W. and Lundstrom, W. J. (1977). Identifying successful industrial salesmen by personality and personal characteristics. *J. Mark. Res.*, **XIV**, 517 29

Lidstone, J. (1975). *Training Salesmen on the Job*. (Farnborough: Gower Press)

Lusch, R. F., Udell, J. G. and Laczniak, G. R. (1976). The future of marketing strategy. *Business Horizons*, **19**, 165–74

Mant, A. (1977). *The Rise and Fall of the British Manager*. (London: Macmillan)

McMurry, R. N. (1961). The mystique of super salesmanship. *Harvard Bus. Rev.*, March–April, 113–22

Moss, C. D. (1982). Industrial sales forces—trends and developments. *Q. Rev. Mark.*, January, 19–25

Rackham, N., Honey, P. and Colbert, M. (1971). *Developing Interactive Skills*. (Northampton. Wellens Publishing)

Robertson, D. H. (1974). Sales force feedback on competitor activities. *J. Mark.*, **38**, 69–71

Roethlisberger, F. J. and Dickson, W. J. (1939). *Management and the Worker*. (Cambridge, Massachusetts: Harvard University Press)

Sayles, L. R. (1964). *Managerial Behavior*. (New York: McGraw-Hill)

Singleton, W. T. (1979). Final discussion. In W. T. Singleton (ed.) *The Study of Real Skills, Vol. 2: Compliance and Excellence*. (Lancaster: MTP Press)

Singleton, W. T. (1981). Management services. In W. T. Singleton (ed.) *The Study of Real Skills, Vol. 3: Management Skills*. (Lancaster: MTP Press)

Strongman, K. (1977). Learning social skills. In M. J. A. Howe (ed.) *Adult Learning*. (London: Wiley)

Vroom, V. H. and Yetton, P. W. (1973). *Leadership and Decision Making*. (Pittsburg: University of Pittsburg Press)

Welford, A. T. (1976). *Skilled Performance: Perceptual and Motor Skills*. (Glenview: Scott Foreman and Company)

15
The French:
A Cross-cultural Comparison

D F AGER

INTRODUCTION

If the average Englishman walks around with a mental picture of himself playing cricket in the middle of an island, then the French equivalent will be of himself eating in the upper part of a regular six-sided figure, a hexagon. The grain of truth involved in such a picture is as awkward to define or refine as is the irritation we feel when faced with the impossibility of communicating across the Channel, whether in a seminar in which people we thought were colleagues seem to completely lack understanding of the first principles of discussion, or in friendly chit-chat which suddenly reveals gulfs of misunderstanding. Yet French and English speakers are brought up within a European culture: we have common ancestors, spiritual in the Greeks and the Christians and even physical in a thousand years of invasions and conflicts; why and whence the problems? Why should it be that the French and the English find it so difficult to work together even on co-operative projects like *Concorde*, that the French should strive so hard to get the Americans out of their country, that the European Community is so frequently shaken by Franco-British disagreements? The present paper examines some of the aspects of the French which the 'Anglo-Saxons' find difficult to comprehend—or to stomach.

SELF-PERCEPTION

Geographical

The 'natural' frontiers of France do indeed form something like a hexagon: to the north the British Isles, lost in fog and rain and inhabited by perfidious public schoolboys and shopkeepers, only merits a point, rather than a complete side; to the north-west the sea, beckoning to colonial adventure, and nowadays to holidays in the French-speaking parts of the world many miles from Europe; to the west abandoned acres of sand dunes, agricultural poverty and sheep; to the south-west Spain, exotic and unreal; to the south-east Italy and the Mediterranean destiny of France—a major direction for love, learning and loot; to the east a safe haven for storing the loot—in times of trouble, whether political or (at least in the past) amorous, Switzerland provides a secure bank, a neutral bolt-hole and a sympathetic abortionist; to the north-east danger—Belgium has its problems, but Germany is a threat, actualized three times in three-quarters of a century. France for the French then sits at the centre of Europe, at the centre of the civilized world, a microcosm, both geographical and psychological:

> The originality of France is to unite and to summarize the main characteristics of Europe . . . this convergence of characteristics explains the diversity of natural landscapes . . . and that of the people.
>
> *(Documentation Française, 1972)*

Within the hexagon the keynote of this diversity is variety in productivity: where the Englishman sees green fields, the Frenchman sees wheat fields; where the population of the British Isles was two million in the eleventh century and six-and-a-half million in the early eighteenth, that of France was twelve and twenty million respectively. A rich and fertile, varied and productive, spacious and welcoming territory, France seems to its inhabitants the natural centre of things.

Economic

Economically, the French are peasants, but middle-class peasants. Hence small is beautiful; large firms, large farms, large forms (in the administration) are anathema. Likewise, savings are in gold. Wealth, once amassed, is for storing and hoarding, preferably in gold coins in a stocking under the bed in case the Germans invade again. Investment in productive industry is a recent invention, and the Frenchman's concern is to pass on his inheritance intact. The first Napoleonic code was that of property and the Communist Party is insistent that its duty is to protect the peasant's right to the ownership of land.

As the peasantry represents the group with the most to gain or lose by revolution, the urban working class is not the point of progress, nor is it the proletariat for the French. The small independent farmer rules the roost, resistant to change, ready to demonstrate in the streets of the local town or Brussels, ready to burn Spanish lorries or destroy Italian wine; the modern Luddite has no history of Tolpuddle martyrs or Tammany Hall and demands that the State protect him and his way of life.

Despite Pascal, Diderot and the technological marvels of the eighteenth-century *Encyclopedia*, France's industrial revolution came late, hence mines and steel are not the traditional basis for France's industrial wealth and there is room for technological innovation.

Historical

The Frenchman is formed with an historical as well as a geographical mould, and the strongest elements within France's history are the Revolution, Napoleon and the invasions.

The Revolution of 1789, in which the Paris mob killed the king and in which Parliamentary debates led directly to action, has marked fundamental dichotomies of French society ever since: the Left and the Right, obviously, although the Left, being the first Left, is now far to the Right of contemporary post-Marxist thought and its representatives co-operate in capitalist government; centralism and decentralization, actualized in the striking phrase of 'Paris and the French desert'; the haves and the have-nots. But the most striking legacies are in the role not taken in public life by the aristocracy, except at local level; there are no local squires, and Agatha Christie's village life, or Lord Peter Whimsey, are fundamentally incomprehensible to the French. By contrast, the local elite is the lawyer, the priest and the schoolmaster, who act in opposition to each other, particularly in politics. Hence, trivially, gamekeepers in France are ineffective and serve wealth not position. More importantly, the money markets which have been the refuge of the English landed gentry when trade became possible for them do not exist in France, and capital generation has traditionally been slow and difficult.

The Revolution had one other sociological effect: the power and prestige of the real winners, the middle classes, whose offspring flood the universities and selective higher education institutions, the 'Grandes Ecoles', who themselves staff the elite positions in government and business, whose priorities and pleasures control and direct the nation's life. Of the nineteenth-century baccalaureate, the 'highest level of secondary education and the lowest of higher education', used traditionally as a certificate of belonging to this class, it was possible to say that it

> did not, in fact, test any real level of intellectual ability or attainment; rather its primary function was to legitimate and sanction a certain form of culture, that of the decent and virtuous 'honnête homme', capable of holding his own in a bourgeois society and of being recognized and respected within it.
>
> *(P. Gerbod, 1981)*

Of the three slogans of the French Revolution, equality, fraternity and liberty, Napoleon, the Cromwell who didn't retire to the country, revised the first, defined the second and channelled the third into ways which were eerily echoed by de Gaulle. The myth of the strong man, the only political power capable of controlling the undisciplined French, has given birth to an -ism of its own, Bonapartisme, and a political party which has survived under the name of Gaullism 15 years after the death of the General. But Napoleon's strongest legacy is the very framework of France: its laws, its administrative system, its structure as a modern State.

There were, of course, two Napoleons: the first, who ruled from 1799 to 1814 and is remembered; the third (there was no second), who ruled from 1851 to 1870 and is buried in Farnborough, in Hampshire, forgotten and ignored. The first codified laws, set up the present system of selection for the Civil Service—the selection of Mandarins by examination, and ruled as a despot, extending French ideals and presence over the whole of Europe by force of arms. His legacy is a powerful body of functionaries, treating the State as all-important and accepted by the citizen as possessing this authority:

> the Civil Servant does not consider himself as an isolated individual . . . but as the representative of an entity which surpasses him and from which he derives his power . . . the State is the symbol which establishes social identity and guarantees continuity, the unity and permanence of the Nation. The Nation–State is the foundation of all authority . . . its symbolic image is a veritable fetish . . . a substitute for God and for the Father . . . speaking for the State, the Civil Servant is merely conveying the precepts of the Law.
>
> *(J. Chevallier* et al., *1980)*

The destiny of France is intertwined with that of Germany, its powerful neighbour. Ever since the sons of Charlemagne agreed to divide up Europe between them, French and German kings and politicians have been at war or have tried to set up a lasting peace. In 1871, 1914 and 1940 they failed, and the invasions from the east have marked the French in ways as deep as those from the west have marked the Russians. The outward effect is a distrust of the police, so often used by the conqueror to enforce his rule, and an expectation of violence in political life, an expectation which is all too often realized, whether in strikes, peasants' protests, political rallies, mysterious assassinations or simply in emotional meetings and rallies, in which the rhetoric is extreme and vigorous.

Cultural

Man does not live, however, by politics and sociology alone; the life of the spirit also contributes to the make-up of individual and national attitudes. France has always considered herself to be at the forefront of artistic development: in literature with the great men of the seventeenth century, in art with the early twentieth, in music likewise; only Paris could have accepted the design for the Beaubourg Centre and then actually built it within sight of

Notre Dame. Pride in achievement is not limited to Frenchmen, but the certainty that French culture is pre-eminent is a characteristic based on an attitude towards the life of the mind which fundamentally opposes Anglo-Saxon hatred for thought with Latin respect for thinkers.

The French respect for thinkers and 'intellectual workers' should not lead us to ignore the effect of fashion, nor to avoid analysing the nature of the 'thought' involved. A perspicacious French sociologist views the intellectual world in somewhat jaundiced fashion:

> One cannot understand French post-war intellectual life without giving Sartre the importance he deserves. As a prize example of the 'literary spirit', and particularly of the application of this spirit in the political domain, Sartre is incontrovertibly the reference, to use the term in its sociological sense, for many of the French intelligentsia. His preference for a rhetorical and pseudo-deductive treatment of empirical questions, his tidy mind, his skill with words, his lack of respect for facts can be found in many intellectuals who have been lionized over the past twenty years.
>
> *(R. Boudon, 1981)*

Whether such a description could fairly be applied to all the country's intellectuals is doubtful; that the 'literary spirit' is very much alive and well is undoubted. The French educational system and procedures reflect deeply-felt approaches to life and cultural values. In the development of the 'literary spirit', the 'rhetorical and pseudo-deductive' approach must fight hard against other traditions and other values: Descartes, Voltaire and the linguistic bias of education all have a role to play.

Descartes, the inventor of 'I think, therefore I am', encourages the French to trust nothing and nobody. Relying on his own judgement and his own perceptions, Cartesian man slowly rebuilds a world in his own image. The contrast between a caring, sharing interdependent world and an individualistic, shrewd, self-reliant and critical approach, organized within a systematic framework, is apparent in attitudes to authority, and Pitts' view of the 'delinquent community' is an entertaining representation of this:

> In France, the secondary school remains a place one goes to solely in order to work. . . . With some teachers, the group spirit is revealed, and barracking, collective joy, fantasy, uproar are let loose . . . a sort of happening where the individual is free to express his will . . . in miraculous unanimity with his comrades. The delinquent community is established, opposing the cultural community.
>
> It is delinquent because it exists only in opposition to established authority . . .
>
> The State gives its orders in the form of a peremptory instruction taking account of all possible eventualities. . . . Any discussion, since it is in its nature illegitimate, immediately becomes inacceptable and rebellious . . . its consequences are:

The French political system is more subject than others to collective demonstrations leading to contained violence which does not threaten symbolic or administrative frameworks.

The citizen conforms, but speaks as though he does not believe; he has no public commitment in the process of decision making.

(J. R. Pitts, 1981)

This detachment from decision making, or from the responsibilities associated with decision making, is fascinating. The propensity of Anglo-Saxons to believe that laws are made to be obeyed is observed with some horror by the French, who honour many laws, particularly, of course, those relating to tax collection, more in the breach than the observance. Such autonomy, individualism and self-reliance, is inculcated from the first school exercise in 'forming judgement', a process in which the child is encouraged to *'trancher'*, to identify clear, black and white points of view, and to plump for one or the other of these clear-cut opposites. Grey compromise has no part to play in the French educational system.

Voltaire's famous phrase at the end of *Candide*—'That's all very well, but we have to cultivate our garden', although reminiscent of 'I'm all right Jack', is, in fact, qualitatively different. The canny peasant looking after his own is disregarding, in *Candide*, a grand philosophical statement, not being selfish towards others; and Voltaire's commonsense approach to the realities of life is often echoed in the Realpolitik of French diplomacy or the down-to-earth contrast, not unique to the French, between talk of disarmament and the sales of Mirage fighters.

The French educational system is language-based, that is to say, the typical exercise at primary school level is dictation and at secondary school level the 'explication de texte', a process of commenting on selected pages from great works in a set order and pattern. The aims of education, however, are not merely to encourage the young to read and write well, they combine the State aims of forging a nation by eliminating local variation in language with class priorities in establishing and maintaining the elite. Although today the education of the elite is mathematics-based rather than classics-based, the point remains that the techniques involved require students to acquire a spread of knowledge, a nodding acquaintance with great thinkers, writers and characters, rather than the narrower, more specialized coverage required by the British educational system. The aim might seem to be the development of the *honnête homme*, a citizen familiar with and able to speak on most subjects, not afraid to put forward his own ideas and robustly to defend them.

THE USE OF LANGUAGE

Within this range of attitudes and against a historical, economic, political and social setting so different from that of Anglo-Saxon man, the Frenchman evolves, expresses himself, lives and dies. The skills he displays in expressing himself and in interacting with others, whether of his own or of other cultures, are learnt, displayed, practised in many ways, most obviously through the manipulation of spoken and written language.

In order to manipulate spoken or written language the most obvious requirement is to have something to say, and to organize that something in a sequence. At this level one of the greatest differences between French and non-French culture and educational tradition manifests itself: at school we are asked to write an essay and the subconscious model is Hazlitt; they are asked to organize a dissertation and the subconscious model lies in the Greek and Latin tradition of rhetoric, a tightly organized sequence of introduction, thesis, antithesis, synthesis and conclusion, a sequence whose rigidity contrasts utterly with the disorganized and random thoughts of the nature-lovers that we are. What then exactly is a dissertation in the French sense?

A fundamental test used in many examinations and in most of the 'concours' (competitive examinations used for entry to the Grandes Ecoles, for admission to qualified status in many professions, and for all State-controlled professions (the majority)) . . . attacked in recent years as a formal and arid exercise . . . the dissertation is nonetheless fundamental to many activities. It has three aims, corresponding to the three needs of any developed communication . . . identification of the basic elements of a question . . . covering all aspects of a question . . . elaborate the coverage in an intellectually satisfying way, so that the logical process adopted by the author in presenting his analysis . . . enables the reader to understand and to accept this analysis as correct.

Such precise objectives impose a rigorous method . . . the first principle: the subject, the whole subject, nothing but the subject . . . the second principle: proof, and not idle chatter . . . the third principle: be personal, but not partisan. . . .

On the question of the plan . . . no one has ever imposed the three-part model. Nonetheless, if a student only finds two stages in his argument he will do well to check carefully that other aspects have not escaped him . . . on the other hand if he identifies five, six or seven stages, he must be sure that he is not exceeding the limits of his subject and perhaps recast the same idea in different ways. . . . Certain logical approaches are possible: a dialectical method, permitting the analysis and evaluation of a point of view . . . a progressive method, illuminating a process of definition . . . a comparative method, establishing the relationship between items . . . enumerative methods, replying to specific questions—where, what, how, how far?
(P. Jeoffroy-Faggianelli and L.-R. Plazolles, 1975)

Such immensely precise advice indicates how important this particular linguistic form is within the educational and professional life of the country. Certainly the formal training of the higher echelons of the Civil Service, of those who will go on to staff universities and research institutes, and of those who now call themselves 'Superior Administrative Cadres', will not merely include such exercises but be based on them. Pity the product of an educational system which prefers the rambling inconsequentialities of the typical British A-level essay question when he meets, perhaps in Brussels or at the United Nations, minds which have cut their teeth on such procedures. Pity, perhaps, also the product of the system who is able to present, dissect and analyse any topic, force it into the mould and squeeze out the approved compromise answer at the end, compromise, that is, lying exactly half-way between the two extreme positions which have been previously rationally discussed.

Many other message forms exist in French culture, of course: the lecture, the speech, the letter, the tract; as in any other culture they have their norms and their requirements. Because of its importance in contemporary life, and before examining the detail of the symbols, the words and sentences, which make up messages, we could perhaps pause for a moment over publicity and advertising.

It is a truism that different cultures react differently to pictorial representations. Nonetheless a cursory glance through any French publication, a newspaper or weekly magazine, will show that in many if not most cases cigarette advertisements, or those for cars or other artefacts of our contemporary civilization, are very similar to those appearing in the *Daily Express* or *Newsweek* or *Time*. Some aspects of lifestyle differ, of course, but the USA will be positively viewed and many 'European' attitudes accepted as not too exotic.

Analysing or creating advertising messages appropriate for the French is a job for specialists, of course: indices of readability, of concision, of dynamism, of interest help to identify the impact of the message, which itself has to be consonant with the frame of reference of the target individuals and groups. Merely saying that advertising in French avoids the use of the otherwise necessary 'form' words (of, the, at . . .) and makes heavy use of 'full' words (mainly nouns) and certain 'key' words (new, bargain, free, modern . . .) is insufficient to enable us to distinguish between the good and the ineffective advert. But nonetheless these linguistic norms, the expectation that advertising language will be different from ordinary language, forms part of the frame of reference within which one can assess the effectiveness of the publicity message.

The symbols themselves, the words and phrases the Frenchman has available in his armoury to assist him in communicating, are of course, different from English, not merely in their form but in the way they are grouped and rendered available and in the way they are called on to perform in the act of communication. The French language does not possess the wealth of vocabulary of English nor its double keyboard—the words of French or Latin origin contrasted with those of Anglo-Saxon or Germanic origin—an opposition which enables English to offer many subtle contrasts, particularly in class-related usage or in the opposition between abstract and concrete. Hence, French often appears to the English as a language full of abstractions, preferring the theoretical to the concrete, the theory to the data, the general to the particular, and also the logical to the intuitive. Not that French appeared ready-made from Latin—its history has been just as chequered as that of English, particularly in the words and expressions it has borrowed from other languages over its development. At the present time it is suffering massive invasions from Anglo-American and absorbing, badly, new words and expressions, ill-digested and causing much resentment to the purists. Scientists are finding that their work is not recognized unless they publish in English. Even international conferences held on French soil are addressed by French scientists now in English.

Another striking problem for the French language is the amazing contrast between its spoken and its written forms. A letter written by an average intelligent child of 15 or so can be guaranteed to contain mistakes in spelling. There are at least eight ways of spelling one of the common verb endings, and although French does not have problems of the 'tough, cough, plough, through' variety, these are actually quite rare in English, and French does have major problems in coping with the conventions of its written form, conventions which date in the most part only from the seventeenth century and which are still occasionally adjusted by ministerial decree.

The French language is highly valued, regarded as a major contribution to the artistic and cultural inheritance of mankind, and as an object of considerable value in itself. Hence, not merely the many and repeated condemnations of what are seen as attacks on it by foreign aggressors, such as the Anglo-American terms taking over in the worlds of commerce, of science and of technology, but also the general acceptance, particularly since the Revolution of 1789, of the necessity to oust regional languages and dialects in favour of the language of Paris. Local terms have proved remarkably resilient in fact. Although the national language was understood by less than one-third of the population in 1794, dialects had not completely disappeared, even from the area around Paris, until around 1925, and certain regional languages (Breton, Basque) have not gone and in fact have regained some of the ground lost in the last 20 years or so. Nonetheless the point remains that whereas received pronunciation of Oxford English is a class phenomenon, regarded with scorn particularly by males north of Hatfield, Parisian French is regarded as the norm, acceptable and to be admired.

Not merely is Parisian French admired in itself, those who are expert in the manipulation of the cultural symbols represented by words and phrases are themselves admired:

For those who possess 'style' much will be forgiven. There are, of course, many different kinds of style. It's a question of presence, of movement, of tone, but above all of the mastery of words through which the individual, teacher or pupil, will be accepted as both a unique individual and also as member of an elite group.

(J. R. Pitts, 1981)

Admired also are politicians who are able to deploy their linguistic skills; a detailed analysis of the language of Giscard d'Estaing shows the extent to which his televised debate with Mitterand in May 1974 contributed to his win in the Presidential elections:

> Having hammered home a dozen times the binary opposition yesterday–today, you–me, V.G.E. can thrust home the final barb without fear of appearing discourteous—'Mr Mitterand, you are a man of the past'; and the effect of a single well-chosen phrase: 'I find it shocking and hurtful to take for oneself the monopoly of feelings *(le monopole du coeur)*. You, Mr Mitterand, do not have a monopoly of feelings.'

(P. Lehingue, 1980)

COMMUNICATION BETWEEN INDIVIDUALS AND IN GROUPS

Stated attitudes towards the symbols and signs of language indicate the values a society holds, and the use of those symbols in interaction between citizens is significant in revealing the extent to which that same society carries into practice its own beliefs. France was one of the first European nations to create a revolution, to overthrow despotic and autocratic rule. It replaced this regime with the concept of the nation, the voluntary association of free men who wish to put aside regional and personal differences to create political and social unity. In the process, regional languages were to be discarded as relics of an aristocratic past; French was the language of liberty, Breton the language of obscurantist maniacs. French could not, however, as easily put aside the range of expressions it contains to express relationships between individuals, whether these are relations of respect, of affection, or of intention, and the range of linguistic devices which enables individuals to convey information, to indicate their own status and provenance, or to control the nature of the interaction in which they are participating, is, for example, noticeably different from the range available in English.

Languages are not, of course, static:

> Among the European countries in which the language distinguishes the two forms of 'you', the France of thirty years ago used the familiar form most rarely (more so than Germany, Spain or Italy). It liked politeness forms and titles, and did not restrict the external forms of respect. . . . In Japan, Frenchmen of 50 feel a lot less out of place than most Europeans. But there too, change is visible; practically all in the workplace can now be addressed by *tu*, even between the sexes and the hierarchical levels. First

names can be used (a habit borrowed from the United States and felt as such at first). Boys and girls of student age greet each other by kissing on both cheeks (a popular, peasant custom, but for peasants only used between relatives).

(J.-D. Reynaud, 1981)

Such subtleties in the external forms of relationship (constant handshaking is another one—the rules completely baffle the average Anglo-Saxon until he realizes that the gesture is a ritual for initial contact rather than leave-taking) reflect norms of politeness which run deep in the society and the language. The use of *Monsieur*, or, more particularly, *Madame* and *Mademoiselle*, frequently during conversation between comparative strangers or even between, for example, neighbours who have known each other for years, reflect the degree of social distance which the Frenchman feels it appropriate to maintain between himself and others.

Wylie has shown also that physical stance, gesture and personal space reflect the private person who is the Frenchman:

When moving during conversation, the French rock from front to back, contrasting with the American lateral movement . . . a conversation in France reminds one of the reciprocal movement of fencers . . . the French rarely put their hands in their pockets. They often keep the upper arm pressed against the body, but have incredible flexibility in the wrist, elbow and hand. . . . Hands are used to indicate conversational rhythm. . . . The difference between the gait of Frenchmen and Americans is so marked that it is easy to pick out an American in Paris a hundred yards away . . . the French seem to move along a narrow corridor; their personal space is much more restricted. . . . Body tension gives the movements of Frenchmen a certain brusqueness, a sort of staccato rhythm which is distinctive, not merely of bodily behaviour but also of French communication norms.

(L. Wylie, 1981)

The apparent rigidity of the French often makes them appear to American eyes as formal and unfriendly; less so to the British, who are famous for their reserve. Nonetheless the French certainly feel uncomfortable in the presence of Anglo-Saxons who lounge about, leaning on the nearest wall or table with their hands in their pockets, casually and in what seems a barely polite fashion.

Likewise, the Anglo-Saxon is often disconcerted by the apparent vigour and forcefulness of French conversation itself. The Frenchman leans forward, his shoulders jutting into the group, making his points in stabbing motions of the fingers and waving his hands in incomprehensible gestures, shooting his cuffs and occasionally shrugging his shoulders and forcing his chin forwards and upwards, expelling breath in a 'bof' or a 'pouf', which contrasts violently with the English drawl, 'er, um', or the American drawn-out 'well'.

Incomprehension is complete when the Frenchman starts playing different rhythms with different parts of his body. Wylie again:

> If one watches a slowed-down film of Frenchmen talking, it is possible to observe a one-second rhythm with the hand, while the head is showing a different rhythm to indicate the significance of the point being made, the sound being emitted in well under a second. In addition, the French are able to greatly increase the speed of gestures, or to slow them down.
>
> *(L. Wylie, 1981)*

These bodily indicators of interaction are of course supportive; the rules of conversational interchange applicable to two-person conversation are what really worry the poor Anglo-Saxon. Not so much the openers and closers, the *Bonjour* or the *Au revoir* (or more usually nowadays the Italian *Ciao*), as the problem of taking one's turn in the conversation. English and American clues are quite obvious, at least to those who have been brought up within Anglo-Saxon culture and have learnt them as cultural norms: intonation drops and the voice dies away, eyes look and invite, eyebrows rise, there may be a change in the body orientation of the partners; in France the rules are quite different and must be learnt all over again. Wylie comments that: 'Among the French it is by no means rare that the second speaker does not wait for the first to finish before speaking, starting on the last or even the penultimate beat, or even on the one before', and it is a common experience for the American or English person to find it extremely difficult to adapt to this procedure, thus constantly finding himself unable to participate in a conversation without what in Anglo-Saxon terms feels like unpardonable rudeness. Likewise, he must be prepared for an apparently friendly interlocutor to 'interrupt' at inopportune moments or to misread the cues to take his turn. Within Anglo-Saxon norms the 'interrupter' is a neurotic, an extrovert, a dominant male (Beattie, 1982), and it is hence easy to regard all Frenchmen as attempting to dominate, even though on their own terms this is merely the normal procedure for interaction. The need to interrupt, to make one's point in the conversation, is the need to participate, but 'participation' for the French is defined as the need to express oneself, one's own point of view as an independent being normally in competition with others.

By contrast with English, the French language does not avoid the use of the first person singular pronoun; the language requires that pronouns be used with verbs always, and forms like 'seems so' or 'think it's OK now', although only possible in conversational English, are altogether impossible for French. This being so, the pronoun 'I' has to be strengthened in some way in the French language in order to be used to stress the identity of the speaker, and it is usual nowadays to find that instead of the simple *je*, *moi je* will be used. However, this boosting of the personal pronoun seems to fit quite well into conversation in French and, incidentally, it of course boosts the importance of the speaker. This boosting process happens in at least two other ways in

French: the subjunctive is, for example, used after 'I don't think that . . .' but not after 'I think that . . .', and the subjunctive, as we know, expresses a mood of doubt; and the intonation patterns of French, quite unlike those of English, do not permit emphasis—French has to emphasize by using additional words, by rephrasing and adding to the length of items. Whereas English can say 'I think so' and stress any one of the three elements by intonation, French has to recast the sentence to boost up the particular element.

One final major way in which the norms of French conversational interaction differ utterly from those of English lies in the expression of various moods and feelings. Doubt, anger, fear, joy; the approval or disapproval of what has been said, and its acceptance or rejection by the speaker; surprise, disbelief or disgust all come through in English by a mixture of linguistic clues—principally intonation; non-verbal indications, such as gesture or facial expression, and semi- or para-linguistic features, such as heavy breathing or a high voice. In French, many of these clues are quite different and again the characteristic French staccato intonation, with a stress on the penultimate syllable of the phrase (not on a 'stressed' word) and without the pitch differences of English, is responsible for much of the difference. Listening to a Frenchman speak can be a tiring experience for an Englishman; this constant high-speed rattle on the same level, with apparently arbitrary rises and falls in the voice and no obvious end to the sentence:

> The melody of the French phrase, the continuity of the vowel chain, the duration, obviously and noticeably equal, of syllables and the relative weakness of stress upsets many foreigners, more used to a stressed or more rhythmic sentence. And it is perhaps by this that one first recognizes a foreigner speaking French; a German, an Englishman, an Italian, unconsciously destroy the natural melody of our sentence patterns.
>
> *(G. Galichet, 1961)*

For a Frenchman, of course, the opposite is true: the Anglo-Saxons drawl, lazily swallowing half their words in such a way that comprehension is decreased; they raise their voices, but don't indicate what's important and what isn't; and they seem to have no opinions of their own.

Disagreeing with the previous speaker is an obvious case in point. In English, at least in polite conversation between comparative strangers, it will be usual to introduce one's comment by some such phrase as 'On the other hand' or 'Well, perhaps it's not quite so simple as that . . .'; French will have no qualms about putting the boot in straight away with something like 'I (stressed) think that . . .' or 'You're wrong . . .', followed by a detailed exposition of exactly why and where you're wrong, and what the speaker's opinions exactly are.

It could well be, in fact, that it is in expounding a point of view, explaining, 'pontificating' generally that the Frenchman's conversation takes off. Give a Frenchman the chance and he'll tell you in great detail everything you ever wanted to know about anything: displaying knowledge, monologuing or telling, as opposed to talking, is anathema to the British, although less so to the Americans.

SUCCESS: THE GOOD AND THE BAD COMMUNICATOR

Hence, for the French, the good communicator is he who can get his word in edgeways. Although the situation may seem to the bemused Anglo-Saxon anthropologist somewhat like that which apparently prevails among the Subanun, who have to display superior linguistic prowess in order to earn a drink and gain the respect of their fellows, the French still value conversational interchange highly enough to want to do it. And those who are good at it are prized by their fellows.

In order to be able to recognize someone who is good at a job one must be able to define what is the measure of success, and success in a communication situation is presumably measured either from the point of view of the sender of the message (he got his message over—a political speaker would be a good model), or from that of the recipient (he got the information he wanted—a journalist/interviewer could be the model). In a conversation the two participants are both senders and receivers alternately, so the measure has to include some notion of the effectiveness of the feedback mechanism (I disagreed, and then we agreed on a new line—the model would be the negotiator). Added to this is the whole area of the obvious as opposed to the less obvious (we were talking about the theatre, but really I wanted to find out if he knew about Jack and Jill, and to see if he was the sort of chap I could tell trade secrets to—the successful participant here could be an industrial spy). And, finally, there is the question of 'face' (Goffman, 1955) and motivation generally (he made me feel stupid—the most obvious model is the relationship between the sexes, a couple on the way towards marriage or on the way from it). Measuring what we mean by a good communicator as opposed to a bad one should presumably contain some element of all these strands. In observing French society from the outside it would seem that those who seem to be regarded by the French as successful conversationalists are those who come nearest to the model of the politician—i.e. those who can get their message, their point of view or their feelings, across best.

How does this good Frenchman do it? In Anglo-Saxon society it would have to be by force of personality. Only the dominant can get his message across against the other messages that are being sent when the norms of society do not permit the imposition of the message. Not necessarily so in the competitive society of autonomous individuals, which is the picture of French society we have painted. It's not just a matter of shouting louder than the other chap when all the chaps are shouting equally loud, but of formulating a message which persuades. So one aspect of success must lie in the presentation of the message, a presentation which is clear, coherent, consistent, cogent and convincing. General de Gaulle, like Winston Churchill in England, must go down in history as one of the great representatives of his country. It was apparently de Gaulle's habit, when he was entertaining the president of some comparatively minor country, to dazzle the interlocutor by a monologue covering all aspects of French foreign policy, reviewing every quarter of the globe in half an hour and dismissing the bemused guest after a display which had apparently revealed the secrets of world diplomacy. Whether the display could truly be called conversation, or would be recognized as such in the Anglo-Saxon world, is doubtful.

Associated with this taste for rhetoric is the taste for maxims. Because the French language, when contrasted with the English, lacks precision—that is to say its words are more general and can be used in different contexts with different senses—French tends to like the grand general statement, the *bon mot*, the maxim, the definitive formula:

> One tends to speak in ready-made formulae, in cliches. Bally notes that the Frenchman is characterized by his liking for the ready-made formula, for maxims struck like so many medals.
>
> *(G. Galichet, 1961)*

The good communicator will be he who uses such grand statements of general import, who discovers the general message in the particular case; above all he who discovers the abstract in the concrete, and generalizes, as quickly as possible, from the specific.

The poor communicator, by contrast, is recognizable to the French as the person who has no ideas of his own, and who has no coherence—*pas de suite dans les idées*. What is more, even if the poor chap does attempt to express himself, he will be unable to 'defend' himself against the ideas and opinions of others. One of the aims of education, for many parents, is in fact to inculcate the ability to defend oneself against others, to put forward a point of view and maintain it in the face of attacks.

CROSSING THE LINE

There are many obvious differences between French and Anglo-Saxon culture, and many commentators feel that the gap is too big to be crossed. Two more examples:

> We were able to observe that the French were indeed less inclined than the English or even the Italians to accept the discipline of group-work. We are less well-prepared for it than the others. The whole of our education prepares us for competition . . . We do not work with others but against them; the less information they have the less likely they will be to beat us in the race.
>
> *(P. Gourgand, 1969)*

and again, in discussing social networks, the authors of the latest edition of the French government's statistical survey of social trends note that there exist some particularly closed groups, as measured by intermarriage. These include the liberal professions, leaders of the commercial world, the self-employed, artists—that is most of the elite—in addition to traditionally closed groups like miners, fishermen and smallholders. Closed groups within the country do not lead to open communication networks with strangers or foreigners.

If French society is closed, 'blocked' as it has been described, communicating with its representatives, and particularly with representatives of its elite, will be no easy task. For the Anglo-Saxon to succeed in so doing requires him to adopt the norms of the French, or for the French to adopt our norms, or for there to be some form of compromise. If we assume that our two participants are not really interested in learning about each other's societies, but wish to exchange cognitive information and are interested in indexical information and in interaction management only insofar as these other aspects of communication enable them to exchange across the barriers, the compromise will involve, from the Anglo-Saxon side, willingness to move at least part-way towards French norms. The implication is that we are prepared to understand the reasons for the French norms, observe the characteristics of communication in French, and adopt some of these characteristics.

Which ones? Let us assume that the conversation is in English, or pseudo-English, and that there are no problems of linguistic understanding. Advice could then be limited to dealing with openers, with listening, with monologuing and with the niceties.

The Anglo-Saxon can with advantage be more brusque, more personal and more definite—use of the personal pronoun 'I', use of the negative, either directly or by implication, avoidance of intonation as a marker of one's feelings or of stress, but also care in the outward forms of politeness, particularly in initiating conversation.

It is difficult for the average Anglo-Saxon not to be somewhat overawed by what appears to be the wide general knowledge of the French and also by their apparent superior intelligence. The latter often derives from the habit of abstraction, of adopting the general statement, of drawing the general case from the particular—and sometimes of doing so without bothering about the intermediate step of analysing the particular case. The former has its origins in a mode of education which examines extracts, which covers trends and movements rather than individual authors or problems. In both cases there is no reason why such an approach could not also be adopted by the English or the Americans. It has not been, and it is often necessary to listen critically to French speech in order to identify the vague generality and the superficial understanding which may lie behind the tag from Plato or the breath-takingly wise maxim. In interrupting, too, French norms will accept both speaking at the same time as one's interlocutor and starting to speak before an apparent sentence ends.

When the floor is ours, six hints seem to work. Firstly, that organized statements go down better than apparently pointless remarks. It is quite surprising to discover how many statements in English do not seem to adopt the obvious order of items in the sentence, for example, subject, verb, object. Neither does much of French, as a matter of fact, but the French love of clarity and simplicity makes this a preferred order, and systematic, if somewhat boringly obvious, coverage of the point is more effective than allusive side-swiping. British understatement, associated with the stiff upper lip and all that, is completely incomprehensible to the French. If you wish to stress something to a Frenchman, you stress it, not the opposite.

The general statement, the abstraction, goes down well also; move out of the particular into the general as quickly as possible. Maxims, fine turns of phrase, aphorisms and elegance are most definitely grist to the mill, rhetoric and overstatement likewise. What to many an Englishman sounds like flowery, effeminate and rather woolly playing with words sounds to many a Frenchman like a pleasing and acceptable aid to understanding: monosyllabic utterances are out, polysyllables are in. English has a considerable and well-developed Latin-based vocabulary, and most teachers of English counsel against using it. For the French the Latin-based words are easier to understand than the Anglo-Saxon ones, so the long words are better than the short ones. Top of the list are Latin-based words ending in -tion or -sion.

Until recently, at any rate, the main entertainment of the French was talking, so the Anglo-Saxon will be expected to talk a lot, by our norms. Silence is not regarded as the refuge of the super-intelligent, wishing to avoid contamination with lesser minds, but rather the opposite; roses that are born to bloom unseen are just plain ignored. And two niceties to end the list of do's and don't's: in humour, wit rather than bananas, boobs and bums, although this is not to say that French humour cannot be extremely crude on occasions; and the liberal use of politeness tags, such as the name of the interlocutor, his title or position, avoiding any casualness in address.

The list is inevitably limited to aspects of interaction which are amenable to conscious control, which can be learnt and practised, and which go some way towards a sort of international average of acceptability. How far, in individual circumstances, one or the other interlocutor will wish to go towards the norms of the other's society is difficult to tell; in doing so he will be gradually adopting a different persona. The French have fascinated the English for centuries, through wars, love affairs and negotiations; at many times their attitudes have been the opposite of ours, and if it were not so the world would be a more uniform, grey and miserable place:

The French may have changed their ambitions and material interests, but their basic character-traits, built around individualism, social mistrust and desire for formalism and routine, are inevitably slower to change, and so is the legal and official framework of France which derives from the French character.

(J. Ardagh, 1970)

References

——— (1972). La France: Documentation Française

——— (1981). Données Sociales: INSEE, 4e edn.

Ardagh, J. (1970). *The New France*. 2nd edn., 15. (Paris: Pelican)

Beattie, G. W. (1982). Interruption in conversational interaction. *Linguistics*, **19**, 15–35

Boudon, R. (1981). L'intellectuel et ses publics: les singularités françaises. In J.-D. Reynaud and Y. Grafmeyer (1981), 479

Chevallier, J. (1980). L'idéologie des fonctionnaires. In J. Chevallier *et al.* (1980), 3–58

Chevallier, J. *et al.* (1980). *Discours et Idéologie*. (Paris: P.U.F.)

Galichet, G. (1961). *Physiologie de la Langue Française*, 115. (Paris: P.U.F.)

Gerbod, P. (1981). The baccalaureate and its role in the recruitment and formation of French élites in the nineteenth century. In J. Howorth and P. Cerny (1981), 54

Goffman, E. (1955). On face-work: an analysis of ritual elements in social interaction. *Psychiatry*, **18**, 213–31; reprinted in J. Laver and S. Hutcheson (eds.) (1972). *Communication in Face-to-Face Interaction*, 319–63. (London: Penguin)

Gourgand, P. (1969). *Les Techniques de Travail en Groupe*, 20. (Toulouse: Privat)

Howorth, J. and Cerny, P. (1981) (eds.) *Elites in France*. (Paris: Frances Pinter)

Jeoffroy-Faggianelli, P. and Plazolles, L.-R. (1975). *Techniques de l'Expression et de la Communication*, 91–4. (Paris: Nathan)

Lehingue, P. (1980). *Le Discours Giscardien*. In J. Chevallier *et al.* (1980), 167

Pitts, J. R. (1981). *Les Français et l'Autorité*. In J.-D. Reynaud and Y. Grafmeyer (1981), 285–99

Reynaud, J.-D. (1981). Introduction. In J.-D. Reynaud and Y. Grafmeyer (1981), 15

Reynaud, J.-D. and Grafmeyer, Y. (1981). *Français qui Etes-vous? Des Essais et des Chiffres*. (Paris: Documentation Française)

Wylie, L. (1981). *Joindre le Geste à la Parole*. In J.-D. Reynaud and Y. Grafmeyer (1981), 319–22

16
Learning Conversations: The Skill of Managing Learning

L. F. THOMAS

INTRODUCTION

It is the aim of this paper to explore how far a 'skill theory' of conversation can shed light on the process of effective teaching. For hundreds, if not thousands, of years the art of teaching has been analysed and discussed. The belief that great teachers are born not trained persists despite numerous attempts to formulate and empirically evaluate some science of teaching. Socrates and Confucius were revered for their outstanding powers as teachers. Jesus Christ is often acknowledged, even among the ungodly, as the greatest teacher who ever lived. Great teachers spend their lives conversing with people. Occasionally they talk at people; and since it is relatively easy to record such set pieces as the sermon, the speech, the oration and the lecture it is these that get published and are passed down as 'The Teachings of . . .'. Recording the essence of conversation is infinitely more difficult. Despite the quality of what was being taught even Plato could only reproduce Socrates' teachings as a series of rather clever, if slightly unfair, question and answer games.

Teaching cannot be viewed as one coherent skilled activity without stretching and thus distorting the meaning of the word 'skill' well beyond its normal usage. Outstanding teachers have a whole battery of 'skills' at their disposal. They can counsel, instruct, design learning situations, raise interest, tutor, direct attention, create learning opportunities, evaluate, present a topic, organize a laboratory, lead an encounter group, explain or clarify a problem; and manage learning.

TOWARDS A THEORY OF SKILLED BEHAVIOUR AND EXPERIENCE

Until quite recently the description of conversation has been solely the province of the 'arts'. Novelists, poets and playwrights occasionally produce beautiful examples of the conversational process. But it is in the nature of art to conceal the means by which its results are achieved. It may even be that it is essential for the best of art not to examine how it is produced. Even Shakespeare, who has been valued for his capacity in this direction, left no recipe for how to reproduce his success in capturing the essence of conversational exchange. Indeed, his achievement itself is in the nature of a mystery since each reader of a play recruits their own experience to the interpretation of its meaning. Every great stage interpreter of Shakespeare's plays has in some way to construct and breathe life into a new conversation from the script which the playwright left as evidence of what he had in mind. It is perhaps the artists' understanding of this recreative necessity which is their most significant contribution to our understanding of the process of conversation.

The purpose and method of science is different. It is to create public, demonstrable knowledge of the topic being investigated. Sometimes this may appear tedious and it makes for slow progress, but it has the inestimable advantage of enabling one scientist to build directly on the work of another. Gradually a coherent body of knowledge emerges. Despite what have appeared to be insuperable difficulties there are now signs that this is beginning to happen in the study of conversation. The psychology of skill is a useful explanatory paradigm with which to start.

All descriptions of skill are eventually forced to include some reference to the perceptions, thoughts and feelings associated with behaviour. They all return to some version of Miller, Galanter and Pribram's (1960) plans and images. They return to the intentions and purpose of the skilled performers, to their understanding of tools and materials or to some other form of cognitive model; and to some evaluative system which sets personal standards and acts as the basis for defining criteria against which success or failure can be privately assessed.

Already—with its hierarchical structure and its need to describe the constructions of experience—the theory of skill has moved a long way from the linear sequence of behavioural units described in work study. The organization of behaviour is seen to reflect the organization of experience. The selectivity of perceptual set is seen to reflect the anticipatory nature of a model of reality which can be run faster than reality itself. Thus the skilled ball player has a model of the way in which tennis balls, footballs, baseballs or cricket balls move. This model 'automatically' enables him or her to anticipate the flight of the ball (i.e. to 'know' where it is going before it gets there).

For the computer buff the analogy is to the simulation or modelling programme which has been constructed to reflect the reality of the specific situation or series of events it purports to represent. This model can be used to monitor the present reality and then run forwards in time to anticipate the future. This type of programme is used in various forms and complexities of process control. The more sophisticated versions use various 'records of past experience' (i.e. the match and/or mismatch between their predictions and what actually happened) to improve their model of reality and thus their future performance.

Such modelling facilities are at their best when the reality is man-made, e.g. a manufacturing process, and therefore fully known and easy to represent. They are less accurate but are rapidly improving in those 'predictions of nature' where the situation is already well monitored and described and where the scientist (at least in his role as scientist) assumes that there is no other intelligence intervening in the control of events, e.g. in the meteorologist's models of the weather and in the astronomer's models of the heavens. This 'computer model' analogy is useful in extending our theory of skill. The hierarchical organization of behaviour can be seen as an over-simplification. It was a first approximation to the human computer model, that is the cognitive model. The behaviour produced as the cognitive model drives the human organism, in the context of a partly predictable environment, reflects the organization that might be represented as a programme composed of a complex and variously tested set of routines and subroutines. From one perspective the cognitive model represents the relevant segment of reality, from another perspective it is the mechanism via which the skilled person carries out his or her intentions with respect to that reality. It is the means by which ideas are put into operation.

The computer analogy has proved exceptionally fruitful in offering the theory of skill existing and quite widely shared forms within which to grapple with the complexities of experiential organization. Unfortunately, as is always the case, the analogy can be pushed too far. The computer programmer knows the computer language in which he is working. Most of the people who study cognitive organization have a scientific if not a behaviourist background. This has led them to believe that the cognitive model can best be described by the observer of the behaviour who then formulates a view of the model which could or might result in that behaviour. The skilled person's cognitive structure is described in the language of the skills analyst. This is the prevailing error in most of the attempts to systematically examine skill in this way. It is a hangover from the behavioural era.

The assumption is made that even when experiences differ they can still be described within one shared descriptive system. This assumption is reinforced by those professions which spend years systematically practising the sharing of certain experiences/behaviours, e.g. ballet, boxing and building technology, whilst imposing a specialist descriptive language upon its proponents. This view of experience as having the same dimensions within everybody, individuals differing in terms of where they lie along each dimension, is the next major hurdle to be traversed in our search for an adequate theory of skill.

Psychotherapy has also been faced with this same issue. Freud gave a giant impetus to our understanding of mental illness by developing a language in which to explore the experience with his patients. The psycho-analyst believed that the experiential organization of his patient was always best understood when formulated in the 'id, ego, super ego', etc., language of psycho-analysis. Psychotherapists are now moving away from this type of constraint as more and more evidence accrues to demonstrate the inadequacy of each and every attempt to develop one universal descriptive language of human experience. Gradually as these lessons have been absorbed many psychotherapists came to the conclusion that each person can only properly explore and reflect upon their own experience if they do so in their own terms.

Having explored alternate languages for describing the psyche of others, more and more of them are turning to the client for the forms in which the client's psychic organization is best represented. In parody this is like the computer programmer at last asking what operating system assemblers and compilers are loaded in her or his machine before attempting to converse with it. But that really is a parody, since psychotherapists have no reason to believe that the client's language is one already known to them.

Carl Rogers' (1961) solution to this dilemma was 'client–centred therapy' in which the therapists reflect back the language of the client to the client until they learn to reprogramme themselves. Again, Carl Rogers was perhaps the most extreme advocate of this view, refusing to offer his clients anything but their own words as a resource for describing their own experience. George Kelly (1955) took a similar view. He suggested that each person has their own set of personal constructs (dimensions of experience) out of which they attribute meaning to events. He developed a technique, the repertory grid, which can be used to make the language of the client explicit. Kelly decided that each of us has unique personal experience, that we search after meaning and develop constructions of experience which are viable for us in our own times and places. In Kelly's scheme we each develop our own repertoire of personal constructs which serves as a resource out of which we construct our experience and thus attribute meaning to events. He further believed that these constructions serve to anticipate future events and our construing of the consequences of our constructions of meaning validate or invalidate them, allowing us to develop or revise them the better to achieve our purposes. Kelly's theory of personal constructs is in many ways very similar to our theory of skill. The difference is, however, crucially important. For Kelly the way to understand a person's behaviour was to so fully enter into his or her construct system, to so fully enter into his or her system of personal meanings that the behaviour was then merely a natural exteriorization of the client's way of looking at things. The last step in developing our theory of skill is to recognize that the only adequate form in which to represent the experiential organization of skilled people is the form in which they each construct their own experience.

SKILL AND THE FULLY FUNCTIONING PERSON

The word skill has become somewhat debased in its professional psychological usage. The craftsman, the scientist and the artist are all seen as more than skilled. The capacity to express oneself with unusual competence, whether on the football field, as a carpenter or as a sculptor, is thought to involve more than skill. Here the argument is that the personal 'skills' of the behaviourist have gradually pre-empted the professional usage of the work 'skill'; this is because the severe limitations of their model of man has restricted their most productive work to the study of relatively uncomplicated skills. This is artificial in two ways. On the one hand their personal models of skilled activity have produced a selective perception which is blind to the creative 'problem identification' and 'problem solving' activity implicit in even the more repetitive of skills, e.g. the person with a 'knack' is usefully construed as someone who has identified and solved a series of inter-related problems which most other exponents have never conceived. On the other hand complex activities such as painting, gardening or inventing the theory of relativity are either reduced to absurdity by a 'do it by numbers' approach (including some descriptions of 'the scientific method') or they are placed outside the useful span of the word 'skill'.

An implicit purpose of this chapter is to suggest that skill, competence and creativity may be seen as a continuum which would be better understood if it were partitioned in other ways. Here it is argued that a more adequate theory of skill, competence and creativity must be constructed from both behavioural and experiential evidence. This allows a more complete description. It accepts that the individual's conception of the seemingly relevant reality is a crucial component in explaining the structure, timing and synchronization of her or his behaviour. But it also recognizes that their reflections upon an analysis of their behaviour is essential to a proper understanding of their constructions of experience, e.g. their perceptual selectivity and their ability to anticipate.

George Kelly (*op. cit.*) has suggested that each of us is our own 'personal scientist' constructing our personal realities from replications of our experience. He suggests that we are constructing our own theories of reality from the raw materials of our experience, that we act (behave) on the basis of these theories refining, validating or invalidating them until we achieve sufficient understanding to meet our needs and achieve our purposes. In this view perception is merely one function of the construing system and behaviour is another. Neither is comprehensible apart from the whole. The hierarchical description of behaviour proves useful in so far as it is compatible with the hierarchical structure of the personal construct system as this is expressed in the cognitive and sensori-motor structures of the body.

This leads to the (currently) final component of this outline 'theory' of skill, competence and creativity. Most theories of skill are framed largely in terms of task analysis. They are constructed from the point of view of the job to be done. Conversation with almost any effective on-the-job practitioner in 'the art of helping others to acquire skill' will contain much that contemporary psychology would partition off under headings such as personality, motivation or the emotions. Any theory should offer some explanatory system which includes the whole person in relation to the task. Reactions as well as reaction times are relevant. The creative foundry moulder and the skilled composer of music both accept themselves as part of the system which is the task-being-done. Rogers expresses this as the fully functioning person having increasing trust in his (or her) own organism.

The computer scientist would talk about the hardware and firmware of the system as well as the software. Lorenz (1977) expresses his view of 'life as a process of learning' in part with the following words: 'The physiological mechanism whose function it is to understand the real world is no less real than the world itself'. Polanyi (1953) talks of the 'tacit knowing' of the scientist as a function of the whole person. Thus the cognitive model of reality on which skill is based should include a relevant model of self as well as a model of the task in the work situation. To the extent that a person's cognitive model fails to anticipate his own reactions to doing the task it will fail to incorporate them into the experience of the task-being-done. The result is a failure to synchronize the pattern of internal reactions with the structure of the external activity; and less than fully skilled performance will result. This is equally true for the soldier under fire, the primary school teacher with a 'difficult' child, or the carpenter with a 'feel' for his tools and materials.

CONVERSATION AS A SKILL

The behaviourists' studies of the laboratory rat were based on a 'model of learning' which always pre-supposed that learning was doing the task as it was defined by the experimenter, i.e. learning meant running a maze, discriminating shapes or pushing a lever at the 'right' time, etc. Ethologists studying animals in their natural habitat watched learning happen for needs and purposes that arose out of the animals themselves. Theories of social skill vary as widely as theories of animal learning. The encounter group, behaviour modification and transactional analysis each embody theories or models of 'other people'. Each model produces a different model of social skill.

In attempting to apply our theory of skill, competence and creativity to the processes of conversation we are faced with a peculiar dilemma. In conversation the referents of the model of relevant external reality may be construed as entities which are modelling other conversants whilst they are being modelled. For purposes of first order explanation only, it may be useful to think of three types of participant in a conversation. The *type A* conversational participant models other people, often very elaborately, but allows little or no room in their models for the possibility that the other is modelling him. Conversational participants *type B* model the other as having a fixed or fully established model of them. Whereas participants *type C* model the other as actively modelling them.

> *Type A*, as psychologists, will tend to treat the other as object. The *type B* will tend to produce a psychology of individual differences and *type C* will tend to produce a humanistic psychology.

But within each type the nature of the model of the other can vary considerably. Hence some of the complexities of conversation. Here it is neither relevant nor feasible to expand on these possibilities, although the reader might like to contemplate how people modelling others through various popular or unpopular theories of man would or do converse about learning. Here we will focus on two components of this modelling:

(1) The teacher's and the learner's model of the learner.
(2) The teacher's and the learner's model of the conversational process.

Teachers may operate type A, B, or C models of their students. They will also have convictions about each student's:

> capacity for learning certain subject matter;
> the best conditions for learning; and
> the processes for learning.

Together the teacher's models of the learner and the learner's model of himself create a conversational frame which largely defines the quality and amount of learning that they will achieve.

PERSONAL MYTHS AND THE UNDERSTANDING OF LEARNING

The learner will always have some assumptions, prejudices and/or understanding of his or her own learning. Such personal models may be formulated:

> as convictions about capacities or incapacities for learning different subject matters, e.g. 'I have no musical talent', 'I am no good at mathematics' or 'I am good with people', etc.

> as convictions about the best personal conditions for learning, e.g. 'I like background music' (or complete quiet), 'I can only work for twenty or thirty minutes at a time' or 'I have to have three or four hours before I can settle down to studying', 'I have to be in a relaxed position when I read' (or 'I have to sit at a desk if I want to concentrate'), etc.

> as convictions about the optimal processes for learning, e.g. 'I have to write it out to remember it', 'I learn best by talking with other people', etc.

Most people have arrived at these convictions about their own learning, the models of themselves as learners on less than adequate evidence. They have either been convinced by somebody else's assessments of them, e.g. parents or teachers, or they have been offered less than optimal opportunities to learn and have generalized the experience as a commentary on their own methods. Such assumptions can very easily become self-fulfilling.

The teacher also develops assumptions, prejudices and understandings about the nature of learning. Sometimes teachers have one set of models for the learning in their students and another for learning in themselves.

MODELS OF THE CONVERSATIONAL PROCESS

In addition to beliefs about learning, teachers and learners have assumptions, prejudices and understanding of the process of the teaching/learning conversation.

One difference between people's approaches to learning is about awareness and the freedom to negotiate. There are those teaching/learning situations in which the nature of the conversation is assumed but not discussed. These are those in which the method is made explicit but not negotiable, and there are those organized learning events in which the nature of the teaching/learning process is itself a subject for negotiation.

Although there is not space here to elaborate upon the wide range of personal myths and assumptions which exist, it will be obvious that there is great variety and flexibility in the scope and nature of the models which individuals may bring to the teaching/learning situation. Many seemingly valid models are demonstrably merely self-validating.

What is needed is some meta-theory of learning conversations which simultaneously offers sufficient agreed structure within which to construct the learning/teaching event whilst maintaining the freedom to discuss and negotiate the nature of the personal models which both limit and enable learning. The remainder of this paper attempts to outline one such model of a 'learning conversation'.

LEARNING CONVERSATION

Most people are disabled learners, but, having no agreed referents, they do not know how slowly and badly they learn. Believing their capacity for learning to be inborn, e.g. a matter of intelligence and personality, they make no attempt to increase it.

Even senior managers and professional specialists differ in their capacity to learn from experience;

Manual skills have a reputation for being difficult to acquire.

Not everybody who goes on a training course will extract the same benefits from it;

The skills of identifying and solving significant and relevant problems within a realistic time span are not as widespread or fully developed as many would wish;

Technical experts sometimes have difficulty in learning to manage people;

All of us have some learning disabilities. Most of us have many.

The universality of inhibited or undeveloped learning capacity goes unrecognized only because so many of our peers are equally disabled. Expectations are low. The occasional exception is classified as a maverick or a high flier. This does nothing to change the general level of expectation—of what can be learned, by whom, how thoroughly and how quickly.

At school, in further education, at university and at work the problem of 'improving learning' is generally misconstrued. The usual response to a lack of success in organized learning is that teachers and trainers attempt to improve the methods of instruction or to simplify the instructional materials. The usual response to a lack of success in learning on the job is for the manager to raise the selection standards or to send the learner on a course. These methods for tackling the difficulties which people experience in acquiring new attitudes, new skills and knowledge can, and often do, cope rather cumbersomely with the immediate problem. They would not continue to be used if they did not. But they do nothing to increase the disabled learner's capacity to learn more effectively in the future. By placing the primary responsibility for what gets learned with the trainer or the designer of training materials this approach leaves the learner more dependent on good instruction. Indeed, effective instruction can, by artificially simplifying the learner's task, have the unnoticed side-effect of leaving the learner more vulnerable and unable to cope creatively with the challenges in his or her less protected future.

There is another approach. The disabled learner can learn-how-to-learn. This is very different from being trained-how-to-be-trained or being taught-how-to-be-taught. The theory and practice of learning conversations has been developed over the last fifteen years within a sustained attempt to study human learning in its many natural habitats. The effort has been made to look at learning from the learner's point of view. This has enabled the author and his colleagues in the Centre for Study of Human Learning to develop a systematic methodology for helping people to increase their capacity for learning. The speed and extent of this increase is often quite startling to both participants. Follow-up studies over two years show that the change is sustained and is, therefore, probably permanent. A wide variety of projects in education, industry, commerce and government agencies has resulted in the development of an effective technology for reflective learning. This technology adds selective power to the various phases and stages of the learning conversation.

Whilst the occasional lucky learner may unconsciously hit upon some successful strategies for learning, disabled learners only become more fully functioning as they are enabled to reflect upon their own learning activities. Through the learning conversation they become able to recognize, represent and thus control their own processes. They become more self-organized. In any effective conversation, control is passed back and forth among participants as they recognize the nature of what each has to contribute. But all participants are not equal. Most conversations are asymmetric. In the early stages of the learning conversation the learner provides the evidence on which the collaborative research into the nature of her or his learning is based. The manager of the conversation guides and controls the discussion and the exploration of it. As the learner's awareness of his own processes increases, the manager of the learning hands over control of these awareness-raising activities to him. He (or she) then begins to encourage learners to challenge their personal myths about their own learning capacity. The learners are encouraged to change the emphasis of their attention. The learning conversation moves into the next phase. They begin to explore how the learning can be improved. The manager encourages them to explore alternative models of their own processes and to develop and test in action personally acceptable theories about how they can learn more effectively. Gradually the manager also hands over control of this exploratory activity to the learner until eventually only the quality of the learner's personal investigation remains under the manager's guidance. The total conversation is phased to enable the learners to obtain insights which allow them to conduct more and more of the conversation for themselves. The ability to conduct most of a learning conversation with yourself is the essence of 'how to learn'.

The process of a conversation can be distinguished and described separately from its content. In any job or topic area, learning needs and purposes can be clarified and agreed, tactics and strategies can be discussed and monitored, and criteria for judging the quality of outcomes can be constructed and applied. The conditions for creative conversations require that the content of an exchange is modulated according to a shared understanding of how the conversation will be conducted and that this model of the process itself remains negotiable. Such conversation is rare. People value it when it does occur, but they can rarely create the conditions to make it happen. Each of us can identify our own special events in which we had this rare experience. It can be recognized by the experience of constructing, exchanging and negotiating personally relevant and viable meaning. Such experiences have been defined by Maslow as those in which the criteria for appreciating them can only arise out of the experience itself. They are both self-referent and self-assessed. People may achieve such creative conversation within themselves. This is the focus of self-organized learning.

The conditions in which such experiences are propagated and grow demands a different approach from that of instruction. The final arbiter of the effectiveness of learning is always the learner himself. To be truly conversational, the technology of learning must allow relevance and viability to be assessed by the learner. The criteria and referents used by the learner may be challenged and renegotiated but they cannot be ignored, denied or arbitrarily over-ridden without destroying the sources of self-confidence and self-sustaining effort. The learning conversation encourages and enables the growth of this capacity for self-organization.

A TAXONOMY OF LEARNING CONVERSATIONS

In its *tutorial* mode the learning conversation leads the learner to the formulation of a personal learning contract in terms of *purpose, strategy* and *anticipated outcome*. After an attempt has been made to carry out the contract the review leads the learners to reflect upon their learning competence. Poor learning performance may come about in two very different ways. Learners may have wanted to achieve the contract and yet not have had the skills and competencies necessary to formulate and execute the contract effectively. The *learning-to-learn* mode of the learning conversation leads them into a self-diagnosis of their learning strengths and weaknesses and into conversational activities designed to help them achieve greater capacity for learning. Poor performance resulting from lack of interest leads into the *relevance* conversation mode. Here the learner is asked to identify long-term needs and purposes and to differentiate these into shorter-term recognition of the relevance or inappropriateness of the current learning contract. It is this part of the conversation which can save days, months or even years of alienation, misery and mis-spent effort. The relevance conversation can identify the personal structure of a topic or a job situation and thus help learners chart their own paths to involvement in it.

Choice of specific techniques to be recruited into the learning conversation depends upon the nature of the application. Learning skills, learning situations and topics to be learned may all require special techniques for awareness-raising.

CHALLENGING THE ROBOT

Achieving new levels in learning performance usually involves serious personal change. It involves the disruption and breaking of existing skills and the establishment of new attitudes and personally strange ways of thinking, feeling and behaving. Many of the techniques used in the learning conversation have been specially recruited and developed for such controlled interventions. But however carefully the conversation is developed the process of significant 'learning-to-learn' will always involve a 'learning trough' in which anxiety and feelings of inadequacy combine to push the person into preserving the safe status quo.

It is useful to talk of each learner as having a set of personal learning robots: the learning-by-reading robot; the learning-by-discussion robot; the learning-by-doing robot; the learning-by-listening robot, etc. Each of us has been so habituated in our own ways that we are completely unaware that each of these modes of learning is itself a learned skill. Each learning skill has become so automatic that it is no longer under conscious control. Special techniques are required to challenge the robot, bringing the skill back into awareness and thus available for revision and development. But the disruption of existing skills produces a drop in effective performance. The learner feels that he is getting nowhere and becomes frustrated and anxious. Part of every learning conversation is concerned with offering the learner support through this learning trough.

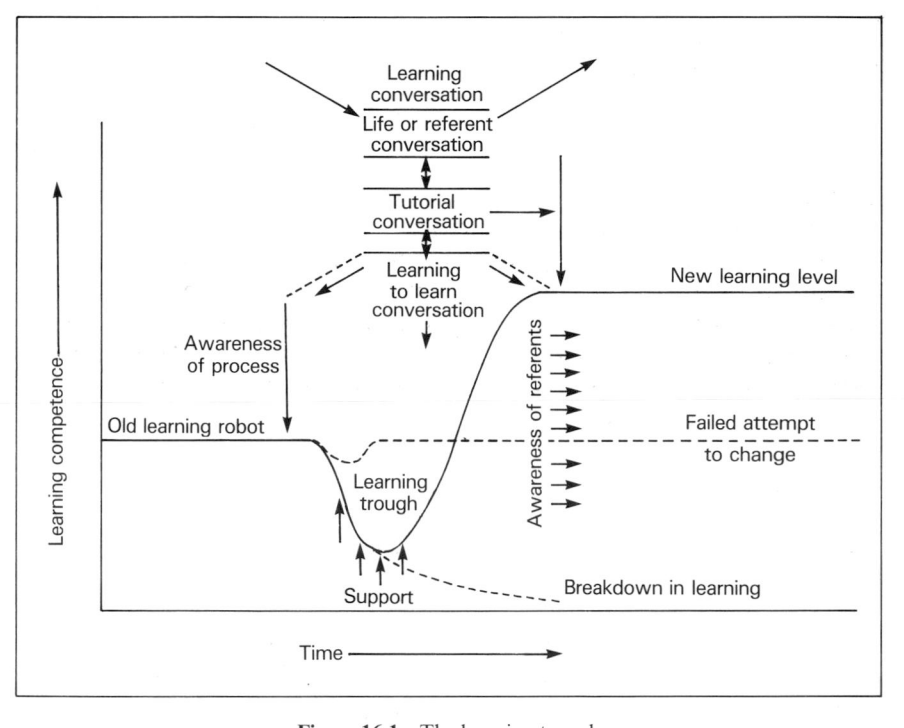

Figure 16.1   The learning trough

THE NEED FOR THREE RELATED DIALOGUES

The change conversation can be seen to contain three entwining dialogues. *The first dialogue* serves the purpose of raising awareness of the learning process. *The second dialogue* offers personal support to the learner, particularly when he is experimenting with new methods of learning and feels vulnerable after having abandoned his habitually safe techniques. *The third dialogue* helps the learner to identify standards: in himself, in other people, and in the situation, which can serve as referents for the quality of the learning which he is attempting to achieve.

The first *process* dialogue taps unconscious habits and helps the student to become aware of his own learning style. In most areas of activity, for example in manual skills, social skills, reading skills and management skills, people have little or no understanding of their own learning processes. Records of learning behaviour can be used to talk the learner back through his experience. These can be as elaborate or as informal as the situation demands. Careful reconstruction of the experience serves to raise awareness on subsequent occasions. Gradually a personal language for describing learning develops. The Kelly Repertory Grid can serve as an awareness raising device for many different tasks, from interviewing to industrial inspection, in which perception, judgement, thought and feeling are of central importance.

The second dialogue *supports* the learner through this process of change. It is as yet largely a matter of sensitivity and intuitive understanding on the part of the manager of learning. However, the work of Carl Rogers and B. F. Skinner together offer some indicators of the ways in which this personal support should be offered. Rogers' technique is to create a very attentive but relaxed and accepting atmosphere in which there is no evaluative comment. His studies show that this frees individuals to experiment and explore their own processes in ways that are normally too threatening for them to attempt alone. Skinner's behavioural reinforcement techniques enable a person to define new patterns of behaviour which they can then be carefully guided into achieving. Some of the 'precision teaching' techniques in which learners observe themselves and provide their own systematic reinforcement seem to be bridging the gap between experiential and behavioural techniques. These two seemingly disparate approaches can be variously adapted and combined to produce a powerful range of methodologies by which the individual can be freed, supported and guided into new ways of behaving. But teachers must explore their own resources and develop those 'mixes' of methods which are most effective in enabling them to support change in others.

The third *referent* dialogue aims to enable learners to appraise their own performance, but to do so they need to identify examples or referents which they can use as a basis for comparison. The manager helps the learners to identify such examples either in outstanding performers of the skill which they wish to acquire or as measures of quality and/or speed which they can apply to their own activities. Whatever examples learners identify in their own environments they must remain free to use them for their own purposes. In the end, the learner comes to use his or her own previous performances as the basis for evaluating their improvement and should be encouraged not to restrict themselves to the existing norms nor to be discouraged by the outstanding performance of more experienced people.

THE MANAGEMENT OF LEARNING

If we are to encourage people to learn from experience, to think about their needs and purposes, to plan their strategies, to evaluate their success, and to review, revise and improve their methods of learning then inevitably we are emphasizing self-organization. Self-organized learners expect to go on learning, to make independent judgements and to question. This makes them potentially more useful and productive. Everyone can learn to adapt and develop. This depends on the recruitment of procedures which facilitate personal growth.

An emphasis on the 'process' of learning rather than the 'products' of learning enables the development of a 'language' for negotiating changes in learning capacity. This language is itself content-free and once acquired enables individuals, often for the first time, to take control of the ways they learn from experience. In the crisis-ridden conditions which prevail in much of contemporary society, where 'the valued learning products' of today can easily become the chains restricting tomorrow's growth, the development of a language which enables a way of thinking about personal learning processes becomes an important selective factor in the struggle for personal and industrial survival.

The special tools for challenging the robot contribute to the development of this language in which these dialogues can be conducted. The dialogue signpost separate roles for the manager of learning as an agent for change. People do not necessarily learn from experience; it depends on the meaning they attribute to their experience and on their capacity to reflect and review it. Much organized learning has tended to disable us as learners and the onus is clearly on teachers and trainers alike to provide a context within which learning conversations can be nourished and sustained.

LEARNING MANAGERS

The emphasis on self-organization and the practice of learning conversation has serious implications. Who are to be the managers of learning? Is it the training or personnel department's job? Is it the job of every manager to see that his department becomes a more effective learning system?

Managers of learning can play a key role in any organization. They can become the catalysts for change at all levels in the company. Such managers will need guidance in their own development and will also need encouragement and assistance in providing an organizational context for all participants to grow and change. To act as 'managers of learning' people will require new skills, sensitivity, a wide knowledge of learning methods and considerable resources, and above all, they will need to be self-organized learners themselves. Industrial and commercial organizations must meet the challenge involved in enabling staff to adapt themselves to the changing scene. For an organization to achieve creative growth and change it must work as a system of corporate, self-organized learners. Some of the techniques and philosophy described in this chapter can be recruited to achieve this. A fully participative corpus, made up of supporting self-organized groups, is feasible. To meet the demands of today's society and the challenges of the micro-processor revolution which is almost on us the trajectory to growth must involve the management of people as self-organized learners and fully-functioning beings. Only by moving into this unexplored terrain can industrial society survive and grow.

Bibliography

Bloom, B. S. (1970) (ed.) *Taxonomy of Educational Objectives*. (London: Longmans)

Ferguson, J. (1970) (ed.) *Socrates*. (London: Macmillan) (with Open University)

Harri-Augstein, E. S. (1978). Reflecting on structures of meaning: a process of learning-to-learn. In Fay Fransella (ed.) *Personal Construct Psychology*. (London: Academic Press)

Harri-Augstein, E. S. and Thomas, L. F. (1977). *The Art and Science of Getting a Degree*. (London: Brunel University)

Harri-Augstein, E. S. and Thomas, L. F. (1978). Learning conversations: a person-centred approach to self-organized learning. *Br. J. Guidance Couns.*, July

Harri-Augstein, E. S. and Thomas, L. F. (1979). Self-organized learning and the relativity of knowing: towards a conversational methodology. In D. Bannister and P. Stringer (eds.) *Constructs of Sociality and Individuality*. (London: Academic Press)

Heaton, J. M. (1968). *The Eye: Phenomenology and Psychology of Function and Disorder*. (London: Tavistock Publications)

Kelly, G. (1955). *Psychology of Personal Constructs*, Vols. 1 and 2. (New York: Norton)

Lorenz, K. (1977). *Behind the Mirror: A Search for a Natural History of Human Knowledge*. (London: Methuen)

Miller, G. A., Galanter, E. and Pribram, K. H. (1960). *Plans and the Structure of Behaviour*. (New York: Holt)

Newell, A. and Simon, H. A. (1972). *Human Problem Solving*. (New Jersey: Prentice-Hall)

Pask, G. (1975). *The Cybernetics of Human Learning and Performance*. (London: Hutchinson Educational)

Piaget, J. (1969). *The Mechanisms of Perception*. (New York: Basic Books)

Polanyi, M. (1953). *Personal Knowledge*. (Chicago: University Press)

Rogers, C. R. (1961). *On Becoming a Person: A Therapist's View of Psychotherapy*. (London: Constable)

Strongman, K. T. (1977). *The Psychology of Emotion*. (London: Wiley)

Thomas, L. F. (1979). Construct, reflect and converse: the conversational reconstruction of social realities. In D. Bannister and P. Stringer (eds.) *Constructs of Sociality and Individuality*. (London: Academic Press)

Thomas, L. F. and Harri-Augstein, E. S. (1977). Learning-to-learn: the personal construction and exchange of meaning. In M. How (ed.) *Adult Learning*. (New York: Wiley)

Thomas, L. F. and Harri-Augstein, E. S. (1981). The dynamics of learning conversations: a self-organized approach to management development. In T. Boydell (ed.) *Handbook of Management Self-Development*. (London: Gower Press)

Vernon, M. D. (1969). *Human Motivation*. (Cambridge: University Press)

17
Final Discussion

W. T. SINGLETON

SOCIAL INTERACTION

It is clear from the preceding chapters that the exercise of social skill always takes place within a continuously developing process. The participants are communicating and learning. Their behaviour is governed by other events which took place before they met and the consequences of the meeting extend into the future, not only for those concerned, but also for others who are not personally involved. To make sense of their highly integrated and very complex interaction it can be examined in terms of context, communication and learning. It must be accepted at the outset that this separation in the interests of clarity may not do complete justice to the essential unity and homogeneity of the interactive process.

The context

The context is dominant to the point where each participant can be regarded as functioning as a representative. The teacher represents the educational system, the doctors and therapists represent the health services, the policeman, the judge and the referee represent law and regulation, the salesman and the negotiator represent the needs of their parent organizations and the Englishman or Frenchman inevitably represents his own culture.

Ager demonstrates that the Frenchman in conversation is using the conventions of his own language with accompanying body expressions of posture gestures and the phasing of exchanges. Behind all this are the methods of thought instilled by a particular kind of formal education and the equally potent, if less formal, foundation of the person identifying with his image of his own country and himself within it. It was suggested in the Introduction

283

that any person engaged in social interaction continually consults himself as well as other participants. It becomes a little clearer why the concept of self is such a complex one. The self incorporates the residue of the individual's personal history, not only in the sense of his experiences but also because he often has a role within the meeting which has been created by previous social interactions between himself and others. He may have received anything from a general orientation to detailed instructions. This is at its most manifest for the negotiator whose instructions may be based on the agenda of the meeting and the salesman who may have been provided with a plan on how to conduct each of his meetings.

Within the context also are the factors which arise from personal and environmental circumstances. S. J. Singleton emphasizes that the patient is in hospital because of the seriousness of his plight, in addition to which he is outnumbered and in a state of undress. From the professional's, as opposed to the client's, viewpoint, Slattery mentions the difficulty of practising in an alien environment—the industrial culture. The remedy is to widen the context, to recognize that there are valid objectives, such as productivity and profit, but not to compromise on style—for the doctor it should always be the individual who is considered rather than the holder of a defined position in the organization. Hay mentions the preliminary encounter with the receptionist and the unfamiliar depersonalized waiting-room environment as factors which influence the interaction with the general practitioner. Caney also notes that the patient is conditioned by the medical atmosphere: the apparatus, the smells, the uniforms and so on. The person assumes the identity of 'patient' and the 'sickness role'. Paradoxically the patient who is very ill can have a very close relationship based on physical contact with a physiotherapist who is providing, say, respiratory assistance and it is only when the patient gets better that the normal 'social distance' is resumed. Correspondingly the psychotherapist can have a closer relationship with a more seriously disturbed client, but again normal social distances will be established as the client recovers. There would appear to be implicit rules about the closeness of contact and communication which regulate what is seemly in a particular context. The relationship between the policeman and the criminal which the policeman may deliberately develop to facilitate communication can be misunderstood by outsiders.

Potter lists the plan preceding the sales encounter as one of the three main phases of the process. The salesman can and should be trained to use this approach. Moorhouse suggests that there is some role conflict for the salesman in that he acts as an intermediary between the parent organization and the customer without having control of either customer requirements or organizational resources. This is one aspect of the general situation of the 'boundary keeper'. Loveridge points out that the boundary keeper often finds it desirable to disguise his personal identity behind a uniform or a ritual. Negotiators attach great importance to the procedure, e.g. 'free collective bargaining'. Salesmen have standard clothes, cars and procedures.

In the law courts and the police force also uniforms and rituals are used. Referees and linesmen have whistles and flags respectively as well as uniforms. These are used in standardized ways. They are rituals, but the ritual is, as always, a part of the business of communication.

Communication

During social interaction much of the communication depends on style and emphasis rather than mere content. The referee uses the sharpness of his whistle blast and his verbal directions to indicate the degree of positiveness of his interference in the game. This will result from factors such as his assessment of whether a transgression of the rules was deliberate or accidental, whether 'gamesmanship' is involved, whether a rule has been flouted in the letter or in the spirit and so on. All this emerges from the sometimes distant observation of fast physical interaction at a time when the observer himself may be running rapidly. Thornhill implies that development of these skills is one of the functions of the extended training by experience and graded promotion to more senior games where more skilled and experienced players are being monitored. Goodfellow describes how the experienced teacher can interpret the sideways look and the brightness of the glance to detect whether or not there is something amiss and even whether it is mildly mischievous or malicious. On the other hand, for a passive pupil, further exploration may be required to determine whether this is due to reluctance, inadequacy or just a retiring disposition. Passivity is the enemy of communication; while there is activity there is always the possibility of communication. Hence the irritation with another person who refuses to react: 'say something or do something!' is the common cry of anyone wishing to exchange information.

The intention not to communicate by passivity or withdrawal itself expresses an attitude which is disturbing to the other party. This and other attitudes seem to be readily understood. S. J. Singleton notes that a condescending or dismissive attitude will always be detected. Wells emphasizes the importance of never patronizing or appearing to patronize. Condescension achieves the opposite of what is seen as one of the main tasks of a judge— namely to establish a frame of mind to speak fully. Using a different terminology, Moorhouse talks about 'perceptual reciprocity'. This includes the willingness to reveal your model of the situation so that the other person can accept it, modify it and return it—this is the process of 'mutual construing'.

W. T. Singleton considers that the job of the university teacher is to communicate beliefs and enthusiasms rather than facts. This requires the devising and shaping of pictorial and symbolic models. The model which is being built and developed simultaneously within two or more minds is inevitably at least one stage removed from what is actually being said. It is achieved by a process described as observing the other, not only directly, but also as a mirror of oneself. Thomas describes the same process on a wider scale as understanding the person by entering into his construct system.

Hay reminds us that communication can be impeded because the two participants attach different meanings and more widely a different significance to particular words. This is not just because of any differences in educational or social background, it is also because the outcome of the exchange has only professional consequences for one party but personal consequences for the other. In these circumstances it is hardly possible to think of the development of the same model, but nevertheless there can be a mutual empathy. The doctor can imagine what it must be like to receive bad news about health and the patient can imagine what it must be like to have to convey such news. In this more complex sense they are again sharing a common model of the situation. This recognition of a shared experience is commonly described in the phrase quoted by Caney as 'getting on the same wavelength'. It is analogous to the more formal negotiating situation where, as Loveridge puts it, people test needs and objectives against those of others. Goodfellow mentions the sense of the needs of others as one attribute of the good teacher.

Learning

Another attribute of the good teacher appears in the structuring of the environment most appropriate for a particular learning process. W. T. Singleton makes a similar point in stating that a teacher cannot transmit a skill, he can only persuade the learner to make the effort to acquire it himself. Goodfellow is suggesting that one aspect of the persuasion is in the sensitive creation of the environment, another, appropriate for very young learners, is to instil a repertoire of habits. Thomas considers that for many adults this repertoire is not adequate and therefore much learning, even for mature students, is learning how to learn. The optimal process is described as a creative conversation with oneself.

Such a conversation has much in common with a conversation between two people. The information exchange is used as a basis for understanding the model which the other person is using and 'understanding' itself implies building up a similar model. As Thomas puts it, perception is one function of the construing system and, as Moorhouse puts it, conversation is a process of mutual construing. This is a basis of Thomas' typology of conversational participants. Those of type A neglect the possibility that the person being modelled might be modelling the observer, those of type B assume that the observed has a fixed model of the observer, while those of type C accept that mutual modelling is taking place. It is difficult for a physical scientist to escape from type A because such science assumes that there is no intelligence intervening in the way the physical world works. Thus when psychologists attempt to imitate the rigour and respectability of physical science they are inevitably driven into behaviourism. However, once we accept that learning takes place, that is models are changing and developing then, even for manipulation of the physical world, the characteristics of the manipulator become part of the process.

Learning in this sense is not something restricted to the classroom and the training school. It is a process which goes on whenever there is any activity even of a routine kind. It is minimal for a repetitive¹ task not requiring conscious intervention. A well-established model may simply guide the person through a sequence, but even here there will be some minor perturbations which perhaps leave the model slightly more flexible as well as marginally better established. For a social interaction of any kind there must be learning involving the task of constructing some analogue, not only of what at least one other person is saying and doing but also what that other person is thinking. Hence the importance of the teacher, lecturer or trainer. It is not the statements but the models behind the statements which must be detected, absorbed and recreated if learning is to be consolidated.

SKILL APPRAISAL

Assessment of success in social interaction is very difficult even for participants. In the case of the sales encounter, salesmen are trained to detect what Moorhouse calls 'buying signals'; these provide the information on the necessarily precise timing of the 'sales closure'. Even in the highly formalized situation of a law court, Wells describes the judge as an imperfect creation administering an imperfect system.

Social encounters are usually open-ended and often deliberately so. Goodfellow describes education as an open-ended process subject to constant modification as a result of teacher–pupil interaction. In situations as diverse as selling and therapy, Potter and Barker respectively stress the importance of avoiding closed questions which require a simple definitive response; these tend to create a hiatus within an interaction. Barker quotes the observation that clients often seem to benefit from spontaneous unnoticed interactions rather than positive interventions. W. T. Singleton considers that the social interaction required between examiners can easily be overformalized to the detriment of the quality of decision-making.

A single social encounter cannot be evaluated without a knowledge of the favourability of preceding conditions. W. T. Singleton considers that a good lecture requires commitment, security and self-confidence on both sides. Potter attaches great importance to the plan formulated before the encounter and Thornhill mentions the need for the referee's calm period before the game as a necessary preparatory phase. Correspondingly the long-term consequences of an interaction may look very different from the apparent success in scoring points within a negotiating situation. Loveridge finds it important to distinguish between the short-term spot-dealing situation and the longer term contingency contracting. Thomas considers that people do not necessarily learn from experience—it depends on the meaning attributed to the experience and on the capacity to reflect and review it. To put it another way, an important conversation does not end when two participants go their separate ways, each continues the conversation with himself.

A 'critical incident' approach to the analysis of an interaction might miss the essential skill of at least one of the participants. Cumberbatch and Morgan point out that the skill of the policeman is not so much in coping with physical aggression but rather in avoiding its occurrence—the ability to 'de-escalate'. Similarly, Thornhill points out that conflict on the field of play can be created by the incompetence of the referee.

More generally, there is a delicacy in effective social skill which precludes the direct approach to assessment. S. J. Singleton and Potter both mention, in their very different situations, the avoidance of the blunderbuss approach as an indicator of skill. In the medical situation this is evidenced by selectivity in what needs to be investigated, in the sales situation the buyer's needs are identified as precisely as possible and there is concentration in the way the product meets these particular needs. Just as Goodfellow and Thomas stress the importance of the conditions for effective learning so also does Hay emphasize that the task of the general practitioner is not so much to positively restore health but rather to supply the necessary conditions so that the patient's health will restore itself.

Loveridge sees the task of the professional negotiator as one of finding out as precisely as possible what the opponent's needs are and what price he is prepared to pay for them; this is happening on both sides simultaneously so that it is very difficult for an observer to disentangle what is going on. As in ball-games, a participant cannot demonstrate his repertoire of skills unless his opponent has a similar repertoire developed to the same standard.

All this is a consequence of the dynamic interactive nature of social encounters. Sometimes it can be detected physically; Hay mentions the dance-like pattern of movements seen in a slow-motion film of a clinical interview. More usually it has to be deduced from inferences about what provokes what at several levels of abstraction, from the words and gestures used through the models to the needs and motives and at several levels of time-scale from the immediate exchange to the long-term past and future.

It emerges that social skills are best appraised or analysed by the practitioner. He plans what he is going to do, he does it and he assesses the consequences of what was done. In each of these phases he also introspects about what he is doing and why he is doing it. Skills analysis of social interaction is another version of a social interaction. It involves conversation with others and with oneself, it is one formalized version of the learning process and of introspection.

SOCIAL SKILLS

Social skills are employed in communication with other people. There is evidence that communication has taken place when the recipient modifies his behaviour or his attitude. Thus communication usually involves seeking a response from another. There are one or two apparent exceptions to this, e.g. the radio talk, which will be discussed later. The response may vary from something trivial like the answer to the question of what the time is to something profound like an admission of a change of belief.

Communication is clearly not restricted to the use of the lexicon. There can be communication by posture, by facial expression, by body movements and by touch. When there is no visual contact, as in a telephone conversation, communication involves variables such as changes in tone, pauses and other variations of tempo as well as selection of words. Within the use of words there are, in developed languages, many different ways of ostensibly saying the same thing, but choice is dictated by the desire to indicate an attitude or an emphasis which is too subtle to be incorporated in formal grammar or vocabulary. There are overtones in speech and writing as well as in music. As Ager points out this is just one of the difficulties of obtaining full communication between two people who do not share the same native language. In practice it is surprising that such communication does not fail abruptly more frequently. This is probably because there is a good deal of redundancy, a particular choice of words is reinforced by a posture and a facial expression and in listening to someone not using his native language the listener takes account of discrepancies and makes due allowances.

For this reason two-way television communication is better than telephone communication but is still not equivalent to being in the same room for contextual reasons which will be taken up again later. For the moment there is a challenge in attempting to explain how something such as a talk on the radio or even the written word has any success at all. Starting from the principles that multi-sensory inputs are needed for full perception and that feedback is integral to the practice of social skill, then one-way communication between people ought to be very difficult. There are a number of partial answers. Every author likes to receive book reviews or comments from his readers, all radio speakers welcome letters relating to their talks. In addition, such communication can be regarded as using up capital acquired in extensive two-way communication acquired before the one-way communication is undertaken—books or radio talks based on lectures given to live audiences are much easier than those attempted *de novo*. Finally, one-way communication is a tribute to the skills of the reader or listener who can reconstruct the message from the partial data available.

The process of communication has much in common with other kinds of skilled performance. The initiator has a range of objectives from immediate to long term, he generates an hypothesis about how to achieve them. The stored record of the hypothesis consists of an action and a prediction of the consequences of that action. After initiating the action he compares the actual consequences with the prediction. This is true for anything he does and anything he says. It applies equally to driving a golf ball and to a verbal gambit in a negotiation.

The skilled communicator, like the skilled golfer, does not consciously select the detail. He sets the immediate objectives to himself and the rest fellows automatically. In the case of the golfer this is the precisely timed and phased posture and applied muscular forces. In the case of the communicator the use of words, the posture, the expression again proceed in a precisely timed and phased fashion.

Communication is as much a function of the listener as it is of the speaker. The speaker has the initiative and the listener can respond positively by indicating acceptance of that initiative. On the other hand the response may be creative, it may be a rejection or at least a radical reorientation of what the speaker is saying. Hay is presumably thinking along these lines when he discusses the role of the general practitioner as an interpreter of myths. Similarly, but more concretely, Slattery suggests that the medical role as a listener may be to detect the need for help with a psychological problem which underlies the superficial request for help with a trivial physiological problem. Sometimes the plea for help may be so tentative that the listener may be almost afraid to respond positively in case he snubs the speaker. Barker discusses this situation in psychotherapy where the therapist attempts for a time at least to be a 'blank screen' on which the client can paint a picture as he sees it. This approach comes from the theory due to Kelly, also described by Thomas, in which communication needs to be based on an understanding of the constructs of the client. However, personal construct theory is about how the individual structures his world but not about how it is or could be structured by other people, including the therapist.

There has to be some sharing of constructs for good communication and it is perhaps peculiar to the clinical situation that the constructs of the speaker are accepted as they are at least in the early stages. In most communication, including science, activity is based on building mutually agreed constructs. To obtain agreement there has to be extensive creative effort at both ends of the communication channel. Elementary teaching is similar to the clinical situation in that the constructs of the teacher are accepted, but more advanced teaching requires correspondingly more creative effort on the part of the learner. This is presumably what Goodfellow means by sharing lessons rather than adapting the respective roles of giver and receiver. Similarly, her concept of the balance of authority and relaxed contact is something which the skilled teacher achieves on the basis of awareness of the optimal kind of communication required. The complete sharing of models which are entirely mutually acceptable, satisfactory and fitting is what W. T. Singleton refers to as the collective mind in action. Several authors use the word 'empathy' to describe the process of acquiring and the achievement of mutually agreed models.

Social skills then appear to have much in common with other skills in that an internal model in the form of a continuously developing schema is used. Development occurs when a hypothesis is generated and then checked against reality by the use of feedback. In the case of social skills reality is not only physical events, such as verbalization and gesture, it is also the schemata in other people's minds which control their attempts to communicate. Social skills, like other skills, are structured and characterized by key features. The key features of social skills are the constructs which are attributes of the self.

OPERATIONAL UTILITY

In principle, social skill theory should be the basis of social skill training. There is currently extensive interest in social skill training as a form of psycho-therapy, as an aid to interviewing (from the clinic to the industrial selection board) and as a part of selling technique. At present most of this training uses techniques which indicate that theoretical knowledge is inadequate, viz. role playing, case studies and use of proverb-type rules. It can be successful because the fundamental rules which govern success in any training are followed, namely provision of incentives and provision of relevant knowledge of results.

Insecurity about concepts can lead not only to non-optimal training but also to extensive susceptibility to outside influences. For example, Cumber-batch and Morgan mention the tendency for media myths to be absorbed into police culture. They are somewhat pessimistic about the understanding of police skills achieved so far, suggesting that the elements of the skills are currently captured by the novelists rather than the academics. Some police skills would appear to be very difficult to provide by formal training, for example, the extensive use of discretion in whether or not to enforce the law and the objective to present an image of effectiveness which is regarded as even more important than to be effective for the particular case. Such behaviour demonstrates high-level social skills which at present can only be acquired by extensive experience. The main impediment to the use of training is that such behaviour is so contextually dependent. The policeman, like the schoolteacher described by Goodfellow, needs to know the neighbourhood and to have an acute sense of time and place. The policeman, the schoolteacher and indeed all social skill practitioners also need, as Goodfellow points out, to anticipate the lines of development of a situation and to steer it accordingly. Cumberbatch and Morgan use the term 'resourcefulness'.

However, all this is itself a beginning which can make some contribution to the design of training courses and also to assessment—the awareness of what is important in the skilled practitioner who works with, through, and some-times against, other people.

Technical aids to communication, telephone, radio and television, appear at first sight to make little difference to the problems of conveying a message. This is true if the message is factual or trivial, but it becomes less true as the level of associated social skill increases. Comedians, for example, invariably need a live audience as well as a television camera to ensure that factors such as timing and situation development can be kept optimal by feedback from the audience. There is current discussion about how far private television channels can provide a substitute for the business meeting. It seems unlikely because so many of the contextual cues will be missing. The preliminary chat before the meeting, the communal lunch and even the prospect of a social evening together are potent factors in relation to what happens at the meeting itself. It ought to be possible to develop principles of what can and cannot be expected when there are restrictions on communication imposed by particular technological devices.

More widely, social skills are the glue which holds society together and the principles and structure of a satisfying organization or society must depend on at least an intuitive awareness of how social skills operate. If this awareness could be clarified it should make some slight contribution to organization theory, government and politics. Unfortunately most people involved in any complex socio-technical system find it difficult to articulate what they want from it or what they should attempt to put into it. This would seem to make proceeding by definition of objectives an unproductive method, but there are several factors which make it feasible to function in a reasonably democratic fashion. That is, to allow participants to have some say in their own controlling organization. Most people are much clearer about what they don't want than they are about what they do want. Thus negative guidance can be proffered, but so also can some positive guidance in that most people can make a reliable choice between sets of objectives spelt out by others. The task of political leadership is to provide a range of feasible alternatives. This demands social skills not only in arriving at possibilities but also in presenting them to the public. There is increasing dissatisfaction with the performance of politicians, possibly because they place too much emphasis on acquiring economic parameters rather than social parameters. The responsibility lies with students of social skill to make whatever expertise they have available to policy makers.

In general, individuals are aware that a situation is unsatisfactory before they can identify what is wrong and certainly before there is any vision of what might be done about it. There is a will to do something as yet unidentified. This adds again to the complexity of considering objectives as the boundary definers for skills. The remedial approach to the feeling of things being wrong is to attempt to analyse the symptoms of what is wrong. This usually involves some comparison with an abstract idealized model. It is then necessary to attempt to clarify what to do in terms of possible ways forward. For an organizational issue of any scale there is so much uncertainty that few individuals can make progress alone. Hence the need for social interchange and the development of a collective view; i.e. most people spend a lot of time discussing the defects of their organization with fellow members. This should be an interesting and productive field for the application of principles of social skills.

RESEARCH NEEDS

Research in this field is far from easy; it is not clear what should be done next or what methods to use to progress understanding of this topic.

The use of the many variations of the Repertory Grid can make a contribution, particularly in the understanding of how an individual structures his world. Nevertheless social skills, in common with other skills, have characteristics which transcend individual differences and it is these characteristics which we need to be able to identify more precisely in order to improve training and assessment methods.

The standard skill procedures of task analysis and skills analysis still apply. The use of task analysis is valuable in clarifying some aspects of the context which is so important in social skill. For example, social skills are often practised in combination with technical skills. This is clearly true for all the medical and paramedical people and Loveridge specifically mentions it as a characteristic of industrial negotiation. There is also some dividend from appreciating the relative parts played within a time slot or sequence. For example, Barker describes the use of 'talking turns' in the analysis of the clinical interview.

A number of key words occur in many chapters; it would aid understanding if we knew more precisely what we mean by terms such as empathy, style, rapport, feeling and awareness. All these, of course, are gestalt-type concepts not susceptible to reduction but perhaps susceptible to better definitions and distinctions.

It would be useful to explore why it is that some perceptual aspects of social skills are more universally established than others. For example, S. J. Singleton and Wells both mention the ease with which even people who do not otherwise communicate easily can readily detect condescension on the part of an interlocutor and can also detect when the other party, even a very senior one, has 'got it wrong'. The concept of authority and authority gradient is one interesting factor related to social interchange. Thornhill mentions the distinction between authority and power (the latter involves coercion) and describes one typology of authority: legal, charismatic and traditional. Authority is related to leadership and there has already been extensive research on the latter, albeit using this type of social skills theory.

Another contextual aspect is that identified by terms such as duty, service and responsibility. This has not been a fashionable research area for the past

40 years or so. This relates back to the concept of objectives described above. It is probably the key issue because the identity of a skill always relates to its purpose. The extensive development of skill psychology or other field theories of human behaviour awaits the development of appropriate mathematics which incorporate the principles of structure, the developing of structure in time—that is the process and the sense of unified direction which we call purpose.

CONCEPTS OF SKILL

As befits the variety of human behaviour there are many different attempts to develop our understanding of it. These vary from the orthodox physical science methods of the deductive/analytical kind used by the physiologist through to the more speculative intuitive/gestalt approach. Skill psychology .is of this latter kind. At present the search is for patterns: periodicities or morphology. The approach is a developmental one, the emphasis is on the continuous nature of learning.

A skill is a hypothetical construct used to explain why performance changes with experience and why some individuals are more effective than others. The characteristics of skilled performance are movement towards an objective, resistance to perturbations and economy of resources such as energy, information and effort. The appropriate cues are selected and accepted, the appropriate actions are taken with precise timing.

The mechanism which supports skilled performance is conceptualized as a set of schemata, that is continuously developing models of reality. There are a great variety of these schemata within a mature mind and a particular one comes forward to match any situation which that individual becomes a part of. The unitary mechanism supports all the functions which are separated within more reductionist psychology: perception, learning, memory, decision making, thinking and action. Attitudes, beliefs, motivation, personality and even self are inferred entities to do with the range and style of the available schemata.

A schema in use is being modified continuously by feedback following actions; actions themselves are initiated as hypotheses. A record of what is likely to happen is stored and compared with what does happen as detected by the senses. The schema is modified accordingly having accepted the new information. Thus, anticipation is an integral part of the control of skilled behaviour. Errors are significant because they generate new evidence, particularly about the limits of the possible flexibility of actions.

The more primitive but more creative models of reality are 'inside looking out': the individual acts as a body, the body image can have extensions. There are also 'outside looking in' models where the individual considers himself as one unit within the scheme of things and which develop in time and space as localized bits of reality. The model bits take account of the past and the future, the lock on to real time is through action and feedback. For the human adult, because of the dominance of visual inputs, the basic models are pictorial, but there are confirmatory supplements from other senses. Models also involve symbolism used for abstractions, generalizations and learning. Symbolism makes for economy of storage and search resources.

Social skills which appear in interactions between people employ the same mechanism of developing schemata. They are highly symbolic because the essence of social skills is exchange of information. Communication between people is almost entirely symbolic; that is there are standardized but arbitrary meanings for words and gestures. The uniqueness of social skills is in the sets of key features which structure the models (personal constructs) and in the need to take account of other intelligences.

Models are hierarchically organized: at the bottom of the hierarchy are simple actions involving integrated joint movements, at the top are intentions. The concept of a master programme directed by needs or purposes is an illusion fostered by the relationships between the set of schemata and their orientation towards reality. Models are mapped on to reality or, in the case of social skills, on to other models of reality. The skilled person can be thought of as a map-maker and as a navigator finding his functional way by using his own map in the context of the particular developing situation. The model or map develops in harmony with the situation but is sometimes ahead of it and sometimes behind it. The past is fixed but modified by the present, the future is laid out as a range of possible developments and a matching set of behavioural options. Paradoxically so-called perceptual skills are organized around output options and motor skills are organized around input options. This ensures a full matrix of connections between them.

The characteristic of the highly skilled person is that he is at one with the situation because his model maps fittingly on to the reality.

All this is highly speculative, but the study of psychology is a skilled activity which in common with all skills requires hypotheses which can be tested against action. The relevant action is communication with other skilled individuals by structured observation and conversation.

Author Index

Bold numerals refer to names cited in reference lists at chapter ends

Subject Index

advertisements, cultural differences 256
assessment 287, 288
attitudes 16–18
  cognitive style 17
  and communication 17
  physiotherapy 105, 106
  pupils and teachers 28, 29

behaviour, instinctive 4
behaviourism 120
  rat model 272
  reinforcement 279
behaviour therapy and homosexuality 133
beliefs 16

Cattell's Sixteen Personality Factor
    questionnaire 15
central authority and labour relations 209
children
  compartment concepts 28
  description 55
client-centred therapy 270
client-psychotherapist relationship 130–4
cognitive strategies 20
communication
  breakdown 243, 286
  complicating factors 59
  components 289
  cues 7
  doctor–patient 62, 63, 77
  doctor–patient, non-verbal 57, 58
  France 258–62
  French and English compared 258–62
  good, definition in France 262, 263

interorganization 240–2
listener role 290
non-verbal 57, 58, 109–12, 221
  conscious 110
occupational physician 96, 97
one-way 289
referee 180, 183
selling 220–2, 235, 236
technical aids 292
competence and skill 271
computer 272
  analogy with skill 268, 269
conciliation, judge role 171, 172
constructs 23
  and convenience 23
continuity 1, 2
contracts 199
  business, US 208, 209
  long-term 200
  open-ended 208
  renegotiation 200
conversation
  asymmetry 276
  description 267, 268
  dialogues, entwining 278, 279
  learning 274–81
  modal types 272–4
  process description 276
  relevance 277
  skill 272, 273
  skill theory 267
  taxonomy 277
counselling practice, theories 24
creativity and skill 271
cure 54